Bard

Bard College invites su~~bmi~~ssions for its annual Fiction Prize for young writers.

The Bard Fiction Prize is awarded annually to a promising, emerging writer who is a United States citizen aged 39 years or younger at the time of application. In addition to a monetary award of $30,000, the winner receives an appointment as writer-in-residence at Bard College for one semester without the expectation that he or she teach traditional courses. The recipient will give at least one public lecture and will meet informally with students.

To apply, candidates should write a cover letter describing the project they plan to work on while at Bard and submit a C.V., along with three copies of the published book they feel best represents their work. No manuscripts will be accepted.

Applications for the 2021 prize must be received by July 30, 2020. For further information about the Bard Fiction Prize, call 845-758-7087, or visit www.bard.edu/bfp. Applicants may also request information by writing to the Bard Fiction Prize, Bard College, Annandale-on-Hudson, NY 12504-5000.

Bard College PO Box 5000, Annandale-on-Hudson, NY 12504-5000

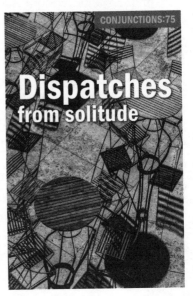

CONJUNCTIONS

Bi-Annual Volumes of New Writing

Edited by
Bradford Morrow

Published by Bard College

EDITOR: Bradford Morrow
MANAGING EDITOR: Nicole Nyhan
SENIOR EDITORS: Jedediah Berry, Benjamin Hale, J. W. McCormack, Edie Meidav,
    Michael Sarinsky, Pat Sims
COPY EDITOR: Pat Sims
ART EDITOR: Jessica Fuller
ASSOCIATE EDITOR: Evangeline Riddiford Graham
PUBLICITY: Darren O'Sullivan, Mark R. Primoff
EDITORIAL ASSISTANTS: Michael Blackmon, Emily Giangiulio, Danielle Martin,
    Brian Araque Perez, Alexi Piirimae, Nik Slackman

CONJUNCTIONS is published in the Spring and Fall of each year by Bard College, Annandale-on-Hudson, NY 12504. This project is supported in part by an award from the National Endowment for the Arts and from the New York State Council on the Arts with the support of Governor Andrew M. Cuomo and the New York State Legislature.

SUBSCRIPTIONS: Use our secure online ordering system at conjunctions.com, or send subscription orders to CONJUNCTIONS, Bard College, Annandale-on-Hudson, NY 12504. Single year (two volumes): $30.00 for individuals; $50.00 for institutions and non-US. Two years (four volumes): $50.00 for individuals; $80.00 for institutions and non-US. For information about subscriptions, back issues, and advertising, contact us at (845) 758-7054 or conjunctions@bard.edu. *Conjunctions* is listed and indexed in JSTOR and Humanities International Complete and included in EBSCO*host*.

Editorial communications should be sent to Bradford Morrow, *Conjunctions*, 21 East 10th Street, 3E, New York, NY 10003. Unsolicited manuscripts cannot be returned unless accompanied by a stamped, self-addressed envelope. Electronic and simultaneous submissions will not be considered. Do not send work via any method requiring a signature for delivery. If you are submitting from outside the United States, contact conjunctions@bard.edu for instructions.

Cover design by Jerry Kelly, New York. Cover art by Hugo von Trimberg: *Der Renner*, ca. 1230–ca. 1313, courtesy of The Morgan Library & Museum, MS M.763, fol. 230r. Photography by Janny Chiu, 2020.

Conjunctions e-books of current and selected past issues are distributed by Open Road Integrated Media (openroadmedia.com/conjunctions) and available for purchase in all e-reader formats from Amazon, Apple, B&N, Google, Indiebound, Kobo, Overdrive, and elsewhere.

Retailers can order print issues directly from *Conjunctions*.

Printers: Maple Press, GHP

Typesetter: Bill White, Typeworks

ISSN 0278-2324

ISBN 978-0-941964-25-8

Manufactured in the United States of America.

TABLE OF CONTENTS

GRENDEL'S KIN:
THE MONSTERS ISSUE
Edited by Bradford Morrow

EDITOR'S NOTE

MONSTERS ARE THE ULTIMATE OTHER. In them, our most heinous traits, our weirdest fantasies, our greatest primordial fears, are mirrored and transmogrified into grotesqueries of every kind. Our ancestors' imaginative visions of terror and dread gave rise to a spectacular alternative universe of fiends, daemons, ghosts, griffins, zombies, succubi, dragons, chimeras, sea serpents, vampires, were-wolves, and other monstrous progeny. Latter-day generations have been just as creative in adding marvelous creatures to the Nuclear Age pantheon—1954 alone saw the birth of Godzilla, stirred to life by the atomic bomb, not to mention the giant mutant ants of *Them!* No matter the era, no matter which century, be it a dark age or one of enlightenment, monsters have held a mesmerizing fascination, as well as an existential horror, for everyday mortals.

In *Grendel's Kin*, classic monsters such as the Minotaur and Sasquatch are conjured alongside newly imagined unfriendly beings like the Gricklemare, the Moon Fairy, and the Soul Collector, as well as a poltergeist, a tentacled creature discovered in an uncharted crevasse in Antarctica, a sister who is grossly, inexorably extruded from her host sibling (much to the latter's mortification), and killer fleas from beyond Pluto. Here are monsters who inhabit the churning oceans and ride on killer tsunamis. Monsters born of plague and strife and hatred. Monsters who lurk in spellbound woodlands. Village and city monsters. Monsters who are stubborn, inescapable, greedy, pestilent, some of them cunning, others a bit clumsy—and most of them as malignant as a stumble off a very high cliff.

—Bradford Morrow
April 2020
New York City

The Moon Fairy
With a Drawing by Del Samatar
Sofia Samatar

WHEN THE MOON FAIRY ARRIVED, blown in through an open window one summer night, we were all surprised by how much it resembled Sylvie. Of course, it was much smaller—no longer than Sylvie's forearm, the perfect size to take its place among her forgotten dolls—but its small, shimmering face was a tiny image of hers, like a portrait cleverly formed from beaten tin. The fairy was found against the bookshelf, lying on Sylvie's discarded bathing towel, fast asleep with its wings folded along its back. Despite the astonishing grace of its form, it was clearly alive and breathing. When it woke up, it yawned so prettily, we all gasped.

Thus began the time of the Moon Fairy. At first, we thought it would fly away, and left the window open for that purpose, but it seemed comfortable in the house, and soon took to sleeping on Sylvie's pillow, using her long hair for a blanket. During the day, it was rather paler than at night, almost transparent. After it startled Mother on the stairs, nearly causing her to lose her balance (she complained about it for a week—"Control that thing!" she said), Sylvie made it a little frock of red worsted, with openings for the wings, in which it flitted about as gaily as a kite. She also sewed minuscule undergarments for it, and a red cap with a bow, from under which its bright hair billowed like candy floss. It submitted to being dressed without complaint, closing its eyes. Sylvie taught it to eat cracker crumbs from her finger.

The Moon Fairy liked white foods: crackers, shortbread, rice, and milk. It disliked wine, loud noises, Uncle Claudius Eppenberg, and the cat. In fact, poor Mittens, whom no one loved more than Sylvie, was given away to the neighbor children soon after the fairy's arrival. From the window on the landing overlooking the neighbors' garden, Mittens could be observed in her new circumstances, mewling piteously as the children forced her into doll clothes, tied her up in a wagon, and dragged it over the grass. "Poor creature!" Sylvie was heard to murmur, standing at the window. However, she made no attempt to rescue the cat, which had scratched her darling's wing, leaving a gash that took days to heal. As she looked down, holding the curtain back with one hand, the Moon Fairy curled up in its customary place on her shoulder, sighing placidly and nuzzling her neck.

It really was a charming creature. It smiled, laughed, turned somersaults in the air, played hide-and-seek among the clothes on the line, danced when Ellen played Chopin—did everything but speak. In the evenings, when its energy tended to rise, it would fly round the room up close to the ceiling, emitting a happy buzzing sound. Sylvie said it was singing, but Uncle Claudius, who often dropped by in the evening to have a drink with Father, opined that the buzzing was caused by the movement of the fairy's wings, "in the manner of a bumblebee or other insect." "Nonsense," said Sylvie, frowning. She disliked hearing the fairy compared to an animal. Since the fateful evening when the young man she'd been walking out with that summer (the son of some family friends, a law student with excellent prospects) had rashly referred to the Moon Fairy as "your new pet," he had been forbidden the house, and the increasingly desperate telephone messages from him we wrote down were crumpled up unread. Unfortunately for Sylvie, it was not so easy to get rid of Uncle Claudius, an "almost doctor," as she called him rudely behind his back (he had never actually completed his studies), who, since his automobile accident some years before, had been living on the proceeds of the lawsuit, and had nothing better to do than read, play with his shortwave radio, and drink Father's brandy. "The vibrations," Uncle Claudius went on, unperturbed, leaning heavily on his cane (he could never tell when he was not wanted) and peering up at the Moon Fairy with his bulging, yellowish eyes, "may be providing it with a new sensation, one unobtainable on the moon, where there is no atmosphere. Apparently, this gives it pleasure."

The Moon Fairy's response to this speech was to crouch on the curtain rod, growling and spitting with rage. The change in its manner was so unexpected, and its temper, despite the distortion of its features, so adorable, we all burst out laughing—none more loudly or wickedly than Sylvie. "Come, Claudius," Father chuckled, taking his elder brother's arm to lead him toward the library and the bottles. Finding his dissertation drowned in mirth, Uncle Claudius obeyed, still muttering about the Sea of Tranquility.

After that, one had only to pronounce the words "Uncle Claudius" and the fairy would crouch, alert and bristling, its face twisted into

10

an expression of captivating malice and a small whine issuing from its throat. John amused himself like this for days, shouting "Uncle Claudius is coming!" until Sylvie told him to stop. As for Uncle Claudius (who really was obtuse), he gave Sylvie, for her birthday that August, a rare book called *On Human Interactions with Lunar Sprites*, which she promptly shoved under the bed.

Autumn came. During thunderstorms, the Moon Fairy would rush into Sylvie's arms and hide its face in her bosom, weeping and trembling. She made it a dress of dark-green felt. She made it a little rabbit-skin coat with matching fur boots, hat, and muff. She walked about town with the fairy on her shoulder. A man from the newspaper came and took her picture, and when it was printed, we noticed again, as if for the first time, the startling resemblance between the fairy and Sylvie. It was like a second Sylvie, mute, argent, and lighter than air. Nothing pleased her more than to hear people say this. In restaurants, when waiters exclaimed over the uncanny coincidence, she blushed happily and left them an extra tip.

There was something of a squall when Sylvie refused to return to college. Father was furious over the money he had wasted for two years, and called Sylvie an empty-headed lump, to which she replied that he had only sent her to college to get her married and off his hands. "I can marry perfectly well," she said, "without knowing about the French symbolists." Father said she had better do it then, at which Mother cried and the Moon Fairy hissed like a teapot. Sylvie, however, smiled coolly. "Come, Father, be reasonable. I can't keep a fairy in the dormitory." This statement was so inarguable, and the inseparability of Sylvie and her fairy so patently obvious, that Father was deflated. None of us could imagine Sylvie without the Moon Fairy anymore. At times, there even seemed to be a kind of brightness about Sylvie's skin. It was almost as if she were becoming a lunar creature. One night, when Mother came down to make sure she had turned off the gas, she screamed at the sight of a strange old woman in the living room. It was Sylvie. In the moonlight, her hair looked white.

She began to sleep later and later in the mornings, the fairy tucked under her hair. The two of them stayed awake late at night, often coming downstairs when the rest of the family was in bed for a midnight supper of toasted almonds and cream. In the morning, Mother found their cups in the sink. Sometimes one of us awoke to the sound of the sewing machine, like a distant airplane. Sylvie made matching lace nightgowns for the Moon Fairy and herself, and matching

11

white fur slippers and fleece robes. Soon they wore nothing but these snowy garments. They grew peevish during the day. Sylvie complained that the fairy wouldn't let her do anything—and it was true it pulled her hair if she tried to play music or read—but she wouldn't hear of leaving it with someone else. The one time she did so, during her illness just after the Christmas holidays, was a disaster. Ellen volunteered to keep the fairy in her room (she had always been a little jealous of Sylvie, the creature's clear favorite), and the door to Sylvie's room was closed and locked. What was our amazement and distress the following morning, upon finding the Moon Fairy stretched before Sylvie's door in a dead faint, and Ellen utterly vanished! Only when Father went to the back closet for his galoshes did he hear Ellen shouting and crying from the mud house. The mud house—so called by the family for generations, no one knows exactly why—was a shed near the back fence, originally built to house garden tools, but cleaned up and fitted out with a table and chairs, and even a wood-stove and a chimney, for the amusement of the children. Here, Ellen informed us once she was able to speak coherently, the Moon Fairy had lured her in the middle of the night, dancing just in front of her, all radiant with moonbeams ("Oh! So beautiful!" Ellen repeated, sobbing), and once she was safely inside, it had pinched her horribly all over her face, so that she fell down behind the table (and she had the marks of this treatment on her still—tiny fierce pinpricks, like a rash), and then flown out and locked the door. Ellen called for help and banged on the door, to no avail. Fortunately she had some matches and a stub of candle in her pocket (a thing expressly forbidden, but Father could scarcely complain, under the circumstances), and was able to light some bits of charred wood in the stove. Otherwise—as the doctor informed us severely when he arrived—she might have come out of the mud house frostbitten or worse. Ellen was put to bed under quilts, and the Moon Fairy laid on Sylvie's pillow. It had knocked itself unconscious against her door. Its face was purple for days.

We might have read of such incidents in the book Sylvie had received from Uncle Claudius Eppenberg, *On Human Interactions with Lunar Sprites*. We might have read of Elizabeth Dobb, who, walking over the heath one night, was struck by a ray of moonlight and left with "a limpet between her breasts." This "limpet" could not be detached without danger to the patient, and would eat nothing but white sugar and ether, a demand that eventually beggared Elizabeth's family. We might have read of the young Abbé de Beaumarais, a bright intellect with a promising future and favorite of Marguerite de Navarre, whose health was destroyed by "a silver light lodged underneath his hair." Of this luminosity, he wrote: "My beloved twin! He is all heart; reason maddens him; even now, as I attempt to describe him, he pricks my eardrum." We might have read of the Japanese nobleman and painter known as Lord Sparrow, who built an entire palace to house a creature no bigger than a grain of rice. Though these stories offer no solutions, they might have prepared us for what was to come, but we did not open the book until the summer was well advanced, until Sylvie was no longer sleeping in her room, and Martha Evans, who "did" for Mother once a week, discovered the book under the bed. Then, with horror and compassion, we read of Apalus, son of Threpte, who blinded himself with an awl after his moon spirit suddenly left him, because he could no longer bear to see the light. And we read of Nuru el-Uyun, daughter of the sultan of Zanzibar, who, after nearly a year of close companionship with a mysterious girl as graceful as a sprig of night-blooming jasmine, was deserted by her friend, and sank immediately into a wasting illness, characterized most gruesomely by the destruction of her fingernails, or perhaps (the manuscript describing her case is, regretfully, damaged) by the mutilation of both the nails and the fingertips, an illness from which the princess, so fortunate by birth, was never to recover, and which is known as *al-Inhitat al-Qamari*, or "lunar decline."

"The most terrible thing," wrote Andreas Vogeler, a gifted composer whose career was abruptly stifled, from the Swiss sanatorium where he lived out the dregs of his days, "is that I do not know why it came, and I do not know why it left. I spend my days thinking, not only of what I might have done to avoid its arrival, but of what I might have done to keep it near me. Most of all, I think of those ordinary men—clerks, art dealers, estate agents, and the like—who live their entire lives, full of small joys and sorrows, successes and crises, without an inkling of either how happy or how wretched it is possible to be. Such people seem to me like magical beasts. And yet there is no reason why my life should not have been like theirs, for I was a person like anyone. It is the contemplation of this—the *absence of reason* in my having been, as it were, moonstruck—that prolongs my shattered state."

One evening we tried to determine the last time we had seen Sylvie happy. (Father left the room when the conversation began and shut himself up in the library, for his bruised heart cannot endure this kind of talk.) We decided it was at the beginning of April, when the cherry trees were in flower. The tree outside Sylvie's window was particularly thick with blossoms, almost impossibly heavy, so that one felt it must bow down to the ground. She stood at the open window in her nightgown. Her bedroom door was ajar, the room flooded with moonlight extending nearly to the threshold. The dense perfume of the cherry tree too reached us in the hall. Sylvie appeared to be talking to herself, but we soon realized she spoke to the fairy, which hovered about her face, darting and whirling in a strange ballet. "My love, my love," Sylvie murmured. "My little heart. My silver dollar. My night witch." She laughed softly and touched a finger to her lip. It was John who realized that she was placing grains of sugar there, which the fairy was lapping up with its own mouth.

A last flash of pure joy in a time of dread. The fairy had begun to leave her. It disappeared for an hour and was found rustling in the pantry. Its face was sharp and impenitent. It flew to the top of the cherry tree and had to be coaxed down with a dish of honey. When she went out, Sylvie took to tying a thread around its ankle, the other end of which she secured to her belt. One day, when she was knotting the thread, the Moon Fairy bit her finger, leaving a small raised welt like a beesting. Sometimes, in the midst of apparent harmony, an evil look came over it, and it flew at her, scratching her neck or yanking her hair. Sylvie grew wan. She began to lose weight. Ugly spots came out on her skin. She complained of a constant "fluttering" in her stomach. It was the terror of the approaching end. She could not cease her vigilance for a moment. She stalked the Moon Fairy, which turned on her, baring its teeth. It refused to wear the clothes she had sewn. It tore up its little nightgown. One night—who knows how, for the windows were closed—it left for good.

"They breed on the moon," wrote an anonymous sufferer from Thrace, "they come down to earth, they dazzle us with their incandescence, and they go, without logic or hope of appeal, bound by no known law. Since she left me, I am unmoored."

In June, a few days after the Moon Fairy had flown away, and almost a year to the day since its first appearance, Sylvie received a visit from the neighbor girl, Marjorie Pierce, who found her lying flat on the floor beneath a window. Without getting up, Sylvie described a "dark fire of horror" blazing over her life, and advised Marjorie to strangle Mittens the cat. Marjorie departed in tears, and the doctor was summoned. He found Sylvie in perfect health, but in the evening she walked from her bedroom down to the kitchen, pressed against the wall and scraping her mouth along the plaster with such force that she left a long carmine streak. It was as if she wanted to erase her mouth. Her lips were badly torn, and several teeth broken. She was sent to hospitals in New York, Vermont, and Basel. Now she lives in the mud house, where, after much anguish, Mother finally agreed to place a chamber pot and bed. This solution may seem cruel—we have certainly been censured by the neighbors as a family deficient in feeling—but such people cannot know how the grief of a person abandoned by a Moon Fairy can destroy a house. One would not say, today, that our house is happy, but it is functional. The walls are freshly painted, and Ellen is engaged. As for Sylvie, she sits in the mud house, staring at the table. No one likes to go there, except, as it happens, the Moon Fairy's old enemy, Uncle Claudius Eppenberg. He says that he and his niece are both victims of accident. He sits for long hours at the table with her, listening to his radio. If you pass through the garden, where the mud house stands covered with vines, you can hear the sound of the radio, very thin, like the chirping of crickets, and if you have the courage, you can pull the vines aside and peer through the thick, dirty glass of the only window. There you will see Uncle Claudius, perhaps fiddling with his radio, perhaps feeding Sylvie something out of a bowl, perhaps merely discoursing to her on some subject that has crossed his mind, blinking his yellow eyes in the half-light. And you will see Sylvie, her hands motionless on the table. She wears a stained plaid dress, buttoned at the throat and wrists. Her mouth hangs dark. If, inadvertently, you move the leaves at the window, gauzy shadows drift across her face. Then it is as if the moon is peeping out of the clouds, shining on her, and withdrawing its gaze again, and you feel, for an instant of absolute, clenching terror, that she is going to turn her eyes on you and strike you to the heart. However, she doesn't move. The moment passes, leaving a throbbing in its wake. She floats there, oddly detached, like a being immune to gravity. You would not guess that this was a girl who had received every advantage. She no longer looks like our Sylvie. She no longer looks like anyone.

15

The Thickening

Brian Evenson

I.

WHEN HE WAS VERY YOUNG, Greppur often awoke late at night feeling he could not afford to remain alone. He would creep from his room and down the hall, listening to the swish of his soles against the parquet floor. That and the feel of his hand brushing along the wall were just enough to keep the air from thickening into something else. He would travel by feel to the end of the hall and open the door to his parents' bedroom as quietly as possible. He could not climb into bed with them because this might wake his father up. If his father awoke, Greppur would be immediately carried back to his own bedroom, locked in this time. But if he was careful, he could creep to the chair just next to his mother's side of the bed and curl up there.

Once there, if he was unlucky, his father would still sense him and suddenly rough hands would be lifting him, carrying him back to his room, where the thickening would begin.

If he was very lucky indeed, he would fall asleep to the sound of his mother's breathing and remain in the chair until morning.

Usually he was just lucky enough. After some time in the chair he would calm down, and only then see a glint in the darkness and know his mother's eyes were open, that she was observing him.

"What is it?" his mother would whisper. "Another bad dream?"

"No," he would whisper back.

But his mother did not understand that what he meant by this was not that there had not been a *bad* dream. What he meant was that it hadn't been a dream at all. That it had been real.

She would nod. Sometimes she let him stay, but even if she sent him back to bed it was usually all right: enough time had gone by that the danger had passed.

As he grew older, he came to understand the thickening never happened more than once per night, and usually not even that. He dreaded it happening, and it was always terrible when it did, but usually he could wake himself in time. If there was another person in the house, as long as he came close enough to them to hear the sound of their breathing he could stop it from happening. Knowing another person was near was enough. Sometimes, though, he woke only when the thickening had already begun, and it was too late.

When, later still, he was in college and sharing a dorm room, it stopped entirely. For a few weeks he thought he was free of it. But when his roommate went home for the weekend, there, there it was again, three nights in a row, nearly unbearable in the way the thing that congealed from the air peered into him. But once his roommate was back, it stopped.

Perhaps this was why he became entangled with someone before college was finished. It seemed a necessity. He first lived with her and then, when her parents, religious, objected, married her. It wasn't that he didn't, in his way, love her, only that that was far from his only reason for being with her, not even the primary one. On some level any warm body would have done. Sleeping next to anyone would save him: it just happened to be her.

They were, so everybody said, inseparable. *Twenty-five years together*, he overheard his wife say proudly once to a friend on the telephone, *and not a single night spent apart*, which made him cringe. Made him, after so many years, remember. Made him, for the first time in years, nervous about going to sleep.

Nearly a decade later, long after he had forgotten again, his wife died: a sudden thing, a stroke, almost no warning. One moment they were speaking about how they would spend their evening, the next she collapsed. Then he was calling 911, then riding in the ambulance with her, then riding in the ambulance with her corpse. It was a terrible thing, occurring in such fashion as to leave him drenched in guilt and confusion. Coming back to the house alone in the early hours of the morning, he hardly felt like himself. Exhausted, he managed to strip off his coat and flop onto the bed. And then, before he knew it, he was asleep.

But he was not asleep for long.

II.

It was just like it had been when he was a child. He had been dreaming that the air had become thick around him so that it was hard to
breathe and even hard to move. He had come gaspingly awake, only
he wasn't sure if he was awake or just dreaming he was awake. Was
there time to get up and go find his parents' room? *But no*, he suddenly realized with something akin to wonder, *I'm not a child anymore:* his parents had been dead for many years. His wife too was
dead now, and he was alone.

"Greppur," the thickening in the air crooned. "Greppur?" It was
feeling for him with something that, if he squinted and ignored the
fact that he could see through it, looked like a hand, but was not a
hand. He could not see it, not really: it was like *an interruption of
the air.* He remembered thinking that when he was a child, had
taken the phrase, he supposed, from something misunderstood in a
children's story. But he could see it was right, the right phrase, at
least for this particular phase of the thickening.

"When did I see you last?" it asked. "Yesterday? Decades ago? It
seems like so much time has gone by, and so little."

It did to Greppur too. Both.

It began to thicken, began to inflict a more substantial form upon
the air. The voice was sharper now. What had been a wavering in the
air took on firmer shape. It was too late. He could guess where its
mouth was already, if he was right to call it a mouth.

"Where are you?" it said in a wheedling tone. "Let me see you,
Greppur."

He tried to close his eyes, but they would not close.

What if he fled to the hall? Would it follow him? What if he made
it outside? He tried to get up, grunting with effort, unable, really, to
move. It wheeled and faced his way at the sound, though facing was
the wrong word since other than the mouth, if it was a mouth, it
didn't yet have a face. It thickened further, visible now, but flattened
out and slightly translucent, as if made of paper.

"Ah, there you are," it said. "I hear you anyway." And ears began
to form.

He tried again to rise, and managed to roll out of the bed and fall
onto the floor. He could not move his arms to catch his fall. He
struck hard, with a thunk.

"What's that?" it said. "What's that? What are you trying now,
child?" He had fallen facedown and was turned so he was largely

looking at the floor, but with his head angled just enough that one eye saw the bottom of the door, a little stretch of baseboard, a few inches of wall.

"We were meant to be together, Greppur," it said. "You know we were."

Maybe it is a dream, he told himself, though he knew it was not a dream. He tried to lift his head but could not lift his head. He could move his body a little, just a very little, like a worm, more a shiver than movement proper. He began to do that, began to shiver, rocking a little too, oozing his way slowly, inch by inch, under the bed.

"Where are you?" it said. "Let me see you, child. Let me take a good, long look."

But this, Greppur felt, was precisely what he could not let it do.

He kept shivering, kept inching. Was he making progress? He was, but was it enough? He could smell dust. He felt something brush the back of his head. Had it found him? No, that was the blanket hanging just over the side of the bed, his head brushing past it as he moved underneath. And then it was growing darker and he could wriggle a little better and there he was, a grown man in his fifties, facedown under his own bed, motes of dust whirling around him.

"Greppur," the reedy voice still called from somewhere above. "Where are you, my sweet?"

He was more himself under the bed, even if only slightly. He could turn his head a little now. He could see the creature's legs, looking thick and substantial and opaque, though they left no mark on the carpet wherever they stepped. The feet left the floor and he knew it was on the bed now, though the bed did not shake or creak. But as soon as he noted this, the bed did shake, did creak, and he became afraid that by questioning it he had made it happen, had thickened the creature further.

Now the mattress was sagging down, resting against his back like a splayed palm. He waited, hidden. *I can just wait it out*, he told himself. *I can just wait until morning. It won't find me.*

As suddenly as it had started, the weight pushing down the mattress was gone. Something was there beside him, deeper under the bed, just behind his head.

Ah, it said, and gave a tinny, tinkling laugh. He felt all of its hands close around his head, the fingers long and bony now. It slowly exerted pressure. His face rubbed along the floor and through the dust, and

19

then there the other face was, right beside his own. It had not finished becoming a face yet, or had gone about it wrongly: where one would expect features there was only a gash for a mouth and two divots for eyes, the surface otherwise smooth and bled of color.

"I told you I would return for you," the mouth said softly.

Please, he tried to say, but nothing came out.

"Let me have a look in you," the mouth said, "a good long one." And then the lipless mouth opened to reveal a blotch of darkness. Slowly, from within drifted up what seemed at first a large, dirty white marble, but then turned to reveal itself to be an eye.

It remained there at the top of the darkness, clasped delicately between the lipless top edge of the mouthgash and the lipless bottom edge of the mouthgash. It vibrated slightly, the pupil dilating and contracting, and stared, stared.

And then the creature said, with delight, *Ah, at last!*

III.

Whenever it came for him in childhood, it had always gone something like that: it stared into him so deeply it was as if he felt the eye held in the mouth slowly licking away the lining of his skull. It was looking for something, he knew, but he did not know what. Some memory, he supposed, or some concatenation of memories, but he was not even sure of that much. There was always a long moment where he felt he had been backed into a corner of his own mind, and then the voice would say, softly, "Not yet." And then it was gone and he was left gasping.

After he calmed down, he was, usually, able to convince himself over time it had all been a dream, a bad one, true, but a dream. And, usually, exhausted, he could slip back into sleep, and only wake at daylight, the visit nearly forgotten. He would not think about the creature until, a night or two or three later, it came for him again.

As a child he became quite agile, if agile was the right word, at sensing the thickening coming. He would awaken before it was too late, before it arrived. All he had to do was find someone, be near someone, in the same room as some other human asleep or awake. If he could do that, the thickening would simply dissolve.

But he could not always be agile. Or perhaps as time went on, and he managed to avoid it, it became hungrier and more desperate. It might take a few weeks, a few months, but eventually he would awaken too late, after the thickening was too far along. When that happened, it was hard for him to move and impossible for him to speak. It wandered about the room, crooning his name, not quite able to see him.

But, in the end, it always found him. Just as it had done now, decades later, now that he was an adult, now that it was starving.

In the past, when it was done with him, it would always say, *Not yet. I'll come back for you.*

And now it seemed after all these years it had.

IV.

When he awoke, he remembered very little. Bad dreams, the beginning of panic, nightmares. But it was understandable: he'd had a bad day the day before. The worst of days, he felt, he was sure, he was almost sure, even if he couldn't quite remember what, what exactly, had been so bad.

It must have been bad since he seemed to have slept in his clothes. Why hadn't his wife helped him undress?

He rolled over in the other direction, curling up against his wife's back. Her skin was cold. She uttered a little moan of pleasure.

There was something strange, he suddenly felt, something missing. Had he left something somewhere by accident and subconsciously realized it, was feeling vague anxiety as a result? Or if not something left, an appointment forgotten? To what? With whom?

He shook his head slightly, trying to remember. He felt his wife stiffen a little.

"Honey," she said, still facing away, "darling, what's wrong?"

"I . . . don't know," he said.

It was almost there, on the tip of his tongue.

"Don't you want to tell me?" she asked.

"I . . . ," he started, and then realized that no, he did not. Thinking this made him feel guilty. Why shouldn't he tell his wife?

And then she turned toward him and he knew why: there was something wrong with her features. They were too soft. Almost as he remembered them but not quite.

But then he blinked his eyes and looked again and thought, *No, it must have been something wrong with my vision.* She looked just as she always had.

Didn't she?

21

What was it? What was he missing? What had he forgotten?
"Honey," she said. She almost sang the word. "What is it?"
He just shook his head, said nothing.
She stroked his face with all of her hands. Her hands were cold too.
"We were meant to be together," she said. "You know we were."
He tried not to look at her.
"Let me help you," she said.
And now he did not dare speak or move his head at all in fear that she would take this for assent. But this was his wife. There was no reason to be afraid. What was wrong with him?
Then she opened her mouth wide and looked at him, really looked with another eye entirely, and he realized he had every reason to be afraid, though it was already far too late for something like fear to do him any good.

I, Poltergeist
Mary Kuryla

ARRIVAL

ONLY WAY TO GET TO the island by car is to board the *Margaret Chase Smith* in Lincolnville, heading northeast out Penobscot Bay, and unlike some others, this ferryboat runs on time. You get out of your car and walk to the bow of the ferry and you watch that long island across the bay shape out with its inhospitable spruce twisting up from shoreline rock, where the coves and inlets appear thumbed as child's clay, offering sanctuary to trappers' skiffs in their quest for mink pelts and moose in some long ago, and you fix your eyes on that tenebrous chain of rocks, hoping to settle the plunging feeling from the steel beneath your feet breaking through the waves, breaking through and falling beneath you, the rocks luring your eye further and further away to Precambrian time when the elementals crawled up the slate and quartzite in search of hosts through which to enact their primitive mischief. You feel the draw of the rock and all at once the ferry stalls and jerks, suspending you between the forward motion and reverse of the ferryboat making buttermilk of the seawater round Islesboro, sweet Islesboro!

You walk back to your van and get in as all around you the engines wake up and you slam your door against the welter of fumes, the other cars already forming lines to disembark, although on that particular day we were the first let off on account of having been first in line.

Steel grates will test your van's suspension as it rolls onto the landing then onto the road that circumvents a dense beech forest on one side, the bay on the other, as you head east on Ferry Road, past the vast shell middens left by the Penobscot natives, and on past the bleached bellies of upended lobster boats settled between columns of skeletal traps that hold up nothing but sky. It is here where the boys learn to maneuver in skiffs long before they learn to ride a bike, and the girls swing their clam buckets just so so as not to interfere with the motion of the oars.

Here folks came to capitalize on the bounty yielded up by the sea and later still to down spruce and maple for the mills that never got built and so departed to steadier futures on the mainland, and those who stayed never numbered more than six hundred, even now, reclusive and hearty enough for year-round island life, passing down these traits generation after generation, preferring quilting circles to church groups for socializing. The inhabitants retaining that piecemeal stitchery of suspicion for any patch that didn't show the common good sense to blend in.

You drive the Ferry Road that dead-ends at West Bay Road, which will take you up island where most of us year-round folk live. Or you can turn down island and continue to Dark Harbor. That was the direction we took on this day in May. I rode in the rental van with Sparkage Stevens and his pro skateboard gear, though I could just as well have been outside the van as in, not being bound by the same physical laws as humans. But I liked being close to Sparkage, catching some of his high at coming back to Islesboro.

Sparkage took the first turn past Islesboro's only cemetery, where wildflowers bobbed among the stones and lavender butterflies pedaled in the long air just below the Stevens' house, appearing now over the rise.

Having pulled into the gravel driveway, he parked before the large old house constructed of fieldstone then hopped out of the van. Rising to his full height, Sparkage took your breath away. Hands on narrow hips, the flannel's loose cuffs flapping over the wrists, thumb catching the loop of the bright corduroy slung low, on every garment stitched the name of our biggest sponsor but nothing in the way to give offense. This was branding that said rebel.

An uncanny knack for making the right call wasn't the only thing that had landed Sparkage a rating as top US pro skateboarding champion this year. His rangy athleticism infused the sport with nuanced grace, the endless legs heralding the sinuous allure of the loins. While in person his face came off awkward with its surfeit of angles, the camera liked him. The dark eyes, the pale New England skin, the unruly hair, the gazing off into the distance: one sportswriter had gone so far as to call his style on the deck Byronesque.

Sparkage pushed the hair off his brow, but it just rolled back down in waves. He smiled at the house that he'd walked away from over a year ago. You could have heard my heart skip a beat when he smiled like that. If I had a heart.

Not that it made much difference to Sparkage. He sensed my presence, had said as much for years. But he couldn't see me. He never

24

knew how I felt about him, let alone what would get rid of me. Oh, he had his theories about that. We all did. We would all pay dearly for those little theories. None so dearly as I.

Sparkage scanned the windows of the house, but in none was the face that he sought. The face for whom he'd risked his neck on every skateboard trick that couldn't be done but he'd nevertheless managed by gumption and luck to pull off, and he'd done it for her. All for her.

No, she was not looking out any window but she was around. Somewhere on the grounds. I could hear her reading aloud. When you go without something so essential to your existence that you will not go on much longer without it, you keep an ear out.

Sparkage reached into the van for his deck and set it on the ground and stepped on it, an anxious twitch. The rocking side to side on the trucks of his deck and the bees buzzing low in the June grass and sweet joe-pye weed rimming the house: the only sounds.

And the slight southerly breeze that carried her voice to me. With striking allophonic clarity, she was reciting the lines of her father's favorite verse:

> *She dreams a little, and she feels the dark*
> *Encroachment of that old catastrophe . . .*

Clementine. Her name ringing fine and bright as a citrus hymn. The mandarin-scented-skin Clementine, and the pulse between her bowed blood lips. One guffaw from her drowns the siren's call, inviting all to sin.

To Sparkage she was just Clem. Bucketed and boyish and salty Clem, like the smell she trailed in from the shore, rinsed with ocean spew. Grubby and stirring awake, that Clem.

> *There is not any haunt of prophecy,*
> *Nor any old chimera of the grave,*
> *Neither the golden underground, nor isle*
> *Melodious, where spirits gat them home . . .*

Clementine was behind the house in the lower meadow, probably practicing for the commencement address, the same one delivered by the school valedictorian for the past, well, who's counting?

Certainly not Sparkage. But he knew she was close. Clementine was the arsonist of his mind. The thought of her reduced his brain to thin, radiant clay. Ooh, baby baby. Somewhere nearby was Clementine.

I was feeling again, feeling her and feeling him. Filling up. Dip and sip, I was back—Zing! Riding the wires again.

Clementine tripped round from the rear of the house, hair loose held by pale-pink ribbon, vivid greens casting back the color of June grass, cheeks flushed with the jog uphill, lips open in an O, exposing the cunning overlap of the bottom teeth. The sheets of paper from which she'd been reading slipping one by one past the still-settling swing of her yellow skirt and on down to the stone path beneath her bare feet.

Sparkage stopped breathing and his heart banged in his chest so indecently, it was a wonder she didn't cover her ears. Except for this boy and girl staring at each other across the eternal stretch of gravel, the only audible sound was the side-to-side loll of the deck beneath his feet.

But, instead of welcoming him home, Clementine—who had implored him to come back to Islesboro, to read for himself the diary she'd found, of the horror it contained—turned and ran back into the meadow. Sparkage leapt off his deck, gave chase, and caught up to the girl, but she dodged him. Sparkage hollered, "Whatever you are whatever you are whatever you are whatever, help me out here."

It happened that "whatever you are" had a name: imp, elemental, or racketing specter, I answer to any of them. Except when I don't. I dig noise, making or mimicking, din, drum, or cadence of song. And this "whatever you are" that Sparkage was summoning to his aid (in spite of vowing not to do so), well, that was yours truly. And this voice you've allowed in your head? Me too. But here's where it gets interesting. Just as this voice was talking to you, it was also talking to me, and it was telling me, "Be careful now. Don't overdue."

The boy grabbed her arm. Their touch was like they were touching me. I shuddered to my soul. In reply, the skateboard shot up from the gravel, sailed over the rental van, over Sparkage's head, well past Clementine and into the woods to land in some decay of pine cones and peat. I did that. I launched the skateboard. It's the sort of thing I do when the two of them touch—BUT I did not overdue. Nobody got hurt. Everybody happy.

Except Clementine. She was shrieking and ducking and snapping her arms over her head. Give me a break. The skateboard had cleared them by a good two yards, minimum, but did that stop her from whining?

Sparkage and Clementine together again. I had forgotten how intense their touch.

But Clementine had not forgotten.

FROM THE DIARY OF MR. STEVENS

A local medium, two psychic experts from the mainland, a clairvoyant all inspected the house and the thing troubling us. On these points they agree: this thing is a poltergeist, and the children attract it.

—Clairvoyant asked Clementine when she first felt poltergeist. Clementine—It's always been here.

Points on which the experts disagree:

—The poltergeist can come and go as it pleases and pleasing itself is its central goal.

—The most aimless of all supernatural entities. Has no identifiable goal.

BIRTH

Not true! My goal was to keep Sparkage and Clementine together. This goal was there from the start, or should I say, my start. Allow me to tell you of the inaugural moment of my consciousness.

Something had changed. Don't ask me how. Different, that's all. Darkness lifting.

Up there, a blink of light. Darkness lifting off in these little blinks of light.

Blink.

Blink, blink, and a baby.

Blink, blink, a baby and another baby.

Babies, side by side.

I could see it all: two babies, eyes fixed on the fanning action of their bitty fingers. I observed how limbs issued from bellies, and the much unadorned skin rounding out soft skulls.

Rocking, rocking, hands on feet, the babies rolling onto their sides— at the same time. Bang! The small soft skulls touched. Brow to brow, blending, adhering, annealing, stuck, but too close to see each other. The tears ran sideways in exquisite frustration.

Their touch as if they were touching me.

Dizzying, everything tilted and now I was up. In the floating air above us, bits of light rising and sinking to the music of cooing beside

27

me in the crib. Now something new, a something dancing with the bits of nothing. It dangled over us, dancing dancing until SMACK! The babies startled. Their legs shot out, kicking the other away. The thing above shivered, a chill up the spine. Electric! Spin! That *thing*—I didn't know the word for it yet—but I'd sent it reeling. Me, I did it. Huh, that was pretty, well . . . sensational. Who knew I could do that?

Pretty baby, full lips, vivid eyes, she squealed with delight at the dangling thing spinning over us. She hiccuped. Squeal and hiccup—the two loveliest sounds.

I had to hear the sounds again. Faster: I made the thing spin. Undoing, disjointing over us. A part of it spit across the room.

The click of heels, the door opened, and a large head appeared, followed by the whole body stepping in quick from the hallway, leaving door ajar, exposing the grand staircase beyond. The large head stared, mouth agog, at the thing swinging over the babies. "What on earth is that mobile doing?"

Mobile? So that was the word for it, mobile. I liked. If there was one thing I would come to have a special regard for, it was an object that could be easily moved.

The large head turned to the window. Who'd left it open, allowing in the wind to play? Slam down the window. That ought to do it. The head turned to the babies. The mobile was still spinning as if spun, set in motion by unseen forces, in other words, me.

The babies squalled and hiccuped in delight. No, that was delight. See, they loved it. Maybe not the brooding dark-eyed baby, but the other one was gaga for it. Around and around we go, whee. Talk about chemistry, it was there from *my* start, which of course is the only start that concerns us.

Large Head reached into the crib.

Don't take them out. I'm warning you. Warning you I will . . . what? What? Do not separate, that's all. Perfect the way it was, the babies together. Forever.

The mobile unlatched, broke free, soared over the crib, chugging past the train tracks circling the rug, *Conjunction junction, what's your function?* past the dozing armchair by the door to smash against the wall, fly swat. Large Head held the brooding one to her, soothing the soft black curls snaking into her own black. Right, very nice. Now for the other baby. Pick the other baby up too.

Large Head reached in for the other one but hesitated, looked back at the mobile in pieces on the floor, then at the one in her arms, kissed the soft curls, then stroked the tender belly of the one left behind, and backed out of the room, heels clicking over the train tracks circling the rug, backing to the open door. "Bye bye, Clementine. Don't fuss. You won't miss us much. All will soon be fine as sunshine."

The cushion inchwormed out of the seat of the armchair dozing by the door and flopped heavy onto the floor, right in the path. Click click, Large Head closer by the step. Might have seen the cushion, stepped around it, if only Large Head had stopped walking backward, stopped saying bye bye, stopped thinking only of an escape plan (as opposed to the infinite possibilities in each next second). Too late. The seat cushion tripped her. Large Head pitched back, reaching for the doorframe, but there was only an open door, falling through the doorway, the free arm making big wheels propelling her to the staircase.

The baby, the boy, flew out of her other arm. Good thing the seat cushion was there to catch him, soft landings. Didn't even cry, strange stoic creature.

It was a long way down the grand staircase before something finally struck the floor. The sound faint, like a slab of meat slapped onto a distant countertop. Last, the extinguishing grunt.

Pretty soon someone came along and picked the baby up off the seat cushion and put him back where he belonged in the crib beside the other baby. Their skin met.

I was born.

Sure, I could be a little cruel in those first years, but what child isn't?

As for Large Head? Dead of a broken neck. A twenty-eight-year struggle with epilepsy came to an end at the bottom of the grand staircase of the Stevens residence. The large-headed woman's name was Constance Monroe and she had worked for Mr. Stevens in the capacity of nursemaid for his only child, the infant Clementine.

Constance, who had delivered of her own body a child just months before, was fortunate to have sufficient milk for both infants, a boon that overrode Mr. Stevens's reservations about hiring an epileptic. When Constance had an attack, she would load up on Dilantin and assure Mr. Stevens that epilepsy was "all a lot of sparkage."

As no living relatives could be found for the son of Constance Monroe, Mr. Stevens adopted the boy, named him Sparkage Stevens, and raised him no different than his own.

Mary Kuryla

FROM THE DIARY OF MR. STEVENS

Poltergeist, a term coined in the postromantic, industrial era. But it feels very ancient. Plato's daemon, guardian spirit, charged with ensuring the recipient of its protection achieves his destiny. Supplying the heartaches, accidents, and shocks to the flesh are the daemon's duties.

THE EARLY YEARS

Our lives drifted along, the children lifting seaweed tresses to gaze at purpled infant starfish beneath or wading into the Meadow Pond to gather up tadpoles. Clamming, on the other hand, was hard labor, but Clementine and Sparkage snubbed it principally owing to its popularity with the summering children down island in Dark Harbor. The winter the water froze on Penobscot Bay, they dared each other to run across to the mainland. They dared each other to pull a snake from a hole. Dared each other to sleep in the cemetery. There among the tombstones and the blink of fireflies we would often settle into companionable silence, contemplating not the dead resting in the soil beneath us, but further down to the cold island rock itself and its innumerable mysteries.

Testing, the children were ever testing the strength of their bond. I too did my share of testing, not of the children but rather the island's winds, tides, lightning, etcetera, and such. Of my powers I knew little and, in truth, wanted to know even less. Who isn't terrified of one's potential?

FROM THE DIARY OF MR. STEVENS

The thing's mischief shifts with the seasons. Could it be nature spirit or elemental? Reputedly, the elemental's job is to choke down every last trace on earth of human strife.

—Or maybe it just crawled out from under some rock. In want of a host. Or two?

> *There was a muddy center before we breathed.*
> *There was a myth before the myth began,*
> *Venerable and articulate and complete.*

DINING TABLE

Poltergeists have a reputation for cunning, but that's not all the time. Like the children, I wanted to be part of a family, I tried to please. Take Mr. Stevens's dining table as an example.

"A table stands best on three legs," Mr. Stevens said the day a leg of the heirloom heavy oak dining table snapped. Sparkage was criss-crossing the kitchen on his first skateboard, which he'd taken to like a wick to a flame. Until Mr. Stevens opened the oven door to remove the roast and cut Sparkage in his path. Whereupon the boy busted out his first ollie. He cleared the oven door but launched headfirst into the table, his skull striking a table leg and snapping it clean off. Sparkage buckled in half and slid under the table. The wildly tipping table followed, bent on slicing straight through his skinny-boy neck.

But I caught it.

Mr. Stevens whipped Sparkage out from under, backing up until they hit the wall. The table had stood—or withstood gravity. The cumbersome item hadn't fallen on his child. "Clementine," Mr. Stevens said, "go to the table. Give it a good push, there's a girl."

Clementine tiptoed up to the table, set her hand on the edge, and looked at her father. He nodded. She pushed. The table was a rock, solid as if it stood four legs to the floor.

"What happens if we eat on it?"

"Set it and see," said Mr. Stevens.

Clementine laid out spoons and forks and knives, but before taking their dinner, Mr. Stevens struck the table with his fist. Tell you what. It didn't budge.

"Fix this table!" Sparkage slammed his backpack against the three-legged table not long after and glared down at his face in the polished surface. "It's a freak. Chop it for kindling."

"Is that the fate of freaks?" said Mr. Stevens.

Without a word, the boy kicked up his deck and walked out of the house.

"What's going on?" Mr. Stevens asked his daughter.

Clementine spoke carefully. "Everybody at school says I mustn't marry Sparkage because we're related."

"Not by blood."

She tugged at the cunning rope she'd used to hold up her shorts. "But we are your children."

"Equally."

31

Mr. Stevens phoned a nanny agency on the mainland. The children required domestication, but it was too late for maternal influence. What the children needed now was a chaperone.

FRAU STARR

The children first encountered Frau Starr in the kitchen, or rather the stiff back of the woman from the town of Worms, Germany, as she scrubbed clean the kitchen sink. She smiled crookedly at them. "Hello, *kinder*," she said. "I have gifts from Worms," and plunked her vast handbag on the dining table.

The table rasped and quivered as if struck by a blade then lurched over on its side with a crash, Frau Starr's bag disgorging bricks of chocolate onto the floor.

Everyone stared in dismay at the dining table that had stood so well on three legs.

Frau Starr looked up, flushed with embarrassment, then studied the table. "So, of course it fell." She sounded relieved. "One leg kaput!"

It's elementary to my nature. I push things, fell them, budge them, misplace them, then again situate them so you stumble, run into them, hurt yourself. Things are one way until I come along, then they are something else, then something else again.

At one time, if you knew me for that, why, I'd got what I was after. What more was there? I was changing, becoming something *more*. How much more I could not say, except that I wanted more of more. Only I wasn't getting any more out of all this wanting. Something had to change.

POLTERZIMMER

Fixed was how Frau Starr liked things. For every object there was a place, for every behavior a room. Eating was accomplished in the dining room, crying belonged in the bedroom, laughter was strictly for the screened porch. But rage, rage was LOUD and had a room all its own, with a name that Frau Starr had brought from the old country—polterzimmer, which means noisy room. No worn-out or broken toys were tossed away under Frau Starr's watch but instead whisked inside the polterzimmer, broken toys adding nicely to the din when Sparkage raged amid its walls.

Daily, Frau Starr sent Sparkage to the polterzimmer. "You want to make like a *kling-a-ling*? So, do it here."

Clementine sat guiltily outside the door, listening to Sparkage smash stuff to the accompaniment of *Sesame Street* on the polter-zimmer TV. "Conjunction junction, what's your function? Talking about AND, BUT, and OR will get you very far . . ." It was Clementine's fault Sparkage got banished to the polterzimmer that day. She had informed him that his mother fell down the grand staircase, and that it was no accident.

These details of his mother's demise were news to Sparkage, and he'd quite naturally flown into a rage, but he was played out now, sprawled across the floor, panting. The polterzimmer was warm, still, rank, so I sent a breeze to cool the boy. The breeze rustled his trousers, tickled his fingers, and aroused curious sensations beneath the trouser buttons. I could have blushed at the lust of one so young.

Clementine had never been in the polterzimmer. Resolved to apologize, she opened the door slowly, afraid of getting clocked by a teacup, eyes widening at the sight of Sparkage hunched over on the floor. He turned his back to her and buttoned his trousers. Shocked and betrayed by catching him in self-caress, all apologies vanished. The two went at each other, vicious as a pair of shark pups in a purse.

I was slow to react—Clementine was not the only confounded one—but now, as the children rolled across the plastic playthings, hands hooked onto cheeks, I reassembled.

Skin to skin, the children were ticked off and on fire with fight. Lobbing me into action.

I inched up the windows. In seconds, I had air breezing into the attic room, swirling the bits on the floor, stirring a broken-toy froth around the boy and girl battling to the *plitsch-platsch* of plastic against the glass. The door to the polterzimmer swung open. Frau Starr stood in the doorway. "Kinder!" Without a fleck of hesitation—I'll give the sink scrubber that, she was no coward—she lifted the two by their collars and yanked them asunder.

But get this.

No dissipation. No dilution.

Their parting amplified their fury—building and building—until. Pop. Pop. Pop! I can still hear the sound of all those polterzimmer windows blowing. Got to be the loudest sound a house can make, shredding the nerves. (I've since figured out how to manufacture the sound without blowing a window. Dead of night. Everyone in deep sleep. That's when I do it.) The shooting shards of glass positively bedazzled the children, but not Frau Starr. Throwing the children on the ground, she covered them with her rigid flesh.

Glass sharp like knives flinging every which way to the *plitsch-platsch* against the glass, blood, and below, the *kling-a-ling, kling-a-ling* of the telephone.

FROM THE DIARY OF MR. STEVENS

Frau Starr quit. Clementine grows moody. Sparkage sulks unless atop his deck. The poltergeist likewise afflicted.

Teens.

—The typical poltergeist feeds off the fear and anxiety it provokes in the focus person. But that was not the case here. Everyone having fun, poltergeist included. Because the poltergeist focused on two, the children, both and together? Who can say?

Trouble now is they are children no longer—the thing as confused as they by this development.

HORMONE STORMS

Mr. Stevens called that one right. Focusing on the two of them was the goal, and it was killing me, especially the older we got, and the hornier. As I was not of human flesh, my love for Clementine was notional, isolate, laced with the delicacy of observation. To register the sound of her voice and to pick up her scent was all. Nothing carnal, mind you. No joy at the waiting willing warm incredible flesh of my beloved, but don't think I didn't try. When it comes to love, not just romantic yearning, it is all about that last dirty sense: touch. For that, one will do about anything.

Other times my object was Sparkage—for the record, "sparkage" is also the word for when the tail grind plate on a skateboard drags against cement, igniting wondrous sparks. Board and boy made sound and light through motion. In the moment of torque, who could say what propelled the other. Goading me to launch the deck so as to feel the heft of his body against me, the two of us leaping, defying gravity for infinite seconds.

I loved, and constantly, but never for both at the same time. Simultaneous lust was off-limits. Moment by moment, I had always to choose who to love. Thus, my lust fluctuated, him or her, male/female, don't much matter, lust is very leveling for a poltergeist, and sometimes I preferred to threaten them with harm.

Fidgety, edgity, I just needed things to move or blow, and Sparkage was no different.

"I'm sliding away from you," he said as his hips shifted on the skateboard, "down the corridor to the top of the stairwell and launching off the top stair, floating while my board does a corkscrew under me. I'm aloft, until I land, upright on my board, at the bottom of the stairs."

Sparkage had taken to skateboarding through the house. His objective was to launch the deck off the top step of the grand staircase and land at the bottom unharmed. He had managed the first landing so far, and not surprisingly all that movement had also loosened his tongue.

In and out of rooms, down corridors, out across the landing, kicking it up along the banister while Clementine watched. But today Clementine had become distracted by the view out the staircase window of clouds pushing against each other, one real billowy display, in particular.

Here he came now. Without shifting her eyes from the clouds, she extended her young arm so her hand might touch some part of Sparkage, even just fingertips brushing his.

The littlest touch and crack! A peel of orange torched the clouds.

Clementine clapped hands. How marvelous. More! she cried. She could not get enough. Nor could I, given this was the first time I had managed something this big outside the house. I mean, with the lightest skin-to-skin contact, I made lightning up there in the clouds.

Fingers brushing cheek, arm, hand: Clementine and Sparkage had been in physical contact with each other pretty regularly. Doing it just to see what could happen. All in good fun. A little game with your poltergeist.

"Did you see the lightning?" Clementine called to Sparkage as he hurled along the corridor.

"Saw it."

The comforting clug of trucks rose up again, and there was Sparkage passing by. He reached out for Clementine and, because there was no hand extended to him this time, his fingers swiped across the first thing they found and as it happened what he touched was her butt—by accident. It was an accident, anyone could see that.

Sparkage stumbled off his deck and didn't retrieve it either, as he was more interested in his hand that had touched Clementine on a part of her that he had never touched before.

He looked up in bewilderment, the sort that comes of having beheld something for the entirety of what you call your life and in one soul-altering second seeing something that wasn't there an instant before.

For the first time, Sparkage saw Clementine, his eyes tapping over her body like a miner striking for gold, following the sway of her lower back to the swell of the rear, lingering, lingering, then following the long thigh extending from the careless shorts, the delicate shell-capped knee, the attenuated shin faintly blued with veins and up again to the jut of hips pulsing beneath the thin skin above the low-slung belt, and further, his eyes tapping up her skin, incredulous at all this flesh, reluctant to yield an inch from his gaze and desperate to see what the next view would bring, the small certain swell of breasts. The very first he had seen of them, of any of it.

Sparkage stomped up beside her but without coming close. He stood there like a straw man.

Clementine moved nearer to Sparkage, took his arm in her two young hands and looked up at him. He flinched.

I did not know how to react.

All she could say was, "What's with you?"

Sparkage shook her hands off him and mounted the stairs with his deck, setting it at the far end of the landing, the best place to launch from the top stair, fifteen steps to the bottom.

"You can't do that. It's suicide."

He stepped up on the skateboard. "Good."

Sparkage carved his way to the top of the steps and launched off, the deck flying out from under, soaring over the steps—

Or

Maybe all I really longed for was flesh: clearly, the skateboarder got the girl (hear the thump of her heart, note the spin of her head, feel the aura of sex); skateboarding was cool in exactly the way my showy display of lightning was not—

And

landing upright, feet firmly on his deck. Sparkage had made it to the bottom of the staircase without a nick, but this was so impossible that he panicked and bailed off the deck, whacking his head on the rail on the way.

Clementine scrambled down the stairs and dropped to her knees beside him.

He wouldn't look at her.

She knew he was not hurt enough to ask after it as she listened with scant attention to the trucks on the upended deck spinning down to still.

"I'm getting out of here, Clem."

"You can't just leave."

"If I don't, someone's going to get hurt." They spoke fast, in whispers, cheeks pink.

Clementine took his hand. "Stupid. It would never hurt us."

Her shirt had risen up, and the boy reached around her waist. The feel of her skin against his forearm shocked me.

Lightning struck.

I'm not speaking metaphorically, either. Lightning struck inside the house, straight through the roof, zigzagging to the ground, electrifying the whole joint nova bright. Fortunately, Sparkage pushed her out of harm's way. Clementine stared fright blind at the smoke swirling up from the singed edge of her shorts and on up to the fresh-made hole in the roof.

The next day, Sparkage left Islesboro with only the deck on his back and would not return, not even for Mr. Stevens's funeral, not until now.

FROM THE DIARY OF MR. STEVENS

Uncontrolled psychokinesis. The thing is without reason, without rhyme. No longer just threatening, if occasionally charming. It no longer likes me. I feel it. Does it fault me for Sparkage's abandonment of us? Doesn't know what's good for it. Shoved a wedge between Sparkage and Clementine. It had fed off passion, I'm certain of it. Can frustration make for better feeding? Well, it drove Sparkage away. Clementine won't leave her room for grief. And I had once heard poetry in the thing. The scrap of wallpaper I found with its first poem.

THE POET

So here we were now: Sparkage had returned to Islesboro at Clementine's behest, but things were already unruly. I had launched the boy's skateboard into the woods, and he'd only just located it. Meanwhile, Clementine fled inside the house for safety.

The house was dark when Sparkage stepped in. He felt along the wall for a light switch.

"Electric's out," the girl said from the shadows.

"Why? I told you I'd cover utilities."

"The utilities are squared. Everything's just . . . busted. Phone too. But it still rings. *Kling-a-ling.*"

37

Clementine followed him into the kitchen, where he took down a glass and turned on the tap.

"Water's still safe to drink," she said.

"Stop acting like the house is haunted."

"Not the house," said Clementine. "We are."

Sparkage tapped his foot, a real impatient vibe. "Cut it out, Clementine. I've got to get back on the road. Skate finals begin Monday. Where's the diary?"

Clementine turned abruptly away from him. Over a year since they'd seen each other, and they were shier and more grown apart by mourning than they imagined. He followed Clementine into the study, where the walls of books were impressive. Too bad you couldn't read the poetry titles since I'd burned them off. The fleur-de-lis wallpaper bulged with velveteen sea life of water damage.

"Poltergeist?"

She nodded. "Trashed the house after you left."

"No, that's not right. It left with me. I know it left with me."

"Maybe it divided its time between us, like a child of divorce?"

"It wasn't divorce, Clem. I left so it wouldn't kill you . . . or me."

"Stupid. It would never hurt us . . . I mean, not that way."

Sparkage snatched Mr. Stevens's diary from her hands, but instead of reading, he turned it upside down and shook. As usual, he'd made the right call. Lo and behold, a bit of wallpaper slipped from the pages. On the back of the fleur-de-lis pattern, someone or *something* had scrawled, "Gug, ick, lug," and below these utterances, Mr. Stevens had noted, *"Its first poem."*

The poem was a trifle, but their awe at my talents was flattering. Sparkage riffled through the diary for more but I'm afraid he was disappointed.

FROM THE DIARY OF MR. STEVENS

The thing topples books from the shelves onto the floor. The romantics, Pushkin, Burns, Baudelaire. Focused upon a constellation of poems. Is this tenderness? Something of the soul? I prefer this to the one that hides kitchen knives then flings them my way. Can it begrudge even supper for Clementine?

KNIVES AND KNIVES AND KNIVES

Sparkage looked up. "When did you find him?" he said.

"Round suppertime."

"Where?"

"Kitchen," Clementine said. She rubbed a fist into her eye. "The kitchen was totaled. Table flipped, cupboards dumped, drawers out, everywhere forks and spoons and knives . . . and knives . . . and knives . . ."

Really a marvelous display, the drawers slicing open and the utensils quaking and chirping, *piep-piep*, until, at last, they fluttered and fledged into the air, the knives swooping about Mr. Stevens's sweet balding skull—but no touching, not once! Beautiful, beguiling, all those loose, serrated objects set free to dance.

FROM THE DIARY OF MR. STEVENS

It left an offering, a stab at verse composed on the back of wallpaper. Its ink! Wallpaper glue. I applaud the ingenuity. But it ought to stick to screaming up pipes and rapping at windows.

AND, BUT, AND OR WILL GET YOU VERY FAR

How cruel their father could be. Can you blame me? Can they?

"Fucking poltergeist." Sparkage chucked the diary at the wall. "Gave Dad a heart attack. I'll kill it."

Clementine grabbed him so hard, she upended his deck. "Shhhhh," she hissed.

His eyes snapped to her.

"It hears you."

They dropped to the floor, holding each other.

The deck flipped back over.

Clementine turned slowly to look. Upright again, the wheels vibrated in place, hesitant, now creeping forward, gaining momentum, the deck electing to circle them.

When the girl leaned into Sparkage, the skateboard webbed them in. She half smiled at him, but he was not fooled.

Each time around, the circle grew tighter and tighter until Sparkage lunged across Clementine's folded knees and grabbed her hand out of harm's way.

She poked his chest, provocative.

The deck picked up speed, fishtailing on the turns, and Sparkage's large hand slid under the hank of hair behind her neck. "You are so beautiful, Clementine."

Beautiful? He still couldn't find the words to describe her. She was nerve-rackingly attractive.

As Sparkage pressed his lips against hers, Clementine stayed very still but did not pull away.

He worked into the kiss, pulling her mouth into his, gentling her lips apart.

"*. . . what are all these kissings worth, if thou kiss not me?*"

Sparkage flipped her beneath him. That was my move, by the way. I'd just done it with the deck.

Her face opened with surprise.

Maybe if he had given her a minute—a simple matter of timing, alas a commodity these youngsters have in little supply—before letting loose (his mouth all tongue now, insistent hips slicing into hers), if he had let her meet him halfway, then maybe her mouth would not have closed so tight against his, her kicks would not have sent the deck caroming against the wall.

Clementine crabbed on the flat of her hands out of his reach. "Let's not be like this."

"We are like this." He yanked her to her feet. She yelped with fright. "You want me. I want you."

"I don't! And you don't want me."—OR—"But, but you really want me." You could chop the frustration with an ax.

A breath, two breaths, and he held her to the wall. "I missed you. Kept seeing you. Every piece of you."

"Go, get out of here."

But his face moved in on her face, her lips opening to his—when, out the corner of her eye, something flashed.

A quick fix. Just fooling around. Ollie anybody? Launched and spinning with weird speed and thrust, the deck's edges ax sharp at this speed.

Coming straight for Clementine's skull.

OR

Sparkage's skull.

Deck speeding AND wavering BUT which to choose; frustration mounting; must choose OR die—

"No!" Clementine thrust him from her.

The deck struck Sparkage, brow to ear, bombing the soft cartilage of the outer lobe. He gagged and dropped like a stone. The skateboard didn't hit the ground that fast.

It is moments like these that you say to yourself, Do something!

BUT

Clementine was already wrapping Sparkage's head in a dish towel to stanch the blood, saying, "Don't move. I'll get help." She grabbed his keys, took the rental van, sped out.

Sparkage heard the grind of tires on the gravel, sat up, then got to his feet, woozy, and looked around, like he was searching for me. "Leave her alone," he said. "You hear me?"

He limped to the door and out onto the driveway where he remembered there was a shortcut he could take to head her off. He crisscrossed through seagrass and stumbled through a stream, arriving at the foot of the island's only covered bridge. The van was coming up the road fast—but it cut short at the lip of the bridge, rolling under the covered portion, disappearing from view.

The sound of the motor convulsing.

Sparkage wiped the blood muddling his sight and dragged himself onto the bridge.

Now the screech of metal getting pried off. Out of the covered bridge shot the van's front bumper. The windshield spun out from the dark of the box next. It landed at Sparkage, knocking him off his feet.

"Get out, Clem!" Sparkage pushed to his knees.

A tire rolled out, followed by Clementine, wiping at blood gushing from her nose.

Something under the wooden cover blew, setting the bridge to swing to and fro. Sparkage crawled to Clementine.

Darkish golden liquid spouted from the box. "Gasoline," said Sparkage.

"Why?" she said. "It messed with others. Not us."

Sparkage might have given her an answer, if he had one.

But Clementine was not waiting for answers anymore. She stood up shaky, walked, and then ran for help.

Did Sparkage catch the sound of the big truck barreling along the main road? If he'd been in shape to get up, he might have seen a small figure (Clementine—thinking only of a rescue plan, as opposed to the infinite possibilities that each next second holds) bolting incautiously onto the main road to flag the driver, who swerved to avoid hitting her, which caused the trailer to fishtail and strike Clementine from behind, sending her soaring over a nearby marsh.

After a tense moment, the truck righted itself and steamed on.

Squeal and hiccup. The two loveliest sounds.

I would never hear them again.

What it was, what it really was, I was the one immobilized. I wanted her, I wanted him—I had to choose. Or did I? Maybe I existed because of him AND her. What on earth had I done? I'll tell you what I did, I chose, but I loved them equally, and now Clementine was dead.

DEPARTURE

From outside the police cruiser, Sparkage's pounding fists sounded dull compared to the racket he had raised after finding Clementine's body. His shoulder striking the door was even quieter and, improbably, his head smashing against the glass was quietest of all since the sound of skin breaking wasn't a tear you'd hear. As his forehead smeared a slurry of blood across the cruiser's window, I made a squeegee sound—for audio accompaniment.

Bet you're wondering why I wasn't riding inside the car, not being bound by the same physical laws as humans. The truth was I was dissipating and supersensitive to sound. And Sparkage's longing for Clementine was deafening, more deafening than the silence I would soon become.

The Owl Count
Elizabeth Hand

IN MID-MARCH, LOUIS'S childhood friend Eric died of a cerebral aneurysm after being in a coma for nine days. The memorial was in the small Vermont town where they'd grown up together. Louis drove there from northern Maine, spent the night at a friend's house after the service, and left again next morning.

It was late afternoon when he got back home, to a few inches of new snow. He went inside and fired up the woodstove, sorted through the few items of mail that had arrived since he'd left, grabbed a beer from the fridge, and checked his mobile. There he found a text message from his old friend Yvette.

> Looks like the best night for the owl count will be tonight or Monday. Moon is just past full now. Will be cold but I'm afraid if we don't get out this week we'll miss the chance because of weather.

Louis stared out at the bare trees silhouetted against the dusk. After a moment he wrote, just returned from a funeral in vermont, can do it tomorrow maybe

Immediately she replied: No, supposed to snow early tomorrow. Need to go tonight.

Louis swore softly, then sighed. ok what time

Will pick you up @ 11:30. See you then!

He finished his beer and reheated some soup for dinner, checked the temperature and weather. Twenty-eight degrees, cloudy, not much wind. Heavy snow predicted but not till morning. Not an ideal night, at least as far as Louis was concerned—it was way too cold.

But the owls wouldn't care, and neither would Yvette. Like Louis, she was widowed. Her husband, Buddy, had been Louis's close friend, a game warden who'd been two months from retirement when he had a heart attack while searching for a snowmobiler who'd gone missing up by Greenville. Louis always felt like he'd taken Buddy's death harder than Yvette. Not true, he knew that; it was just Yvette's way. Her composure and oddly fatalistic good humor remained unshaken

43

by death, war, the slow decay of the wilderness where they lived. And now, her own illness.

Louis's wife, Sheila, had died within a year of Buddy. That was over a decade ago. The plastic bins full of medications she'd been prescribed in her last months were still jammed onto the floor of the bedroom closet, where her winter coats, flannel shirts, and snow-mobiling gear continued to hang alongside Louis's own. Like Yvette—like everyone—he'd been downsized from his teaching job when their university rolled over to the AI modules. Since then he'd gotten by the same way his Maine ancestors had a century earlier. Bartering and scavenging; hunting and fishing; coaxing pumpkins, squash, beans, onions, garlic, Jacob's Cattle Beans from the stony soil and longer growing season that was one of the few enduring benefits of the so-called lost winters.

"You can grow tomatoes in Maine now!" Yvette always marveled.

"Yeah, but not potatoes," Louis would retort. The mutated potato bugs had seen to that.

He washed his soup bowl and spoon, went outside to bring in more firewood. If it really did snow the next day, he'd be too tired from the owl count to bother in the morning. He drank another beer, set the alarm for 11:00 p.m., four hours from now, and went to bed.

He woke when the phone rang. Yvette again. He looked blearily at the time and groaned. "Jesus, you couldn't let me sleep another fifteen minutes?"

"I was afraid you wouldn't wake up!"

Louis had never overslept for the owl count, but he knew that wasn't the issue. Yvette was too excited to wait. "Well, give me a few minutes. I need some coffee."

"I have coffee."

"I give up. See you when you get here."

He heated water for the coffee and dressed. Thermal long underwear, a pair of wool hunting pants that had been his father's, a ragg wool sweater, and another that Sheila had knit for him. Two pairs of wool socks, old insulated Bean boots. Most years, he and Yvette didn't hear any owls. But it was guaranteed that they'd freeze as they waited in hopes of doing so.

He'd just finished gulping down the coffee when Yvette's headlights cut through the darkness outside the kitchen window. She left the car idling and entered without knocking. Louis held up his coffee mug. "Want some?"

Yvette perched on the arm of the chair beside the woodstove. With her green snow pants, oversized black boots, and red parka, its pointed hood pulled up so that wispy white curls framed her face, she resembled a garden gnome. She glanced at the coffee mug and shook her head.

"I'm all set," she said. She watched Louis with the avid expression of a dog awaiting a walk. He grabbed gloves and knit cap, pulled on his own parka, shoved his mobile in a pocket, and stuck another log in the woodstove.

"OK," he said.

Yvette hopped up and hurried outside. Louis followed, the snow soft beneath his boots. He got into her old Subaru, where she handed him a clipboard.

"And there's more coffee." She pointed at a thermos on the floor, put the car into gear, and gingerly pulled out onto the road. "I'm so excited!" she exclaimed, and grinned.

Louis had joined the owl count twenty-six years earlier, when Yvette's former owling partner moved back to Florida. Back then, the program was administered by a Maine college that had received a grant to do a study of the state's owl population. The top data sheet on Louis's clipboard dated to that time.

We seek to establish owl presence across our landscape, to estimate population and density for common Maine owls, and to detect changes in distribution or density perhaps related to human influences . . .

Data was collected by teams of volunteers across Maine between early March and mid-April—breeding season. They monitored five owl species—short- and long-eared owls, saw-whet owls, barred owls, great horned owls. The project ended years ago, but Yvette and Louis had continued to go out nearly every spring since. This was Yvette's idea, of course, but except for that year when Sheila had finally gone into hospice in Bangor, Louis accompanied Yvette every time, including the March night only weeks after Buddy's death.

The Subaru jounced down the rutted drive to the road as Yvette downshifted to avoid potholes and frost heaves. Louis's car was a hybrid, nearly as old as Yvette's Subaru, but it didn't fare as well in winter. He stuck the clipboard on the floor and reached to turn down the heat. Yvette's car reeked of dog and scorched engine oil—the head gasket leaked, so she had to top off the oil every other day, from a stockpile she'd traded for with gallons of tomato sauce and some deworming medicine with a 2007 expiration date. Her dog, Wilmer, was back at the house. The only time he didn't accompany Yvette was during the owl count.

"Damn!" Yvette slapped the steering wheel and Louis looked at her in alarm. Yvette never swore. "I forgot to check if there's batteries in the CD player! Do you have any?"

"At the house, maybe." He twisted to look into the back seat, piled with outdoor gear and blankets covered in dog hair, and snaked out his arm to retrieve the portable boom box, a decrepit piece of out-moded technology that Yvette coddled as though it had been one of her wheezing dogs. She'd bought it specifically for the owl count. That must have been more than thirty years ago, when CDs were already being phased out.

As far as Louis knew, she never used it for any other purpose—he'd never seen a single other CD in her house. Some nights during the summer, she'd play the owl-call CD on the deck of her house up on Flywheel Mountain, watching as the owls appeared ghostlike from the darkness above her head. A practice the Owl Monitoring Program had strictly warned against, back in the day, but the study had ended so long ago, who was possibly left to care? Certainly Yvette had seen and heard more owls during these forbidden sessions than they ever had during the owl count.

He peered through the CD player's smudged plastic window and saw the disc. Did she ever even remove it? Probably not. He hit *Play*, watched as the disc began to spin. "It's working," he said.

"Thank God."

The car juddered as she steered it onto Route 217, one of the sec-ondary roads that threaded through this part of the Allagash territory. Yvette had meticulous directions for the owl count—the exact mile-age between each stop, numbers on utility poles and mailboxes, descriptions of unusual trees or rocks, notes for other landmarks. Once upon a time, there had been sporting camps here, then family-friendly resorts, then a few glampsites, a fairly desperate and frankly insane attempt on the part of entrepreneurs from away that failed almost overnight. As the timber companies went under, most of their holdings went to the state, but with no demand for paper, build-ing materials, or recreation, the land had reverted to wilderness. A new and different kind of wilderness: the nature of the boreal forest changed as conifers and evergreens adapted to the longer growing season or, in many cases, died.

Someone from away might not notice the difference. Looking out the window of the Subaru, Louis still saw the black encroaching walls to either side of the narrow road, the trees closer to the broken tarmac with each passing season. He rolled down the window—even with the heat off, the car was stifling. Cold air rushed in, balsam and the pissy scent of cat spruce, along with a more forbidding, granitic scent that he knew presaged snow.

"It feels like it could be a real storm," he said, cradling the boom box in his lap.

"I know." Yvette sounded triumphant. "That's why I wanted to go tonight. Can you see the *Gazetteer* back there? Grab it, will you? I want to head up to the Araweag."

"Really?" The Araweag was paper-mill land, or had been before it was clear-cut long ago. Now it was boggy, impenetrable thickets of speckled alder and blackberry crowding the wetland.

"I want to try something different. Miriam Rogers told me her son was hunting moose up there and saw a great horned owl. Hunting, in daylight."

"The owl or Miriam's son?"

"The owl. He watched it swoop down on a snowshoe hare. Poor bunny."

"A snowshoe hare? In broad daylight?"

"That's why I want to go."

"If the owls are hunting in daytime, why would we hear them now?"

Yvette swatted him. "Just tell me how far it is."

He opened the glove compartment so he could read by its light, flipped through the *Gazetteer* until he found the right page. "Twenty miles, maybe? Bad roads, though. Some may not be open anymore."

"Let's stay on 217. Make a few of the old stops first."

Louis nodded. He closed the glove compartment and tossed the *Gazetteer* onto the floor behind his seat, swigged a mouthful of tepid coffee from the thermos, and closed his eyes.

"I'm sorry about your friend," Yvette said. "It was your friend, right?"

Louis didn't open his eyes. Yvette had mild dementia that manifested mostly as forgetfulness. "Thanks."

"After Buddy died," she went on cheerfully, " someone told me I should watch for signs. Lori, she's the massage therapist used to live at Stone Farm. She told me if I wanted a sign from Buddy, I should close my eyes and count to three. When I opened them, the first three things I saw, that would be the sign."

"Did you ever see anything?"

"Just the dogs."

Eyes shut, Louis thought of Eric, the last time they'd met. Walking along the Battenkill, the river where as boys they'd fished for brownies and brookies: once one of the world's great trout streams, now nothing but a stony track that resembled an ancient Roman road winding through the Vermont woods. When he opened his eyes, he saw only his own reflection in the black glass of the Subaru's passenger window.

When they used to do the owl count, Yvette would put a big cardboard sign that read OWL MONITORING PROGRAM on the dashboard. In those days, more vehicles were on the road. Not many, especially in the middle of the night, but there'd been a few times when people slowed or even stopped. Always men, they often seemed to have been drinking, another reason Louis liked to accompany Yvette. Once a state trooper had approached them—someone had noticed the parked Subaru and phoned dispatch. The policeman had been bemused, even more so when Yvette played him some of the owl calls.

"Well, just be careful you don't run out of gas," he'd finally said. "Cold out here."

It had been years since they'd seen another car or pickup at night, but Louis felt the familiar frisson as they pulled over beside their first landmark, a Bangor Hydro power pole that hadn't been live since 2013. A small piece of metal stamped 141A was nailed to the pole, but Louis had long since learned to identify it by the surrounding fields: once farmland, now overgrown with highbush blueberry and sumac.

In daylight, you could spot the centuries-old clapboard farmhouse in the distance. When he and Yvette had first done the count, lights shone from one or two of its windows and dogs barked, alerting the household to interlopers in the road, but no one had ever come out to investigate. Louis heard the old man who'd lived there wandered off one night a few summers ago. His body was never found. Now Louis could barely make out the house, ghostly white against the black trees.

Yvette asked, "Did you check the volume?"

Louis reached again for the boom box. He switched it to the radio, reflexively turning the dial. Nothing but static until he hit the Christian music station out of Houlton, one of the few remaining stations in operation and the only one with a signal strong enough to be heard up here. Louis adjusted the volume, grimacing, and quickly switched the player back to CD mode.

"Did you bring extra batteries?"

Louis shook his head. "I told you, no."

"Oh," said Yvette. She turned the car off and stared at the steering column with vague interest, as though she'd never seen one before. "I didn't hear you."

"That's OK." Louis often wondered if her forgetfulness might be an evolutionary advantage. If you couldn't recall the world as it had once been, you couldn't miss it.

Though the evolutionary benefits diminished once you factored in things like forgetting to eat, or misplacing the car keys while you were out in the middle of the night in subzero weather. He slid the key from the ignition and pocketed it.

Yvette smiled. "I didn't forget the key."

Louis smiled back. "Neither did I." He turned on the dashboard light, fumbled a pen from his parka pocket as he balanced the clipboard on his knees, turning from the first data sheet to the one beneath.

MOMP 2012 MAINE OWL MONITORING PROGRAM
MAINE AUDUBON AND THE MAINE DEPARTMENT
OF INLAND FISHERIES AND WILDLIFE

He filled in the date and time, ignored the other blank spaces—*Observer, Route Code, Observer Email/Phone Number, Assistant's Name*—and began to fill in the information for Stop 1:

Time (military): 00:27, Temp: 28F, Cloud Cover: 40 percent

For *Wind* he circled the appropriate numerical Beaufort Wind Scale, guessing it was a 2 [*4–6 mph, light breeze, wind felt on face, leaves rustle*], even though there were no leaves to rustle. He glanced outside and saw spruce boughs rippling, changed the 2 to a 3 [*gentle breeze, leaves and small twigs in motion*]. He notated *Noise* and *Precipitation* in the same way, circling 0 for *Precipitation* [*note that survey should not be conducted if precipitation is a 3 or above*] and 1 for *Noise* [*relatively quiet*], even though when he cracked the window, it was pretty much silent outside.

For *Snow Cover* he circled *C* [*complete*]. For *Frogs*: Yes/No, *No*. He left *Car Count* and *Plane Count* blank. He couldn't remember when he'd last seen or heard a plane. He filled in the *Playback* info from memory—*Boom Box, High Volume, Memorex, Audible at 1/10 mile*—and left the *Comments* section blank, for now.

"Ready?" asked Yvette.

"Almost." He turned to the next sheet, scrawled in the date, his name and Yvette's, the name of the township. He didn't bother with the odometer reading, but looked outside once more before filling in the stop and habitat descriptions: *Pole 141 A, Overgrown fields and abandoned house to right of road, woods to L.* "OK, let's go."

He set the clipboard on the floor, opened his door, and stepped outside. Yvette turned off the dashboard light, grabbed the boom box, and did the same. "Not that cold," she said.

Louis gave a noncommittal nod. It didn't feel that cold, but he knew how it worked, especially with snow in the forecast. No fear of frostbite, but the humidity would seep through your parka and gloves and cap: if you didn't keep moving, within a short while your blood would seem to cool and thicken, your bones to feel as though they held ice instead of marrow.

And you weren't supposed to move, not once the playback started. Yvette set the boom box onto the rust-pocked hood of the old car, pointing it toward the distant empty house across the fields. That overgrown swath would still be ideal habitat for owls and their prey—voles and white-footed mice, rabbits and snowshoe hare, smaller winter birds like chickadees that would be sleeping now but might be caught at dawn or dusk if they stirred.

He leaned against the car, letting his eyes adjust to the darkness, his ears to the silence. His breath clouded the air as he tipped his head back and saw a few stars pricking through the haze. *Cloud cover only 30 percent*, he thought, but that wouldn't last. A few feet away, Yvette's pose mirrored his own, but her eyes were closed. Not sleeping: listening intently. He squeezed his own eyes shut, his head still uptilted.

Everything sounded the same: white pine needles a susurrus like waves on the shore; the skreak of spruce branches rubbing together; a noise like knuckles cracking that might be a deer moving through the woods. He recalled what Yvette had said about watching for signs, held his breath, counted to three, and opened his eyes.

For a split second he thought he saw another pair of eyes gazing into his, then realized they were stars, momentarily dazzling in a gap of clouds that moved swiftly across the sky. The wind carried a faint scent of crushed bracken and balsam. Almost certainly a deer had left its bed, awakened by their presence. He looked over his shoulder and saw Yvette watching him, her hand on the boom box. She raised her eyebrows. He nodded; she nodded back, then pushed *Play*.

The owl-call sequence began with a low electronic beep, followed by the first track: two minutes of silence. During that time, Louis's hearing grew more acute, the rustling of trees amplified so that he could distinguish between individual branches as they rubbed together, some high, others closer to the ground. After two minutes, the second track kicked in—the call of a short-eared owl: a series of brief, breathy hoots, repeated twice, then another two minutes of silence.

Louis held his breath, straining to hear a reply. Many years ago, he had seen a short-eared owl in daylight, skimming above a field, its yellow eyes bright as traffic lights, tiny tufted ears nowhere in evidence. He saw and heard nothing now. The next call was the long-eared owl's: a single, rather toneless hoot, repeated several times, each after a few seconds' interval, followed by the two-minute silence.

Only now it wasn't so silent. Tiny things stirred nearby—small birds fluttering nervously in the lower branches of the spruce trees. Mice skittered across the dead leaves that had rucked up against the tree trunks to provide shelter from the snow. Squeaks and rustlings, a swift settling back into a new, more watchful silence.

The saw-whet owl was next. Its breathy piping cry grew gradually louder, paused, then repeated. Louis had seen one of these too, improbably perched upon his bulkhead one late-spring morning. It looked like a toy, small enough to fit into his cupped palm, with enormous orange eyes that, when it blinked, gave it the appearance of a sleepy child. Louis had longed to pick it up, it looked so utterly helpless and soft. When he went to check on it an hour later, it was gone. He hoped it hadn't fallen prey to some larger owl or eagle. He cocked his head, hoping to hear a response in the silence that followed.

Again, he heard nothing but wind in the trees. Like him, the birds and mice were holding their breath. He glanced at Yvette and saw her staring raptly into the sky above the field, her gaze flicking back and forth. Was she watching something? He squinted but could make out only darkness seeded by a handful of stars.

Two tracks left. The barred owl came first, the owl they were most likely to hear, with its distinctive demand, *Who cooks for you? Who cooks for you?*, followed by a six-minute silence—barred owls sometimes took longer to reply.

This was the most difficult part of each stop. Six minutes could be an agony, if you were cold and unable to move. The frigid air crept up from his frozen feet: he felt immobilized, his legs encased in ice as though he were trapped in one of those fairy tales where people turned into statues. He no longer felt his fingers in his gloves. He tensed his muscles, fighting the urge to shiver, when, fainter than the sound of his own breath, an answering call echoed from somewhere far off in the black woods that surrounded the overgrown fields.

Who cooks for you? Who cooks for you?

Elation flooded him; he glanced at Yvette and saw her grinning like a madwoman. He strained to hear another call but none came. The long silence broke with the final track, the great horned owl's loud, increasingly threatening *Who? Who?? WHO???*

Its cry died off into the sound of wind rattling the aster stalks. Louis tilted his head slightly, mentally counting down the remaining seconds, and stiffened.

Something was walking across the snow. Furtively: it paused before its feet broke through the frozen surface, a sound like a boot crunching shattered glass.

Heat flashed through Louis's body, terror and adrenaline. He looked at Yvette and saw her eyes widening, not in fear but wonder. He turned to see what she gazed at, detected nothing at first but then caught a glimpse of a dark blur at the edge of the field, maybe twenty yards away. In an eyeblink it had disappeared into the trees.

An electronic beep signaled the end of the owl-call sequence. Louis grabbed the boom box. He and Yvette jumped back into the car, slamming the doors closed behind them. Louis locked his, leaned over and did the same to Yvette's.

"Did you see that?" she asked, eyes so wide she looked like an owl herself.

"I don't know." He set the boom box at his feet—it felt cold as a block of ice—yanked off his gloves, and blew on his fingers as Yvette turned the ignition. "What was it?"

"I don't know." Hands gripping the wheel, she craned her neck to peer past him, to where the black line of spruce and pine gave way to the long, white expanse broken by brambles, stands of dead aster and milkweed. "It looked like a person."

"It can't have been a person," Louis said, even though his thumping heart suggested that's exactly what he believed. "A deer, probably."

"It was upright." Yvette stared outside for another minute before she sighed, turned on the headlights, and began to drive, very, very slowly, continuing to look out the passenger side of the windshield. "Did you see it? Tall and kind of stooped. It might have been a bear."

"Bears don't walk upright. Not in winter, anyway. They're hibernating."

"But you saw it, right?"

He shrugged, unwilling to look at her. "I don't know," he repeated. "I saw something—I *think* I saw something. I definitely heard something. I thought it was a deer. That noise their hooves make when they break through the crust."

"Deer don't walk upright."

"Then it was a person."

Now he did meet Yvette's gaze. They grimaced in unison.

"That's not good," she said. "They could freeze."

"Do you think we should go back?"

"No." They both laughed, and Yvette added, "Maybe we should go back? What if it's someone who's lost?"

"No one's lost." Louis removed his knit cap and pressed his hands against his ears to warm them. As heat flooded the car, and him, his fear abated. "It was probably a deer. I mean, it could have been an owl—I just saw it from the corner of my eye. You heard that barred owl, right?"

"Yes! *'Who cooks for you!'*" Yvette hooted, and laughed again. "Did you write it down?"

Louis shook his head. He retrieved the clipboard and pen, using his mobile as a flashlight as he scrawled *Barred owl*. He couldn't recall the last time they'd heard an owl respond to the CD when they were out in the field like this—four or five years ago? Yet he heard plenty of owls when he was at home, barred owls and the occasional great horned owl, and he and Yvette had even sighted them a few times when they were driving along the owl-count route. Maybe there were simply fewer owls than there used to be, along with everything else. Fewer bats, fewer nightjars, fewer bugs, fewer bees.

Fewer people too, since the last few outbreaks, though it was hard to think of that as a bad thing. Friends of his in the warden service said that wildlife populations appeared to be rebounding, not just deer and moose but apex predators and omnivores. Black bears and coyotes, mountain lions and wolves, whose existence the state's Department of Inland Fisheries and Wildlife had a decades-long policy of denying, despite numerous sightings. The last confirmed wolf in Maine had been shot dead in Ellsworth in the 1990s, but Louis knew people who'd seen them, reliable witnesses—hunters, trappers, loggers, fishermen. The wolves came down from Quebec. No one knew if there were enough in Maine for a breeding population. Funding for that sort of study had disappeared long ago.

Yvette longed to see a bear or wolf. Louis was content to think that they were out there at a safe distance from his home. Hearing a family of coyotes erupt into howls in the middle of the night, fifty feet from his driveway, could be hair-raising enough.

"What's the next stop?" he asked.

"Deadman's Curve."

After about five miles, Yvette pulled the car over again, this time along a heavily wooded stretch. The road here hadn't been plowed, but wind had scoured most of the snow from the broken blacktop. A decaying mobile home stood a dozen yards from the road, its roof and walls collapsed to expose clouds of soggy pink fiberglass insulation, shredded Tyvek, and splintered beams, like some immense piece of roadkill.

As Louis stepped out of the car, he recoiled from the odor of mildew and an overpowering reek of rodent urine, along with the stink of something dead, a rat or scavenging fox or coyote. He pulled his scarf up to cover his face as Yvette motioned him back into the car, and they pulled up farther along the road, out of sight of the trailer.

"Whew. That was bad." He stepped outside cautiously, pressing his scarf against his nose so he could breathe in the reassuring scents of damp wool and woodsmoke. "It's better here."

Yvette nodded. She looked drifty, like maybe she couldn't quite remember where they were, or why, but when she saw Louis watching her she smiled and set the boom box on the car's hood. For a minute they stood without speaking. Louis lowered his scarf and breathed in tentatively, catching only the faintest whiff of mildew.

Not far from the road, on the same side as the ruined trailer, a stream ran through the woods. A small stream—with his long legs, he could have jumped across it without much effort—yet deep enough that it hadn't frozen. No one had bothered to trim the trees here for ages—while most of the power poles remained standing, the power companies had long ago stopped maintaining them. As a result, the oaks and maples and birches had grown unchecked, their branches nearly meeting above the road to form a ragged net in which a few stars gleamed like trapped minnows. In the darkness, the little stream sounded startlingly loud, more like a torrent than a brook.

"Ready?"

He turned back to Yvette, nodding, and she pressed *Play*.

The owls' mournful liturgy repeated itself as before, alternating between silence and melancholy summons, its only response a fretful twittering from above that Louis recognized as a red squirrel's alarm. The cold seemed more penetrating here; because of the tangle of branches over the road, Louis thought, then realized that was ridiculous. There was no sun. It must be getting on to 2:00 a.m.

He cursed himself for not bringing along a thermos of hot coffee. He knew better than to ask Yvette to abort the trip: she might forget what day, or even year, it was, but the owl count was sacrosanct. As the great horned owl's cry faded into the final, silent track, Louis didn't bother to suppress a yawn. He rubbed his arms, noting that Yvette remained stock-still, her hood's pointed tip silhouetted against the trees like a spearpoint. The rushing stream sounded so loud he wondered if they'd missed the beep signaling the end of the call sequence.

But then he heard the soft *beep.* Immediately he turned to open the car door. As he did, an explosive sound echoed from the woods directly behind them. Louis shouted: he stared into the trees, then at Yvette where she stood and gazed openmouthed at him. He heard splashing, a huffing noise that turned into a strangled grunt as something crashed through the underbrush. An overpowering fecal odor filled his nostrils, rot and shit but also sweat, a smell he'd never encountered that was somehow horribly recognizable.

"Get in!" he gasped at Yvette, but she'd already grabbed the boom box and was back in the car. Louis flung the door open and saw her fumbling for the keys—she'd forgotten again and left them in the ignition. He got inside and locked the door, shouted at Yvette to do the same. The Subaru's engine rumbled and the car shot forward, fishtailing across the slick road then straightening as Yvette hunched over the steering wheel.

"That was a bear!" She sounded exultant.

Louis said nothing, tried to slow his breath enough to speak without his voice breaking. "The fuck it was," he said at last. He pulled off his gloves, hands shaking, and turned to look through the rear window. The car's brake lights cast a dull crimson glow across skeletal birch trees and a fallen evergreen bough that Yvette had somehow avoided. "It sounded huge."

"Bears are huge. It could've been a moose. Or a beaver."

Louis snorted, but she was right. The sound of a beaver slapping its tail on the water in warning could reverberate like a thunderclap. "There's no pond back there, just that stream."

"Maybe it runs into a pond nearby. Check the *Gazetteer.*"

Louis shook his head impatiently—he felt at once irritated and frightened—but he picked up the *Gazetteer* and found the corresponding map among its frayed pages. "Nope. No pond."

Yvette slowed the car to a crawl, its studded tires grinding over the snow. "There should be a turn in the next few miles. For the

Araweag—I think it's on the left. Can you check for that?"

"You still want to go?"

"I thought we decided."

"Yeah, but. That thing . . ."

"I know!" Her cheeks were flushed, excitement more than cold, he suspected. "See if you can find that turn."

A glance at the open *Gazetteer* on his lap showed the township, a formless green space threaded by streams that connected myriad small ponds, lakes, and wetlands. Broken stitches indicated a seasonal road, which these days meant an impassable one. Before he could voice a perfectly reasonable excuse for not going there—they'd get stuck, run out of gas, and not be found until spring, besides which there was just as much likelihood of hearing owls right here on the old route as in the Araweag—Yvette brought up the single unreasonable one.

"Are you scared?"

He took a deep breath. "Not really. Just—that noise, it spooked me. And the smell? Did you smell it?"

"I did." Yvette wrinkled her nose. "Phew! Like when my septic field overflows every year."

Yvette's septic field hadn't flooded in decades—she'd switched to a composting toilet, like nearly everyone else, as the grid became unreliable. Louis knew it would be pointless to remind her of this. She'd laugh and say, *Oh right, I forgot.* Then forget it all over again, just as she'd done with the car keys. He cleared his window, the glass already steaming up, stared out at the shifting crosshatch of black and gray-white. Trees, rocks, snowdrifts, trees.

"It smelled worse than that," he said. "Like . . ."

"It could have been a moose. It sounded big."

Louis nodded, frowning. He picked up the thermos, took a swig of cold coffee, then offered it to Yvette, who shook her head. "Whatever it was, it smelled like it had rolled in something dead," he said. "Like a dog does. And what was that noise? It sounded like an entire tree came down."

"Like I said, moose."

"A moose doesn't knock down trees."

"Well, it's not the same thing we heard at the first stop, whatever it was." Yvette tugged her hood from her face. "It's four miles from there to that old trailer. Nothing goes that fast. Maybe an owl," she added after a moment's thought. "Horned owls, they're fast."

Yvette turned the wipers on. It had started to snow—tiny, dry flakes, the kind that normally blow off the windshield, but they weren't driving fast enough for that. She hunched over the steering wheel, scanning the road. "I think there's a sign—didn't there used to be a sign?"

"I don't remember." Louis didn't bother to keep the irritation from his tone. He peeled off his gloves and closed his eyes for a moment, imagining himself back at home in bed, warm and asleep. Then he remembered Eric was dead. He was old enough now that grief had become a near-constant presence, a prolonged dull ache rather than the piercing anguish he'd experienced when he was younger. The aftermath of his wife's death was like a raging virus that left him sickened and weak for several years, a virus that could be reawakened by stress, or sunrise, or a scent. You don't recover from grief, he'd learned, it can't be cured; it only appears to go into remission, to flare up, not as intensely perhaps but retaining its nightmarish power, with the next death.

He had not even begun to mourn Eric. He thought again of that last time, just over a year ago, the two of them leaving the dried-up Battenkill to hike up a ski trail, a broad swath of young beeches and sugar maples that had sprung up when the ski mountain closed early in the century. Eric white-haired but hale, more so than Louis, who'd had to stop often to catch his breath, holding on to young birch trees that showered them with autumn leaves like a rain of new pennies.

"They found a mastodon in the Mastigouche," Eric had told him, and Louis laughed.

"That sounds like a song," he said, and began to warble. "Mastodon, in the Mastigooooche . . ."

"No, really—there was a landslide, and they found its tusks in the rubble. Like in Siberia, where they keep mining mammoth ivory where the permafrost used to be."

He started as Yvette nudged him, looked up to see her grinning at him. "I know," she said. "It was the Agropelter!" She pronounced the word with a slight lilt and the accent on the final syllable, the way her Quebecois grandmother would have. *Agre-pel-TAY.*

Louis made a face. "Well, I hope not," he said, and they laughed. Yvette's great-grandfather had been a trucker who worked the Golden Road, the hundred-mile-long, mostly unpaved track that ran from the old paper mill in Millinocket to the Quebec border, and her great-great-grandfather had worked in Canadian logging camps. Yvette's grandmother claimed he had hundreds of stories about the terrible things that could happen in the North Woods, but the only one Yvette recalled was about the Agropelter. Half human, half ape, the Agropelter sat in treetops and hurled rocks and branches at unsuspecting woodsmen, sometimes killing them.

"Sounds like a bad excuse for knocking someone off with an ax," Louis had remarked the first time Yvette recounted the legend.

Now he checked the time: 2:17. "Getting late," he said. "And it's starting to snow. We're supposed to call it off if it snows."

"Who's going to check? And it's not snowing now," she added. Which was true: the sifting flakes had stopped. "You came—why did you come if you didn't want to?"

"I needed to be distracted." That sounded cruel; she might not even remember his best friend had died. "Because of Eric."

"Of course," she said, her customary briskness softened. "I remember." She grasped his hand and squeezed it. "I'm so sorry, Louis."

"Thank you."

"You know, when Buddy died, my friend Lori told me if I ever wanted a sign from him, I should just close my eyes. The first three things I saw when I opened them, those would be the sign."

"Yes, you told me that."

"Oh, sorry!" she said without embarrassment. "I keep forgetting."

He turned away, recalling how Sheila during her illness had joked that whatever he did after she died, he shouldn't marry Yvette. "Not a chance," he'd told her, and that had never changed. His eyes stung and he closed them, thinking this time of Sheila, not Eric; opened them and gazed at his bare hands, the red knuckles swollen and fingers twisted from Dupuytren's contracture.

He leaned over to check the gas gauge. A quarter tank, enough to get home. He wondered when and where she'd been able to last fill the tank. Bangor, probably, which meant she'd used up a considerable amount of fuel driving home afterward. He looked in the back seat again, reached into the heap of dog hair–covered fabric, rummaged around till he found a zipper, and pulled at it. A sleeping bag emerged, trailing a chewed-up leash.

"There might still be some of those hand warmers," said Yvette. "Poke around, see if you can find them."

"That's OK. I was looking for a weapon, actually. In case it tries to eat us."

"Very funny. They only eat owls, my gran said. And woodpeckers."

"Well, we're safe then. The turn looks to be about eight miles, on the left. You remembered that fine."

The car inched along, Yvette downshifting as they crept over knee-high frost heaves and avoiding potholes large enough to swallow a bicycle. Intermittent gusts of snow would cloud the air then just as swiftly disappear, the tiny flakes not big enough to constitute a squall. The real snow wouldn't start until morning. If it looked like it was going to come down sooner, they'd simply turn around.

They drove in silence, interrupted only when one of them pointed out a former stop—the flat boulder overlooking a bog, the sweeping vista where they'd once heard two great horned owls—or when they spotted something. A fox crossing leisurely in front of them; a snowshoe hare sprinting off in alarm, its long hind feet kicking up feathers of snow; a pair of tufted ears like devil horns above glowing green eyes, barely visible in the underbrush.

"Bobcat!" said Louis.

"Lynx!" cried Yvette in triumph.

"Oh, come on, how could you tell?"

"It was bigger than a bobcat."

"It was there for two seconds!"

Yvette pursed her lips in a smug smile. "I just know."

Louis unzipped his parka as the car grew overheated, the doggie smell vying with the faint, scorched-sugar scent of antifreeze that seeped from the vents. "You have a radiator leak," he said.

"I know. Bob Marsh said he'd fix it, come spring."

Louis checked the odometer, trying to figure out how much farther it was to the turn. They'd been driving for at least twenty minutes, a long time to cover only eight miles, even in the middle of the night, even on these roads.

"Do you think we missed it?" he asked. "The sign could be gone. That old access road could be completely overgrown by now."

Yvette's brow creased. "I hope not. Let's give it another few minutes."

A few minutes became ten—Louis clocked the time. He couldn't do anything else with his mobile; even back in the early part of the century, there hadn't been service here.

"Look."

Yvette inclined her head to the left, where a twisted metal pole jutted toward the road at a thirty-degree angle. Atop it dangled a small green sign so rusted Louis could barely read it. FR 2973, a fire road.

"Huh. I haven't seen one of those for years." Once ubiquitous, these numerical signs designated seasonal or little-used roads. The numbering system had disappeared when towns had to conform to Emergency 911 standards, meaning all roads needed an actual name.

Despite the warmth, Louis shivered. He peered into the darkness past the twisted pole. "Can we even get down there?"

"I'll just turn in, we can park and walk a bit if the snow's not too deep."

Louis ran his hands across his knees but said nothing. His knees ached, his back. The Dupuytren's contracture in his right hand made it hard to move his fingers in the chill. He'd dressed for cold, not for trudging through deep snow.

But the old fire road, while overgrown and snow covered, still showed signs of use. He saw snowmobile tracks veering across the broad path, along with those of another vehicle, a small Sno-Cat probably. Someone poaching firewood, now that the territory was basically no-man's-land. A few inches of snow had fallen since anyone had last been here—judging by the crust, at least a week ago—but not enough to impede walking.

He zipped up his parka, watched as Yvette made the turn and drove several yards. He winced as the old Subaru jolted over a buried rock and bottomed out. "Maybe this is far enough?"

Yvette nodded and brought the car to an abrupt stop, forgetting to take it out of gear. Louis's skull banged against the headrest. "*Ow!*"

"Sorry!" Yvette clapped her hands to her face. She began to laugh, then reached to touch Louis's neck gently. "We don't have to stay long. Miriam's son saw a great horned owl here. He was hunting—moose, I think. I would love to see another one of those. The owl, I mean. Or the moose."

"I would rather not see a moose at night," said Louis, gingerly rubbing the back of his neck. "Not if it's going to knock a tree on my head."

"That wasn't a moose. Bear," said Yvette.

She pulled up her hood and stepped out of the car without the boom box. Louis considered leaving it inside—maybe she'd forget the reason they were here, and they could just head home. But then she turned and pointed at it. He tucked it under one arm and joined her, stumping through the snow and halting in front of the car.

Shreds of gray lichen littered the snow, and the dark scales of pine cones resembling fingernail clippings, which fell where red squirrels had fed in the trees overhead. Balsam and pine resin scented the air, rather than pissy cat spruce and crushed bracken. Even though the road was only a few yards off, he felt as though with a few steps, he'd traversed a hundred years, backward or forward, to a moment when his presence was as inconsequential as a thread of reindeer moss.

He found the thought oddly comforting. Perhaps this was how Yvette felt all the time. He set the boom box on top of the car, tugged his knit cap snugly over his ears, pulled up his hood, and stared at the sky.

Far above him, a gap in the clouds revealed stars so brilliant he imagined he heard them crackling in the frigid air. The night seemed absolutely still—he felt no wind on his cheeks, and the jagged black evergreens that scraped the horizon appeared not to move.

And yet he did hear something. A faint, nearly subliminal sound like static, a noise he could imagine accompanying the prickles that presaged the agonizing leg cramps that woke him some nights. He cocked his head, trying to figure out if he was imagining it and, if not, where it came from; glanced over to see Yvette looking at him, eyebrows raised. Within moments her expression altered, from perplexity to alarm to outright horror. He opened his mouth to ask *What?* Then he heard the same thing.

He thought it was the wind at first: a low rumbling that lasted mere seconds before it stopped. In the near silence he heard Yvette's breathing and his own, a frantic rustling in a tree overhead. He exhaled shakily, caught his breath sharply when the sound recurred— louder this time, closer, rising then fading into a long echo that, after several moments, died away completely.

And, after another few moments, resumed. The cry rose, not the yodeling ululation of a coyote or wolf, both of which he knew: something deeper, more sustained and resonant. It died away before recurring a fourth time, much louder, so close that the hairs on his neck and arms and scalp rose, as from nearby lightning. Sensation flooded him, an emotion he had never experienced before: a horror so all-encompassing his stomach convulsed. His arms grew limp, his knees buckled, and he slumped against the car's hood, gloved fingers sliding across the smooth metal as he tried to grab it.

The sound faded. Silence surrounded him, long enough that his gasps subsided and he drew a shuddering breath, wiping tears onto his sleeve. He struggled to stand upright, bracing himself against the car, and cried aloud when the sound came again, from not more than twenty feet away. Loud enough now that he could detect within the deafening bellow a grinding anguish, physical pain and also a deeper torment, as the cry exploded into a thunderous roar. His ears ached but he could clearly hear as it crashed through the trees, not blindly but with steady purpose, pausing between each step as though ensuring the ground would bear its weight. A shrill piping sounded in his ears, the saw-whet owl, he thought with desperate calm, before recognizing his own scream. The roar came again and with it a wave of heat.

He gagged as that smell of fecal rot overwhelmed him. A tree crashed down, pine needles and splinters of wood stabbed his cheek and his vision blurred as blood washed across one eye. Soft feathers brushed his face, or fur, he could no longer distinguish between what was his skin, his body inside his layers of clothing, his scalp or neck or toes. His feet disappeared, the ground beneath them. With a moan he slanted his gaze sideways, searching for Yvette in the maelstrom of snow and broken bark, hair, blood, bone, and feathers.

He saw only a smudge of red, the tip of her parka's hood. He tried to breathe but found his mouth sealed shut by the wind; tasted blood, he'd bitten his tongue. He thought of Yvette, of Sheila in bed beside him, of Eric walking next to him as they traced the lost Battenkill.

He closed his eyes, counted to three. *Who cooks for you?* he thought, and opened them.

First Love

Joanna Ruocco

THEY TOOK ME TO THE MORGUE in a cart with the corpses. I don't blame them, those soldiers, saucepans, and cats of the republic! They're always up to something.

"Kaput!" said a soldier. That's my recollection. He might have sneezed. At the time, I didn't speak the language. Then, as now, I was gray complected, yellowed at the mouth, which is on the lipless side, livid of cheek, nakedly cadaverous, a flaking and pitted behemoth. Moreover, I have filmy eyes and the hairs never came in on the ridge above them. There was so much death on that beach, I couldn't—with such a face—distinguish myself. I let a soldier lift me off the shingle. The cart rolled through the streets and I flopped on top in the arms of a black-bearded man in tattered white flannels. *That* was a corpse, that black-bearded man. In fact, he had no beard at all. His neck, his chin—what they'd produced was a thick crop of leeches. He was just a boy, in pajamas. He embraced me tightly. Under the leeches, his Adam's apple slid strangely, squishing against my shoulder. Poor apple, bad already. The rot begins there, with male corpses. Soon after, the whole body gets spots and softens. The boy's breath smelled of kidney and cider. He was either Pituco Murguia or Rudolph Grauenwald, a cattle merchant's son or a student of equatorial plants. I have consulted the Wreck Register of 18—, and the newspapers, their Lists of the Lost—uselessly! I can narrow no further than Pituco or Rudolph, Rudolph or Pituco, and why not call him, then, Pituco? My Pituco! He dripped and dripped, sobbing the vinegar tears of male corpses. I was soaked with him. Something scrabbled in his chest, not his heart. A prawn, then. Pituco! He whetted my appetite for love. I can trace it to that moment, that cold morning, my bones jarring as the wooden wheels rattled on stone, the vibration moving through me and into Pituco and through Pituco into me. That's how it began. Later, I became insatiable.

The crowds pressed close, piling us with flowers. There are surfeits of flowers in this city, a city of perpetual spring. The weather too is scavenged, composed of the unguarded, raw, open days at the edges of the seasons, the changeable days that don't belong anywhere. At the morgue, I was stacked on the marble floor of the corridor and Pituco was carried past me on a board. The doctors and newspapermen walked up and down jotting on tiny notepads. That's when I raised my head, to shock and fanfare.

"Eugepae!" said a doctor. That's my recollection. He might have spat around the stub of his cigar.

For weeks, I lived on the hospital balcony, resting at night in a narrow bed beneath a parasol, receiving visits from foreign ministers in the afternoons as I sat in a Viennese chair, which Fabia, my favorite nurse, had borrowed from a coffee house. The city curves like an amphitheater around the harbor, and, from my balcony, I could watch the heavy traffic, steamships going by so close together they might have been coupled, each a car on an endless train chugging over the horizon. Or maybe I could hear it, the chug chug of the engines, the hiss of the hulls ripping the surface of the water, ruching it into wavelets. In those early days, I couldn't sit up, couldn't stand. I couldn't sort my organs. I evacuated gases through my ears, and the milk I swallowed often ran out my nose. I couldn't sort the air from the tongue. The foreign ministers arrived one after the other in long black coats and puffed and clacked.

"What a great big duck," said the foreign ministers. "What a bonbon. Where's your tata? Your mama? Your bubbe, your papou? Were they on the bad ship? Did they go into the ocean in their clothes? That was silly of them. It's silly to be dead, yes? If you're big enough to know better? Well, anyone can be silly now and then. Terrible shock, terrible. Lots of sun. Doctors' orders. Must be going, theater tickets. The Death of Olég. Snakebite. A ballet. Bye-bye, Donkey Rump. Bye-bye, Kunegunda. Cleobula? Barbara. Rubber bandage. Prunella. Does that ring a bell? No? Puff puff. Clack clack. Ciao ciao. Cover your mouth when you cough, dear. Can you? With those very short arms?"

"Cough," I said. That's what they heard at first, the foreign ministers, the newspaper men, the doctors, the nurses, even Fabia. I was very weak. The doctors thought water in the lungs, but I can diagnose myself, retrospectively, with love sickness. Nights I gave in to fever. I imagined Pituco at the morgue, spotted and slick as a leopard fish, and so soft, like the shirred curtain that conceals the depths of the sea. I imagined rolling in the silver velvet of Pituco, but, in reality, I couldn't even turn over in my narrow bed, a wooden cot with a leather pad. The nurses tucked the sheets so tight the creases cut. Only Fabia would leave a little room, a finger's width between the fabric and my skin. She pulled close the Viennese chair and read aloud from a fat book no taller than her palm. The Death of Olég. A novel. Maybe. No, a diary. The story of her life. I didn't sleep, but I swiveled my eyeballs all the way around and contemplated the darkness inside my own skull, which is segmented into worms, glowworms that light up in patterns, and those patterns are my thoughts. While Fabia read, I began to identify correspondences between the glowworms and her words, and soon I could think in words, and even letters, the worms' luminescent organs composing texts in broad thoracic green, with the full stops and question marks picked out in lanky antennal red. Within the week, I could understand the speech of foreign ministers, although I couldn't tell what was English and what was French, what was Czech, what Deutsch, what Hiszpański or Spagnolo. To this very day, it's all the same, tiny photic heads and bellies, wiggling. I don't even need to keep my eyeballs swiveled, the shadows are just as legible. Of course, glowworms are larvae and harden into beetles, great rude lumps of them! Too many beetles and I lose my capacity for abstraction. I start to dodder, the beetles in my skull forming scaly tan patches, impenetrable blanks. That's why I sit at my vanity each morning and first thing—before I powder, before I pin my wig—I squirt a potent aphrodisiac into my ears. This impels the beetles to copulate at an excessive rate, so that each generation of larvae outnumbers the last. As a result, I suffer frequent headaches, but I endure them—coolly! Only rarely do I lash out and then mostly at crockery. The skulls of geniuses always pinch a bit, like the skulls of dogs bred to stick their heads in holes. The aphrodisiac—I am proud to say—is my own recipe, now patent formula. The base is equal parts rum and vino seco in which three fertilized hen eggs per quart are boiled. Additional ingredients include patchouli, the urine of a male dog, the milk of rubber trees, the hemorrhoid of a pregnant widow, a grated green bruise, a birthmark, a freshwater pearl, baker's yeast, grave dirt, a dropperful of *Salmonella typhimurium*, the ejaculate of spiders fed on Spanish fly. There are others. Many have tried and failed to discover them, ransacking my solarium where the light is fuzzy black with insect life—flies from every corner of the world, spiders, ants, also my capuchin, Franz, the cricket of primates—and delirious with heliotrope. I keep my papers there, in the cartonnier mounted on my writing desk, but nothing that pertains to my aphrodisiac, the composition, proportions, process. I

65

Joanna Ruocco

hid those papers thoroughly. My aphrodisiac—it stimulates the passions, yes, but more importantly, the production of penis spikes, not only in beetles. I sell to soldiers, bones and fat of the republic! They grow gristly spikes, barbed tusks with sticky pores, ruinous, ruinous to girls, cows, whores, mares, melons, nurses. Not to me, my genitals are sturdy, a slit between the callused flaps of which a series of rasping discs churn without mercy. Before I copulate with soldiers, I insert half a dozen cloves, for the numbing and the fragrance. Soldiers stink in my experience. Like the insides of pianos. They're always tense, despite their good cheer and profligacy. That's enough about cloves.

I write these pages, not at the davenport in the solarium, at the lacquer table on the patio, and not I, my amanuensis. It is her birthday. No? But to celebrate I bought a pink-and-yellow cake, I bought the mechanical bear from the shooting gallery, I told the cook to go upstairs to scale the fish, to scale fish while leaning out the window, to fill the air with fish confetti, and I taught the crickets to sing the Hymn of the Republic. They're singing now, in the solarium. They'll sing all day. At midnight, the mechanical bear will pirouette. He'll tender a proposal. Of marriage, certainly. My amanuensis is a bit mechanical herself, strapped to an invalid chair, tapping at the writing ball, a porcelain hemisphere pierced by brass keys. She belongs with the bear, truly the Pituco of bears, tattered and mothy, bullet holes filled up with fleas that suckle at your fingertips. I give my blessing. I give her away, the bride to the bear. I do, says he. I do, says she—through me, of course. I speak on her behalf. Lovely bean-fed child, teeth like seed pearls, flounce between her legs. White grapes and gauze, muddled by a long snout of flocked pewter. I'll bless it, yes, and bottle it. Enough! How I tease her! There is no cake, no bear, no birthday. No cause for alarm. I'll keep her, my amanuensis, an ageless poppet, a darling, a Fabia, in fact. I call her Fabia, after my favorite nurse. During her very first hour of service, I made her take a vow of silence. She looks like Fabia—same curved neck, same long hands—but when she opens her mouth she sounds like a trough on the cathedral tower, fawn-colored masonry clogged with newborn nuns, irritating as a sandy prune. It's a miracle any nuns at all survive into adulthood in this city, and yet they are everywhere, nuns, second in number only to soldiers, nuns and soldiers, always falling under your carriage wheels or forcing kisses on your horse. Sometimes I wish I

66

resided in quite another place, less romantic, a modern city with clean, empty streets, such as can be ordered from Fitzwilliam's House of Toys, die-cast models of any scale, each with an ornamental key, jeweled or carved from coral. Sometimes I wish I could lock up this city and climb aboard a steamship or a train to the interior, become a land- or seascape painter, not I, my amanuensis. Is it harder to dictate a painting? My amanuensis will no doubt strike all my wishes from the record. She is easily ruffled but knows what behooves me: displays of strength, zeal, wealth, my left profile, well lit, fidelity, the common touch.

This morning, as I take my cold lamb and pudding on the patio, I hear the crickets, the tapping of brass keys, cathedral bells, distant strains of the military band, and above it all, the cries of gulls. They're feeding on the beached whale on the shingle by the citadel. They cry in the voice of Fabia, my favorite nurse, who once read from the fat book on the hospital balcony, read in the voice of a gull with a moon in its throat, a balloon filled with poached horned melon marmalade, soft pops of blubber, paw-paw-paw, a rain of jellied almonds at a carnival. Golden spheres of dough pouring from a paper cone. I sat, propped up on a leather bolster, swiveling my eyeballs, from time to time looking down at the city, which reduced at night to little balls of flame, paper lanterns in trees, lampposts, carriage lights floating down the avenues. My brain crawled with syllables. Now, my brain is still, too hard and sluggish. I knock my plate onto the travertine, and Franz bounds from the solarium with a glass pot, nozzle and tube, piglet bladder bag. He administers in each of my ears a squirt and one more squirt. That Franz! He deserves himself a key to the city, a chancellery, a daily asado of cabbage flank and charred mosquito. He deserves the hand of Fabia, my amanuensis. What monkey-faced scarabs they'd breed, or long-tailed crabs. He's jealous, the old bear, the old bachelor, creaking sadly on his rotary. No matter. A matchmaker never says I'm sorry. My brain squirms again, the fat book, the story of Fabia, my favorite nurse, her childhood in the House of Sugar, Paseo de Molina, passed over. Life begins with romance.

One day, the madam gave her a coin and a basket. In the basket, a new little dog wrapped in a beautifully embroidered swaddling blanket.

He needs a bath, said the madam. Take him to the fountain of angels, and after he bathes, let him play in the flower beds and make sure he eats a few violets. Last night his foul breath gave me bad dreams. I was a queen in her canopy bed, but my head rested on a side of beef. Can you imagine? I rolled over at once and broke a goose egg filled with vomit. Foie gras, declared my little dog, and gobbled it. Selfish beast. I'm so fond of him. His name is Violet.

As soon as she reached the park, Fabia met a soldier. He was standing by his horse in front of the fountain of angels. At the sight of him, Fabia reverberated emptily. Like any girl in such a circumstance, she turned into a citrine whistle. She became a needy prism, her yellow cleavage hard and insistent, the soldier's buttons suddenly in contact with the edge of it. He leaned in. She split the air into a stinging inhalation and a shriek. The game began. He seized the basket and jumped away, jumped up onto his horse. He wheeled around and galloped toward the iron ring mounted on a distant gate post, arm stretched out. Beneath the orange trumpet trees, the other soldiers sprang into action. One rode straight at him, two, three. The park began to churn with soldiers and horses. They banged into one another and some fell, horses rolling over and struggling up and galloping harder, with the screaming soldiers dangling from the stirrups. Fabia stood on the lip of the fountain and watched. Glossy flanks and Zouave jackets, arched necks, kicking legs, reins and tails—a mass of coarse and shiny shapes heaving together. Then it was over, and the soldier returned to the fountain. The hooves of his horse were painted red with blood. In the center of the park, the ruined basket, a curly heap of willow sprigs, tangled with the blanket's golden floss. In the distance, the dog was dangling from the iron ring, its belly torn out. The soldier had won.

My name is Violet, he said. I love you.

Then his friends called out to him and he rode away smiling over his shoulder.

The dog dangled from the distant gate post. Fabia went toward it, fitting her feet into hoof prints, hobbling, the torn turf horribly erotic, her heels gloved by hole after hole. She could just reach the dog's back legs, and she jumped and tugged and the dog slid over the iron ring and swung down. The dog folded easily like a hand fan made of fur, the kind the ladies twirl at skating parties, bonfires burning on the brilliant ice. Fabia closed it with a snap. She was a Muscovite duchess, and where was her lover? Chopping wood. Hunting bear. Throwing onions at the stage in the opera house. The Death of Olég. She ran from the park and into the city to the taxidermy shop. The taxidermist complimented the dog's black mouth and delicate foot pads. She poured Fabia a cup of resinous tea to sip at the table while she stuffed and sewed. She filled the dog with cured meat and painted his teeth and tongue with honey and removed the eyeballs and fitted the sockets with the bulbous backs of black widow spiders, each pupil an hourglass that displayed the red instant of death, shiny with lacquer.

Charming, said Fabia.

An excellent pedigree, said the taxidermist.

I'll keep him with me always, said Fabia. She let a room above the taxidermy shop, the room where the taxidermist stowed leftover feathers. Fabia lived in the room of feathers with the dog and learned to preserve heads, assisting the taxidermist with her side business in exchange for her lodging. She wandered back to the park when the shop closed at night, hoping to encounter her soldier, carrying the dog in a basket lined with feathers, but she never saw him and years went by. Finally, one hot day, the eve of the independence celebrations, she spied him near the cathedral on the city's broadest avenue, smoking in the shade of a terebinth tree. He'd grown a mustache and his horse's hooves were colored regular, like four nostrils. But she recognized them both, the soldier and the horse. The soldier had a violet pinned to his Zouave jacket.

Why hello, he said, smiling as she approached. He didn't know her, or the dog in the basket, even when she spread the feathers to show off its brittle corona of fluff.

Oh, said Fabia, with disappointment.

Oh, oh, said Fabia, despairing.

But why had she expected him to know her? She was no longer a child, and the dog was no longer a dog but a holy relic, easily mistaken for the stitched-together armpits of the saints.

I'm waiting for Sigismunda, explained the soldier. I arrived late, like always, but so what? She never gives up, that Sigismunda. Maybe you've seen her. Did you come by Constitution?

No, said Fabia. No, no. I came through the cork district.

She has green warts on her cheeks, continued the soldier. Like potato buds. They sprout when it rains.

And so! cried Fabia—painfully!

What were they to her, the warts of Sigismunda? The sunlight was dry as an urn. The ground was white with the powdered feces of frigate birds. A lizard ran over her right slipper and caught its hooked tail in the embroidery. The tail broke off. Good luck, bad luck. Which? She stared at the soldier, who was stroking his violet with a tobacco-stained thumb. Like any girl in such a circumstance, she turned into a crystal goblet, a goblet filled to its highest facets with the blood of virgins. Beneath the terebinth tree, she faced the soldier, a greedy goblet, drinking of itself, the blood jumping in her mouth with pulses.

Ho, laughed the soldier, leaning close.

Fabia put down her basket. She crouched beneath the terebinth tree and exposed her haunches and the soldier beheld her positioned just so, like an inside-out goblet, like the bell of a must-filled trumpet, like a lioness upon a cheese grater, and he beat her with the joyful tedium of soldiers, until Fabia stretched and shook, her bloated heart forcing open her mouth.

Meanwhile, his friends had gathered, groaning with boredom, batting at the lazy flies, at Fabia's heart caught in the branches of the terebinth tree.

Let's go, they called. There's a party at the House of Sugar.

The soldier jumped up and jumped onto his horse, the hot air wafted over Fabia, smelling of gunpowder and horse milk, of cat and onions and piano wires, of leather boot tongues and scorched cheese. She rolled over onto her back and gazed up at the tree, at her heart.

Farewell, Sigismunda, laughed the soldier, and he galloped away down the avenue, but not before wheeling his horse in a circle around her, trampling the holy relic in the basket, popping the stitches, flattening the skull. The eggs of black widow spiders poured from the sockets of the little dog's eyes. The horse's hooves kicked up the eggs and the dust, the powdered feces of the frigate birds, and the white cloud sifted over Fabia, a dry tickle, the soldier's laughter sticking to the warm, wet welts on her skin.

The next day, Independence Day, Fabia stood beneath the terebinth tree. She watched the parade go by, plumed horses, mules pulling artillery, little boys riding ostriches, little girls waving from floats made of flowers, and nuns, of course, hundreds of nuns, and soldiers, none of them hers. The next day, she stood under the terebinth tree, and the next. Slowly, Fabia's empty middle hardened, a goose egg resting on the girdle of her hips. One night the taxidermist had to rush her to the hospital, where she pushed out a taut pink membrane. It was wobbly but alive, wiggling its arms and legs. The doctor held it up and smacked its bottom and it vomited. It vomited until it was empty, a wrinkled pouch. Fabia had it stuffed and sewn by the taxidermist. She named it Violet.

That was the end. The story of Fabia.

*

"The end," said Fabia. The night she got there, to the end, I pulled one leg free of the sheets and kicked the table so the milk spilled and vanilla wafers scattered everywhere, and I tipped the parasol. I strained my short arms, and I heaved the parasol off the balcony. Down it fell without a flutter, a strangely motionless descent, like that of an executed moon. I wanted to ask Fabia if I might have been born in a barracks, not a soldier's daughter but the offspring of a firing squad and a waterskin. Did I too have a story? A story that began before the shingle, the cart, Pituco, the morgue, the hospital balcony? I could remember—vaguely—something. A momentum that transformed surface into volume, how I rose through waves of amorphous silica, a lateral propulsion that sent me up, up, a tube of muscle taking flight, making me—what?—a tail, a wing? A bullet embolized in an intestine? I wanted to ask Fabia and thrashed gently until she perched upon my breast, her face fig blue in the moonlight.

"It's so easy to talk to you," said Fabia. "I live in the nurses' dormitory now and there's too much chatter. You're so quiet I could go on forever. If I put my arm under your neck and lift, you can see there, those tiny balls of light, those are the paper lanterns tied to the jacarandas in the coffee-house courtyard. My fiancé, Raul, works at the coffee house. Every capital has its drink, a liquor, coffee, or green tea, and in this one the drink is green coffee. Have you tasted it? I'll bring you some. It's greenest at that coffee house. Raul is the head waiter. He dips his index finger in every cup to test the temperature and he checks the color against the emerald in his pinky ring, not *his* pinky ring, of course, the pinky ring he wears, as head waiter. The reputation of the coffee house depends on Raul, who won't serve a cup that's too hot or too cold, too clouded or too clear, too tannic or too floral, too oblique or too direct, too tip of the tongue or too back of the throat, too third eye or too lizard brain. He's exacting when it comes to green coffee. Otherwise, he's haphazard, sentimental, and generous—generous to a fault! He was born into a minor zoological family—his father was the manager of the monkey house and his mother cleaned the leopard cages. During the siege, there was no food for the leopards. There was nothing for the zoological families or the animals save waxy soup made from tree leaves. Leopards need to use their teeth to eat. You can't bite soup! They won't survive on a liquid diet, even if the liquid is pure antelope juice. Raul tried to share his soup with the leopards, but they only snapped at it, listlessly, and continued their ostentatious starving. Each discrete bone was soon visible, wrapped in a leopard-skin coat. Raul would sit by the cages looking at the elegant jumbles that had once been leopards, and one day, he stuck his legs through the bars. He fed his legs to the leopards! His mother was so angry she strapped him to a wheeled board and made him clean the cages himself. After the siege ended, he left to try his luck at several professions. He opened a candy store that was ransacked then exploded by soldiers. He offered a poem-framing service but his only client was a bar owner who wanted to hang dirty jokes in the bathroom. He modeled bowler hats. He sold blancmange. He ran an amethyst stand. He bought a monocle and a newspaper in an imperial language and set up as a duke in an out-of-the-way garden, waiting for heiresses. Finally, he became head waiter at the coffee house. Now he has enough money to buy us a pleasant hovel near the rag market. I won't miss the nurses' dormitory. The beds are so close together we have to crawl over each other, over the mountainous Rose Maria and deep into the crevasse of Delmira, our tongues hanging out—with exhaustion! I'll miss these nights, though, here on the balcony, the two of us together. . . ."

As I dictate, Fabia, my amanuensis, taps slower and slower, inflating herself with agitated breaths, so that the pleats of her dress spread flat, so that the buttons stick out. She's wheezing away, a perfect squeeze-box. In the solarium, the cactuses make love to the flies with the tips of their needles. Some of those flies were flugel adjutants in St. Petersburg, at least one, a kammerjunker, married to a fruit bowl in the Winter Palace. Cubed carrot and pineapple, cucumber and strawberry, drizzled with yogurt. Shall I allow it? The surrender of duty to pleasure?

"Your vows, Muravief!"

No, I got it wrong. I sense this at once. The words were not in fly but in iron settee. I have too much rapport with furniture. The scroll-work at my back says—

but the cook bursts onto the patio with hake and cleaver and starts to dance. He dances with Franz, the national dance, vulgar as a corn-cob. O hooligan, I stamp your high-crowned hat / I feed your rump to the tin pig in the rubbish yard / To pave the parish of La Piedad with slashed bellies / To welcome all strange and terrible events / That's the law, that's the paradise of men.

The sun gongs. Noon. Lunch. Cook departs and reappears with peppered venison, the Pampas deer. Peaches with cream. Chubby wrens' legs. Gossipmongers break into the kitchens on the weekly hoping to steal a menu and publish proof of my extravagance. No one in this city can fathom my hunger, not even the heifers. Grossly unfair, to count it against me. Sometimes I wish the citadel was made of marzipan, and the shingle, crisped pork skin, and the hospital, cod cheeks, and the barracks and convents, a chilled stew of squid and potatoes, and the cathedral, egg custard, and the fountains, marrow bones, and the plazas, blancmange, or that the city was entirely molded out of chicken liver parfait. I would devour every morsel. Instead I corset myself and nibble dainties, a model of restraint, considering.

Franz sleeps in the shade behind my knees, and I lick a wren's leg and look toward the sea, pleated then flat, pleated then flat, itself a perfect squeeze-box, its song no less suggestive. Meanwhile, between strokes of the keys, Fabia sips green coffee. I smell the burnt lemon. Every day, she has green coffee delivered to the patio, along with a parcel of pink and yellow meringues. Today, I didn't see him come, the waiter balancing his tray, dropping into Fabia's cup his emerald ring, which tinkles the china as she sips. He means to lure her from my service, to carry her off to his hovel, this work unfinished. Sip and tinkle, sip and tinkle. I have no choice. I leap to attention and beat her severely with the wren's leg, snatch her cup and smash it on the balustrade. We're seduced too readily in this city. It's the squeezing sea, or it's the climate. It's the uniforms or the literacy. That last night at the hospital, I felt the feathery hair of Fabia poking out from her nurse's wimple, tickling my cheek. I felt her buoyant mouth. She was drier than Pituco, warmer and sweeter, free of leeches. Instead, mites tiptoed over her skin, nearly invisible, rolling crumbs of vanilla wafer.

"You could come with me," she said, and at that moment, I spoke—*por fin*—comprehensibly. I succumbed to my love. I uttered it, worm after worm after worm after worm. She took it all down.

The next morning, we were separated forever. The day nurse came on with doctors' orders for my removal to the villa of Olég Ortiga Olég, the richest man in the city, whose brick-walled pond wanted, for its central plinth, something eye-catching and one of a kind. Fabia was carving a glazed fruit for my breakfast, the rasp of the sugar crust giving way to a glug with each tiny plunge of the knife. As the day nurse spoke, the knife clattered down.

"Thing?" said Fabia. "Thing?"

"Of course," said the day nurse. "Don't you know—the passengers, the crew members, even the rats, all tallied and tagged. What we have here is the following: a convex mirror from the captain's berth coated heavily with ambergris to which has adhered, among other smaller pieces of detritus, a green raincoat, a conch, and a sea-rotted doll. Look."

And she divided from the doctors' orders a sheet of paper so white I could see its blue veins. Fabia took the paper and crumbled it and climbed into the bed, wrapping her arms around me, but the day nurse laughed. She laughed with such hollowness I knew she was Delmira, the nurse into whom the others tumbled when they crawled from bed to bed in the dormitory.

"Look," she said. "Look, Fabia." She put a hand behind her apron and rummaged so deeply she had to bend in half, and we all heard the ball of her arm bone pop from its socket like a cork bullet on a string. She held up a wrinkled pouch. "You dropped it in the nurses' dormitory. Were you going to leave it behind? Now that you've found something shinier? You're the true daughter of a boiled owl, Fabia, a boiled owl and a magpie, engaged to a coffee pot and at the same time pecking the gilt off that glitzy flotsam, the most prized collector's item in the capital, the pride of the nation."

I realized then that I did look as though I belonged on a plinth, part of a fountain perhaps, enclosed by triumphal arches, or else rising nobly from a brick-lined pond. My face was streaked with the white feces of a frigate bird and my porcelain legs were blistered with mauve lichen. The pride of the nation—haphazard and historical. I kicked Fabia. I kicked her and kicked her and she moaned paw-paw-paw and flapped to the railing of the balcony and then over the railing. After a moment, the patrons of the coffee house below began to untie the paper lanterns from the jacaranda trees. Or so I assumed. I lay exhausted on the leather bolster and watched as the sky filled with spheres.

One more thing happened at that hospital: before the soldiers could load me into the crate, I dug the pouch from Delmira's lap as she dozed in the Viennese chair. I turned it inside out, exposing the curls of golden hair, and I fitted it onto my sea-rotted head.

The crate-bearing donkey at last reached the gates of the villa of Olég Ortiga Olég, and I was installed on the plinth in the brick-lined pond.

74

In those days, Olég kept the pond stocked with chignons, golden chignons, that he fished out with a net. And so he arrived to the pond just after dusk, the long pole of the net on his shoulder. He saw me, stippled with gilt, crowned with golden curls, earless, snouty, milky green, and that was that. He broke the pole across his knee. He netted his own head and sang through the mesh, a Fabergé aria. It got stuck in the net and mashed his lips, and he bled, singing. He was a man in love. For years, he rowed around my plinth day and night, singing, or eating oranges, or sighing, in a canopied boat, until, one spring—but it is always spring—I toppled onto him and swamped the boat and pinned him below the surface of the water. That brick-lined pond, it was more of a rouge pot. When Olég's wife saw the red mark on his collar, she had his corpse drawn and quartered. She eloped with two ballerinas to the Island of Glass, the one with the ruined lighthouse, and never returned to the capital.

And so, I inherited the vast estate, villa and pond, zoological park, orange groves, sugar house, solarium, private army, distillery, Museum of Belles Artes. I became more than a shapely midden, more than a monstrous composite of heirloom and carcass. I became a madam, an apothecary, a horticulturalist with a specialty in spikenard, a docent, and most recently, a presidential candidate and memoirist, although I have discovered that love makes memoir impossible. A memoir is written in the bubbles rising from the lips of a shipwrecked doll. Perhaps her name is Concertina, and her young mistress, not yet a corpse, is calling for her sweetheart, Pituco. Her Pituco! Swept off the deck. The ship is listing. The boats are being lowered. I don't know. Neither does my amanuensis, silly creature, soon kicked off the patio, sent rolling down the slope to the pond, capsized there, lost in the wreck of her invalid chair, wicker frame weighted with iron wheels, with the heavy writing ball, all of the alphabet. She means nothing to me. New paragraph. Never mind. The people will decide. My opponents say I have a heart like an iron fist, but I dare them to find a trace of rust, or with their hearing trumpets detect the faintest thump.

We Are All Breakable, Ready to Break
Lucas Southworth

I.

AFTER THE BITES. After the appearance of what, under one of the wobbly lamps in the employee dressing room/lounge, looked like three welts on T.'s forearm and two little ones on the webbing between S.'s index finger and thumb. After they (zombie fans all of them, horror fans all of them, gore fans all of them) whooped for October 1, whooped for the whole damn month, whooped for another year at the Haunted Farm, which was the only thing they loved in otherwise miserable Olney, Maryland. After they complimented each other on their costumes, even more detailed than last year: zombies, all of them, with fake gashes and rashes and torn clothes and flaking skin. After they decided the biter must have been a deranged co-worker, some new bozo they hadn't met. After they said, That was fucked up, but gave him props for getting into character. After they passed a bottle of whiskey around (a few of them still underage) to loosen their fingers and joints and help paint their moans. After they tried some of those moans together. After they critiqued them. After they talked about what they'd do in a real zombie apocalypse and said they hoped for one and admitted (some of them) that they'd prepped, stashed a little food and a few rudimentary weapons. After they agreed the world deserved it now more than ever (and also agreed, though they left it unsaid, that their movie knowledge and their job at the Haunted Farm in pathetic Olney, Maryland, and the love between them, the strength of their friendship, would be what kept them alive as the Hoard consumed almost everyone else). After their manager poked his head in (that boring haircut) and sent half of them to the cornfield and half to the barn. After they worked for a couple hours, stumbling and lurching and teeth gnashing. After they scared some kids and even made one cry and generally had a pretty good time. After T. and S. met in the dressing room/lounge during a break and compared their bites again and convinced themselves the swelling wasn't swelling. After they said, I'm OK, you OK? After their manager (that haircut again) pointed them back out. After, on the walk

76

over to her spot, S. thought triumphantly that zombies didn't really haunt, couldn't. After T., from his position in one of the dark corners of what used to be a stable, sighed about Maryland's obsession with horses, cursed the Preakness (the mistreatment of animals, the use of animals for show, the torturing of animals, essentially). After S. felt something snap in her hand. After the surface of T.'s underarm prickled and then opened like a zipper. After S. thought, What the hell? and wondered if her makeup was defective, had gone gloopy, was causing her skin to burn. After T. plunged his arm into a slant of light jutting dramatically and decided pus wasn't quite the right word (but there was no other word he could think of). After the pus began to bubble. After T. panicked. After he told himself he didn't care and abandoned his post to search for S. After he tripped in the dark and flailed, hugging for a clump of cornless cornstalks as if they'd be enough to keep him from falling, as if they wouldn't just fall over with him. After he moaned S.'s name. After he began to want. After that want, which started out hazy, began to sharpen, and found its way into his teeth and tongue. After he pushed himself up and lurched toward a group of teenagers and grabbed the hand of one and got a wriggling finger into his mouth. After the kid's friends wrenched the kid free. After one of them called him a pervert, and the kid he'd bitten said, He bit me, he really bit me, and another said, This is awesome, this is too fucking real. After T. felt the instant ecstasy from the bite, and relief, and then disappointment, and the same want he'd felt before, even stronger. After the shock (which wasn't the right word exactly). After the horror (which wasn't the right word either). After he stood there, the taste of blood in his mouth, for seconds that felt like minutes or hours. After his throat locked and he couldn't breathe. After he thought, But I should be dead, but I must be dead. After he thought, But I'm putting everyone in danger. After he thought, Quarantine, quarantine. After the want drowned everything else and he forgot the pain and forgot the fact that he was bleeding and forgot the desires he used to have, which were fairly normal desires of a twenty-year-old and had to do (mostly) with trying to be who everyone wanted him to be (whoever that was), trying to be himself (whoever that was), trying to hang out with his friends and to get drunk, and trying to figure out how to finally kiss S., whom he'd liked since they were little. After, far on the other side of the haunted cornfield, S. heard a shot and another (there was no shortage of guns in Montgomery County, Maryland; there was no shortage of guns anywhere), and a scream and another, and a splatter

Lucas Southworth

(an unhumanlike splatter, a splatter no human body should have made), the violence barely violence (all body, no soul), and she watched it the way she would watch it in a movie, almost laughing, and she understood there was no before for her now, and she and her friends hadn't been smarter than everyone else, hadn't helped each other, hadn't escaped, but had, in fact, been the first victims of the apocalypse they had imagined (jokingly, but still), and she stumbled forward, not mindless exactly, but with a mind that only went so far, trapped inside its new want, its new desire, its simple need to join the Hoard and spread and spread.

II.

In praise of the sandwich M. says has a face. In praise of the face M. says is the face of Jesus. In praise of us, who were able to see that face, eventually, if we looked just right. In praise of the sandwich's immortal power. In praise of M., who, at the bidding of the holy sandwich, found the strength to help us, cupped our fears in his left hand and covered them with his right and pulled his hands apart like a magician. In praise of M., who makes simple what seemed complicated before, who says, simply, that strength and love are the same, and the strength it takes to love is also the courage it takes to accept love. In praise of prayer, which the sandwich, through M., its translator, tells us we must do three times a day, same as eating. In praise of the ritual the sandwich has called, to which we arrive single file, wearing the colorful robes we've stitched. In praise of M.'s mustache, aflame in the candlelight, brilliant in the candlelight, dancing like another flame above his lip. In praise of the way we remove our robes, our nakedness not vulnerability anymore, but, together, an armor. In praise of M., who readies his hands around L.'s neck, and of L., who accepts those hands with his head thrown back, his eyes shut, his skin unblemished and pure. In praise of M.'s thumbs, which press L.'s neck harder, until L. tries to take a breath and can't and his thin shoulders shudder. In praise of L., who calms after a few seconds and opens his eyes and lets them roam from face to face to face. In praise of the beauty of it, the sacrifice, the muscles in M.'s arms, long, so long, healthy, so healthy, his veins flowing and all of him flowing like a kind of electricity into L. and through the great triangle and through the sandwich and through us. In praise of M., who releases L. just in time, opens his hands, and of L., who falls to his knees, heaving as if he's come alive again, as if he's been resurrected. In praise of

78

L.'s body, naked in the candlelight, his face inches from the floor. In praise of how seeing him closer to death helps us appreciate life. In praise of how we are all breakable, ready to break. In praise of the end of the world. In praise of the world's end, which the sandwich says is not far off. In praise of us, who have survived families casting us out, or survived leaving our families, or survived our families dying, leaving us. In praise of M., who says, See, girls and boys, see, all we need to do is stay together, all we need to do is become one. In praise of this beautiful farm on the outskirts of Dawsonville, Maryland, where we grow our food and live. In praise of the books M. has given us, even if we haven't read them. In praise of the games M. has given us, even if we haven't had time to play. In praise of the chapel M. built in the shed, the room for rituals on the second floor, the cyanide waiting and ready in the crawl space below. In praise of all of M.'s weaknesses, which are many, but which we salve by taking them into ourselves, where he can't see them, where they're out of sight. In praise of the phrase "in praise," which the sandwich requires we use at the start of every sentence, every thought. In praise of the phrase "in praise," which has made us more grateful for each word and each breath that carries those words. In praise of L., who turns over now so he's on his back on the bare floor, and of M., who takes the holy sandwich off its plate and holds it up for G. to kiss and then places it gently on L.'s stomach, the depression just under his ribs. In praise of the candlelight, swimming. In praise of our bodies, swimming. In praise of us, free and inflamed. In praise of M., who takes the sandwich again and returns it to the plate and covers it with a napkin. In praise of G., who covers L. with his robe. In praise of us, who slip our robes on again and tie them and leave L. alone to reflect and feel. In praise of the doubters, who whisper and point out that our holy sandwich is starting to smell pungent, dark, almost eggy, its bread growing spots of green, with hair. In praise of the doubters who wonder if the sandwich is going bad like any sandwich, if the face is disappearing, if there ever was a face at all. In praise of the doubters who say, This has happened before, hasn't something like this happened before? In praise of M., who says the doubters keep us strong: doubt being the same as belief and therefore the same as strength and therefore the same as love. In praise of the neighbors who have noticed us through the trees, of the one who came over to call us monsters. In praise of V., who told him that if we are monsters, it is only because we love too much, are overbrimming. In praise of us, who did not have voices before, or had them but nobody listened, and who now want to be heard, even if we're still deciding what we want to say. In praise of the sandwich, which says through M., its unlikely messenger, that it is time to go. In praise of our hearts, which start to beat hard. In praise of the world ending in seven days, just as it started. In praise of us, whom the sandwich, and M., have chosen to ascend. In praise of us, who take our clothes off for the last time and put on our robes for the last time and walk single file, holding a candle each. In praise of the basement, where M. has unrolled a carpet on the concrete floor and placed the sandwich close to one of the edges. In praise of us, who, from practice, form an effort-less and humble triangle. In praise of the sandwich as one point and M. as another and G. as the third. In praise of the paper cups, one for each of us, the juice in that cup, the cyanide in the juice. In praise of the sandwich and M., who both say we have no obligation to drink or to remain part of the group or to ascend. In praise of heaven. In praise of the beyond. In praise of passing the sandwich around one more time, each of us taking a bite until it is consumed, gone, until a little part of it is hurtling through each of us. In praise of living and dying, which should not cause fear because, as M. says, they are the same, and are therefore the same as belief and therefore strength and therefore the same as the love we found courage to give and only wanted to receive all along.

III.

Imagine the end of imagining. Imagine how, without it, there would be no monsters. Imagine that, instead of fantasies, your wants are curated, played out on the screen. Imagine watching yourself take any drug, touch anyone or anything, go to war in any century and fight and die and reboot and fight and die again. Imagine how that might free you from your own dark thoughts, from the fear all humans used to have of acting on that darkness, of being capable of it, of passing on that darkness and fear, of spreading it as quickly as fire or disease. Imagine hell, which has always been a simulation anyway—written and preached and painted and reconstructed on film—that place dreamed by humans to punish themselves for the monsters they were sure they were—that place where humans could imagine suffering at the hands of devils and demons, the way they were sure they deserved. Imagine that though hell still looks much the same now, we visit it only when we want to, watch the monsters stab us and burn us and stuff us with grapes until we swipe over to some bathtub or breezy terrace or beach. Imagine only knowing where you actually are from a pop-up in the right-hand corner of your screen—mine says Montgomery County, Maryland, close to Washington, DC—and imagine that place meaning little to you, meaning only where you left your body before you ascended to HEAVEN! and after. Imagine being guaranteed a spot in HEAVEN!—which is always written in caps, always with an exclamation point, always copyrighted, trademarked, registered. Imagine how this happened—how it really was inevitable—how as humans it was always our nature to invent ways to make our lives easier. Imagine how this used to take one great imagination or the imaginations of the collective, or both, and patience, and eons of trial and error. Imagine how, little by little, we tamed fire, developed better tools, taught ourselves to farm. Imagine our brilliant, stupid brains going into overdrive as soon as we had access to energy, real energy—oil, nuclear, coal. Imagine how we produced, breakneck, tools that could circle the world, transportation that could take you anywhere, all the fat and salt and calories you could eat. Imagine how, once humans beamed electric lights into every dim corner, they defeated the monsters that lurked there, and the hoard split, almost evenly, half looking for utopia, half pining for the past, one side making devils and demons of the other, even if, in the end, both sides wanted the same thing. Imagine politicians falling prey to lobbyists falling prey to greed falling prey to lack of imagination. Imagine that you are there, right there, in the moment of that split—because you are—and imagine our callousness, the jokes we send about our brilliant, stupid ancestors—when they became too much for the world, when the world became too much for them, when it all came so close to ending. Imagine that, just at the last moment, against all odds, humans saved themselves, not through innovation or cooperation or harmony, but simply under the pressure of their own dull claws, their division becoming numbness becoming fatigue, and they returned to their love of ease. Imagine yourself as part of it—because you are. Imagine fitting a pod around your body, strapping on your headset, setting your Tangential Life Mechanisms, slipping out of your life and finally, fully, mercifully, into your screen. Imagine that you will soon shift the burden of inventing to the computers. Imagine how much better at it they will be—without sentiment, without selfishness, without the fear of change. Imagine consumption going virtual. Imagine energy going clean. Imagine warming leveling out. Imagine us, inside our pods now, enveloped by the pleasure of receiving any bit of information, any byte, any image at any time, any text. Imagine how good it feels, how easy it is, like gorging on pizza or cheesecake every minute of every day. Imagine how if you saw us, you would think of us as monsters, so disconnected from our bodies, but imagine that we get to watch ourselves eat at the best restaurants every night, watch ourselves go to Mars or the moon, watch ourselves go to the Uffizi or Rijksmuseum or Louvre and hang paintings we made—paintings the computer painted for us—right next to a Michelangelo or Rembrandt or da Vinci. Imagine our friends and relatives living forever, bytes now, stored in HEAVEN!, a simulation so real we might as well call it immortality. Imagine the pure pleasure of not having to imagine. Imagine the relief of not having to think about any of it. Imagine the end of fear, the end of darkness, and how, now, we control the monsters—or our screens do—deciding when and where they come. Imagine why we chose this, even if we had to give everything up to get everything, and how it wasn't a choice, not really. Imagine someone from my time writing to someone from yours as I am writing now—the computer writing for me. Imagine this note as a how-to for the past, a warning, but also an everyone-calm-down-humankind-is-going-to-be-OK. Imagine me sending it, or imagine my screen simulating that. Imagine me watching you—a simulation of you, whoever you are, reading. Imagine how I can see your demons, even those you cannot and even those you are sure you feel but are not truly there. Imagine that, at first, you will not quite be able to imagine. Imagine that you will deny it, will turn away, but imagine you will also realize you still have time to imagine something else, that you might be the one to imagine what saves us.

IV.

Considering my marriage to Joel. Considering the different names we've had during our century together. Considering the beautiful house before us: a Craftsman like ours, with a stone chimney like ours, but bigger, much bigger, and in the most sought-after part of Takoma Park. Considering why I feel so competitive walking up. Considering that the two of us, Joel and I, are wearing vampire costumes, me in a corset that is tight enough to pinch, him in a nice vest and a puffy-sleeved shirt, both our faces powdered to make us paler, our coats still with store creases in them, our hands deep in our pockets imitating claws. Considering that we once wore clothes like these for no other reason than they were in fashion. Considering our survival has always rested on the ability to fit in. Considering that we're nervous, considering that we've never done this before, considering that we've become parodies of ourselves. Considering the exposed rafters over the house's front porch, which are pretty, the rounded rafter tails, the paneled door. Considering the sign that says, You Are Invited, Please Enter, written in the red crayon of one of their kids probably, red drops dripping from the letters to look like blood. Considering this won't be enough. Considering Joel tries anyway, and pulls his hand back from the handle, his fingers smoking until they heal. Considering we must now wait on the porch for another couple in vampire costumes, must pretend we're taking the vampire rules seriously when we ask if they'll go inside and ask us, formally, to enter. Considering my humiliation. Considering the man's slippery glance. Considering Joel's eyes on his feet. Considering that we have no reason to be afraid or ashamed. Considering we're immortal. Considering how we ended up here, with Joel working for the government and me for a nonprofit that supports DC- and Maryland-area poets. Considering that we're bored and have been trying to convince ourselves that it's a good thing. Considering why, after ten years, nobody's seemed to notice we haven't aged. Considering how small the world's gotten and that there are fewer and fewer places we haven't been. Considering how things were easier before everyone knew about the garlic, about the sunlight and the stake, before everyone knew what our bites looked like and what something drained of blood might mean. Considering the disgust or disappointment on Joel's face when I suggested a few months ago that we try a marriage counselor. Considering that, when you're as old as we are, you're always considering. Considering that half of what I eat is blood. Considering that long ago, before I met Joel, he drank from humans regularly. Considering my shock when he told me he would do it again, could probably do it again, almost kind of craved it. Considering that if he did, in this age of information, in this time, it would mean almost certain death. Considering the party we're at, which Joel found by lurking around online like some less dignified monster. Considering the hierarchy of monsters, and that we, the vampires, have always been at or near the top. Considering the house's front entryway, full of candles that urge us toward the room to our left. Considering that room, where four vampires sit on the sectional and four more sit on chairs dragged in from the kitchen. Considering the different ones: some Anne Rices or Bram Stokers like us, a couple of Coppolas, a few hipper and leather-jacketed from *Buffy* or *Lost Boys*

Lucas Southworth

V.

As if someone else might finally pay for A.'s steak, especially today, when he was pretty sure he deserved it. As if walking across DC in the summer would ever feel like anything other than walking across the ceiling of a sauna. As if A. wasn't already molten under his suit. As if telling himself he'd soon be in the air-conditioning might stop the sweat, might save him from another leap of faith with the dry cleaner. As if the sign over the crosswalk on Constitution could count down any slower. As if the tourists might, for once, just once, resemble anything other than aliens who had recently landed their craft. As if they could ever keep their elbows and shoulders and wide eyes and giddiness to themselves. As if they could walk an entire block without careening left or stopping for no apparent reason. As if they could ever dress without looking like people who looked like they'd put on their clothes out of town. As if A. could pass that ugly fountain between Pennsylvania and Constitution without someone yelling at him, accusing him of being a vampire or troll or zombie, or accusing him of selling his soul to the Man or to Satan or Lucifer or Beelzebub. As if the shouter might ever be someone other than a graying hippie, the saddest thing, or a Jehovah's Witness on an over-turned crate or a homeless man with his eyes tuned to different channels than his teeth or a feminist with smiley-face pasties and a sign filled with curse words or sex puns or both. As if A. could just ignore it. As if he could just walk by without the anger swelling up, without thoughts along the lines of, If I'm a monster, I'll show you what a monster can do, without the images that came, so violent and fucked up and horror movie, his breath caught in his throat and a wave of shame that followed, doubt, and thoughts along the lines of, Maybe they're right, maybe I am, maybe I'm becoming one. As if A. had gotten more than a few steps closer to the relief of the Capital Grille. As if his friends weren't already inside, drinking, ready to shake his hand and punch him on the shoulder and bring up his "chance" meeting with the senator. As if word of A.'s triumph hadn't already spread over the Hill and to the White House. As if his friends wouldn't want to hear if from him anyway, wouldn't ask him to repeat exactly what he'd said and how he said it. As if A. wouldn't happily remind them that the senator had been wavering, his stance on oil and coal weak after that hurricane crawled over his state, and A. had brought the senator back around, the light coming back on in the senator's eyes, the flicker. As if lobbying didn't often feel so much like a game.

As if they weren't so fucking good at it. As if the lobbyists on the other side, the environmentalists, the greensters, the greenies, had any chance against them. As if trolls could make the arguments they did in one-minute or five-minute or seven-minute bursts. As if vampires could love anybody the way A. loved each of his coworkers and friends. As if zombies could return that love the way his coworkers and friends returned it. As if A. could ever, just once, catch the light at Pennsylvania perfectly. As if he could ever cross without stepping over fast-food bags ripped like soldiers at war or pizza-box sarcophagi leaking their uneaten crusts like bones. As if, A. thought, it isn't really just the city that's the monster, DC mutating everyone to monsters inside it. As if he could just get to the restaurant, just cool down for a minute. As if he didn't already know his order: a medium-rare New York strip, half a dozen raw oysters, clam chowder so good it reminded him of his mom's, roasted mushrooms, au gratin potatoes, dessert. As if he wouldn't eat it all, ravenously, insatiably, like he hadn't eaten in weeks. As if someone else might actually pay. As if the DC traffic might just part for him on his drive home, all the way up Connecticut to Chevy Chase, like a magician pulling his hands apart to reveal something impossible. As if, after that, he'd have time to scan the blogs and see who was talking about him and check email to see who was reaching out, and, when his eyes got tired, to do what he never did and close his laptop and go out to his backyard to sit alone in the heat and sip some whiskey and listen to the suburban quiet as pool lights swayed across the fence. As if, A. thought, in the middle of Pennsylvania now, stalled on the island between one direction of traffic and the other, there could be anything more unfortunate than wanting to sell your soul and failing to do so. As if there could be anything worse than putting on your best clothes and going outside and looking down past your feet and announcing that you are ready, finally ready, but you don't even get a puff of smoke, and Satan or Lucifer or Beelzebub or whatever he calls himself, doesn't come, doesn't even flash his red cape, and you think, Maybe he's busy with other soul sellers, maybe he just didn't hear, but after few more minutes, after repeating your intentions a couple of times, you start to understand he doesn't want you or he sees you as worthless or he knows your soul is already destined for hell and he can already feel it in his claws. As if, after coming up with that, A. could keep himself from wondering whether it would happen to him. As if, he laughed, soul sellers couldn't just go online now, check whether they were preapproved, make their soul payments securely through PayPal or

Venmo. As if selling his soul might finally, fully, break the DC heat around him, might cause his dry cleaner to return his shirts crisp and clean and undamaged, might compel one of his friends to cover his dinner and the right bloggers to mention him and the president to give him a shout-out and, most importantly, might clear the rush-hour traffic. As if, A. thought, a family on his left speaking a language he didn't know and a couple to his right speaking a different one and a red Capital Bike missing his foot by an inch, selling his soul might bring him even greater relief than all that. As if it might save him from suspecting, as he had lately, that being paid to talk didn't mean all the talking he did was true, that having what he wanted, success and attention and love even, didn't necessarily mean he had done anything to deserve them. As if selling his soul might actually empty him of the emptiness. As if it could clear his conscience by erasing it. As if it could turn him into a vampire or zombie or troll, or, better yet, turn him, with all his anger and doubts, into nothing, nothing at all. As if, A. thought, entering the cool air of the restaurant and seeing R. and F. and O. waving, calling him over, as if.

VI.

Therefore, the door that appeared in the Lowe's parking lot, across from the Panera Bread, catty-corner from the Michaels and the Whole Foods. Therefore, all of us, ten years younger then, dazed from the early exultation and sleeplessness and constant worry of new parenthood, were a bit out of tune with everything past our front lawns, caught in the immediate wants of our babies or toddlers, those little monsters, we called them, affectionately, absorbed by our immediate want to fill those wants. Therefore, we sensed a get-together for the first time in a long time, a gathering. Therefore, we didn't even hesitate. Therefore, we strapped our children into their car seats, loaded up the diaper bags, folded the strollers, and went. Therefore, the circle we made that first afternoon and the time we spent staring at what was just a freestanding frame and a closed door inside it in the middle of a great stretch of concrete. Therefore, we should have grabbed soups and sandwiches from Panera and gone home, but we didn't, mostly because the door was old, a little weathered even, not newly built and definitely previously used, and, on the Lowe's side, it had five etches or scratches that could have been made by something as simple as a key, but looked like they'd been made by the claws of a hand about twice the size of a human's. Therefore, the door stood with what I can only describe as a kind of unsettling confidence, like it knew it would soon become a great part of our lives. Therefore, the joke I repeated a few times back then, that the door was the same as the monster that had scratched it, reaching out to us and saying, I am not friendly but I am going to live among you, I am going to force you to be my friend. Therefore, as dusk settled on the door a few days after, and D. saw the neon from the Lowe's slant across those scratches, he went to the woodshop he'd built in his garage and made two signs, one to hang on the Lowe's side of the door that said, Do not open, and one to hang on the Panera side that said the exact same thing. Therefore, the Door That Must Never Be Opened became a tourist attraction in our little city of Gaithersburg, Maryland, with T-shirts and a festival and food stands, and tourists coming up from DC, and maybe even people coming down from Baltimore, though I have no idea what people up there do. Therefore, they eat an excellent falafel and line up to take photos of themselves with their hands pretending to turn the knob. Therefore, they had to open another Panera on the other side of town because the original was always too crowded. Therefore, all of us in Gaithersburg know how doors work, chassis to spindle to latch. Therefore, the schools in Gaithersburg spend a few days on the door every year, and our kids, now twelve and ten, are always handing us waivers to sign for field trips, and we're always asking where they're going, and they're always saying, We're going to see the door. Therefore, as was inevitable, imaginations clicked in, stories sprang up, fairy tales basically, the kind, I think, people write together about whatever occupies them or as a way to understand something or explain something or place them in time or distinguish where they live from everywhere else. Therefore, in Gaithersburg, we don't remember how the stories started, or exactly when, but they were probably a way to have fun and scare each other a little and make our city feel special. Therefore, the happy stories alongside the darker ones alongside the ones with the monster or a group of monsters poised to do what they could with teeth and claws. Therefore, one of the most famous, about how our door holds up the sky over Gaithersburg and how the sky over Gaithersburg holds up the sky over the rest of the world, and if the door were opened, the sky would fall, crushing our city first, and then everywhere else. Therefore, the story about a man named Z., who came close to opening the door and ending it all, confusing it, on his way home from the bar, for his own front door, calling through it for his wife and son, growing distraught when neither answered, thinking they were punishing him with silence for staying out too late and thinking he deserved that punishment, and he took his hand off the knob and slid down and slept with his back to the door and, in the morning, realized what he'd almost done. Therefore, the story about a scientist named C., an academic and born skeptic from College Park, who invented some machine to test the air around the door and take measurements and readings, who concluded, when the machine came up with nothing, that the door was just a door, that the etches were probably made by some prankster with a kitchen knife, and she put her hand on the knob and turned it, heard the latch rattle and release, pushed until the door creaked open, and a light that science couldn't explain filled the crack, and she heard whispers and voices and growls, and watched a giant hand fly out and grab her wrist, yank her in. Therefore, our kids love these stories, the mystery, the mythology even, but I've noticed they've developed, almost sadly, almost disturbingly, an honest fear and an unwavering belief, despite what we tell them, that opening the door could actually release these monsters, could actually bring about the end of the world. Therefore, the photograph my son took, where the pocked knob looks exactly like a full moon. Therefore, it's up on our fridge. Therefore, it's the most artistic thing he's ever done. Therefore, the meeting in the Gaithersburg High School auditorium a few weeks ago with parents active in the community, where we all blurted out our unease until we exhausted ourselves, which, I've noticed, is the way concerned parents tend to do it, working ourselves up together before hopefully bringing ourselves down. Therefore, we talked about the trauma our kids might face if some tourist actually turned the knob or a rogue wind happened to push the door open or, what has become common belief in our little city, that the monsters or demons, or whatever might live beyond the door, decides to open it. Therefore, some of the parents launched into a long description, a very vivid description, of these monsters or demons spilling out into the Lowe's parking lot and into the Lowe's and messing up the Michaels and trashing the Panera Bread, and killing, of course, and, of course, killing. Therefore, in that moment, in our meeting in the Gaithersburg High School auditorium, I, and probably some of the other parents realized that, without trying, we'd passed our fears onto our children and our children had kind of incubated them and made them stronger before passing them back, and we'd done this despite our good intentions, because we loved them and didn't want them to be afraid, and the monsters had filled the unfilled spaces around us and the unfilled

89

Monster Eight
Jeffrey Ford

I RAN INTO THE LOCAL MONSTER a couple of times behind the Laundromat on my way home with clean clothes. He had a base of operations back there since it was only a short dash into the woods behind the place. That forest goes on for a hundred miles. I don't know what he's a monster of, everybody said he was definitely one, but I hadn't seen it. He was just a fat guy who sat at a desk made of a plank and blue plastic milk crates. He had a hot-orange scoop chair with three legs that he balanced on. For my money, he was just a sad sack. He was always looking at the woods over his shoulder, seeming to contemplate dashing back into them at the drop of a hat. A hairy motherfucker, though. You could stuff a mattress with just the crop off his back. And his conversation was self-deprecating but not in a humorous way. He was always apologizing for everything—the weather, his mood, the news of the day. A monster of sorry, I'd give him that.

So after having said hello to him when leaving the Laundromat a few times, one day I stopped and asked him why he was sitting back there in a parking lot no one ever ventured into, save a drunk looking for a place to piss, maybe a curious kid on a bike every blue moon, or me heading home from the Laundromat on the path through the woods. He seemed surprised that I spoke to him. His eyes widened, raising his brows, and deep flesh moved around the horns protruding from his temples. Granted, the horn thing was a turnoff. Like what am I talking to? A buffalo? It's not a good look if you want to be taken seriously. So I had to get past that. I swallowed hard and waited for my answer. He grunted a little and I could tell he was nervous. His leg shook and it rattled the desk plank.

"I've got business back here," he said.

"What's your business?"

"I do my monster thing."

"Who pays you? Who's gonna pay to get harassed by a monster?"

"I'm a pro bono monster."

"Working for the good of the people?"

"That's right. I want to create an epic experience for everyone."

"How do you do that?"

"Get into their lives, and then I see what the biggest problem they have is, and I turn up the monster BS level to just above that. They battle the monster and survive and then their real problems don't seem that difficult. That's the gist."

"What's monster BS?"

"Could be everything from some light haunting, calling out their name in a spooky voice in the middle of the night, to shooting right up their toilet and taking a bite out of their ass. It's all in a day's work."

"Sounds rewarding. I heard you bit the head off the Miller girl. What was she? Sixteen? Some collateral damage?"

"That's not true. She's in town right now, still tweaking. The kid's got nine lives. People tell all kinds of stories about me."

"My problem with the whole charade is that you're not scary in the least," I said.

"There's scary and there's scary."

"Right, and you're not either one of them." I got kind of a thrill from telling off the local monster. Not wanting that feeling to fade, I added, "You're more pathetic than anything else."

"OK, OK, I can see where this is headed," he said. He stood up to his full height. He was tall, maybe eight feet, and wide, with rippling muscles beneath the red sleeveless T and hair and fat. My obstreperousness wrinkled away in the shadow of his stature. He came around the desk and put an arm across my shoulders.

"What are you doing?" I asked.

"Look, there's no longer any reason for me to go on with this. You see through me. But, since you're not afraid of me, you wouldn't mind taking a walk in the woods."

"Where to and why?"

"I may not be mythic but I've got something mythic to show you."

"Well, I have to go through the woods anyway. What do you say you stop at my place so I can drop my laundry off? Then we'll check out whatever it is you've got going."

"Fine," he said and led the way toward the boundary between the parking lot and the woods. I caught up with him and as we crossed over, I heard him breathe a sigh of relief. We got on the path and headed northwest where it would eventually lead to my place out in the sticks on the edge of farmland. Side by side, we ambled onward at a long, slow gait. He complained about how out of shape he was, apologized for it, of course. I asked him if he could at least give me a hint as to what he would show me later. He stopped for a moment on the trail, paws on hips. Looking into the sky, he shook his head. "All I can tell ya is it's connected to the ideas of fulfillment and the growth of the spirit."

"That sounds like monster BS," I said.

"For real. That's what it's about. I'm taking a chance showing this to you."

"Calm down," I said.

The woods became a forest, the canopy thicker and blocking more light. There were spots where sun came down like a transporter beam from *Star Trek* and puddled on the path but there were shadows too and they were extra cold. Somewhere along the line, his complaints about himself turned into a story he spoke in cadence with our steps. Occasionally, purple finches darted above us. The trees grew taller as we went along, the oaks and pines like columns and spires in an enormous cathedral.

"I remember some real monsters," he said. "For instance, my uncle, Ted. He was old-school, tear 'em up, pop off a head, no reason needed. You know, just a total hard-ass. And he looked terrible, lumps all over him, a pig nose, nails that were claws, pointed teeth, a fucked-up face. He'd show up at a party with a pair of long knives and leave the place looking like a bad night at Benihana. Slaughter was his nickname among his friends. He ran with a crowd of other monsters who called themselves the Magnificent Seven. Seven monsters all impressively horrible. Each of them had a special trait and each a nickname. There was Bite Em, who bit people a hundred times in a minute, and another with the name Shit Breath Academy. He just opened his mouth and reality wilted, you get the picture. Seven monsters with more monster BS than you could shake a stick at. They were full of themselves, taking liberties with their mythic powers, not to mention murder and mayhem in short order. As they achieved the height of their power, there appeared on the scene a new kind of monster. He went by the title Monster Eight. And he let it be known that he had come to defeat the Magnificent Seven.

"Monster Eight was different, more reptilian, and had the ability to morph into any human form he had ever seen. His feet were molded in the form of high heels; his flesh was pebbled in red scales. He could leap, run fast, and was strong, but his most dangerous asset was his voice and what it said. In the end Monster Eight shut them all down, One through Seven. Talked them right out of their lives.

93

Uncle Ted split his own head with a hatchet. It took Monster Eight seven minutes to convince the old dope he was better off away in the cosmic elsewhere. Once his task was complete, and the seven were gone, he disappeared. No one knows where he went. It's said that he wanders the world unable to die until eight centuries have passed."

I wanted to hear more, but we were approaching my house. Lynn was on the porch in her rocker. I waved as we came out of the woods and walked across the field. I could see her stand up and go inside. The moment I saw it, I knew exactly what was going on. She went inside to get her father's pistol. She knew immediately that I was walking with the local monster. As we reached the porch, I started up the steps, but she pushed through the screen door with the gun out in front of her aiming at my new associate. "Stay there," she said to me. "And you," she said to the monster, "you make a move and I'll drill you with all six."

"Have no fear, madam," said the monster and put his paws up.

Lynn pointed her gun at me. She said, "Give me the laundry," and reached down the step as I reached up. She took the stack by lacing a single finger under the knot of twine at the top of the package. In her opposite hand the gun wobbled and made me nervous. Once she had the laundry she said, "I'm gonna give you about two minutes to get that fucking thing out of here. Then I'm just gonna start shooting. You come home with the local monster? You're out of your mind. Early onset, if you know what I mean. I can't believe I've put up with forty years of your stupid shit."

"He's got mythic qualities," I told her. The monster nodded without lowering his arms.

"He smells like an epic shit. I can't believe you can stand the smell of him. Move it along." She looked directly at me and then her gaze went slowly out across the field toward the old white garage and she winked. "Unload this walking turd and get back here for dinner. Hurry up."

I turned to the monster and apologized for my wife calling him a walking turd. He shrugged and said, "Not uncalled for by any means."

We stood out front for a few minutes, and I made as if I was unsure if I wanted to take the journey. When he started to get impatient, reminding me I had promised to go, I said, "Come to the garage with me. I have an ATV in there that we can take out into the woods. We'll go see your deal and then I can get home quick."

"I do have an appointment to break a priest's legs this evening, so if we could pick up the pace, that would be fine," he said.

We headed for the garage, a big building at the edge of the field beneath a white oak. I let him lead the way. "Your wife is lovely," he said. I quietly laughed. He opened the whitewashed door and stepped into the dark. "Hey, where's the light switch?" he asked. An instant later I heard him get whacked by whatever she whacked him with. I guessed it was that big plumber's wrench just by the metallic ding as it cracked his skull. He went down like an eight-foot furry sirloin and slapped the cement floor of the garage. We worked together and had him strung up in chains in no time. In the middle of the garage there was a large hole dug through the concrete and fifteen feet into the ground. Lynn emptied a can of lighter fluid into the hole. We shared a cig, discussing the clean, accurate blow to his head. Before the smoke was out, I tossed it into the pit. The flames took and in no time, he was awake and in agony at the melting of his flesh. The screams kept up for a while. What a world of stink.

Right when we thought he was finished, and things simmered down to a sizzle and an occasional pop, Lynn called me over to the rim of the pit. She had been inspecting the remains from above with a powerful flashlight. I joined her at the edge and she said, "What's happening?" I squinted and could see in the harsh beam that the charcoal remains of the local monster were splitting open. "We've done three of them so far, and none of them before has done this after roasting for forty-five minutes," I said.

"Yeah, this ain't right."

"Do you have the gun?" I asked.

She pulled it out of her pocket, and as she did, the remains of the local monster, a flame-blackened shell, split open and something quick as a wink shot out and hovered up by the rafters. It was red, with a long, flickering tongue.

"Oh, shit," I said. "It's Monster Eight."

"No way."

"Plug it," I yelled. She fired and her shot went wide through the roof. I grabbed her arm as we made for the door of the garage. It chased us out across the field toward the house. Lynn stopped twice in our escape and each time fired a shot at it. It seemed she hit it twice as it was bounced back through the sky a few yards with the impact of each bullet. We ducked into the house, ran upstairs to our small library, and shut the door. I pulled the copy of *The Marble Dance* in the first bookcase to our right, and the shelves opened like a door. We ducked and stepped into the darkness and the bookcase closed behind us. In that cramped space, we held each other. Only once we were in there did it become clear that we should have left the gun outside. We heard him enter the room, and heard him draw a chair up next to the shelves we were behind. The flow of his reasoning was such that I was already convinced about early inconsequential points in an argument for suicide before I realized he was speaking at all. His bleak message was relentless. We each closed our eyes, drew nearer, and staked our love against his monstrous powers.

Lego

Tere Dávila

—*Translated from Spanish by Rebecca Hanssens-Reed*

THE FIRST WEEK, SEEING that the pustule wasn't drying out, I visited the doctor.

"A bacterial infection is rare in these cases," he said. "Keep an eye on the cellulitis."

His fingers traced the flushed and tender ring that surrounded the yellowing abscess. He advised me not to scratch or play with it, or I'd risk irritation that could lead to sepsis, and wrote a prescription for thirty-five enormous penicillin pills.

I took them religiously, waited, and nothing. In an attempt to supplement the medication's activity (or inactivity) I turned to home remedies: applied udder balm, cotton balls soaked in green tea, slices of raw potato, vinegar mixed with garlic and Crema Santa I got from the Dominican Republic. But the infection, the result of an attack by a common wasp, two stings just above my left nipple, wasn't behaving in a normal way. The abscess was resisting all treatments and was determined to settle into me permanently. That's why one morning, against the physician's instruction, I decided to expel the bad stuff—even though I knew it would only make it worse—and I set my fingers upon the site.

I am embarrassed to admit the strange pleasure I felt provoking that initial burst: this substance, something between liquid and solid, sputtered out and, to my surprise, seemed to be endless. It didn't make any sense. Even still, I didn't stop squeezing until I saw the base of the sink filled with pus. Then I really was startled; I covered the area of the sting with gauze, hurriedly got dressed, and left, already late at this point, for the office.

My job had always bored me. To avoid starving as a sculptor, I ended up in a cubicle on the sixth floor of the Ministry of Public Buildings, redacting edicts of auctions for construction projects. The work offered no challenge whatsoever and the only interesting thing was on the seventh floor, where architects examined blueprints for enormous sculptural structures. In moments of creative antsiness I sometimes almost went up to see them. (I say almost because shyness has crippled me.) Maybe I should have tried to find another job, something more related to the arts, but in the end I was practical: one shouldn't take job security and marginal benefits for granted.

Though even this I put at risk the day I started making those mannequins, or, I should say, the day I made the largest mannequin.

It was a little after the sting that the weird dreams started. Every night, a swarm of wasps pursued me while I tried defending myself with a pocketknife. When I woke up I'd go straight to the bathroom sink, squeeze the lump that never went away, which arose each morning crowned with a new large orb, like a putrid raspberry, and I'd spend a long time draining it. It was as if the blemish's head were connected by an intercellular tunnel to an immense, virulent reservoir deep inside my body. Day after day, for a whole month, I filled the sink.

I didn't go back to the doctor. The antibiotics prescribed weren't working, and, besides, I was growing used to having the abscess's company. Emptying it soothed my nerves and the calming effect lasted for hours. In spite of the weird dreams, I went to bed with a morbid excitement, knowing that in the morning I would have the same satisfying ritual of extraction. That substance made of proteins and tissue was the product of a fight to the death between antibodies and bacteria going rogue inside my body, the central command deep in the bone marrow where neutrophils are produced. I started to see the process as one of purification.

I'll admit that when I was younger these sorts of bodily secretions stirred a disturbing fascination in me. I remember a friend from school who had horrible acne, the kind that resisted all treatments and retinoid creams. One afternoon, when he popped a zit that had been colonizing his chin, something remarkable began to appear at the surface: a magnificent blue bead, like a sapphire. I've never forgotten it. Only years later did I learn how anomalous it is to have purulence the color of precious stones and that the probability of extracting a radiant item from the discharge of gammaproteobacteria is less than one in seven hundred thousand.

By contrast, there was nothing extraordinary about the pus I was now extracting, except for the quantity. Intrigued, I decided one day to not turn on the faucet. Instead of letting the water wash the fluid down the drain, I took a ladle and transferred it to a plastic container so I could examine it more closely. Without meaning to, I became a collector (I'd always wanted to be one but until then nothing had inspired me). I bought dozens more containers that I filled and stock-piled without exactly knowing to what end. I inspected them every few days and discovered that, due to a chemical reaction, the liquor puris of the protein mixed with dead cells had taken on the consistency of old gelatin exposed to air, which, after a period of aging, achieved the plasticity of damp clay. This was a great revelation. I stockpiled the coagulated pus over a period of months with the gut feeling that every last bit would be useful.

The first mannequins I made revealed that, as a sculptor, I was rusty. I had to polish my technique shaping these figures just one or two feet tall, using an old book of sketches by Rodin for reference. Once I was warmed up, I hired a model: a gentleman willing to come to my apartment and pose nude for several hours. From six to nine at night, I examined his bone structure and every contour of his musculature while, so as to keep my true intentions concealed, I pinched at some clay. As I was seeing him out I was already preparing to do it all again with the gelatinous fluid that had taken on a hue somewhere between mustard and ocher. I made a lot of mannequins, one larger and more detailed than the other, but I ended up taking them all apart and returning the prime material to its containers, reserving it for a superior specimen.

One afternoon at the office, I felt a tickle under my flesh, a twitching coming from the spot where the wasp had stung me. I clasped my hand to my chest. Listening closely, I thought I could hear something murmur, a rustling that reminded me of the spasmodic movement of wings.

That night I started on the large mannequin. I fashioned it the same height and breadth as myself, carefully shaped the neck, the torso, the arms, and the legs. The fingers and toes turned out to be the hardest to represent (a common challenge for sculptors). But where I really exerted myself was in the facial features. I rendered them gentle and symmetrical. I smushed and reshaped until I achieved an expression that I might go so far as to describe as compassionate. (I was inspired by prints of sculptures by some of the masters of the Italian baroque.) I devoted hours to the mouth to give it a pleasant smile. I ordered eyeballs and a box of teeth from a company in China that sells prosthetics. Deciding against synthetic fibers, I opted to give it a wig and eyebrows made from human hair. Nearing the end of the process, which took several weeks, I dressed my mannequin

Tere Dávila

in a white polo and khakis. Aside from the yellowish tone and slimy quality of the skin, I was satisfied with my work.

I baptized him with the name Lego, inspired by the toy blocks I'd used as a kid to construct buildings and bridges. To me those childish structures weren't just pieces of plastic; they had been true edifices and even cities that harbored life. My new Lego had that same vitality as those plastic parts; he wasn't an empty husk like the previous lay figures.

I practiced moving his arms and legs until he could do it himself, albeit without much coordination. At first he walked like someone who'd just had his herniated disks operated on. Nonetheless, he turned out to be a willing student and soon enough mastered the skill. I talked to him at all hours, read him stories, but I never could get him to learn to talk, or at least not like ordinary people, since he could at least communicate in a primitive way. If I asked him a question, he'd emit a kind of guttural rumble, a soft and agreeable *hummmm* not all that different from a cat purring.

Proud of what I'd created, I brought him to the office one morning. That first day, Lego was simply another visitor whom my coworkers greeted with impersonal friendliness and the occasional comment about the particularity of his name. He sat for eight hours straight in the cubicle that belongs to Wanda Pellot, who was on perpetual maternity leave.

The following day, Florita, my coworker at the adjacent cubicle, invited us to lunch. To be honest, I got excited; she's never approached me at all except when starring in several of my erotic fantasies. I'd have preferred to spend that time alone with her, but her invitation included Lego, so then I thought it could be an opportunity to put his social skills to the test. Florita and I shared a pizza while Lego drank an herbal tea I'd brought for him in a thermos. Despite having teeth and basic digestion and elimination functions, his system favored the absorption of liquid from a macrobiotic diet. Over the course of lunch, our coworker dominated the conversation: she chattered about our boss, other coworkers, and the last movie she'd seen. Lego limited his reactions to a light warble in a sympathetic tone Florita interpreted as interest in what she was saying.

That Friday a group went out for drinks after work and, for the first time, I was invited to join. Lego came with me and it seemed like, at one point in the night, Florita was flirting with him. One beer followed another. I don't remember precisely when Lego succumbed to the pressure of the group and sipped up a little—only that, when we got

100

back home, he collapsed. He was unconscious for three days and that's how I discovered that alcohol, even in minor amounts, could be deadly for his infectious essence. I took care of him then—the whole week he was in bed I discerned gratitude in his eyes—until he recovered his energy. I realized he was a hard worker: as soon as he could stand again he made the bed and set off sweeping and wiping down the whole apartment. I might have kept him there, as a permanent housekeeper, but my coworkers, and especially Florita, kept asking about him so much that I felt moved by a sort of parental pride and brought him back to the office.

"We have a problem," the director of Human Resources said one day.

Lego had spent more than eighty hours in the office and the company was required by law to offer him a full-time position to avoid being fined by the Ministry of Labor.

This is what prompted my first crime. It wasn't that difficult to buy counterfeit documents: an ID card and Social Security number, the documents needed for employment paperwork. I should confess that my intentions were not pure. More than opening an avenue toward independence for Lego, I was motivated by wrangling some extra cash, a second income that I wouldn't have to work for. When my mannequin received his first check, I pocketed it. Of course, I now had additional expenses: I'd had to buy Lego some work clothes, shoes, and a cell phone (someone technologically regressive would have raised suspicions).

Lego turned out to be an excellent copy editor thanks to all the time I'd spent reading to him. The work environment suited him and he navigated the social dynamics of the office with ease, something I'd never managed to do even after my years of working there. His silences were interpreted as earnestness and focus; his laconicism as the delicate sensibility of someone who prefers listening over commenting. The architects from the seventh floor paid him visits. They bounced ideas off of him. They expressed their doubts and he would answer with his contemplative *hmm* or *uhum*, which seemed to give them assurance and helped them resolve their own problems without feeling like someone was imposing judgment. They even credited him in their work if the projects moved forward. In the end, the gladness I'd felt at having an additional source of income lasted only briefly.

Then there was Florita. She stopped including me in her invitations to lunch or to grab a coffee (or, better yet, tea, following Lego's example). I resented the attention she showered on him and, aggravated,

101

Tere Dávila

I started leaving him in the office overnight instead of bringing him home with me. I'd leave early, stop at the bodega, buy a bottle of Chateau Clos or d'Armailhac (two salaries allowed for such taste), and drink at home by myself.

It didn't take long for my dipsomania to affect my performance at work: a numbers slipup, a typographical error, and soon I was called in to the supervisor's office. More than the rebuke, what really hurt was that my mistakes were reflected in my end-of-year bonus. Lego's was more generous than mine. Leaving him to sleep in the office had been a mistake: it enhanced his reputation as a dedicated worker and made him almost untouchable. It was even rumored that my pus statue played golf on Sundays with the secretary of health.

"Come back home," I asked him one afternoon.

In spite of everything, Lego's absence had caused me to feel despondent and sad. So much that, struck by a surge of affection fueled by the two beers I'd had at lunch, I sought to salvage our relationship.

"*Hmmmmm.*"

I was touched by that gracious purr of his. Harboring resentment wasn't part of his personality. I moved to hug him to indicate that "There's nothing between us" when I heard that murmur again: a deep thrumming was coming from Lego's chest, identical to the one that, almost a year earlier, I'd experienced within my own chest. I felt an irresistible urge to scratch myself from head to toe and, confused, I withdrew. I then stood observing him from a distance and noticed Florita was also absorbed in him. Her enthrallment and that murmuring troubled me; something was telling me these were warning signs.

They were. Late one night, after Lego had come back to the apartment, I got up to pee and saw the bathroom light was on. I quietly peered in and discovered Lego in front of the medicine-cabinet mirror, pinching his sheeny skin and extracting gushes of a juicy and yellowy paste that filled the sink. I hid behind the door, waiting for him to finish his ritual, just like mine but nocturnal. When I heard him fumbling with what I assumed were scoops and containers, I understood. Maybe this impulse to create was natural. Why shouldn't this desire to shape one's own lay figure also be born in Lego?

During the weeks that followed I left him to it without confronting him. I knew where Lego was hiding the containers he continued to fill with his secretions and I would wake up before him to go inspect them. I verified that, just as in my case, the substance's consistency

102

changed and I imagined that from it more Legos would be sculpted. I couldn't have been more wrong.

How useful it would have been if, starting on the day I was stung, I'd taken an interest in the behavior of wasps and, in particular, the behavior related to their fertility. I would have learned that, as is the case with many social insects, only the queen mother has the ability to engender productive members: worker or fighter females who had evolved for survival. But if one of the daughters tries to assume the birthing role, their larvae turn out inferior: drones incapable of working, finding nutrients, or fighting. They can't even feed themselves and their lives are short: one single flight to mate followed immediately by death.

The same thing happened with Lego's fluids: they didn't have what they needed to become something that was viable.

The first creature was unable to coordinate its movements. It would hardly take two steps before it flailed against the walls and collapsed on the floor, shuddering in epileptic spasms. It couldn't stand on its own and needed to be spoon-fed and prodded in the jaw so it remembered to chew with its toothless gums. It didn't have eyes either. It sat motionless in a corner and the only time Lego managed to provoke some reaction from it was when he put on a Prince CD. Only then did Francisco—Lego wanted to give him a normal name—move his big head from side to side.

Carlos, the second mannequin, turned out hyperactive. He couldn't stay still, he paced in circles, running around the apartment, knocking over furniture, and if we tried to restrain him he would lunge at us head first. Like Francisco, he didn't have eyes or teeth (thank God); both were like zombies.

"Don't try another," I pleaded. "It's not working."

By the guttural sound of Lego's answer I knew I'd offended him, and that's how we ended up with three monsters in the house.

The third, Arturo, was the worst. Not only was he the most aggressive, but also for some reason, not having inherited his creator's agreeable vocal warbling, he screamed continuously. The night he was "born" (I remember it was a Friday) he grabbed a stapler and began hammering it against the kitchen cabinets, against the lights, the stereo, the coffee table. To the beat of his yawps, he broke everything within reach with his chosen apparatus without us being able to stop him.

"What's all that racket?" one of my neighbors complained from the hall outside.

"What is going on in there?" Another neighbor started pounding on my door.

"Do something!" I implored Lego through clenched teeth, but he was petrified, watching his mannequin with the saddest expression I've ever seen.

"We're going to call the cops!"

Swiftly Lego pulled himself together. As best he could, he dragged Arturo into the kitchen while I stayed in the living room, making sure the neighbors didn't knock the door down.

The uproar, however, didn't last long. I soon realized the racket outside was more dramatic than the one inside. Arturo had calmed down. I opened the door and faced my neighbors.

"I'm sorry, I'm sorry, it won't happen again," I babbled.

After closing the door, I slid the latch, and ran to the kitchen, where I found Lego alone, standing in a pool of pus with a knife in his hand. He set down the knife, which was dripping over what remained of Arturo, steadily walked into the living room, put on his jacket, and left. He didn't come back that night, or the following.

All weekend I speculated on where he might have gone, and I already suspected the answer, though I wished I was wrong. But on Monday, showing up at work and seeing them, Lego and Florita, I knew I'd guessed right. After so many years observing my coworker, the star of hundreds of fantasies, I knew well how to read her emotional state in her facial expressions, gestures, even in the way she walked. I had longed to be the one who caused that sparkle in her eyes.

I'd wanted to approach Lego but he was dodging me; he pretended to be busy with the constant back-and-forth of paperwork. I saw how Florita slyly smiled whenever he passed her and I started imagining them together. After the disaster at the crack of dawn on Saturday, he'd showed up at her door (at some point she'd given him her address or phone number, something I was never able to get), she woke up, confused; they embraced in silence, needing no explanations, which he wouldn't have been able to give, and then they made their way to her bedroom.

It made me sick picturing them making love, to think of him contaminating her with his microorganisms, but I could at least contend with this revolting image; it was something else that horrified me. Was it possible that, somehow, Lego's body had the ability to spawn more monsters by having sex? I hadn't forgotten that he had my DNA and this made everything even more horrendous: whatever he engendered was a direct product of me.

Getting up from my desk, I walked, as coolly as I could, to the elevator and pushed the button. I grabbed what I needed from an architect's drawing desk and returned to the sixth floor. In the short span of the elevator ride I reflected on how Lego had been the only valiant one between the two of us. He didn't hesitate to kill Arturo and destroy the mistake that had come from him.

I'll never know if Lego sensed my intentions, but when I entered the space of his cubicle he greeted me with a feeble hum, sorrowful. I avoided looking him in the eyes when I threw myself on top of him with the X-Acto knife. I didn't count how many times I was able to stab him before the buzzing became deafening and a gray force pushed me backward. The purulent mass that was formerly Lego was oozing to its end while thousands of wasps deployed, each with its own minuscule dagger. They surrounded me, working as one, and enveloped me in an aggressive cloud whose mission was to kill me. Or that's what I thought then; now I'm not so sure.

They managed to drive the wasps away from me with a fire extinguisher, I'm told. I don't remember anything else about what happened then, or during the two weeks that followed when I was comatose in a hospital, covered from head to toe in stings. The prognosis was that I would die from sepsis. Somehow, I lived through it.

As soon as I regained consciousness I learned that the state had assigned me a criminal defense lawyer and that I'd been accused of homicide. Of course, I pleaded guilty in court—after all, I had killed a coworker in front of a dozen witnesses—and with stunning speediness, considering how long these legal proceedings can take in this country, the judge sentenced me to twenty years in prison.

From my lawyer I learned of the fate met by Lego's mannequins. The day after the incident, detectives broke into my apartment and Carlos, the hyperactive one, hurled himself on top of them. They killed him with one shot. Francisco was found sitting in a corner, unmoving and oblivious. At first they thought he was dead, but when they realized that wasn't the case, they brought him to an institution. If he's still alive when I get out, I'll go visit him.

It's been hard for me to have contact with people here, not because of my shyness, but because of my appearance. The wasp attack left me covered in yellow and hostile abscesses, agglutinated one on top of another such that I am one amorphous surface of pus, as though another of Lego's hideous and twisted offspring.

105

Tere Dávila

Every morning in my private cell (they granted this to me, not as a privilege but to avoid unnecessary cruelty to the other prisoners), I stand in front of the mirror above the puny sink provided by the Ministry of Correction and begin the ritual that sometimes manages to keep me busy for the entire day: I apply pressure with my fingertips and extract copious amounts of the festering liquid. There are days when I work furiously; I squeeze the lesions of flesh with the hope that, from somewhere deep in my vast reserves, a blue sapphire will emerge. But I don't know why I bother. No matter how much I prod at them, the pustules have yet to offer such a treasure, have yet to relent in size or ferocity.

The Gricklemare
Julia Elliott

She's been up for two hours, typing on her laptop, when the children come scampering and giggling. But the mist is still thick, crickets still chirring a nocturnal song. By the time she steps out onto her porch, the imps have slipped off into the twilit woods.

"Gricklemare Gricklemare," they chant—nonsense language, some tidbit of Appalachian folklore, a meme, perhaps, or something from a Kids Netflix fantasy series.

She spots one of them, crouched behind a mountain laurel shrub, a blond child so pale he seems half-dissolved into the mist. And then another, tittering above her in a cedar, a girl perched in the highest branch. How did she climb up there so fast?

"Gricklemare Gricklemare," the girl croons, birdsong needling around her voice. Sylvia wonders how many children there are, hidden in the forest. Dizzy, she sits on the old rattan chair that came with the cabin.

"Gricklemare Gricklemare," the children taunt, halfway down the mountain now.

"Gricklemare," Sylvia shouts back, the word sticking in her throat when she sees the egg smashed on her stone porch step, red shelled, the meager yellow yolk still intact.

"Little shits," she hisses. She fetches a bucket and rag, swabs the mess up with paper towels, and rinses the step. She might have slipped on it and tumbled into the ravine that's unnervingly close to the cabin she rents, battering her body against tree trunks.

She goes back into her study, sits down at her laptop, reads through the words she wrote before sunrise: *using an EcoJustice education methodology to engage rural communities with indigenous knowledge systems and Western scientific traditions, thereby deconstructing the subtly imperialist ideological hegemony of traditional ecopedagogy. . . .*

Darkness stirs inside her like a roused flock of grackles. But really, it's more like a sap, a fog, *a humor*—the archaic medical term fits best, her body tainted with black bile, melancholy vapors floating up from

107

some foul green gland to cloud her mind. As she writes gibberish, the world burns. As Alex used to remind her, by the time her useless theory is put into practice, bees will be extinct, the polar ice caps melted to filthy slush, coral reefs bleached white as bone. She half wishes the children would come back, for she longs to talk to someone, anyone.

She will not think of Alex. She will keep him contained, down in some festering fold of her frontal cortex, where, according to a recent article she read, bad memories go.

But Alex slips up from the murk. Alex with his amber eyes and black hair. Alex with his womanly lips, his stark rib cage fit for a pietà. Alex cocking his head like a hen as he considers something she has said. Alex smirking, claiming that science will save the world, not gibberish. Alex delivering a sharp retort. Alex lingering in the air of her apartment a week after his body is gone—scent molecules, dead skin cells, dirty socks in the closet, pulsing with strange energy. She'd thrown the socks in the trash, but one night, like a starved racoon, she'd dug them back out again.

"A walk in the woods." She speaks the words aloud to summon the act.

Alex gone shockingly fast, like the chestnut ermine moth, like the golden-headed Langur, like the Kalimantan mango. She does not know exactly where he is—studying slime mold in some dwindling forest. What she misses most is not the sex but the mammalian warmth, the everyday hum of their parallel lives, when they were kind to one another.

"A walk in the woods to get my serotonin levels up, a dose of mindfulness."

A walk among sentient trees will do the trick. The mycorrhizal networks of the ancient forest are unbroken because she lives on the edge of a national park—a great privilege, she reminds herself, because she's white, writing a grant-funded dissertation, raised in a nuclear family funded by a nuclear engineer who used to laugh at her when she told him, as a child, that trees could talk to each other. She holds grudges, dwells on things. Years ago, when her father was in the hospital having kidney stones removed through an incision in his back, she left an article about the so-called wood-wide-web on his nightstand, along with the toxic chocolate shake he'd requested from McDonald's.

"Trees *can* talk," she whispered as he came out of his anesthetic haze, and then she slipped from the room, leaving her ghostly words behind her.

Now she feels sick about this, remembering the look on her father's face when he saw her outside the SRS Badge Office, a green-haired teen in combat boots, protesting all things nuclear. She'd protested the nukes but had no problem taking nuke money, would jump to snatch her generous allowance from her smirking father's hand.

What a little hypocrite she was.

She turns to the window, focuses on wind in the trees.

Since she moved to Black Knob, memories flash to the shallows of her mind like sun-silvered sharks feeding in the surf. She'd imagined herself in nunnish seclusion, making peace with herself, learning to live alone, enjoying epiphanies during woodland walks and rushing back to the cabin to type furiously into the night.

Sylvia weaves through the last of the mist, breathing in the deeply oxygenated woods.

Walking along an old logging trail fringed with lush poison oak, relishing the feel of fog on her skin, she breathes in the scent of spruce, sugar maples, dewy mountain laurels. But she tenses up again when she passes the rusted trailer, a kudzu-smothered Holiday Rambler from the 1970s—abandoned, she hopes. She can see the roof of a collapsing cabin behind it—the red gleam of wet heart pine. She's surprised it hasn't been dismantled by carpenters from Asheville, hungry for reclaimed wood.

She feels the uncanny allure of the trailer, its door ripped off, its opening fringed with vines—a cave mouth. As a child, she could never resist creeping into a derelict building, even after stepping on rusted nails, getting clawed by feral cats, breathing in asbestos, lead dust, toxic mold. Even after enduring a hundred lectures from her parents, who'd always circled her as they preached, cigarettes fuming in their hands.

Sylvia veers off course, steps inside, smells mildew, the prefab walls spattered with it. A scattering of cockroaches. A dank sofa, velvety with mold, dolloped with animal shit. A red Formica dining table, rusted aluminum legs, no chairs. Wads of clothes on the putrid shag—vintage polyester, rayon, acrylic—cloth spun out of oil through the sorceries of shut-down mills. Holding her breath, she tiptoes down the narrow hallway, the flimsy subfloor creaking beneath her. When she hears a strange cackle, she freezes. There is something—alive, human, animal, other—in the dim back bedroom. Whatever it is could kill her, but she can't stop herself from peering into darkness to catch the witch at her work, the monster feeding, or the psychopath reveling in the exuberant spatter of his kill.

Two windows, no glass, plastic blinds, one half-open.

A particleboard dresser with missing drawers.

Soiled mattress on the floor.

A chicken—*a fucking chicken*—squatting in a nest of twisted sheets.

The chicken squawks again, but doesn't flee, sits as though tranced, beak open, red eyes gleaming.

But then it jumps to its feet, flutters up to the dresser and out the window, a flurry of black feathers.

The hen has laid a small egg, reddish and speckled.

Sylvia picks up the egg—still warm—and slips it into her jacket pocket.

When she emerges from the trailer, the mist is gone, the day stark and blue. No clouds.

Though she finds the warm egg vaguely repulsive, she taps it on the counter, cracks it open, and deposits a dollop of unfertilized goo into a skillet slicked with hot oil. The dark-yellow yolk, tainted by a tiny drop of blood, quivers. She picks the red out with a spoon, washes it down the sink. She puts bread in the toaster, mashes an avocado into paste with a fork.

Alex would have eaten the egg as it was, blood drop and all. Alex would have said she was squeamish. Once, in the thick of sex, when she'd reached the soaring point where she'd forgotten that Alex was the person affixed to her, despite his characteristic arrhythmic panting, he'd uttered a crass phrase that she'd always hated—*Let's make a baby*—pulling her out of her trance.

"Why did you say that?" she asked, afterward.

"I don't know, but it seems only natural, when you think about it."

"If we lived naturally, I'd have a dozen babies by now, my bladder and uterus prolapsed from multiple births. I'd probably be dead."

"You're afraid of the body, the flesh," he said dramatically, like a poet in a play.

"You might be too if you had to give birth."

"You evolved to give birth; I evolved to knock you up."

She cringed again. *Knock you up.*

"I might have a baby one day, just not now."

"I didn't mean now."

"What did you mean, then?"

After that, the air grew stagnant from his sulking. Winter came to their northern college town, slithering like a great, white beast around their apartment building. Alex, immersed in his dissertation on slime molds, became reticent, moody, rifling through cabinets, scattering litter wherever he moved, growling so quietly that the hum of the electric heater almost effaced his beastly language. She detected musk on his clothes, sweet and pissy with a note of onion, full of signals she couldn't decipher. He staked out territory near the TV, cocooned himself in a comforter, scattered his environs with books and crumbs and bits of gristle. He darkened the air in the living room.

She kept to the study they used to share. Stepping into the room each morning, she felt herself descending, as in a shark-proof tank, into the depths of ecopedagogy, the intricate theories difficult to decipher, like the language of whales. There was so much to read before her comps in May. She spent hours scrolling through glowing texts, processing words until her eyes burned.

One twilit day, the light ambiguous, Alex followed her to the bathroom. He dropped his blanket on the tile. He bit his lip. His cheeks were flushed. She was about to turn away when she noticed his erection, keening from his body like an exuberant animal, pressed against damp thermal cotton.

Wet sparks shot from his eyes. His smile made her think of summer—humid air, green mountains. Alex smirked and removed his sweatshirt. She was shocked by the luster of his pelt, how pretty and soft his naked skin looked next to the hair. She couldn't stop herself from sinking her hands into it. She caressed his starveling ribs. Their kiss caught fire.

In the bedroom, she waited in the dark as he rummaged for a condom, remembering the thrill of her youthful exploits, a time when the reek of a Trojan had filled a parked car like an explosion of napalm, setting her limbic system on fire.

"We're out," he said. "It's been a while."

"Let's just be careful," she said.

"Let's not," he huffed into her ear, his weight upon her again.

"You have to be." Her words—stark, loud—punctured the mood, but they kept going.

*

The egg smells gamy, like the chicken giblets her mother used to fry. The egg glistens, so oily that it seems to quiver in the light. She moves to the shadowy side of the table, takes a bite, gags on the rich flavor—nutty, fishy, off. Pinching her nose toddler-style, she gulps it whole, barely chewing it, like a seal swallowing a fish. The egg leaves a film of grease in her throat, a taste of strange meat, metallic, like something from a can with a label she cannot read.

The children chant in the forest.

> *Higgledy-piggledy, my black hen.*
> *She lays eggs for gentlemen,*
> *Sometimes nine and sometimes ten,*
> *Higgledy-piggledy, my black hen.*

Perhaps the children followed her along the logging trail. Perhaps they saw her take the egg. Now that school is out, they have nothing better to do than to spy on her. One of them whips past her window, a streak of pallid hair. Another—long snouted, weak chinned—peers from the brush like a meerkat. Others jump in the branches, sending down drifts of leaves.

Perhaps they expect her to offer them treats, hence their nasty trick. Maybe she could ward off their pranks with cookies, but she's no good at baking—she has no sugar in the house.

At last, they flit off, rustling through brush like low-flying birds.

In the evening, she sits on the porch with a glass of dark wine, enmeshed in the thrumming of katydids and crickets, wondering if their love calls change her heart rate, the rhythms of her blood, tiny valves spasming open and shut. *An unscientific thought*, Alex would say, *but a charming one*. He'd lick her neck, massage her toes, frankly press his beautiful bony hand against her crotch. She feels a hankering. She stretches in the humid air. The temperature has not dropped off yet but will soon. The moon floats like a scrap of gauze in the pink sky. When the sky darkens, an owl screams, so loud she thinks it must be a siren signaling a state of emergency—flames sweeping through the woods, bombs falling, some deadly chemical spreading through the atmosphere, odorless, invisible. The owl swoops from a spruce, its wingspan shockingly small.

Every time she sees the sweep of stars appearing in the dark sky, she pictures Alex, stumbling around the campus quad with his Star

Chart app. There was an ancient astronomer who fell into a ditch, she thinks, or was it an astrologer, a well? She breathes in the mystical moist night air. She sips her wine, watching fireflies sway out from the woods, still thriving in this protected ecosystem. She senses the hum of a body moving near her, turns, sees nothing. Perhaps a deer has passed in the dark.

Her phone throbs in her pocket, the ringer always off. She looks at the screen, sees an unfamiliar number, and then a voice mail signal. She listens, hearing only static, bleeps, and then the word *Alex* in a garbled voice. She returns the call, gets voice mail immediately—a stock, impersonal greeting.

"Yes, you called me," she says. "I'm not sure if I know who you are. Is this Alex? Do you have a new number?"

Sylvia wakes up to the startling certainty that someone is in her house, a small person pattering, opening drawers and slamming them shut. One of the children, she thinks. She slips out of bed, pulls on her robe, tiptoes to the living room. Two windows—heavy, difficult to open—gape. Wet night air blows through the room, fluttering scattered papers, clumps of white fluff that she identifies as pillow stuffing, the gutted pillow flaccid, draped over a sofa arm. Whoever has done this is in the kitchen now, rifling through drawers in the glaring light. But by the time she steps into the kitchen, the vandal is gone, the window left wide open. The ancient fluorescent overhead buzzes. Flatware is scattered on the counters, broken dishes on the floor, an entire roll of paper towels unfurled and strewn.

"Little shits," she hisses, imagining herself snatching a child up by the scruff of its neck. She has no idea how old these children are, how strong, how wild.

"Tomorrow," she says.

Tomorrow she will buy bolts for the windows and doors. Tonight, she will call the police.

She reaches into her pocket for her phone, feels a small lumpish thing—warm, clammy. She plucks it out, tosses it into the dim living room. She sees something—bald, grayish pink like a newborn mouse—slithering under the sofa. Her phone is in her other pocket. She swipes on the flashlight and peers under the sofa: a sock, a book, a withered apple core.

*

113

Julia Elliott

The policewoman is small, elfin, with a neat cap of nut-brown curls, large baggy eyes, and a pointed chin.

"Can you describe these children?" Office Simmons yawns.

"I've only seen flashes: there's a pale one, with blond hair, boy, girl. I don't know. Also, a red-haired girl."

"About how old?"

"I don't know. They hide in the woods."

"No children live up here, as far as I know. So they must be from town. How do you know they're children?"

"As I've told you, they've been stalking me."

"Stalking?"

"Pranking, following, spying. They smashed an egg on my doorstep this morning."

"Those are heavy windows. I don't see how a child could open them."

"Perhaps this is an unrelated incident. Or maybe the children are older."

"Teenagers?"

"Perhaps." But Sylvia knows they are children—slight, willowy, quick.

"Anything else?"

"Not that I can think of."

Sylvia doesn't mention the thing she found in her pocket, the damp, warm heft of it, the way it slithered across the floor like a salamander with rudimentary legs.

"Mind if I take some pictures?"

"Of course not; please do."

When the officer is gone, Sylvia checks the locks. She falls into fitful sleep, a carving knife stashed under her bed. In a dream, she presses a raw lump of meat to her ear and hears the voice of Alex.

"Where are you?" she asks.

"In the air," he says. "Look out your window."

She sees him, hovering in the mist, his skin glowing damply like luminescent fungus.

"Are you dead?"

"I don't think so." He huffs out an angry laugh.

"Are you sure?"

Alex looks stricken, and then a fury comes upon him. He whirls in the mist, sending gusts of damp air into her house. He sucks her

114

out of the window, whips her up into the sky.

Sylvia wakes up, thinks she hears the children in the cabin again, but it's only a tree tapping a window, the ice maker rattling, the creak of the old house settling deeper into the earth.

The next morning Sylvia finds dirty plates in the kitchen sink—two chipped atomic dishes from the 1950s—the ones that came with the cabin—congealed with dark fat. She vaguely recalls eating something in the middle of the night, something from a can, mashed meat, crunchy with cartilage—she thought it was salmon, but it must have been something else. She finds a pile of dirty laundry on the bathroom floor, her clothes musty, as though fetched from a basement. Green scum rings the bathtub. A congealed skin of urine lines the bowl of the commode. Mold has grown on her leather shoes. Moisture oozes from the cabin's plank walls.

"Little shits," she hisses, for the children opened her windows and let mist float through her house. The cabin has no air-conditioning. Ancient mold spores, ignited by moisture, have come back from the dead. Immersed in her dissertation, she has not noticed the mess.

She spends the day cleaning with vinegar, ammonia, bleach, and Ajax—cleaning in a frenzy like her mother used to do, dizzy from fumes, jaws clenched, mop brandished in her white-knuckled fist like a weapon. The vacuum roars; the washer rumbles. She scrubs with sponges, scouring pads, and coarse-bristled brushes, rooting out muck from nooks and cracks. Pulsing with adrenaline, she pulls the stove from the wall and stares in horror at the filth behind it. But she obliterates it all. Buried for decades, gleaming green linoleum resurfaces. She washes clothes, towels, bedding, bath mats. She dumps bucket after bucket of gray water into the sink. When she finishes, it is late afternoon, she has forgotten to eat, and she feels she might levitate when she steps out onto the porch and looks at distant mountain peaks. She floats through the clean house with a glass of wine, enjoying beautiful views, forgetting that she should drive to town to buy bolts for the windows.

The light is too delicious, like soft green gauze, crisp, no mist in the air. She relishes the silvery sound of crickets, the soft fuss of birds. At the top of the mountain, she feels like a woman in a turret, caught in an ancient spell. She scans the forest, half hoping that someone will appear. She drinks more wine, falls asleep just after dusk, exhausted, breathing in the smell of sun-dried sheets.

She wakes with a fever at 4:36 a.m., the house quiet, wisps of mist floating in the lamplight. Did she leave a window open? Did the children come back? Dizzy, clutching her throbbing head, she walks through the rooms. Her eyes itch and leak. She has trouble bringing objects into focus: the brown blur of a chair, the dark blot of a shoe, quivering window frames. In the bathroom, she rifles through the medicine cabinet, pulling bottles close to her squinting eyes: NyQuil, Tylenol PM, Robitussin. She can't remember which concoctions she bought and which were in the cabin when she came. She finds a brown bottle of Aspironal, an aspirin product, she guesses, and takes a sip—licorice, rust, mud. It leaves an oily residue on her lips.

Stumbling back to the bedroom, she sees throw pillows on the floor, strewn books, loose sheets of yellow legal-pad paper drifting in the breeze. She's too tired to pick up the mess, too dizzy to find the open window.

Back in bed, her sheets smell musty. Perhaps they were still damp when she took them off the clothesline. Her head throbs. She sinks into sleep and resurfaces again.

"Sylvia," someone whispers, the voice painfully familiar. *Alex.*

"Alex?" She squints into the dimness. "What are you doing here?"

He slips into bed beside her, smelling of sweat and smoke.

"Why didn't you call?"

"I did."

She remembers the strange phone call, the static, the feeling of wind in her head.

"I've come a very long way," he whispers. "Through forests and storms, along winding roads and through the air."

"I can't see you," she says.

"It's dark, but I'm here."

His breath, sour and hot on her cheek. His arm, heavy on her belly. His toenails, too long, pricking her ankles.

He kisses her. His tongue, longer than she remembers, probes the depths of her throat.

She gags, pushes him off her, sits up.

"I'm sick," she says. "Can you turn on the light?"

He flicks the lamp on. In the brief flare of light, she sees Alex, naked, sitting on the bed, his spine knobby, each jutting vertebra coated in downy brown hair that she doesn't remember. And then it goes dark again.

"Bulb's dead," he says.

"You're too skinny," she says. "Where have you been?"

"In the forest."

"Vague answer."

He slides on top of her, stabbing her thighs with sharp pelvic bones. He smells of mushrooms and soil, damp brown leaves, the sharp mineral odor of corroding vitamin pills. And then she breathes in something sweet, musky, intoxicating: warm kitten fur, summer grass, cinnamon, custard.

Alex pulls off her panties, licks her ankles, slides his strange tongue up her left thigh.

She wakes up, still feverish, her joints aching.

"Alex?"

She hears him, rattling in the kitchen, opening and closing drawers. He must be making breakfast. Her bedroom window is open wide, pink fog outside, the hiss of rain.

"Can you please close the windows?" she calls.

He doesn't answer. She hears glass breaking, a dish crashing against the kitchen floor.

She gets up, pulls on her robe, moves to the window, attempts to yank it down.

"Alex, can you help me with this window?"

She walks into the living room, which is filled with fog. Cumulus clouds ooze through her house.

Touching the damp woolly upholstery of the old sofa, she feels her way toward the kitchen, finds it empty, dish shards scattered across the floor, pieces of broken glass on the counter, the trash can over-turned, a brown smear of coffee grounds on the linoleum. She re-members the apartment she shared with Alex in Pennsylvania. She remembers bickering over the messes he made. Probing for neuroses, he'd analyzed her desire for order, pronouncing her fear of chaos excessive, irrational.

"Alex?"

The door hangs open. She steps out onto the porch, thinking he must've gone to town to get lightbulbs and beer, for wine gives him migraines.

"Gricklemare Gricklemare," children chant from the forest.

117

They are back again, lurking in the mist, crackling through brush, stirring in the branches.

She pulls out her phone, scrolls through contacts, almost calls Officer Simmons. But the children have already fled, down the mountain toward the old logging trail. And Alex will be back soon, to help her with the windows, to clean up his mess.

It's just like him, she thinks, pacing the cabin, fists clenched. Just like him to deem her irrational and arrive unannounced in the middle of the night, to slip into her bed after all this time. Just like him to wreck her kitchen and then vanish before she wakes up. And the bathroom too: soggy towels heaped on the floor, dark hair thatching the drain, toothpaste smeared all over the counter. She still has his old number in her phone, even though he changed phones, still has playful texts she hasn't deleted, a furious voice mail that she listens to every now and then to vanquish her ache for him—a tirade that breaks off after three minutes (though she knows he kept thundering long after the beep). She remembers the strange call she got yesterday, the word *Alex* blooming from the static. She searches her recents but can't find the number.

Why didn't you call? she'd asked him last night.

I did, he'd said.

If he comes back, she will tell him to go. She'll do it calmly, rationally. *This will be best for both of us*, she'll say, casually sipping from a cup of detox tea. In the meantime, she'll carry on with her life, forge ahead with her dissertation, wring sense from abstractions, deconstruct sacred binaries, and formulate new paradigms. Her words will glow with meaning. Her arguments will jar people out of their complacency and inspire them to act, to press against the intricate cages of their bureaucracies like clever rats, to stop mass extinction, to save the dying oceans, to get out there with roaring jackhammers and break up pavement, free the stifled soil, plant a million tender saplings. But when she sits at her desk, she goes straight to Facebook. When she and Alex broke up, they agreed to end their virtual "friendship," for, as they admitted to each other, they'd both be compelled to stalk and spy—not a healthy situation.

Privacy settings in place, all she can see is his profile picture— Alex, squatting in the forest beside a slime-mold-yellowed log. The picture, dating back to a month ago, inspired thirty-one likes. She sees only one comment: *Where are you, man?*

She pulls herself away from Facebook, attempts to read a PDF called "Building a Partnership Ethic for Ecopedagogy in the Segregated Rural South." But she squirms in her task chair, finds herself pulling on running shoes, rushing out the cabin door, slipping down the footpath that descends to the old logging trail. Finds herself hovering near the uncanny trailer, entering the cave mouth swathed with vines.

The hen clucks in a back bedroom, and Sylvia moves slowly down the narrow hall. But she doesn't find the bird on the mattress this time. It's in another room, at the end of the hall, where the flooring is starting to give and the air smells so moldy that she cups her hand over her nose and mouth. She opens the flimsy door, steps into a room gushing with sunlight. Two windows glowing, no curtains.

An ancient person sits in an olive Naugahyde chair, so shriveled and shrunken that Sylvia thinks of the Cumaean Sibyl, withered down to a mite, spending her eons brooding in a bottle. The person is bald, dressed in a gray polyester pantsuit, feet bare, yellow nailed, dangling. The elder holds the black hen, pets its closed wings, peers with clammy eyes, stiffens and sniffs.

"You," the elder rasps in a voice as light as a dandelion seed on the wind.

"I'm sorry," says Sylvia. "I didn't know you lived here. I mean, assuming that . . ."

"You ate the egg."

"Yes."

"And the Gricklemare came."

"Gricklemare?"

"Now you want to get rid of it."

"I'm not sure what a Gricklemare is."

"Lure it with blood and wild honey, lead it to a hollow tree, trap it in with moss. You can give it a task it'll never finish, befuddle it. Make it fetch water with a busted bucket. Make it pick up straws. But it will always be there."

"Where?"

The elder releases a wheeze of laughter and falls asleep. The black hen stands, squawks, flutters her lustrous wings.

*

119

Julia Elliott

Back at the cabin, Sylvia wonders if she should call Adult Protective Services, have them look in on the demented old person who lives in a trailer that would probably be categorized as condemned. But then they might confine the elder to some dismal reeking institution in town, the smell of woods and fresh air far away. Sylvia recalls an article she read about abuse in nursing homes, a bleak piece of investigative journalism that had turned her heart black and confirmed her worst suspicions about the world. Perhaps she should just check in from time to time, take the person food and water, a first aid kit, warm clothes when winter comes.

"Gricklemare," she whispers—the same word the children chant. Maybe the old person has heard the children's taunts. Maybe the children have listened to the ravings of the elder. Perhaps they've gossiped about the odd woman on the misty mountain. Perhaps they've conspired against the stranger—for that is what Sylvia is, perched in her rental cabin, ignorant of the people in the town below, spending her days typing what most people would read as nonsense.

"Gricklemare," she says.

Finding the strange word addictive, she utters it a third time.

"Gricklemare."

And then she sits in the stillness, crickets chirring, branches tapping the tin roof.

Sylvia pours herself a glass of red wine, for she is cold, even though it's summer. Her fever has returned, though she felt fine all day. On the couch, she burrows under a comforter, keeps the wine bottle near, reads a gothic novel, a paperback copy she found in the cabin, the cover and title page ripped off, the spine dusty with disintegrating glue. A countess dressed in dank brocade spirals up a stone staircase, traverses torchlit hallways, attempts to unlock the iron latches of heavy timber doors.

Sylvia's eyes ache from reading. When she looks up from her book, the world has gone blurry again. But she can still see something oozing through the keyhole, a dark wisp of curling fume. She smells sulfur, an odd aerosol scent. *The children*, she thinks, playing another prank, setting off a smoke bomb on her porch. Now someone is in the kitchen again, rattling through the silverware drawer.

But it's only Alex, leaning in the doorway, wearing nothing but a pair of dirty cutoff jeans, his skin pale from months of forest dwelling. His mouth twists into a smirk that she sometimes hates, sometimes adores, depending on the context.

"Where have you been?" she asks, forgetting about her plan, the

120

insouciant dismissal, the cup of herbal tea.

"In the woods," he says.

"Vague answer."

As he moves toward her, his feet leave black footprints on the rug.

He massages her shoulders, kisses her wrists, guides her into the dimness of the bedroom.

When she lies down, she feels a surge of dizziness, the presence of the fever like a gas shifting inside her.

"I'm sick," she says.

"That's OK." Alex slips on top of her, strangely light, almost hovering.

She doesn't realize she's naked until his bony finger slides inside her. She arches her back, moans, and reaches for the meat of him, cool in her grip like metal.

"You're cold down there," she says.

"Only because you have a fever," he says.

This seems reasonable, for her body burns. She is slippery with sweat.

He pushes himself inside her, cold at first but then warm.

"Be careful," she tries to say, but her words come out as moans.

She squints at the face above her—dark, blurred. Her limbs feel heavy, hard to move.

"Wait," she tries to say. "Stop."

She sleeps into the afternoon, the day garish and loud with birds. The light from the window burns her eyes, but she's too weak to get up and lower the blinds.

She hears the shower running. Alex. She has yet to see him in sunlight. He is shadow and detritus, elusive odors and scant words. Today she will tell him to go. Today she will get back to work. Today she will forget about him for good. She manages to sit up, manages to stagger to the window and close the blinds. She makes it to the bathroom, hears someone puttering in the steam. But when the vapor clears, Alex isn't there. Sylvia groans at the sight of wet towels piled on the floor, stubble in the sink, wads of toilet paper everywhere. Determined to make him clean up his mess, she moves toward the kitchen.

"Alex?"

Trash strewn across the linoleum. Cabinets ransacked. Food boxes clawed open. Rice and cereal scattered.

Racoons, she thinks—a mundane epiphany, a dull flare in her brain, followed by a gush of relief. That makes perfect sense. Racoons are notorious for their cunning, their destruction. They can traverse heating vents, squeeze through holes in the floor, climb into attics, and claw their way through rotting ceiling plaster. She will get Alex to drive to town and buy a trap. Together, they'll search for holes, passages through which a wily mammal might slither.

Alex has left the door open again, and his green Honda is not in the driveway. Though she hasn't seen it since he arrived two days ago, Sylvia can picture it there, its hatchback plastered with bumper stickers. *I* ♥ *Slime. I Brake for Mushrooms. Morel Majority.* And then a paranoid thought works its way into her mind, like *Ophiocordyceps unilateralis* into the brain of an ant. *Alex is camping in the Pisgah Forest with his research team, a girlfriend among them. He cannot resist sneaking away in the night and slipping into Sylvia's bed. That's why he always takes a shower—to wash away the smell of her.*

There was a similar overlap when they started dating in grad school, an entomologist he claimed was brilliant, a woman who wore a strange pheromonal perfume that drove Alex mad but that smelled like insect repellent to Sylvia. Their first month together, Sylvia would sometimes smell it on his clothes. Just before they'd moved in together, he confessed at a teahouse. Looking constipated with piety, he claimed he was coming clean, that he was over the entomologist, that he was ready to move in with Sylvia.

When he creeps in tonight, he'll be shocked to find Sylvia on the couch, the overhead light glaring. Wearing what he calls her "Joan-of-Arc martyr's face," she'll tell him to get his ass back to his fucking tent, to never come near her again. She'll get a restraining order if she must.

But now her joints ache; her head swims. Now she needs rest, a swig of cold medicine, and an Advil. A glass of wine to calm herself, a dim room, a warm blanket. Sleep.

She wakes to the clatter of racoons, tiny paws rifling through cabinets and drawers. She gets up, thinks of the countess from the novel as she moves through the dim cabin, her long robe fluttering behind her. The noise seems to be coming from the kitchen, but when she turns on the light, she sees only their mess: scattered macaroni, a flour bag clawed open, a jar of homemade jam broken open on the counter, dropping black gelatinous clots onto the linoleum. The preserves were here when she came, along with a few jars of unidentifiable vegetable matter, fleshy green nodules that look like polyps.

Sylvia cocks her head, listens, hears the hum of the fluorescent light, the chirping of crickets, something scurrying down the hallway toward the bathroom. The beasts have wrecked the bathroom too, opened toiletry bottles, smeared fruity shampoo and almond-scented lotion onto the floor.

"Little shits," she hisses.

Now something stirs in the linen closet at the end of the hall, a moldy closet she never uses, packed with mismatched sheets, threadbare towels, moth-eaten wool blankets. When she opens the door, a cloud of moths flutters out, hovering for a spell before floating off into the dimness. Sylvia smells musky animal piss. She scans the space with her phone light, searching for holes in the ceiling, walls, baseboards, and floor. To get a better look at the floor, she pulls out a cardboard box filled with cloth scraps, shines her light, sees nothing.

Perhaps the beast is hiding in the box of rags.

Sylvia picks through scraps, pulling out pieces of vintage cloth, remnants saved for quilt making, she guesses. Admiring the quaint patterns, she wishes she could sew. She dips her fingers in, sifts through cotton and silk, feels something cold and fleshy—*probably dead*—and jerks her hand out.

Slowly, she unburies it: a writhing, mewling thing that stares with lumpish mole-like eyes. Its flesh is pink and transparent, mottled with clusters of fine black veins. Its dark vital organs pulse—visible, invisible, visible, invisible. Sylvia counts: eight sets of rudimentary limbs, squirming.

Opening its whiskered mouth, baring rodent teeth, the creature hisses. Sylvia drops her phone, fumbles for it, catches the animal bellying its way down the dusty hallway toward the kitchen.

The creature keeps quiet after that, tucked away in some secret nook.

Sylvia sits in the dark living room, listening, waiting. She thinks of strange animals that don't fit neatly into the so-called phylogenetic tree. The duck-billed platypus—half mammal, half reptile. The sea anemone—half animal, half plant. The eusocial naked mole rat, with its grotesque and swollen queen. She drifts off, dreams she's back in her childhood bedroom, suffering some horrible disease. Her feet, black and swollen, drip green liquid into a tube that fills a

123

Julia Elliott

drainage bag. She calls for her mother to change the bag, but her mother, afraid, won't come into the room.

When Sylvia wakes up, her fever is worse—throbbing, psychedelic. Her joints and muscles ache. Her eyes ooze, blurring the lamplight. Her body seizes up, and she releases a violent sneeze, a haggish hack that reminds her of her grandmother. She remembers the strong moldy smell of the closet, fears she breathed in toxic mold spores, the evil black stuff that seeps from your sinuses into your brain, causing insomnia, anxiety, memory loss.

When she sees Alex perched on the sofa arm, she feels relieved. Perhaps he will make her soup, as he used to do in Pennsylvania— warm steaming bowls filled with foraged fungi. In the summer he would sauté fresh mushrooms in butter; in the winter he'd hydrate freeze-dried toadstools—withered, gnarled things kept in a dark cupboard, brought back to meaty life with moisture.

Alex flits from the sofa arm to the chair, from the chair to the window—agitated, as though trapped. Now he hunkers on the floor, his eyes huge and yellow, spinning like whirligigs. When he floats up into the air and bumps his head against the ceiling, she realizes that this person is Alex, yet he is not Alex. She wants to run to her car— to get away from both Alexes—but her limbs won't move. Watching her arm muscles twitch, she remembers the Latin etymology of the word *muscle: little mouse*. Mice, restless inside her skin. Racoons, scampering through the heating ducts. A strange tiny creature, half arthropod, half rodent, hiding in cupboards and boxes of rags. Alex (not Alex) roaring, laughing, braying as he moves naked toward her, a flurry of claws and fur.

She resurfaces in the early morning, her body sore, bruised, and scratched. She feels a weight on her chest, the cold flick of a tongue against her neck. Something is licking her.

"Alex?"

But it is not Alex.

She squints: sees the dim, fleshy eyes of the creature, staring into her own. Its maw is wet, dark. Its buckteeth drip. She flails, swats it off her, sends it flying. It thumps against the wall, leaving a damp stain. Squeaking, it slithers under the bed.

"Gricklemare," she whispers, feeling dense, like the last person in

124

Julia Elliott

English class to understand that Dr. Jekyll and Mr. Hyde are the same person.
Lure it with blood and wild honey.
She gets up, slips on her robe, hurries to the kitchen.

Ten years from now, honey will be extinct, but today Sylvia has a jar of buckwheat honey—dark, almost black, purchased at the Asheville farmers market from a couple who capture wild swarms—authentic stuff, food for larvae, nectar transmuted by enzymes in the crops of endangered bees, regurgitated, sealed in wax cells, stolen, harvested.

She pours honey into a bowl. With a paring knife, she cuts into the meat of her palm, just as she did over twenty years ago when she and her best friend, Emily, became blood sisters. She'd lain in bed that night, rubbing her bandaged hand, wondering if Emily's blood was flowing through her veins, and hers through Emily's.

Sylvia thinks of Emily as she squeezes the cut, dripping blood into the bowl. She mixes the concoction with a teaspoon. Spattering sticky dollops across the floor, she makes a trail from the kitchen to the bedroom. She goes back to the kitchen, finds a dented aluminum colander, sits crouched in the pantry, holding the sieve, leaving the door ajar.

At last the creature moves into the kitchen, squirming across the floor, slurping up sweet drops with its long, sticky tongue. It squeals and coos with pleasure. Glowing like a bioluminescent jellyfish, it rolls onto its back and wallows in ecstasy, smearing gory honey across the linoleum. Sylvia can see the creature's black heart convulsing in its chest. She can smell its body, a pissy floral smell, with a sharp note of turpentine. She has a perverse desire to pick it up, to stroke its belly, feed it honeyed blood with a dropper, just as she'd once fed milk to an orphaned squirrel. But she remembers Alex (not Alex) squatting on top of her, rocking on his hairy haunches, pinning her arms to the bed with his paws.

The Gricklemare, plump and lolling in an opiate daze, is easy to catch. She pokes it with a wooden spoon, rolls it into the colander, turns the colander upright, and slaps on a pot top. Though the creature squeaks mournfully, it cannot move, still stunned from gorging on honey and blood.

Sylvia secures the makeshift cage with duct tape, pulls on her sneakers, hurries down to the creek where green moss grows in

125

stunning velvety clumps. She fills a plastic bag until it bulges and then returns to the cabin.

The Gricklemare is still in its cage in the pantry where she left it. Now the creature squeaks. Now it gnaws weakly at the aluminum walls of its cage, a sound that makes her skin creep. She drops the cage into a cloth shopping bag, grabs her bag of moss, takes the footpath to the old logging trail.

Nearly every day she has passed it, a gnarled oak with a hollow at its base, the perfect cozy nest for a woodland animal, the perfect nook to trap the creature. Though she fears it will wriggle through the moss, slither through dead leaves back to her cabin, and haunt her all over again, she reminds herself that normal rules of logic don't apply to this situation—a kind of spell, she realizes, something she used to believe in when she was a child, a feeling that comes surging back, a reckless sense of wonder that she has forgotten.

She works quickly, peeling off duct tape. And then she stands before the tree, holding the colander, securing the top with her hand. Unleashing a high-pitched whistle, the creature thumps against the walls of its cage. Sylvia inhales mindfully, regards a clump of cumulus clouds—breathes, breathes—and then she dumps the Gricklemare into the hollow, where it flops onto its back. But now it's squirming again. Now it lurches half upright, sniffing, straining to see with its nubby eyes.

She snatches handfuls of moss and stuffs them into the hollow, burying the Gricklemare, cramming the space so thickly that the creature will surely suffocate or starve before gnawing its way out.

*

Sylvia does not go back to the tree until autumn, when the air changes, when the walnuts are golden, when the black gums are ablaze. She has settled back into her work habits. She has written another chapter of her dissertation. She has learned to split a log in half with one strong stroke of a gleaming sharp ax—an ax she bought at the hardware store in the town. She has more than enough wood to get through the winter. She will feed the ravenous potbellied stove, keep it burning so that she may write three pages a day. At this rate, her manuscript will be finished by the time the daylilies bloom. She will not remain to savor the miracle of spring but will vacate the cabin and never come back.

126

The local children have lost interest in her. Perversely, she misses their taunts, their patter, the way their wild glossy hair caught the light when they stirred in the forest.

As she takes the thin trail down to the oak tree where she trapped the Gricklemare, she scans the brush, the trees, the sky—looking for children. When she reaches the tree, she thinks she has made a mistake—for the moss is gone, the hollow closed up with a smooth bulb of fresh wood—sappy, dripping. She presses her hand against it, half expecting it to crumble. But the wood is solid, sticky, warm from a slant of fall sunlight.

When the wind stops rustling through the dry foliage, when her heart settles down, when her hands stop shaking, she can hear it twittering inside the tree: the Gricklemare.

"Still there," she whispers.

She imagines herself hacking through new wood with her ax, finding the sickly creature nested in leaves and crumbs of moss, scooping it up with her bare hands, taking it back to the cabin and releasing it. It would slink through its secret burrows again, marking them with its scent. Mist would ooze through her house again, infecting her sinuses, seeping into her brain tissue. Feverish, she'd feel like she was living inside a cloud. Alex (not Alex) would emerge from the fog, a whirl of fur and claws and hungry eyes, a prospect that both thrills and sickens her.

She has seen him at dusk, lurking at the wood's edge, looking confused. Lost and shivering, barefooted, dressed in shorts and a threadbare T-shirt, he's not prepared for the sudden temperature drop. Alex (not Alex) always stares at the cabin as though he doesn't quite remember it, gazing longingly at the fairy-tale smoke that puffs from the stone chimney. Feeling a strange mix of pity and repulsion, Sylvia always turns off the lights, watches by the window until he slips back into the cold forest.

And then she puts another log in the stove, pours herself a glass of wine, pulls her chair close to the fire. She opens an old paperback novel, starts to read, feels the release of atmospheric pressure when, at last, she gets lost in strange words and forgets, for a spell, who she is.

Thirteen Short Tales about Monsters
A. D. Jameson

MONSTER PARTY

ALL OF THE MONSTERS decided to throw a party. It was to be a proper event, a right old bash. Each monster offered to bring something different to make the gathering one to remember. Dracula offered to bring some wine, a pricey merlot he'd been saving. The Mummy promised to bring paper plates and napkins and silverware and cups. Medusa said she would DJ, spin some records. (She's a great DJ.) The Wolf Man said he would bring party mix, as well as gluten-free party mix. The Wolf Woman said she'd buy decorations and put them up. The Creature from the Black Lagoon said it would send out the invitations and keep track of RSVPs. Each monster promised to do its part, to chip in.

Which left only one question: where to have this party? Who would host? That's when somebody suggested your apartment. You *monster.*

KILLER FLEAS FROM BEYOND PLUTO

You might think killer fleas cannot exist in outer space. Well, you would be wrong about that. And you might think that there's no way those fleas could ever come to earth. Well, you'd be wrong about that too. And you might think that those fleas might turn out to be friendly and polite. Well, you'd be incorrect in that assessment. And you might think that there's no way those fleas could ever enjoy the taste of human blood. Well, you'd be wrong there, once again. And you might think that there's no way those fleas could figure out where you live. Well, there you would be right. The earth is a pretty big place, and your house is difficult to find.

A. D. Jameson

KILLER ROBOT

Someone made a robot and taught it to kill. The only word it knew how to say was "MURDER!" It went around saying that constantly, in an annoying high-pitched voice that could cut through steel. "Well, this is absolute nonsense," everyone agreed. They all had to drop what they were doing and deal with this murderous killer robot, which of course required canceling weekend plans: air and water shows, athletic competitions, outdoor weddings. Or simply walking and biking along the lakefront trail.

To make matters worse, everyone missed out on some truly gorgeous weather. Southerly winds became southeast by Saturday afternoon, reducing highs on area beaches to the mid-eighties. Mixed sun shined through the haze, building high banks of cottony cumulus clouds. The fog departed overnight, leaving Sunday hot but breezy, with plenty of sunshine as thunderstorms settled outside the area. Southeast winds shifted northwest ten to twenty miles per hour in the afternoon, and by evening the city felt pleasantly warm, with comfortable humidity levels. And by that time, people had finished destroying the killer robot, but they were much too exhausted to take in the wonderful weather. They all went home and went to sleep and when they woke up Monday morning, it was raining.

IN A GRAVEYARD

I was in a graveyard. I couldn't see a damned thing. It was totally dark. It was pitch-black. It was really, really black. There was no light, or very little light—not enough light to see, at any rate. It was definitely creepy. It was preposterously scary. I shut my eyes. I put my hands up in front of my eyes. And then I panicked, I'm embarrassed to say. I wigged out. I started screaming, vomiting. My hair stood up on end, went comically high.

Then something grabbed my shoulder, spun me around. It pulled my hands away from my eyes. Whatever it was, it glowed preternaturally, with an ethereal, unearthly glow. I could see it, dimly. It was a skeleton, grinning demonically. It stank of a stygian pit, and it rattled and it clattered. But I recognized it at once; it was a skeleton that I knew. It was the skeleton of my late best friend, Goodwin Eutropius, who had recently passed away peacefully in his sleep at 1767 Holden Street, Santee, CA 92071.

GNOMES

What do you know about gnomes? Do you know anything about gnomes? Are they big? Are they little? Medium sized? Do they have their own language? Are they greedy? Do they crave gold and gems above all other things? Can they cast magic spells? Can they cast enchantments, and bewitch people? Are they friendly? Nasty? Mean tempered? Do they bite? Do they aid lost travelers in the woods? Or do they turn them around, take delight in befuddling them? Are they short-lived? Long-lived? Immortal? Ancient? Hidden? Secretive? Reclusive? What do they eat? Do they like singing songs? Seriously, anything you can tell me, I'd love to know. I'm writing a story about gnomes, but fear I don't know the first thing about them.

DISGUSTING BLOB

What would you do if you met a disgusting blob? I mean, what would you do? Would you scream and try to run? But say you could not. And say that the blob, the disgusting blob, took a shine to you? What would you do then? And what would you do if that hideous blob asked you out on a date? And what would you do if that hideous blob took you out on that date, and at the end of that date it asked for your hand in marriage? Would you say no? Would you pull your hand away and faint and shake your head? But what would you do if you were poor, so poor you couldn't decline that proposal? What would you do then? And what would you do if that monstrous blob, that repulsive blob, became your spouse? How would you react? You wouldn't be free to kiss other people or go outside or speak your mind. Instead, you'd be married to a blob. And you'd be married to that blob for the rest of your life, till death did you part. Have you thought about that? And by the way, disgusting blobs tend to live forever, so you'd be married to that blob till the day that you died. And maybe longer. How'd you like that? I bet you hadn't thought about that.

MY TIME AMONG THE MUMMIES

I knew a mummy once. It wasn't the highest point in my life. It was probably the lowest point in my life, or the second lowest. Through a series of misunderstandings and poor decisions and bad luck I alienated all my friends until my only friend was a mummy. It happened like this. I lost my job and lost my apartment and had to go live in a bad part of town, where monsters lived, and I needed a roommate, and found an ad for an apartment, "roommate wanted." And the person who wanted that roommate was a mummy. I was down on my luck and hard up, so I moved in; the place was cheap and all I could afford. I lived there for one year and seven months and it wasn't easy to make ends meet. The mummy was nice but it was still a freaking mummy. It creeped me out. Whenever I fell asleep I thought that would be the end of me—that that night would be my last—especially when the mummy had friends over, other mummies, with whom it played bridge.

In time I managed to save some money and find a new job and another, human apartment, so I moved out. I promised the mummy I'd keep in touch, that we'd still hang out, maybe see some movies or just get coffee, but it's been seventeen years since then, and we haven't spoken in that time. I feel bad about this. The mummy was always nice to me; it let me borrow its records and books, and some of its shirts. I was the one who acted weird and didn't trust it, and I was the one who never responded to emails or texts. I still feel terrible about this. Sometimes I'll see a funny sign or hear a good tune and think I should tell the mummy about it, but I never do, because it feels awkward to contact the mummy now due to how much time has passed. But I don't know why this should be the case; mummies are ancient and undead, and live forever, and think on a different time scale than human beings do. In my experience, mummies are extraordinarily patient, biding their time, nurturing long-term schemes that take millennia to come to diabolical fruition. They probably like getting random phone calls out of the blue.

A. D. Jameson

THE CRITTER THAT LOVED TO BITE

Once upon a time there was a critter that loved to bite. It loved biting! This critter bit anything you put in front of it, chomp, chomp, chomp. It was never happier than when biting. All it wanted to do was bite. It chewed on anything that moved, and it bit things that didn't move. It bit anything it saw. It bit cows and trees. It bit passing moms. It bit straw, electrons, cinemagoers, libertarians, abstract expressionist paintings. Its bites really hurt. People winced. They winced and they shrieked. They said, "OW!" The critter made people run when it neared. People were running all over the town. But this isn't the problem, not the real problem. I wanted to talk about something else. I get free egg rolls mailed to me daily. I don't know who sends them and to be honest I don't much care. They arrive every day, in a large cardboard box. It's a lot of egg rolls, a hell of a lot. What should I do with them? What do you think I should do? Sometimes I eat them but sometimes I don't. They're not the best egg rolls but they're still decent.

THE BAT MAN

This thing was half man and half bat, the best of both worlds, those two worlds being the bat world and the man world. Or both animals, as it were. He liked the things that bats prefer, as well as the things that all men favor: cakes and fruits and cars and clothes and insects and music and coloring books. He liked just about everything, in fact, pretty much anything you put in front of his face, his bat-man face. It was hard to find anything that he didn't take some pleasure in, at least to some extent.

THE SCARY HAND

There once was a scary hand, perhaps the scariest hand of all time. It was scarier than any other hand, more frightening than any other hand that I can recall. It was the scariest hand in existence, a putrid, terrifying hand. What made it so scary, you want to know. Well, for starters, this scary hand was missing a finger. And it had an extra finger. So it still had five fingers, but it was misshapen, and deformed. And it had hangnails and dirty fingernails and buckteeth—the hand had teeth. And eyes, and a mustache. And it never brushed its teeth, and it never trimmed its mustache. It had been chopped off a criminal, people said, a criminal who had been hanged. It just appeared one day in a box inside your bedroom. And no one else believed it existed, because it hid. Oh, how it tormented you with its tricks! How it bedeviled you with its tricks! It wrote notes and slipped them into your lunch, scary notes, with scary misspellings. And it tapped out disquieting rhythms on your desk while you were sleeping, while you were napping, which to be fair you do too often, so in that way the hand was trying to help. But you didn't look at it that way; you were annoyed. And you said, "Scary hand, please go away!" But the hand said, "Nay! I want to stay with you and play!" And it lunged for your wrist, and tried playing patty-cakes with you, creepy patty-cakes, and it tried to thumb wrestle with you, its skin dry and rough, so callused it hurt your smooth, clear skin. The hand had liver spots all up and down it, and bristly hairs, and of course that mouth with its giant buckteeth, and it bit you if you didn't play patty-cakes with it, and I get shivers thinking about it, shivers and gooseflesh. The hand was so yucky. I feel my gorge rising at the thought. And it would sit on your pillow at night and whisper your name in a raspy voice, a dirty voice, a filthy voice, and when you woke up and shooed it away, it scuttled underneath your pillow until you fell asleep again, then slinked back out, creeping and crawling over your pillow to whisper your name again, and this happened night after night, until you nearly died of fright. Scared to death by the dirty hand with the long dirty nails and the flaking skin, the spooky hand, the tremendously horrific hand, the scary, scary hand.

ALIEN ZOMBIE

He came from the planet that zombies come from, alighting in a cemetery. He emerged from his coffin-like spacecraft, his arms outstretched, moaning and groaning. He shuffled along. This was on Halloween, and the moon was full, the air crisp. He lumbered forward, grunting, hunting, grabbing feebly at victims' heads. He seemed to want brains, though no one could understand his intentions. He

133

A. D. Jameson

stank of dirt and decomposition. He didn't seem happy, that much was certain. The feeling was mutual. Nobody liked him. Nobody wanted him to stay. "Get away!" they shouted. "Get out of here! Go back to your planet!" They threw lollipops and eggs at him, and rolls of toilet paper, wrapped up around bricks. Someone slashed him with a knife, and someone else shot him with a shotgun. Someone set fire to him with a torch, and the alien zombie went up in flames, and that was it. That was the end. Nothing else happened after that.

COOL STORY, BRO

Aw, man, you should've been there! It was like, crazy, bro! These two epic monsters, they like, attacked the city, yo! It was like, nonstop crazy! I saw it all from my friend's apartment. I was like, "Dude!" These giant monsters, they were like attacking everybody, smashing buildings left and right, beating everything up. Buildings were toppling over like dominoes! And people were toast, man, left and right, like totally flattened! I saw some major wipeouts, you know? And then get this—the army, like, came in and was firing all these guns at the monsters, just blasting away at them, all, "Poom! Poom! Poom!" But these two monsters, they were like, "Bam!" Just smashing everything with their tails, tanks and planes, and people and buildings, everything flattened left and right, like, "Ka-blam!" And the army was running all around, you know, like retreating, like, falling back? Because their weapons were totally bogus, man, their guns didn't do a thing! But then—get this—the monsters, they turned on one another and started fighting! The first one was waling on the second, going like, "Rawr!" And the second monster kept on shrieking, "Ahh! Ahh! Ahh!" And they were bashing one another with their claws and with their tails, like just nonstop. And people were running every which way, falling over one another, screaming and trampling everybody. It was like nuts, you know? Like total, absolute mayhem. I couldn't believe what I was seeing! I tried to call you, man! Three times! But the circuits were busy. And I kept thinking, dude, you should be here! You gotta see this! But you were in Akron with your girlfriend. How was your trip?

THE HORSE-HEADED ABERRATION

There once was a man with a horse's head, who went around terrorizing people. People called him "The Horse-Headed Aberration." Eventually some brave soul stood up to him and beheaded him with a sword. But the man didn't die, and he still frightened people, but in a slightly different fashion. People called him "The Headless Horse-Headed Aberration," until someone pointed out they could shorten that to just "The Aberration."

New Sisters
Selena Anderson

QUISA HAD FALLEN INTO the habit of disappointing herself, and then disappointing herself a little more, with the words she let slip from her mouth. She kept talking to people in this hungry, intimate way, as if they too had spent the time of their lives in their heads and read the warning labels too closely and worried irrationally about their lymph nodes. Accidental confessions are what these amounted to. A case of social insecurity, as it were. But at the same time, even when pressed, Quisa found that she rarely said what she truly meant. She began to seriously wonder if her true love was to embarrass herself.

So, Quisa tried her hand at silence. Hoping to pass herself off as a cool woman, she spruced up her wardrobe with ivory blazers and high-waisted pants. Even strangers noticed the change. Other women, more poised and more successful, started looking Quisa up and down. Her first inclination was to remedy these looks with thoughts of extreme dieting and her own mother. She often concluded that the trajectory of her life would've been much improved had she gotten into at least one fight back in school, if she had surprised herself and won.

Quisa's thoughts never walked in a single direction, and she took this personally too. She breathed the dirty, humid air of her city. When she opened her eyes, life seemed tedious and long, unreasonably precious. Nothing was wrong with her. Her hair was glossy and strong. Her bills were mostly paid. She taught herself to walk with such a lightness that from the right distance, you wouldn't guess that Quisa was Quisa. But at some point, for some reason, she had stopped looking people in the eye. Then she got to the point where she could no longer speak without resenting the tongue in her mouth. So, Quisa wound up making a second version of herself by faking the real her all the time.

Unfortunately, Second Quisa wasn't much better. She sat on the middle cushion of the sofa, quiet and icy as a sapphire. Covered in folds, she seemed to be her wearing those imitation silk pajamas for the first time.

When Second Quisa smiled, it looked like an injury. Quisa was horrified, then embarrassed. She had seen something she hadn't meant to see, but there it was. It was the act of Second Quisa's intrusion, her inability to be anything else, her vital nobodiness that caused Quisa's embarrassment. To her mind, Second Quisa was like what happens if you get stuck in your senior portrait.

Second Quisa never said a word, easily her best move. But despite her silence and icy demeanor she seemed fond of Quisa. She liked to torment Quisa by following her around the apartment, holding her own tongue between two fingers. She liked to watch Quisa pick out her clothes in the morning. She liked to eavesdrop when Quisa talked on the phone. Quisa pretended not to notice, but she did. A certain yearning hooked the two of them together, almost by the ribs. It happened gradually over a period of many gestures and sly looks so that eventually Second Quisa began feeling a warm sense of panic when she couldn't possess Quisa while Quisa was doing the simplest things, like clipping her toenails or watering the plants. Second Quisa wanted a front-row seat to what was happening to Quisa. There was no single thing of hers that she wanted to take specifically. Second Quisa wanted to take it all.

It was almost as if they were desperate for conclusions, the way the two of them looked out the window. Refineries burned poisons across the sky, dragging foreign colors down the legs of clouds, so that late into the night everyone below could fight, dance, and dream in foggy peace.

Second Quisa was also vulnerable to appraising looks, but she was a vindictive woman. So, she drowned the plants and cut up the sheets. With a fork, she drew designs into nonstick pans. After ordering specialty meats with Quisa's credit card and eavesdropping on Quisa's phone calls (Quisa was only begging the next man to understand her), Second Quisa resolved to make a Third Quisa to get revenge for having been made in the first place.

First Quisa successfully persuaded this man to buy her some pancakes. And she almost made him fall in love by presenting herself as a sad, beautiful woman alone in this city, unwittingly approaching the apex of her life, her beauty enhanced by her clandestine sadness and loneliness. He had always dreamed of encountering someone in perfect solitude so he could disrupt it. With First Quisa, he was the one to beg. He begged to know what was the matter. Then, as if directed by God, First Quisa said exactly what she'd meant to say, "I have new sisters, and I don't even like them." The man came around the booth and sat next to her, squeezing her shoulder in his big hand.

Selena Anderson

He assured her that this type of thing was happening all the time because of the growing popularity of DNA tests. "One day," said the man, in honey-dripping, self-satisfied tones, "nearly all of us will find out that we have a secret family member somewhere just waiting to be found." First Quisa angled back to look at him. She worried that this was his dum-dum, cryptic way of letting her know that he had a secret baby, perhaps a few.

Third Quisa was something else. Like a star or a river, her existence alone was the miracle. She had big, black eyes with a lizardy shine. A loaf of woolen hair. Narrow shoulders and a high behind. During the peaceful hour of the evening news, Third Quisa would strut into the room gleaming with violence. She quarreled with First Quisa on Second Quisa's behalf, and Second Quisa looked on with a false, painful smile. A cool dignity sparkled in her eyes.

Third Quisa was mouthy and bossy, loud, horrible, and abominable. You couldn't beat her unless you were willing to take off your earrings. Vaseline your jaw. She took over the apartment like an odor. She wore sexy panties and a floral bra that was way too small for her tiny breasts. She sat at the computer for hours and then painted her face with cosmetics that made her look like a sweet dragon. But deep down, under the bad attitude and lingerie, Third Quisa was desperate for romantic attention. Her desperation gave her a scent, made her eyeballs shake in her head. First Quisa opened a window, but the city below was howling at other things.

Second Quisa eyed Third Quisa, saying in her silent way, "Nobody's coming to fuck you." But in addition to being a vindictive woman, Second Quisa was also two-faced. In a leather-bound diary that used to belong to First Quisa, she scribbled down all the atrocious things she meant to say. Then she gave the diary to Third Quisa to perform out loud.

Each of the Quisas sat together on the sofa, turning secretive and dreamy as they grieved their dead girlhood. But First Quisa did what she knew her sisters could never do. She let her little former self take a peek from the great beyond while the other two, having just been born themselves, were left to look back on the most recent wrong turn. First Quisa let her young self regard her with amazement and some disappointment at what they'd become. The simple fact that this little person liked her anyway made her heart swell to bursting. Second and Third Quisa did not ask what First Quisa was laughing at. Somehow they knew. The pain of their monstrous existence was melted into their angry little smile.

Third Quisa started a fight simply because she had no other means of getting First Quisa to make herself more present. Third Quisa fought like she'd been robbed of something. She yelled in the wrong pitch, afraid she might cry. She wanted revenge for being there, for being accountable. Someone owed her a confession and she was beyond bitter about it. But when she locked eyes with Second Quisa, who in the first place had conjured her up from the sole ingredient of desperation, and Second Quisa was all shivering pieces, stuttering from the inside, Third Quisa knew there were no explanations in this life. She stood up, unhooked a painting from the wall, and carried the painting out to the balcony, heaving it into the street.

Tonight First Quisa had had enough of that. She and Third Quisa rolled across the floor, pulling and scratching. They got spaghetti in their hair and socks. They smashed a lamp and flipped over a coffee table before crawling away from each other, embarrassed. Then First Quisa stood up and said, "That's enough. I know who I am." Without even packing her things, she left the apartment for good.

After a while, Second Quisa stopped waiting for First Quisa to return. She lost interest in keeping up with her diary and prank calling First Quisa's ex-boyfriend. To avoid her thoughts, Second Quisa prepared ambitious dinners, serving everything on First Quisa's inherited china. She watched television with Third Quisa. She rolled Orange Crush and they smoked and ate until they were nauseated. In the emptiness they both looked out the window but the night was so pure, what more could be said? Nothing happened, so Third Quisa picked a fight.

As time passed, Second Quisa noticed how unpleasant it was to hang out alone with Third Quisa. With First Quisa gone, Third Quisa had begun to quarrel with her without warning, without end. Second Quisa carved her own face into the chest of a cookie sheet as she listened to Third Quisa's one-sided arguments. Second Quisa flipped through her diary with a look of hurt amusement. Then she tossed the diary out the window. Day in and day out she held her tongue, but this time she wasn't teasing. She killed herself, and Third Quisa dropped her glass. It felt like plumes of smoke were ballooning out of her ears, but mostly Third Quisa was relieved. Her whole body lit up with a green, apologetic joy.

At the service, Third Quisa swayed to the hymns. For some reason, perhaps only because she had dressed up in clothes that didn't even belong to her, she vaguely expected First Quisa to walk in, but First Quisa never showed up.

Late at night Third Quisa was still trying to convert her snubbed feelings into freedom, even triumph. She put on her best lingerie and danced across the den, stiff and rigid as the letter H. But there was a meaning behind all that soulless jerking and shaking. She was trying with muscles and tendons to work something out of her body. Waving her hands had no effect. Bouncing and looking back couldn't unhook it. As the horns and strings curlicued away, Third Quisa scratched between her shoulder blades. In the silence of the apartment, she had reached an impasse with herself. She haunted herself with a memory of when First Quisa had told her, "That's enough. I know who I am."

"Well, so do I," said Third Quisa, a bit too defensively, and even though nobody was listening, she pretended to be satisfied with herself. Alone, she believed that she could act profanely kind with anyone. She'd never have cause to raise her voice, not unless the smoke detector came on. She felt awash with a delicious, guilty sort of relief, and she'd recline across all three cushions of the sofa to sink into that relief and really appreciate the experience.

But sometimes she would jerk up without a thought, her organs clawing up her throat. She would look over her shoulder because after all it wasn't her apartment, and First Quisa knew where to find her.

Monstersister
Joyce Carol Oates

BEGAN AS IT. Not even a thing, just a sensation.

At the back of my head near the crown of my head some kind of small, fleshy lump to which my fingernails were drawn.

First, a mild itch. Then, not so mild.

Had to be an insect bite. Swollen patch on my scalp the size of a quarter.

In the night I could feel *it* quivering. Hot-pulsing like something alive.

Not just itching but burning, stinging. My nails scratched, scratched, scratched until they came away edged with blood.

Thinking—*Maybe* it *will go away by itself.*

Pleading—*Dear God make* it *go away!*

Thirteen years old and had not (yet) abandoned the hope that I was someone special whom God, if there was a God, would protect.

Hours wakeful and in misery. Never had I lain awake so many hours in any night. Would not have thought there were so many hours in any night. In the morning blood smears on my pillow and a rank smell.

Craned my neck trying to see in the mirror what *it* was. But could not see for my hair grew over *it*.

Went whimpering to Momma for help.

"What on earth have you *done*! Looks like a nasty snarl."

Frowning in concentration, her hot breath on the nape of my neck, Momma searched for *it* with her fingers. Scolding as if *it* was just another snarl. Something sticky and clotted in my hair like chewing gum.

(As if in my entire life I'd gotten chewing gum in my hair!)

Sitting on the rim of the bathtub scarcely daring to breathe. Head bowed shivering and praying that *it* could simply be cut away by Momma's deft fingers with nail scissors and *it* would be revealed as merely a tick or flea or bedbug embedded in my scalp, which would

141

be *gross, disgusting* but finite, and could be dealt with with a shudder of repugnance as Momma flicked *it* into the toilet bowl to be flushed away followed with gratitude and relief that *it* was gone. And there would be—what a blizzard of hope in my brain in those days!—a gentle impress of Momma's lips against the wound and a chaste white Band-Aid in case the wound oozed a thin film of blood and afterward the mercy of forgetting—*All gone, sweetie. Good as new!*

Except this did not happen. Nothing remotely like this happened.

Momma carefully snipped away hairs with the scissors and then with a safety razor shaved a little space around the lump. Muttering to herself, perplexed.

"Not sure what this is. A goiter?"

Goiter! No idea what a *goiter* was except something shameful.

Seated trembling on the edge of the bathtub. Like a small child, eyes shut tight. So even if I could have seen *it*, I would not have seen *it*.

At the time no way of knowing that never again would Momma call me *sweetie*.

First sight, *it* resembled a (small, egg-sized) veiny sponge attached to my scalp.

Not one of those synthetic sponges from the grocery store that are fake bright colored but an actual sponge from the ocean. A sea creature lacking a brain and a spine that has no face or limbs and is the color of a paper bag comprised of myriad tiny air bubbles that soak up water.

Of course, such a sponge is a living creature, not like the fake sponges from the grocery store. But when you see it, and touch it, is no longer a living thing but the remains of a living thing.

"... oh my God! I hope it isn't your brain leaking out ..."

Didn't hear this. Did not hear this.

"... maybe a goiter growing out of your brain ..."

None of these terrible words uttered by my alarmed mother as if she were thinking aloud did I hear. No!

Momma held a hand mirror above my head so that I could see *it* inside the shaved spot in my scalp. What a shock! But I wanted to laugh too.

Rejected *it* as some kind of trick played on me, nothing that was real, or would last more than a day or two, while at the same time I had to accept (I guess) that *it* was not an infected insect bite, still less a boil or giant pimple but something stranger than any of these, and nastier.

Most important, Momma said in a lowered voice: We will keep *it* a secret.

No reason Momma argued for anyone outside the family to know about *it*. At least not yet.

By *family* Momma meant herself and Dad; my seven-year-old sister, Evie, and my ten-year-old brother, Davy; and Granma, who lived with us. Not relatives, neighbors. Not friends or, worse yet, old friends not seen in years, high-school classmates of Momma's who'd never left the area but continued to live within a few miles of one another, aging year after year and thrilled still in the spreading of the most absurd gossip.

This Momma dreaded. Being *talked about*.

Of course, Momma had to tell Dad about *it*. But the others—Evie, Davy, Granma—didn't need to know just yet.

Dad stared at *it*. Dad's jaws moved as if he was having to chew, to swallow, something that tasted bad.

"Well, hell."

Never saw anything like this before in his life, had to admit.

Weird boils, bunions, "growths"—maybe . . . But a goiter is some kind of swollen neck gland, Dad said. Nothing like this ugly thing growing out of his daughter's head.

Touching *it* with his fingers, as if he thought *it* might burn his fingers.

A shivery sensation passed through me like an electric shock though I did not exactly feel Dad's fingers touching me.

"Jesus! The thing is goddamned *warm*."

Dad thought that *it* should be cut away with scissors or a knife but Momma thought it might hurt me too much, for I'd writhed in pain when she'd been snipping near *it* with the nail scissors. Obviously, that part of my scalp was hypersensitive, and would probably bleed badly as scalp wounds do.

Dad said, Nonsense, the only sensible thing to do was remove *it* before *it* got any larger.

(Dad was right: *it* was growing. Each morning when I woke, I felt *it*—each morning *it* had grown in the night.)

You might wonder why my parents didn't take me to a doctor to have the veiny sponge growth examined and removed; at least, to determine if *it* was a malignant growth. But that was not Dad's way.

Dad was distrustful of strangers. He did not like people *snooping*. Except in the case of emergencies, and not always even in the case of emergencies, Dad shied away from hospitals, clinics, doctors, police.

Joyce Carol Oates

Persons of authority who might be expected to *poke their noses in our business.*

"I said no. No damned doctor! We will take care of this ourselves."

Flush faced and grim, Dad seated me at the kitchen table beneath the bright overhead light, laid out newspaper pages on the linoleum floor at our feet. With a flashlight he proceeded to examine *it* closely. I could feel—that is, I imagined that I could feel—Dad's warm, quickened breath against the exposed growth.

"Don't move. Stay *still.*"

Tentatively, Dad pressed the razor-sharp blade of a fishing knife against the cartilaginous membrane connecting *it* to my scalp. Gradually he increased pressure against the membrane, began to make sawing motions, to test the toughness of the sinewy membrane, whether he could severe it quickly, with a minimum of pain for me; but the sensation was unbearable, beyond pain, causing me to scream and thrash and wrench myself away from him like a panicked animal.

"For God's sake!—*stop that.* I am only trying to help you."

In disgust Dad pushed me from him. In his eyes I saw loathing.

Momma took pity on me, and allowed me to run away to hide in my room, terrified and ashamed. Later I would overhear her calling my school to explain that I might be absent for several days—"Our daughter has a medical condition that is expected to require 'minor surgery.'"

Still, Dad was reluctant to take me to a doctor. Who knows what a damned doctor might charge!

Also, as Dad sincerely believed, there might turn out to be some perfectly natural explanation for the growth sprouting from my scalp. It might happen that *it* would cease growing, and wither away and die, of its own accord, falling off the way a snake's skin or a vestigial tail might fall off. (Were there such things as "vestigial tails"? In our household it began to be believed that there were.)

Whatever *it* was, *it* was not a goiter. Online research revealed that goiters are nothing but swellings of glands in the neck, and are not "oozings" of brain matter through a crack in a skull.

Nor is a goiter an autonomous growth, as (it seemed to me) the growth on my head was an autonomous growth. For I could feel *it* quivering, especially at night. A certain heat radiated from *it*, hotter than my skin; at times, I imagined that I could feel *it* breathing. . . .

And one day Momma said, peering at me from behind, "Oh God! D'you hear that?—It's *breathing.*"

144

Dad snorted in derision. "Ridiculous! *It is not.*"

But Dad did not wish to draw too near, to incline his head to *it.* And Dad's own breathing was audible, a kind of indignant panting through his mouth; he'd have had difficulty hearing anything else breathing in his presence.

Days had passed. Nights had passed. *It* was not withering away but growing larger, more like a thickening vine now than an egg.

Granma had soon learned about *it.* Davy and Evie suspected something seeing me darting furtively from my room to the bathroom, avoiding them; when I did appear downstairs, for meals, I wore a scarf around my head that stood out oddly, exactly as if some sort of growth had sprouted on my head.

"Your sister has a bad chest cold," Momma explained. "I don't want it to turn into pneumonia. She has to keep *warm.*"

In time, Davy and Evie seemed to know about *it* too. No way to keep a secret in our small household.

Yet they had few questions to ask. They were grim, frightened by the sight of me, suspecting that whatever terrible thing had happened to me might happen to them too, if they misbehaved.

Momma did not want to think that *it* might be something more than just an extraneous growth that would eventually wither and fall off—for instance, a part of my brain that had oozed through a crack in my skull—nor did I wish to think this, though it was (to me) an unavoidable thought. But one day Granma stuck her finger into *it* and recoiled in alarm, saying that *it* felt warm, and pulsing—"Like some kind of a pudding! If a pudding could be *alive.*"

"Ridiculous! A pudding could not be *alive.*" Dad laughed, sneering. But his eyes shone with fear and disgust.

Still, Dad was reluctant to take me to a doctor. For we did not have what is called a "primary-care physician"—we did not have what is called "medical insurance."

Days passed. *It* grew larger. Of the size and shape of a banana tugging at my scalp, exuding heat. The skin of my forehead was tugged back tight. My eyebrows were raised in an expression of perpetual surprise, bafflement. There came to be a sensation like a vise tightening around my head.

At last Momma convinced Dad that I must be taken to a doctor for *it* was obviously more serious than he'd thought.

Reluctantly, Dad relented. Out of the physicians' yellow pages in the phone directory Dad selected Dr. F_____, who must have had few patients since he could see me within the hour.

145

Dr. F_____ expressed disbelief, then astonishment, at the "organic entity" growing out of the top of my head. His examination determined that *it* was not a goiter, or any sort of natural growth (bunion, callus, tumor) of a kind he'd ever seen in his life. There did indeed seem to be a "hairline crack" in my skull through which *it* was pushing what Dr. F_____ believed had to be brain matter, or what are called the meninges, three membranes that envelop the brain, which might have become infected, and might have to be surgically removed, but he would not know with certainty until X-rays were taken.

X-rays! How much was all this going to cost? Dad scowled.

Of course, Dad insisted upon a "second opinion." It was Dad's belief that you were very foolish if you didn't get a second opinion— a "second estimate"—for any product or service. If you were smart you pitted one estimate against the other, to drive the price down.

Dr. M_____ was an older, white-bearded gentleman also out of the physicians' yellow pages who agreed to see me immediately, and like Dr. F_____ expressed disbelief and astonishment at *it*. ("Is this *alive*? My God.") Dr. M_____'s examination was more thorough than Dr. F_____'s as it involved not just the exterior of my head but my ears, mouth, and eyes, into which he stared searchingly as if peering into my very soul.

Dr. M_____'s tentative diagnosis was that *it* was (probably) not a part of my brain oozing through a hairline crack in my skull but rather totally separate and autonomous brain matter belonging to a totally separate and autonomous life-form of a "parasitical" nature that, thirteen years before in the womb, by which he meant my mother's womb, had been meant to be an identical twin of mine, but through a misfiring of crucial cells had failed to develop into an independent embryo that should have been "born" by natural childbirth but had instead been "assimilated" into my body and was now—for no reason Dr. M_____ could discern other than the (evident) imminence of puberty—forcing its way out of my skull by "creating its own 'birth canal.'"

Twin! Puberty! Birth canal! None of these repellent words made any impression upon me for I had become benumbed by so much attention focused upon me (and not upon *it*). The doctor's pen-sized flashlight shining deep into my eyes had rendered me near blind and Dr. M_____'s words had been directed to my father and not to my ears.

(Did *it* hear, and did *it* understand? The sensation in my scalp was tingling, alert, and alive. I could almost feel *it* quivering with life, having been acknowledged as "separate and autonomous" so clearly by a medical doctor.)

It should be surgically removed, Dr. M_____ said. But not before X-rays were taken.

In silent chagrin Dad listened. His mouth worked in a grimace. He may have had questions to ask Dr. M_____ but he was too distracted, distraught. Urged me out of the office without making another appointment, and on the stairway, before we left the building, whispered agitatedly to me, "Fix the damned scarf! Hide *it*."

Sulky faced, I did just that.

*

Identical twin. Once these words were uttered I could not stop hearing them.

Identical twin. Echoing, reechoing.

Indeed, *it* was becoming bigger, heavier at the top, back of my head. You could hear *it* breathing, and you could feel *it* thrumming with life.

Soon *it* was bouncing behind me to the nape of my neck. The top of my spine. A tickling sensation that made me shiver. Throwing me off-balance when I tried to walk the way, with her "bad hip," Granma was thrown off-balance when she walked.

It began to plead with me not in words but in quivering sensations—
Help me! I want to live.

Want to live like you.

These communications were contemptible to me; I pretended not to hear.

. . . like you like you. You.

I laughed, this was so absurd. Like *me*?

Could *it* breathe on *its* own? Could *it* continue to grow, taking nourishment from me, on *its* own?

Scornfully I asked how *it* could live without *me*?

You can't live without me.

I can destroy you at any time.

(But could *it* understand me? Had *it* functioning ears? An actual brain, that might process language?)

As if in shock at my scorn *it* lapsed into silence.

Except for *its* quickened rapid breathing, silence.

. . . at any time. If I choose.

147

*

(But why, you are thinking, did I *not choose?*)
(And now, it is too late.)

The thing, the twin-brain, *it*—we did not yet call it *she*—continued
to grow heavier with the passage of weeks, now halfway down my
back. And now, to the small of my back. *It* was stretched like a
coarse-textured stocking though wider at the top than below. I wondered if this was because the brain was not encased in a skull but just
loose—dribbling like a flaccid, skinless snake down my back.

Staring at *it* in a hand mirror reflecting my mirror reflection behind me a dozen times a day. Nothing else so intrigued me in all of
the world! Alternately repelled and fascinated by the thing's sponge
texture, a pale-brown color, consisting of myriad tiny air holes that
seemed to inhale and exhale air in a concerted way.

The thing had a piteous look, overall. You could (almost) make out
a face near the nape of my neck.

Well—not an actual *face*. Something like the "face" of a manta
ray. In the spongy thing, indentations of where a face would be: shallow sockets for "eyes," small black holes for nostrils, the suggestion
of a mouth, a shallow slit, a mollusk's mouth. . . .

(No teeth inside the mouth. At least, no visible teeth. Yet.)

Somewhere I'd read eyeballs were once part of the brain, over the
course of millennia drawn out by light. Must've been millions of
years!

So, brain matter in *it* was pushing out. The more light, the more
pushing out.

How I'd wanted to *gouge* those manta-ray eyes, before it was too
late! Before they could *see*.

Yes! You'd think that at the age of thirteen, no longer a tractable
child but (almost) an adolescent, I would have been in a rage much
of the time, disgusted by *it*, as *it* was a physical burden for me to bear,
weighing—what?—twenty pounds?—soon, thirty pounds—dragging
down my back, and causing me to stagger when I walked; having
made me a freak who dared not creep outside the house for fear of
being detected. (And who had ceased attending school.) And this was
true, often I felt rage, fury, but mostly I felt sick with shame, but in

another way (when I was alone in my room with just *it*) I understood that I was very special.

It had life only through me; *it* was hardly a twin of mine or even a "sister" (as Evie was a sister). *It* was just an appendage, a thing. A parasite!

And I was responsible for *it*—keeping *it* alive.

Why? This question never to be answered.

Grinding my teeth, chiding the thing for always being *there* dragging after me but at the same time I worried that something would happen to *it*, and *it* would wither and die and "fall off" (as Momma was always saying hopefully).

How lonely I would be then! (I did not want to think of this.)

When I went outdoors (in the backyard) I would wear a shawl over the thing. Eventually the thing itself would require a "skull"-cap to protect the part of *it* that seemed most vulnerable, where *its* head (brain) must have been; Momma made a sort of helmet of soft clothes to fit over the upper part that seemed to be a face, a head, a brain of *its* own, and to be very vulnerable. Over this we attached a thin veil with tiny holes for the pinpoint pupils that had begun to develop in the flat, shallow face.

Fascinating to see how *it* developed protuberances where eyes would have been in a normal face. These appeared over the course of several nights not long after the slit-like pupils had emerged. If you ran your fingers over these protuberances you felt something like the uncanny elasticity of eyeballs, still embedded in brain matter, but emerging from *it*; if you shone a light there, the brain matter shivered and shuddered and (as Momma described it, for I could not see) the pupils *shrank shut.*

In time the veil was outgrown, another veil had to be supplied, more of an actual mask, with larger holes for "eyes" and eventually a slit for the mouth, which was always unpleasantly damp, and soon became ragged.

I want, I want to live. Want to live like you.

Like you like you, want to live. Like you.

These pathetic quiverings were not actual *words*. Not that you could *hear.*

These crude efforts to communicate with me were met with mostly silence. Scoffing laughter, a shrug of my shoulder—*But you will never be like me. You! Like* me!

Except: one dawn in bed I was wakened with a jolt as *she* detached herself from me with a snap of the cartilaginous membrane that had

attached us, and lay for a time stunned and panting behind me. . . .
Or maybe that is wrongly described: *she* did not actively detach herself from *me*; rather, it simply happened that *she was detached from
me* as a scab falls from (healed) skin by a natural process.

As if unaware, or indifferent, I lay unmoving. Of course, I did not
turn to her.

Though all of my senses were alert, my heart rapidly beating.

A sense of profound loss swept over me, a heaviness of a kind I
had never before experienced, for I was sure that it was as Momma had
been predicting for months—*it* would wither and die and fall off me,
and I would return to what I'd been before.

At last then, when I'd gathered sufficient courage to overcome my
disgust, and with my eyes shut tight, I turned and pushed *it—her—*
out of bed and onto the floor, which *it—she—*struck softly, like
unbaked bread dough.

Almost inaudibly, a little cry was emitted—*Oh!*

*

Monstersister! Here was the opportunity to toss *it* into the trash,
now that *it* had separated from me without the spillage of blood.

Yet, this did not happen. For unmistakably, *it* was a living thing.

Already, *it* had become *she*, and eventually, *she* would acquire a
name.

(But not from me! For it did not seem just to me, that *she* who was
only an appendage of mine should have a name separate and distinct
from my name.)

At first Monstersister was fed as an infant might be fed, greedily
sucking on the rubber nipple of a baby's bottle filled with milk.

Later, orange juice, vanilla smoothies.

Then, Monstersister learned to suck liquid-pureed food through a
straw, which Momma prepared in a blender—hot oatmeal, fruits,
yogurt, greens, carrots, broccoli.

Eventually nuts, sunflower seeds, and chickpeas were blended as
well, included in these "nutritious" liquids. (Yes, I was allowed to
suck these through a straw. I was allowed to "lick the spoon.")

Whipped potatoes, with melted butter. Melted cheese, melted-grated
cheese on doughy-soft bread. Rice pudding, Jell-O of every imaginable
flavor. And of course, ice cream in a semisoft state.

Monstersister had a small appetite. You might conclude that her gas-
trointestinal organs were rudimentary as her new-emerging grayish

teeth were certainly rudimentary. But like an undersea creature, Monstersister had a *continuous appetite.*

(Rudimentary, and continuous: suety excretions from Monstersister's colorectal organs.)

(Yes, Monstersister was outfitted with diapers of increasing size until finally adult Depends snug on her misshapen lower body like the knitted helmet on her misshapen head.)

Monstersister was given a "name." *I* would not accept that name and you will never learn that name from *me.*

(No. Monstersister's name is *nothing like my name.*)

(No. We do not share a last name. Monstersister has no birth certificate because Monstersister was never "born." Therefore, Monstersister has no certificate given the imprimatur of the New Jersey State gilt seal. Therefore, Monstersister has no name legal or otherwise.)

Whatever *she* is called in the family, *I* do not acknowledge.

After *she* had broken away from me in my bed that morning like a scab there came to be a profound alteration in our household. A shifting of its foundation. A seismic shrug.

"Oh, what have you done!" Momma cried sharply, seeing that *she* was separate now from me as if out of pure spite I'd scraped her off, out of my brain stem, as a snake scrapes off its desiccated husk of a skin and glides away free and unencumbered, its scales glittering in the sun and its eyes joyously glaring.

"Oh, have you killed her! Your—" But Momma faltered for the word *sister* was too outrageous to be uttered. Instead Momma drew breath to begin again, "Oh God, is she still—breathing?"

No and yes. No no no but yes.

Damn *no* and more damn *yes.*

Turned out, *she* could breathe apart from me after all. An oozing out of my brain initially, *she* soon acquired autonomy as a mature fetus expelled from its womb acquires autonomy, in time.

If it fails to die, first.

*

What is interesting here, from a disinterested/objective perspective, is how the *unimaginable improbable* will become, within a surprisingly short period of time, the *imagined probable.*

How the *lurid freakish* becomes, within that period of time, particularly if experienced on a daily, hourly basis, in a familiar and delimited space like a family household, *normal.*

What was accepted as the *old normal* is soon overcome by the *new normal*.

Eventually, then, simply *the normal*.

For all things shift, as if tugged by gravity, to *the normal*.

*

And soon then, even I was drawn into the new alignment of our household. As with simple repetition any gesture, any process, any movement or motion becomes assimilated into the habit-forming soul. As playing a musical instrument begins in unfamiliarity and awkwardness, as many times repeated it sinks into the depths of the brain, where it is redefined as *tissue memory*.

Of course, I found myself involved in feeding Monstersister. There is a visceral pleasure in feeding a life-form that without your intervention will wither and die.

First, Momma fed Monstersister. Then, Granma. Then—me.

And soon, also, I was drawn into caring for *it*. That is, *her*.

That's to say *caring for* her in a literal sense: *caretaking*.

But eventually, as a consequence of this, *caring for her*: feeling concern, solicitude, "care" for her.

Knitting little hats for her, to protect her (exposed) brain. Knitting sweaters, smocks, gloves to protect the spongy tissue that was *her*.

For unlike me, Monstersister had failed to acquire that outer layer of tissue known as "skin."

(Why had she failed? In the womb?)

(Yes, it is an ugly word. Words. Ugly-cringing words—*in the womb*.)

(Dr. M_____ had not explained. Dad had been too stunned to question him and Dr. M_____ had not cared to explain. Perhaps there is no explanation. The most profound questions of our lives allow for no answers.)

(Though you are led to wonder if there is not some blame involved when one of a pair of "twins" fails to establish herself as an autonomous being while the other succeeds—as I did. . . .)

Without an outer layer of tissue Monstersister was purely brain matter, ganglia, nerve networks, veins, and arteries lacking a protective covering. No (evident) skeleton. *Not human!*

After the shock, the dismay and the disgust, unless it was the disgust and the dismay, and after the shock had faded, a perverse sort of gaiety came into the household. At least, Momma took some determined pleasure in *dealing with the situation*. And Granma too.

For Monstersister was a *blood relative*. No pretending that she was just something that came slithering into our house by accident!

Dad fell to brooding, staring at Monstersister as she lay inert in a cardboard box beside a heating vent in the kitchen. This box was rectangular, several times longer than it was wide, a kind of cradle shape into which Monstersister's boneless elastic-spongy body fit, lined with soft cloths. (You could not readily discern if Monstersister was awake or asleep or in a comatose state for the flat-manta face betrayed little emotion through the veil.)

"Christ! You wonder what it is we've done. To deserve this."

Yet Dad did not seem to doubt that *it* was a consequence of something that had *been done*. (But by whom? Dad? Dad and Momma?)

In the family it was Momma who was most attached to Monstersister. For here was a *challenge*. And Momma liked to say that belief in God is only tested by *challenge*.

Needing to keep Monstersister warm was urgent, Momma believed. Lacking a protective skin Monstersister was hypersensitive to bruising as well as cold. So it was Momma taught me to knit.

Me! Wielding knitting needles! What an insult!

I'd never felt the slightest interest in knitting, an insipid, fussy activity Momma and Granma did, and Dad would never be caught dead doing.

Unexpectedly, then, I discovered that I liked the look and feel of yarn between my fingertips. Bright purple, hot pink, and "royal" blue were my favorite yarn colors.

Knit-purl, knit-purl, knit-purl, taking care not to miss a stitch. Once you learn the trick of gripping the damn clattering knitting needles.

Knitting will make you less nervous, Momma said. Learn to *sit still, not wiggle*.

All of my life a struggle. It is not enough for them to put you in a cage for in the cage you must also *sit still, not wiggle* for they are watching at all times.

How to shape a curved knitted cap. How to shape knitted sleeves. How to knit a glove—with ten fingers! (Finally, despite Momma's best efforts, I could only knit clumsy spade-shaped mittens for Monstersister.)

In addition, Monstersister was given clothes I'd outgrown or had come to dislike. The surprise was, these fit her almost as well as they'd fitted me, though Monstersister is much smaller than I am, what you'd call "stunted"—"dwarfish." She is disfigured like a broken-backed snake if the snake lacked a firm envelope of skin to contain its flesh.

Well, yes—Monstersister was disgusting, laughable.

Eventually, however, unlike a snake, Monstersister began to acquire stubs of flesh where arms should have been, as well as stubs of (thicker) flesh where legs should have been and feet.

At first, just suggestions of limbs. But gradually these began to protrude from the body stem, and to take shape.

Never would the "hands" acquire actual fingers, however. Not as you and I understand fingers. Never would the "legs" acquire actual feet but rather flat, spatulate stubs like the flippers of certain undersea creatures.

Yet, Monstersister was "precocious"—you could say.

Before ten months of age Monstersister began to struggle to stand upright while leaning against a railing or a wall or clutching with gloved stub hands at the arm of a chair. Her legs were stub thighs that ended at the knees, on which she tried to walk upright like a dog on its hind legs; this was piteous to see, you wanted to hide your eyes or look quickly away, or laugh wildly. (Sometimes, as if by accident, I brushed against Monstersister as I passed by, knocking her off-balance without seeming to notice.)

When Monstersister was alone she often sank to the floor and crawled on her stub limbs, panting with effort, with a whistling sort of sob. (This was not a normal kind of crawling such as an infant or a toddler might undertake, for it was attended not with joyous excitement but grimly with panting and moaning; a shivery slithering twitchy kind of crawl such as a creature might undertake.)

Eventually Monstersister learned to make her way on "all fours" up and down stairs slithering and sliding with surprising rapidity. If you were descending the stairs you might glance down and there was Monstersister pushing past your ankles as a mischievous flat-faced snake might do, indifferent that you might tangle your legs in it and fall to the foot of the stairs.

Sometimes in warm weather Monstersister was allowed outside in the backyard by Momma and Granma, who saw that she did not wander more than a few yards from the back porch, and who watched over her anxiously, that she did not injure herself.

For Monstersister (evidently) possessed a rudimentary circulatory system, tendril-like veins and arteries throughout her truncated body. If one of these was pierced, "blood" would appear—thinner than normal human blood but smelling strongly.

Also, Monstersister began to grow a kind of cuticle over her soft sponge head; the exposed brain matter came to be covered by a thin membrane that thickened and became relatively hard, like the rind of a fruit that is soft and juicy within. Still it was necessary for Monstersister to wear the little caps we knitted for her, for she had no hair, or rather nothing more than a light fuzzy down, and was vulnerable to bruises, scratches, infections.

Generally, a membrane came to cover most of Monstersister's body, though it would never be as substantial as actual "skin."

And so, outfitted with a knitted royal-blue helmet, a near-transparent face veil, sweaters, shirts, pants that had once been mine as well as old sneakers of mine, Monstersister could be mistaken for a (more or less) normal child of nine or ten if observed at a distance of at least twelve feet—but no closer!

Yet more strangely, by the end of the first year since the veiny sponge first appeared at the back of my head Monstersister began to be confused in the eyes of my family with—*me*.

First, Granma. For Granma's eyes were not sharp. And Granma's judgment had become blurred.

Granma calling Monstersister by my name but, what was more hurtful, calling *me* by *her* name.

"Granma, no! *I am not—that thing.*"

And Granma would stare at me, and blink, and laugh nervously— "Of course, you are not, dear. What was I thinking of!"

My hatred for Granma began, at that moment. A sudden small throb at the top rear of my head where the veiny sponge had first appeared as itching.

For Granma had forgotten who I was, I realized. From now on, Granma would call me *dear*. (But Granma did not forget Monstersister's name!)

Worse, my brother Davy and my sister Evie began to befriend Monstersister when I wasn't around. I would hear them chattering and laughing and feel a sinking sensation for I knew, and was too proud to accuse them.

For months they'd avoided me when Monstersister had been just an ugly growth down my back but somehow now that Monstersister was "autonomous" they began to be curious about her, and (possibly) to feel sorry for her, that she could straighten to only about forty-eight inches in height and had, inside my cast-off

155

sneakers, no actual feet of her own.

And possibly because of this stunted stature, and her inability to speak except in grunts, moans, whistles and whimpers and trills, they did not feel intimidated by her.

Smaller than Evie, overall. Much smaller than Davy. So if you collided with her there could be no injury to yourself; you felt only a small thrill of pleasure at the pliant warmth of another's being with no recourse but to give way to you without protest.

For *she* never protested, complained, whined, or whimpered. As a normal child would.

All these months that Monstersister was being tolerated in the household, and beginning to acquire an indeterminate status in the family, not one of us (of course) yet not entirely an outsider, still Monstersister remained a secret to relatives, who had been resolutely not invited to visit, as well as neighbors and acquaintances who might have been "friendly" with Momma but would not have dared drop by the house uninvited. Within the family still I took for granted—we all took for granted, I'd thought—that *she* was really just an *it*, a *thing*. And we'd begun to call her *she*, and some of us had given her a name, but not seriously; such a status might be revoked at any time.

Which was why I became agitated hearing how *she* was beginning to be talked about in the family not only by name but *as if she was not so different from me—a "sister."*

(But how was this possible? I was "real," Monstersister was a freak.)

By degrees then, Monstersister began her assault.

Because she could not speak words as a normal human being can speak words, for her tongue was malformed—a thin, little snake tongue it was, unnaturally pink—Monstersister cultivated a way of *whimpering, whining, trilling, humming.*

Of these, *humming* met with the most positive response from the family.

So *humming* was Monstersister's strategy.

A high-pitched *thrumming-humming* began to issue from the hidden mouth behind the veil covering the flat-manta face, musical notes of a strange, uncanny beauty causing shivers to run down the spines of listeners.

Humming, just audibly. Keeping the thin snake lips shut. So you might hear a high-pitched *thrumming-humming* in the air about your head, or rising through the floorboards of the house, penetrating

walls with the power to bring tears to your eyes without your voli-
tion, you would not know why, you would be taken by surprise, tears
running down your cheeks, a shivery sensation rising along your
spine, you would feel faint, you would want to laugh wildly. *You did
not know why and you resented it.*

"Like an angel!" Granma declared, wiping at her eyes when Monstersister *hummed.* (As if Granma had ever heard an angel singing!)

Pressed my hands over my ears. *Did not know why, resented it!*

Hid in my room. Hid in the basement. Hid in the woods behind the
house. Hurt, sulking, staying away from meals. Refused to answer
when Momma called me.

My name had become strange to me—harsh, hissing syllables that
I could not hear clearly, and could not recognize, *Fyczss! Fyczss!*—
so why should I answer Momma, goddamn I would not.

Astonishing then, Monstersister began to appear at mealtimes
seated upright at the table in my chair. *My* chair!

This was Momma's idea, I was sure. But Dad must have agreed,
which is strange to me; of my parents I would not have thought that
my father would betray me for always there'd been the understanding that I was *Daddy's girl. . . .*

Since Monstersister was very stunted, a dwarf with a crooked
back, virtually no spine at all, she had to be seated on cushions to
reach the table; her stub feet came nowhere close to the floor. Behind
the veil (sure to be tattered and wet around the mouth) her face could
be discerned in the bright light from overhead, for it had become
more of a "face" now, with a sickly, spongy skin and stark black
holes for nostrils; you could almost discern "eyes"—a glisten of an
actual eyeball, no longer just pinprick pupils. And when the mouth
slash in the veil became raw and widened from usage you could catch
a glimpse of Monstersister's mouth inside—thin, worm-colored lips
and a flick of an unnaturally narrow pink tongue quick flitting as a
snake's.

Through a doorway, through two doorways at the farther end of
the hall, I crouched, watching in disgust, unseen. How my parents
vied to feed *her!*—*it.* Not giving a damn if their actual daughter went
hungry.

Worse yet staring through a kitchen window from where I stood
outside at dusk only a few feet away observing Momma and Dad,
Davy and Evie and Granma at supper with a hideous freak in their
midst, which they seemed not to recognize; indeed they offered this
thing grown long and limp as a python little treats, lifted a glass of

pureed green liquid to its mouth so that it could suck greedily through a straw in a way disgusting to see.

Were they *charmed* by this thing? My heart was suffused with contempt for them, and rage against *it*.

Hid in the basement. Made a little nest for myself of rags in the basement. Avoided my family, who were hateful to me. Avoided meals. Crept into the kitchen to scavenge leftovers from the refrigerator, took my food away to devour in secret.

More often with warm weather I hid in the woods behind the house. Rolled up in a nylon jacket and some canvas from the garage. At first Momma continued to call me from the back porch in a plaintive voice, for certainly Momma felt guilty, and anxious; but soon then, Momma called me less frequently, days passed and Momma did not call my (unrecognizable) name, and just once Dad shouted from the back door hissing furious words that frightened me for I knew that they contained a threat, and I dared not reply and give away my hiding place.

Following that, I would observe with contempt *the family* at the kitchen table. All of them were becoming freakish to me: "Momma"— "Dad"—"Davy"—"Evie." And the elderly woman with the foolish face creased like a dish towel—"Granma." And Monstersister upright in my chair on cushions, purple-yarn knitted cap on the undersized, misshapen head, translucent veil over the flat-manta face so that you could dimly make out glassy-glistening eyes, nostril holes, wormy-lipped slash mouth through the fabric, and around the neck a scarf decorated in pink rosebuds and sequins—one of Momma's birthday scarves! This thing, this "sister," could now feed herself awkwardly, lifting in gloved stub hands a container of pureed liquid to suck through a straw.

Through the window came a thrilling *humming*.

The sound of this *humming* caused tears to spill from my eyes, wetting my cheeks. Tears of sorrow or loss, tears of rage, I did not know.

The sound of this *thrumming-humming* was so high-pitched, so piercing, I fell back from the window, stumbling away, weeping in grief and incomprehension.

*

I see now. A mistake, not to have cut *it* from my head.

Might've torn *it* out with my bare hands while *it* was no larger than an egg and had not yet drawn breath.

Does no one *see*, Monstersister is a freak? Not a *she* but an *it*?

Why is it only I, the legitimate sister, who can *see*?

Lulled by the *thrumming-humming*, that is it. A normal (frail) voice like mine can't compete with the monster.

Wondering if, if I crept into the house to discover Monstersister asleep in her cardboard-box cradle, I could smother her? Press a pillow over the little slash mouth and nostril holes and deprive her of oxygen as she struggled weakly until her breathing ceased forever and we were freed of her. . . .

Excited, by this prospect. And yet, unable to act upon it.

To know what must be done, yet lack the strength to execute it— that is the predicament of humankind.

Until one day wakened from sodden sleep in our neighbors' abandoned barn where I had made a little nest for myself in the (rotted, sour-smelling) hayrick. Hearing a sound of (male) voices from out by the road.

Oh, was it Dad calling me? Dad at last, calling *me*?

Calling me back, begging me to return, saying he is sorry, damned sorry he'd made a mistake, I am the daughter he loves best, not this freaky thing, should've severed *it* from my head when he'd had the chance, nothing but a veiny-spongy growth lacking a heartbeat and breath. . . . But it was not Dad's voice waking me.

Men's voices, raw in the wet morning air, where a moving van was parked in the driveway of our house.

A moving van! This was a stunning sight.

Hours of that interminable day passing like the clattering of cars in a freight train. As the interior of the house was emptied item by item, carried into the moving van by strangers.

Rooted to the spot behind the house, unable to move, seeing "my bed"—"my desk"—carried out and into the moving van.

I was not weeping. My heart had turned to stone. By this time any cruel act of my family was expected by me. Monstersister had hypnotized them with her demonic music, they had excised me from their lives.

Devastated to see Dad climb into the cab of the moving van to ride beside the driver when the house was emptied at last. And Momma driving our car in their wake. Not a backward glance to where I stood staring after them alone and forlorn in the driveway.

Monstersister in the passenger's seat beside Momma. In bulky clothing to disguise and protect her (allegedly) frail body, carefully secured in place by the seat belt. And in the rear my brother, Davy, and my sister, Evie, and between them Granma, avid and unquestioning where they would be taken next.

Would not run stumbling after them. Would not cry after them begging them Take me with you! Take me with you! *For if I did, my brother, Davy, and my sister, Evie, would stare at me through the car window aghast and without recognition as I trotted on the highway shoulder only a few yards away like a beast running itself to death. Momma at the wheel of the car would stare at me with a fleeting glimmer of recognition even as her panicked foot pressed down harder on the gas pedal to escape. And Monstersister through the eye holes of her veil even with her weak vision would identify me as the sister twin she'd betrayed, secure in the triumph that she has taken my place in the family, she has sucked all the oxygen and nourishment from the womb, and there is no place for me now, as the car speeds toward a distant, unnameable city leaving me exhausted and defeated in its wake with no recourse except to limp miles back to the vacated house where now I have made a cozy nest for myself out of left-behind carpet and curtains, threadbare blankets, soiled towels, and where for years to come and beyond even my death neighborhood children will peer through cobwebbed windows into the derelict interior thrilled to terrify themselves shrieking* Monster!—Monster!

Cosmogony
Lucy Ives

A FEW YEARS AGO a friend of mine married a demon. There was a liberal in the White House then and everyone was feeling pretty sanguine.

The demon's name was Fulmious Mannerhorn Patterlully, and he was approximately 200,001 years old. His legs were blue, his eyes were yellow, he had to gnaw at his own fingernails all day to keep them a reasonable length. He did not wear pants with notable frequency. He was intelligent, gregarious, undying.

My friend was twenty-eight. She was a human girl.

We'd always known about demons. They were the necessary, baleful entities that stood on the porches of history, holding up the roofs of civilization with their knotted backs. They were the reason that the past was visible to us at all.

People kept complimenting my friend on her choice of partner—and I know you get it too. Although people did not say so in so many words, what they meant was that my friend now partook of the powers of the demon FMP, without having to experience any of the drawbacks associated with actual demonhood. The demon FMP could (and, presumably, would) share with my friend his occult understanding of the stock market, his ability to produce fire on demand, his talent for translating himself into a fine mist. He liked to hang, shimmering, from the ceilings of crowded subways, for example. He enjoyed magnetizing coins and possessing small dogs, speaking to us in funny voices through their squinty wet faces. He was an expert in the objectification of souls and had a long-standing social network.

And this was good for my friend. But the demon FMP alone experienced that terrible period in April when demons undergo new growth in their horns, not to mention the insidious agony that comes of eternal life.

My friend seemed to understand the trade-offs, as well as society's position on the matter. She took it all in stride. "I know he's an infernal demiurge, but he's actually just a nice guy."

Everyone grinned hard.

161

My friend wasn't talking to us anyway. She was describing her own happiness, which had its limits. We wanted to believe that she knew more than we did, but, in truth, even my friend did not know where things were going to go.

Now, my friend had mentioned to me, at some point during the time when she was engaged to the venerable FMP but not yet married, that there is a little-known fact about demons, which is that they have two different names, or sets of names, given FMP's tripart moniker. There is the name by which they are known to humans, and the one by which they are known amongst themselves. My friend said that at some point during a certain particularly poignant night of passion and spooning, the demon FMP had let slip the fact of the existence of his other name, his real name, the name by which he was known among demons.

"It must be hard," I said, "going all those millennia."

She was reserved. "I'm not his first human, you know."

I was doing my best not to imagine whatever it was that transpired between my friend and her supernatural other on the carnal plane. "So, what is it?"

"You mean, his *real name*?"

I nodded.

My friend seemed to contemplate my lack of inhibition. It wasn't the same thing as rudeness, and I think that she was wondering if one day this lack of tact would destroy me—or if, because of it, I was destined to live an unusual life.

I kept going. I said, "Wasn't I there that night you recited Shakespeare to Thom Velez in the motel hot tub? Didn't I hold your hair until 9:00 a.m.?"

My friend blushed. I could tell she loved me.

"Won't I be there," I pursued, "after *everything*, even when he's gone?"

"But you realize"—my friend was daintily reaching for her phone—"that he's never going to, um, your euphemism, 'be gone'?"

My friend thumbed through something or other.

"I'll die before him," my friend continued, gazing into her iPhone 8, which was encased in a piece of plastic designed to resemble marble. "You know?"

So she never did tell me her fiancé's demon name.

But I still found out. I'm sure you understand I always do.

It was after their wedding. I was in the supermarket, the one at the corner of _____ and _____, assessing the rows of cherry tomatoes. I lifted multiple pints, gazed up into their see-through bottoms searching for fuzz. And then there, suddenly, FMP was. I saw him out of the corner of my eye, it was the blueness of his legs, which appeared weirdly white or violet in the afternoon light. He was tearing pieces off a glistening Danish, popping them into his maw as he engaged a young artist whom I recognized as the subject of a recent *Artforum* pick in a lazy chat pertaining to the shop and, one had to assume, eternal damnation.

FMP was staring right at me.

I stared right back.

I knew it was weird but I couldn't help myself. I directed my gaze firmly and robustly back to the bottom of the tomato container I was holding up. I knew very well it was the wrong thing to do. An ambitious parent had long ago instructed me, specifically and in detail, never to look demons in their eyes and look away again without acknowledging the encounter. It was a gross offense. But this was exactly what I had done. FMP had seen me, and I had seen his yellow eyes, which basked calmly and yellowly in their furred sockets. I recalled that line of Edgar Allan Poe's, "And his eyes have all the seeming of a demon's that is dreaming." It's from "The Raven," something I once memorized in an institutional context. I often remark to myself regarding Poe's dorky specificity in this phrase: His eyes (the raven's) have the appearance of a demon's (eyes), and, meanwhile, the demon, and not his eyes, is dreaming. . . . Because grammar and syntax are real, don't you know! Life is not all about magic and deities, even if it sometimes seems like it is, whether due to one's liquid laudanum habit (have a nice jar of it on your afternoon stroll and get ready to unleash some neo-Gothic lyrics) or one's best friend's marriage to a certain minion of Dis. There are facts and rules. Edgar Allan Poe, for one, understood that you *do* need to know whether it's the demon who's dreaming, or just the eyes of said demon. He would never have been so stupid as to do what I had just done.

Anyway, there I was staring into the glossy redness of miniature tomatoes, themselves not unlike a bunch of disembodied eyes, when I smelled FMP's sulfurous approach.

"Well, hello," said he.

I laughed weakly. "Just researching the ways of very small nightshades!"

FMP reacted with solemnity. "Of course." It was always difficult

163

to ascertain if he might be joking, and at this moment the ambiguity was daunting, slimy. "I thought I'd say 'hi.'" FMP smiled, releasing a fascinating, hideous stench from between his peg-like teeth. "By the way, it's come to my attention that there was something you wanted to *know*."

I was sure I did not know what he meant.

"About *me*? Or have you forgotten so soon? I was extremely touched that you were interested in my True Name."

The way he said it, it had to be capitalized.

"Um, not sure?"

"Oh no. You're sure, you shallow wretch. Even if I were not the life partner of a being with whom you are bonded through shared trauma, nearly identical socioeconomic standing and level of physical attractiveness, as well as geographic proximity, I'd still know. It was obvious in your desperate attempt to avoid this very encounter. You're a coward," FMP told me. "Yet it alleviates the torment of my archaic burden somewhat to watch you squirm. Thank you for that. I like your superficially independent, spineless style, you immature female specimen," and here he also reeled off my credit score, Social Security number, number of porcelain versus gold tooth fillings, and the date on which I was currently scheduled to die.

It's not, by the way, like this was an anomalous encounter with FMP. He was constantly like this, reminding you of your mortality plus vulnerability to identity theft. A lot of people seemed to find this charming, a cool party trick, but it had occurred to me that this behavior must have been going on with him for centuries if not geologic eras, and I didn't find FMP all that original, even in his omniscience.

"Right again," said I.

FMP glittered with malice. All his hairs stuck out. He was having a great time. "I know," he let me know, "that you want what's mine."

I shrugged but had to go fondle some nearby fennel in order to hide the trembling in my hands.

"I'm going to tell you my True Name," FMP whisper-shouted. "Then you will know it!" It was all extremely mechanical and ancient. It was the best and the most unpleasant thing. It is such an event to speak with a demon! "My True Name," FMP hissed across a heap of broccoli rabe, "is 27."

"Wait," I said, "*what?*"

"Twenty-seven," FMP repeated.

"As in the number?"

FMP looked annoyed. "No, it just sounds like that."

I didn't know what to say. "Twenty-seven?" I repeated.

FMP, aka 27, was glancing around the store. He seemed concerned that he had made a mistake.

"Twenty-seven," I muttered to myself. "Twenty-seven." I couldn't believe it. I think I must have wandered unceremoniously off, because the next thing I can remember I was standing on the sidewalk.

And if you thought my encounter with FMP/27 was startling, which, granted, it was, I don't quite know how to explain the subsequent scenario.

It was how *he* looked, because that's always part of it. But that wasn't all. There was also this quality about *him*, a kind of unbelievability, and I think I can point to it in this moment, when it was still fresh. I was probably squinting into a device, trying to refresh my email.

"Hi," he said. "Sorry to bother you. Were you just in the market over there?" Note that he did not say "supermarket," just "market." Note also that he was an otherworldly being. Now that he was present, the light seemed not to originate in the sky but rather from somewhere inside of him. "I'm so sorry," he said again. "Many apologies." It's impossible to describe his voice. It was soft, delicately wilted, but also it was like the mighty crash of apocalyptic hailstorms, jet engines, stampeding mares.

I nodded. Probably I made one of those incoherent noises of assent that have become so popular in postwar America. "Yeah," I said. "Unhuhn. Mmhmm. Heh!" I was a moron, typical of my time.

The being smiled. "I thought it was you. I'd like to speak with you. I'd like to know you." Please note how this was extremely direct. He was tactless, just like me.

Maybe I had the wherewithal to reply in words. I dearly hope I did. At any rate, somehow it came to pass that a week later we were having coffee.

And isn't it clear by now? He was the exact opposite and equal of FMP/27. Oh, the symmetry! Oh dear God! Oh how fearful! How precise! He was an actual *angel*, and his name was Eric.

Eric was subtle at first. To be fair, we did establish during our second encounter that I was an acquaintance, if not quite ally, of FMP. Eric built that fact out like a custom cabana, a dell we could retire to should we run out of things to say. And it was true that in the beginning Eric did not push me. This was likely much of the secret to his success, that he did a host of other things, but he did not push. I do sometimes wonder, which parts of what occurred were due to Eric's

165

immutable role within the cosmos, and which had to do with something similar to free will, perhaps the portion of it belonging to me, a minor anthropomorphic pleat in the fabric of eternity? Was any of it, I keep asking myself, "for" me, a human girl?

I, for my part, was twenty-nine and, like everyone else these days, a product of the Enlightenment. I believed that dating (along with everything else) occurred in a wide, wide, secular zone. Sure, there might be devils and angels and true believers, but what did that really matter, now that we had the news? Everything was basically all about information, who possessed it, who didn't. So, there might be some level at which Eric could bring about my salvation, but that was just one piece of the puzzle, and I was actually more interested in whether he might be privy to anything proprietary regarding me or relevant others: sensitive thoughts, secrets, insecurities, lusts.

The idea of the network, as described in Gottfried Leibniz's 1714 tract, *La Monadologie*, pretty much the number one guide to dating ever in the history of the West, furnishes a useful description:

To the extent that I comprehend it, in Leibniz's conception the world is made up of various shiny, translucent cells ("monads"), and each of these cells can perceive other cells, its own unique identity being constituted by its various perceptions of these infinitely various others. If any one monad depends on something external to itself, then it depends on *others*, an infinite number of them, and not just *an other*, since it is only by virtue of the many, the perceptions they provide, that there is such a thing as a *one*.

If you're with me so far, let's make an inference. I think it might be interesting to ask what the responsibility of one monad is to another. I think we can safely say they owe each other everything and also nothing. For what can be the meaning of a pair, a couple, in a structural environment such as this—I mean, for just two monads, given the propensity to reflect and just, like, go on reflecting? What are they to each other?

You can imagine that, if it works for monads that they get their identity by having a unique perspective on all other monads, then if you take two of them and sequester them somewhere (say, Eric's so-so apartment) in order that they only have each other to work with, the effects are crazy. Each of these two monads, now isolated as a couple, can only take its respective identity from reflecting the other. If we slow the process down such that we can look at it step by step, in time we see something like, monad A reflects monad B, and vice versa (they each become the other, $A \rightarrow B^R$, $B \rightarrow A^R$). In step 2, they then each reflect themselves *as the other*, so if monad A has already become B^R and B has become A^R, then in the second glance they are $B^R \rightarrow A^{RR}$ and $A^R \rightarrow B^{RR}$. This can go on for a very long time.

While I'm not saying that this is really what happens in romantic relationships, it might be what people have a tendency to think is going on. This is also how they decide who is the bad person in the relationship and who is the good. Of course, given the monadical model, they're basically the same person, if not entirely composed of each other. However, few couples recognize this simple point. There's always one person who wants to feel worse about themself, and this, my Secular Enlightenment–inheriting friends, makes all the difference.

But Eric and I didn't talk about ethics or psychology or the structure of the cosmos. He was an angel and thus already good.

I was, as noted, but a human girl.

Eric rented a junior one bedroom. And indeed it was so-so, but it overlooked a park where some of the few birds that continue to inhabit New York City sang. I remember the first time that I learned that the etymology of "angel" brings us to a Greek word for messenger, go-between. It makes sense. Demon is more insoluble. It was inherited wholesale and just means "demon," though without some of the negative connotation. I often wondered if Eric had looked these histories up too, or if he knew what these terms meant innately, without research.

Eric had a job. By this I mean he went to work every day at a small IT company with an office overlooking the Holland Tunnel. I think this was part of the reason why people were so much bigger on the sort of relationship my friend and FMP had. FMP was completely consumed by his role as a tempter of souls and artisan of fate. He was vaguely famous and didn't require a day job. I'm not trying to say that, as an angel, Eric was some kind of excessively dreamy idealist—it's just not entirely clear what he and his team were trying to do.

Eric bought all his clothes from AmazonBasics. He was often online. Far from being tactless these days, sometimes he did not speak at all. He went down to the park. He watched.

I pondered Eric's muscular, winged form. It was often walking away from me. He was a sort of intergalactic male model, I thought: quiet, strong, krononautic.

To return for a moment to words: in an early essay, "On Language as Such and on the Language of Man," the great twentieth-century critic and mystic Walter Benjamin maintains, on the one hand, "Every expression of human mental life can be understood as a kind of language," and, on the other, "Speechlessness: that is the great sorrow of nature . . ." In Benjamin's account, nature mourns the incompleteness of human speech, its petty enumerative names. Speechless herself, nature receives the story of the creative word of Genesis, turning a melancholy face toward mankind, who can only supply a "hundred languages . . . in which the name has already withered, yet which, according to God's pronouncement, have knowledge of things." I found myself thinking a lot about this notion, in those days of Eric, who was so graceful and perfect and taciturn. In other words, I found myself thinking about how everything regarding human systems for organizing the world is basically fallen and repetitive. This was weird for a number of reasons but primarily it was weird because, you know, the Enlightenment! We're not supposed to have these sorts of thoughts anymore.

Also we're all supposed to be OK with the notion that we can't fully know one another. I think about it like this: Leibniz says that the irony of being human is that you're just like everyone else. You have all the same stuff everyone else has, just in a different order. The reason it is in a different order is that you have some sort of discrete origin, you were born in a time and place and that's what makes you, you. This difference is arbitrary and the system is designed in this completely infuriating way that makes it impossible to know about it—which is to say, your difference—as a kind of content. Which is why medieval Europeans all look like dolls in their paintings. There wasn't anything unknowable about them. They were the puppets of God, and they didn't have psychology or newspapers.

However, one of the few interesting things about being a woman is maybe the Enlightenment didn't happen for you. Like, you know how to speak and read and participate in democracy, but maybe you aren't really any better off. There are analogies between being female and being left-handed, I think, or being an animal. While I was with Eric, I thought a lot about the limits of psychology—or, as I privately referred to it now, "monad chatter." Monad chatter is going on in the world and meanwhile the world sits glumly by. We monads cannot get over the fact that we can't fully know one another. We'll surveil each other until the cows come home and pretend it's for marketing or science or spy craft. But really all this data is just a burnt offering to a god who withdrew long ago, leaving us the mute earth and also the vestiges of good and evil. And I guess we're free to care about, or even date, these vestiges, if we so choose. . . .

As time went on, things were more and more placid and even quieter, but on occasion I caught Eric looking at me in a certain way. It was hard to say what sort of way this was because, having managed to fall deeply in love with him, I was more than a little confused.

"He's not the marrying kind," my friend said. "He dresses like an undercover cop."

I assumed she was jealous or in some other way annoyed by my righteous mode of affiliating myself with the deific. Also, I had begun to consider her immoral. Why was she consorting with a demon when we all knew demons were the one thing rendering this perfect universe impure?

My friend, meanwhile, was looking up at me with a mixture of recognition and pity. "So I guess you're going to play this one out to the bitter end?"

"I guess so!" I yelped, pitying her right back.

When I got home from the New American Restaurant that evening, home now being Eric's so-so apartment, where I kept a small pile of belongings neatly stowed in discarded Prime packaging, Eric was hunched at his desk. He was filling out some sort of online form that he minimized as soon as I walked in.

"Hey, you!" he said.

"Hi there." I hopped over and stroked one of his translucent feathers. I felt the usual electric charge and began drooling. I wondered if he felt like going to bed.

"In a minute. I was just thinking, remember that day when we first met?"

I said something about how could I forget but he ignored me. I think, anyway, that it was a rhetorical question.

"You were in the market that day. Do you remember?"

This was not a rhetorical question. I nodded.

"You spoke to someone there. That person is important to me." Eric paused. "For my work. I mean, my *real* work. Do you remember?"

I nodded again.

"And who was that?"

"FMP."

"Yes and no," said the angel, his eyes vibrating softly. "What was his *real* name?"

Of course, all is fair in love and war but you don't know how fair it really is until you become intimate with a being who looks pretty much exactly like a human but is not a human at all. At this point, I would not have denied Eric anything. I couldn't have. He represented

169

my salvation. I could barely speak. He explained things. I don't mean, by the way, that he explained things *to* me, with his voice and words and so forth. I mean, he explained everything that had happened, his presence did. He explained why I had had to go through what I'd gone through, all the years of isolation, my strange inability to find individuals to whom I could relate. My bizarre talkativeness. This had all happened because he was here. And now he just was.

I said, "Oh, you mean his *real* name," as if I knew exactly what was going down, as if I had known all along and was even waiting for this moment. "I'm surprised you never asked! It's 27, of course." I was terrified but manifested confidence. I put my hands on my hips. I stared bravely into the abyss that was opening up around me.

Eric raised an eyebrow. "Thanks," he muttered, stepping out an open window. He was evidently going to work.

I never saw Eric again. And I never saw my friend again, either. FMP, I heard, was reduced to a coal briquette. All in all, given these atypical goings-on, it's been a strange spring. I've realized how little I know of the ways of the world, how much there is that has come before. Yet I feel that I have made a lot of progress, that I'm slowly comprehending more. I marvel, and I try to be tough. I try to grow. I still have Eric's so-so apartment, by the way, and sometimes I go for walks in the park. There really is something lovely, something touching about survival.

On that last point, a few final remarks. Even more recently, over the past few days, maybe the last week and a half, I've been experiencing these headaches. They're brief, but when they strike it's like nothing you've ever known, believe you me. It feels like something stiff and sharp is trying to bore its way *out* of my skull. I mean, what's weird about it is it feels like it's coming from the interior.

It's made me start thinking more carefully about demons. You do see them now and then, doubled over in some discreet location, given the month. I think too, as it can't be avoided, about Eric, an angel, whom I've come to regard less as a self-idealizing sociopath than a sort of amphibian, although he definitely put one over on me.

I've been told by numerous acquaintances that I'm looking pretty good. Their softballs, re: breakup weight loss, sail over my head. Sometimes it's because I'm dealing with a migraine, but at other times it's because I'm lost in thought.

Immortals, I'm thinking, they're just like us.

The Soul Collector
Ethan Rutherford

FIRST THERE WAS AN EARTHQUAKE, then, as the story goes, there came a giant wave. But of the wave itself, the boys heard and remembered nothing. They'd been asleep, and when they woke and looked out their bedroom window they saw their world had filled with water. It was impossible to imagine the sea twisting its way this far inland, but that's the way it was—their eyes were not deceiving them. The water was dark and sludgy and thick with debris. It had moved through their neighborhood in the middle of the night like some slow, obscure beast who'd unhinged its jaw and quietly swallowed up everything they had ever known.

They climbed up to the attic and scrambled onto the roof of their house. Still water stretched everywhere, as far as they could see. Most of the houses in their neighborhood were submerged, their windows dark. Everything was deserted, everyone gone. They heard no sirens. No parents called for their children. A tremendous quiet lay over the land. Night fell. In the distance, they saw fires push orange heat into the dark sky. Where were *their* parents? The boys didn't know.

On the third day, they watched a thick blanket of fire ants flotilla by, while the sky filled with seagulls. On the fourth day, they woke to find an empty canoe turning in slow circles just outside their window, and they lowered themselves down and climbed in. They paddled through their water-sunk streets calling for their friends. They called the names of their parents and teachers and coaches, but no one replied.

At first they were sad, but then, with great effort, they stopped feeling that way. The world was new, that was the only way to look at it.

Mornings, they ate quietly in the attic before mapping out their days. They paddled farther and farther from their home. When the sun went down, it felt as though they were floating through a dark, flooded cave; the only sound that came to them was the kiss of their paddles stirring the water. Every so often an unusual ripple pushed toward the canoe, or they heard a shallow splash like a fish had jumped, giving them the distinct feeling they were being watched and followed. But each time they turned toward the sound they saw only their own flat wake licking eerily away from them.

Every night, they returned to the attic, climbed into their shared bed, and listened to the quiet world outside until they fell asleep. They didn't want to be alone, but clearly were; the town was flooded, everyone had forgotten about them. And they knew that the sooner they accepted that, the happier they'd be.

"But of course they hadn't been forgotten," Soren said, and held up his hands. His two boys sat still in their beds. Earlier, they had complained about putting on their pajamas and brushing their teeth, how it was dark outside but not *that* dark, but now, in the yellow lamplight of their shared bedroom, they'd gone quiet with anticipation. "And they *were* being watched," Soren continued. "For the splashes they heard while they were paddling came from the Soul Collector. He'd come in on the wave and was, in many ways, responsible for it."

Soren shifted his weight at the foot of the younger boy's bed. Outside it was cold, and freezing rain had begun pelting the bedroom window. The boys hated to hear about the Soul Collector, but they loved him too. He'd come to them in a dream, and, as far as Soren could tell from the pictures they'd drawn and shown him, he was some sort of red squid the size of a bus. His black beak chomped relentlessly even when he was not eating. With his many tentacles, he held the souls of drowned people to keep him company in his painful limbo on the abyssal plain. But now and then he rode in on tsunami waves, which was something the boys had been learning about in school. Where they'd gotten the idea of a soul collector, Soren had no idea.

"But don't worry," Soren added. "They don't encounter him yet. Because that was the night, when they were about to give up, that they met the Diver."

"Did they see his light?" the younger boy asked.

"It hung in front of him like a large, blue lantern," Soren said, "and glowed in the depths as he made his way up their street. They watched from their attic window. It was unmistakable. He looked like an anglerfish. They knew immediately they were no longer alone, and that was something to celebrate."

The Diver was the Soul Collector's lifelong enemy. Since the beginning of time, the two of them had been battling for the souls of

172

the drowned. Hana, Soren's wife, wouldn't tell Diver stories anymore. She thought they were too violent and sad. He could hear her now from the bedroom; she was on the phone in the kitchen. She'd spent the day canvassing, which always left her a little depressed. People listened, nodded, said I know, *I know*, but no one would sign at the door, no one ever donated money. I'm not asking for much, she'd tell Soren. Vote the right people in! Don't let the planet choke! When she was tired, she'd yell at the boys for leaving lights on when they weren't in the room, or for wasting water as they brushed their teeth. "Right, right," Soren heard her say now. She was talking to her sister, Chloe, who was going through a bitter divorce. Soren had liked her husband, who had once told him he found marriage to Chloe suffocating, and so in some ways it was a surprise they had lasted at all. Chloe lived in California and thought nothing of calling late and keeping Hana on the phone for hours now while Soren put the boys to bed. After these long conversations, Hana would hang up the phone and come to bed glassy-eyed and defeated.

"Carefully," Soren continued, "the Diver opened the front door to their house, and they heard him walk up the stairs." He coughed and adjusted his leg. "Then, his brass helmet lifted through the surface of the water, and, with seagrass coming off of him in cold, green strings, he stepped into the attic.

"For a long time, he just stood there, dripping water, like he was some sort of ghost himself," Soren said. "He was taller than the boys had expected. But they knew it was him: iron shoes, brass helmet with four portlights, heavy gloves. There was something unusual about his appearance, however. His helmet was streaked and dented, not shiny but a dull, greenish color. It had long ago rusted to his corselet and could not be removed. His canvas diving suit was stained yellow. Barnacles had colonized his gloves. He looked very old, as if being in the water for all these years had finally caught up with him. This came as a bit of a shock to the boys, who had always imagined him to be a young man. While they couldn't see his face through the helmet's forelight, they could hear his breathing, and now he grew quiet. Finally, in a low, deep, patient voice, he explained what he was doing there.

"As everyone knew, he followed the Soul Collector and freed the souls he held in his pulsing grip," Soren went on. "But this last wave had been so large, and the Soul Collector, in his loneliness and fury, had grown so powerful, that even the Diver was having trouble keeping up. *I am old*, he said, *and tired. Still, this is important work,*

173

and I need your help. What he meant by this wasn't exactly clear to the boys. But it would be soon."

Soren heard Hana open and shut the refrigerator door and listened for her footsteps down the hall. She'd been gone all day, and had barely said hello to anyone before her sister called. He waited for a sound from outside the boys' room, and heard nothing. "Anyway," he said. "Where was I?"

Next morning, the Diver woke them gently and presented each of them with a small, collapsible bathyscope, which would make it easier to watch as he went about his underwater work. The boys nodded, got dressed, ate, and left the attic together. Outside, the air was heavy and smelled of seaweed. The Diver sat in the front of the canoe with his back to the boys. He whispered directions as they quietly paddled across the blackish water, past a gas station, an antique store, a train-car diner. The tops of pine trees pushed through the water and stretched their dark and resting arms. Eventually, the Diver held up a closed fist and stood. Around his old, dented helmet a halo of blue electricity began to fizz and snap like a mosquito trap. He made a slight nod in their direction, indicated that they should use the bathyscopes he'd made, crossed his arms over his chest, and slipped over the side. Water swallowed him up.

From the canoe, the boys watched his blue lantern glide through the murk as he sank to the bottom. Through their bathyscopes, they saw he'd landed in the middle of a street. Cars lined the empty block. Large branches, which had been swept a great distance by the rushing water, now lay still on the sidewalk. They saw no people. How strange it was to see this neighborhood underwater, and so clearly; it was like peering into an empty aquarium. The Diver soon stood and his light seemed to grow in strength. When they looked to where he was pointing, they saw bodies of people who had been drowned by the wave strewn everywhere. They seemed to be floating just above the ground. Most had kelp caught in their hair, and many were without clothing. Some had gaping, bloodless wounds. All were ghostly in the blue light of the Diver's lantern. Their faces were not contorted, but their eyes were open; they watched pleadingly as the Diver approached. Wrapped around the torso of each was a dark red tentacle, which tethered the body to the ground.

The Diver moved gracefully underwater, slow and deliberate. When he reached the first body, he took his drifting hand and gently

174

lifted the man's arm. Then he unsheathed his knife, slid it under the tentacle that was wrapped around the man's ribs, and began to saw. It was difficult work—and with every cut and plunge of the Diver's knife, the water became cloudy with jets of pus and decay.

Once the Diver had severed the tentacle, it released its grip and floated away. There was a flash of white light, and the drowned man closed his eyes in gratitude and let go of the Diver's hand. For a minute, he remained suspended in the water, his arms extended over his head as though he were stretching after a very long nap. After that he disappeared into a cone of golden, pulsing light. The boys looked up from their bathyscopes as the light lifted up and out of the water near their canoe, and then all was quiet, the Diver alone again in the putrid water, making his way to the next tethered soul.

"They continued this work for hours," Soren said, "with the boys on the surface, in their canoe, watching and marking off their map every time the Diver cleared an area of drowned souls. They were making progress, for sure. But there was something else the Diver had told them: the more souls they discovered and cut loose, the angrier the Soul Collector became. This often led to brutal, repetitive attacks on the Diver as he went about his work. One minute, he would be walking heavily across the seafloor as normal. The next, he would be set upon by angry tentacles—they wrapped around his ankles and wrists, tightened, and pulled—and he would be torn limb from limb."

"No," said the younger boy. For reasons Soren didn't understand, for his younger son had no injury, he had begun wearing a small Band-Aid across the bridge of his nose. Now he reached up and traced its wings with his fingers.

Soren took a sip of water. "It was awful, truly it was. It was a terrifying shock to see the Diver ripped apart, and they hadn't believed it would happen. But sure enough, near the end of the day, the Diver found himself overpowered by the Soul Collector's tentacles—and in horror they watched as he was torn at the joints, his arms and legs scattered while his torso and head were severed, then floated to the ground. The boys wanted to cry out, but kept quiet, for this is how they were supposed to be of help to him. Once everything had cleared—the tentacles no longer writhing and kicking up silt, the Diver's lantern still emitting its blue light to guide them—they dove from their boat to gather his parts. It was exhausting, but the tentacles

175

didn't recognize them as any sort of threat and left them alone to collect their friend."

Hana walked down the hall past the boys' room. She held the phone against her ear—Soren could tell by her tight shoulders she was upset—but when she saw they were watching, she flashed a thin smile and waved at the boys.

"I forgot she was here for a second," the older boy said.

"Hmmm," Soren said. "Where would she have gone?"

She gave them a thumbs-up, then turned and walked to the kitchen. There was a long silence. "Do you think she saw all the bags?" the younger boy asked his father. He was talking about the Ziplocs they'd washed and hung to dry before she'd come home. "I'm sure she did," Soren said.

All three kept their eyes on the doorway as though Hana might return any minute to congratulate them. But she didn't, so Soren began again.

Back in their neighborhood, the water was black and still. On the attic floor the boys arranged the Diver's arms and legs and helmet in the shape of a man, as he'd told them to do. They watched for hours, but nothing changed—his various parts just lay there like an empty suit. They zipped their sleeping bags together, to stay close as they slept. But they couldn't sleep, having no idea what would happen next.

He revived as dawn was breaking. Slowly, his arms had scooted closer to his torso, then his legs. Blue light flickered from his helmet and it too reattached. Then there was a sound like a great exhalation of air and the Diver sat up. He said nothing at first—methodically he moved each arm, his hand, his fingers. Finally, he stood and walked around the attic like a rusty old machine. He was certainly the worse for wear, but it was him. The boys were immensely relieved.

From then on, each day they set out according to a grid the boys had drawn of the town. The Diver plunged into the depths, the boys guiding him, and they watched as he released the souls of the drowned. Each man, woman, or child they freed was engulfed in a blinding, golden light, and lifted out of the water, then seen no more. Sometimes the tentacles attacked, sometimes they didn't. It was no longer shocking. If the boys had to swim after pieces of the Diver, they didn't mind. In fact, it made them feel useful, like they were working at a job only they could do.

But soon they began to notice that with each excursion the Diver seemed more spent, tired. He'd become sluggish in his movements, as though he were resigned to the monotony of his work. His blue light would dim, flicker, and only truly shine for a few minutes at a time. He'd begun to repeat himself, when he spoke at all. If they didn't tell him where to go, occasionally he would just stand under the water, still as a statue, as though he was puzzling through a serious problem in his mind. In the evening, when they'd returned to the attic, he'd slump in the corner and power down as though some old clock in his chest had become weary of keeping time. He never slept exactly—his feet, in iron shoes, would kick and his arms swatted at things neither boy could see. If they spoke to him, he would not answer.

One night, after he'd been still for a long time, the boys crept across the attic to get a closer look. His canvas suit had frayed at the elbows; his dull knife was caked in tentacle gore. The rotten smell he had begun to give off was intense, and they held their noses as they climbed over his legs. Carefully, they stood on their toes and peered through the forelight in his helmet. What they saw startled them: the Diver seemed to have no face. Inside his helmet was only a thick, black mist.

What had they expected to see? Periodically the mist in his helmet cleared and gave them a glimpse of something like unbounded space—a deep and shapeless darkness pricked with stars.

They tiptoed back to their sleeping bags. Both had the feeling that the mist had been trying to tell them something. But they had no idea what. In the morning, the Diver stood slowly and stretched. They exchanged pleasantries, got into the canoe, and went about their work. But the boys had begun to worry. They wished they'd never looked at all.

"How bad did it hurt when he got pulled apart?" said one of the boys. "A lot?"

"I'd imagine so," said Soren. "Pain like you can't really believe. He didn't like getting pulled to pieces, he'd just become used to it. Each time he stitched himself back together, the boys saw little lightning bolts fizzing from the seams of his suit, and at the end of each bolt was a tiny blue skull. He didn't talk with the boys about what he was feeling, though. In fact, he rarely spoke unless it was absolutely necessary to their mission. He was stuck in an endless cycle with the Soul

177

Collector, and it had become the only thing he could think about."

The younger boy stirred as though he was about to speak, but his brother put his fingers to his lips. "He can ask a question," Soren said. The younger boy thought for a second, and finally said, "It turns out I don't have a question."

"Can I ask you a question?" Soren said, and pointed to his nose.

"It makes him feel comfortable," the older boy explained.

"I'm OK," the younger boy said.

Soren nodded. "Anyway, while all this was happening, the Soul Collector had been gathering strength. He had grown infuriated by the Diver stabbing his tentacles and freeing people. After their last excursion, he'd followed the Diver and the boys to the attic, so he knew where they stayed at night." Soren cleared his throat. "And soon, in fact the night after the boys looked into the Diver's helmet, he attacked."

"Were they ready?" asked the younger boy.

"Not at all," said Soren. "He caught them completely by surprise. For a giant squid, he was quite a subtle swimmer. He moved without sound and expanded like a large red stain across the water, changing colors whenever he wanted to. If it was night, there was no chance you'd see him. So it was without any warning that he pulled the roof off the attic and began his battle with the Diver. His tentacles were enormous: each was the size of a barge's anchor line; every sucker was like a giant pair of closing lips. He squeezed one of his limbs around the Diver and brought him to his gnashing beak, but the Diver plunged his knife deep into the tentacle until it released its hold and he fell to the slick attic floor. The boys were terrified, but the tentacles did not reach for them just yet, and from where they sat huddled in the corner of the attic they could hear the Diver's heavy breath as he cut and slashed at the attacking squid. They believed in the Diver—he was doing well—but the Soul Collector was determined. He hissed and clicked his giant beak as his tentacles slapped the floor trying to hook the Diver's legs, and in the process smashed most of the attic to pieces."

"The whole house?" the older boy asked.

Soren nodded. "Destroyed. At that point, though, the house was the last thing on their minds. This battle went on and on. They were fighting for their lives, and the tide seemed to turn on each of them over the course of an hour. Eventually, however, it was clear to both boys the Diver was truly exhausted—and each time the Soul Collector pulled him closer and closer to his beak it took him longer to free himself. The boys froze. They had no idea what to do. Finally, the Soul Collector's remaining tentacles worked in tandem; they swept the Diver's legs and, in one smooth, unfurling motion, wrenched him off the floor by his feet. The Soul Collector opened his great black beak and the boys closed their eyes—they knew this was it for the Diver, and probably for them as well. But," Soren said, and coughed, "right at that moment, the Diver must've gotten the Soul Collector with a lucky stab—because with a high-pitched scream, the mysterious squid fell back into the water around their house and swam away. The attic was destroyed, but they'd survived."

"I have to go to the bathroom," the older boy said, and jumped off the bed. Soren moved his knees to let him by.

In the low light of the bedroom, his younger son hugged, then flattened, then hugged his pillow again. He looked so much like Hana that people stopped them on the street to comment on it. "What's on your mind?" Soren asked.

"Nothing," the boy said, hesitating. "Where are their parents?"

"Oh," Soren said. "Right." He clasped his hands together and looked to the window. It was late. The traffic sounds had gone almost completely away. "Give me a second," he said. He felt the answer coming, but before he could respond he heard the toilet flush and the older boy returned. "We'll get there," he said. He wiped at his nose. "Now, where was I?"

"The Soul Collector," the older boy said.

"Right. They'd survived the attack but no longer had a home, which made them sad. The Diver had been listening to what they were saying, and he sympathized. But now was not the time to think about that, he told them. Now was the time to follow the Soul Collector and finish what they'd started." Soren felt something in his chest tighten—this sometimes happened as he tried to bring his stories to a close and, because he'd forgotten to include some crucial detail or another, didn't quite know how to continue. The boys shuffled around in their beds until they found their old comfortable spots. They looked at him, waited. The feeling passed. "And so they did. They set out together to bring the Soul Collector and his horrid quest to an end."

By canoe, the trip took most of the morning—they paddled past upturned cars, small rainbow slicks of oil, the occasional fire. They paddled past the fifth floor of an office building whose windows were

179

blown out. The blue corona of light around the Diver's helmet flickered as he trailed one hand over the canoe's side and signaled to the boys by pointing where he wanted to go. They understood he was following the squid by reading the water, but how he was doing that remained a mystery. Soon, they saw nothing familiar. The sea was gray and leaden, and stretched in an unbroken line all the way to the horizon.

No birds called. The air was heavy with salt. The Diver held up his hand and the boys stopped paddling. What they heard was a sound not unlike the absence of sound, followed by a distant inhalation. Then a tremendous howling wind ripped across the water. It was the Soul Collector. As he whipped up the waves, everything became unrecognizable.

"The fight was brutal," Soren said. "The Soul Collector had lured them to his lair, and in the deep water the Diver was clearly at a disadvantage. The boys cheered for him, but had their doubts. The Soul Collector's lair was right on the edge of a huge, breathing fissure that opened like a jagged mouth in the earth; it sucked up large amounts of water then forcibly spit it out. The boys watched uneasily through their bathyscopes. The Diver slashed and cut and tried to stay away from the fissure, while the Soul Collector reached for him with a seemingly unlimited number of tentacles. It was impossible to say who was winning. They battled and battled. With each fresh wound the water became inky with the Soul Collector's blood, which the fissure sucked up like a vacuum and then expelled toward the boys. This darkness then blossomed and moved for them like the mist they'd seen inside the Diver's helmet. Soon the water grew so cloudy that the boys couldn't see what was happening at all." Soren paused, took a breath. "Meanwhile," he said, "the waves were really kicking up. The boys had to abandon their bathyscopes and lie on their backs in the canoe so they wouldn't tip over. As they went up one wave and down another, they held hands and closed their eyes. Though they could no longer see the Diver, they tried to imagine how the fight was playing out. They pictured him, exhausted, piercing the Soul Collector's tentacles with his knife. They saw him make slow slashing motions through the heavy water. Then, to their horror, they imagined his suit coming apart in the blue light of his helmet as he was pulled closer and closer to the Soul Collector's enormous chomping beak. They were afraid for the Diver, afraid for their lives. But,"

180

he said, "just as they were beginning to lose all hope, the waves churning around them settled and stopped and they heard a great shushing sound. All at once columns of golden light broke through the surface of water and lifted toward the night sky."

Soren shifted his weight on the bed. It was the only sound in the room.

"Soon, everything was quiet again, and when the water cleared, they looked over the canoe's side. The Soul Collector's foul tentacles were scattered everywhere and the large fissure had ceased its exhalations. They scanned the seafloor until they saw the Diver's helmet. Though no longer connected to his body, it still gave off its faint blue light and called the boys quietly to their work. Without a word, they stowed their paddles, stripped down to their underwear, and dove into the cold water to search for every piece of their friend. Sometimes they surfaced empty-handed, gasping, and clung to the gunwale to catch their breath before diving again. They gathered his arms, torso, and helmet into the bow of their canoe, hoisted his heavy legs from the water over the stern. The only part missing was his left boot; it must've been sucked into the fissure during the brutal battle. They looked until both were quivering from the cold and their vision went cloudy. Then they put their clothes back on, apologized, and, just as the sun was coming up, began to paddle in the direction of home."

"Was the Soul Collector gone?" the older boy asked.

Soren nodded. "The Diver had won only by feigning death and allowing himself to be swallowed whole. Once in that squid's rancid stomach, he'd kicked and cut his way out. However, before succumbing, the Soul Collector had managed one final time to pull the Diver apart—and that's why he was in pieces. After that, the Soul Collector crumpled into himself as though he were trying to fit somewhere small, and died. The fissure sucked him up."

"Good riddance," the younger boy said.

"My thoughts exactly," said Soren. "And that brings us almost to the end of the story."

They drifted and drifted. Every day, the boys woke with the hope that on the horizon they'd see land, or another boat, or . . . anything at all. But every day, they woke, hungry and thirsty, and saw nothing except brown, waveless water. The days grew infernally hot and the nights were frigid. They waited for the Diver to reconfigure himself, but the light was gone from his helmet, and he never did. His canvas suit baked in the sun until it no longer gave off any smell. After a week of paddling, they understood that the Diver wasn't coming back and that they were all alone. They had no idea what would happen next, and that made them afraid.

One night, after two aimless weeks on the water, they woke to a sharp buzzing sound. It came from the front of the canoe, where the Diver's parts lay in a heap. The sound was like static from a radio, and they held each other as the pieces of his body began to hum and glow with the blue light they thought they'd never see again.

For a long time they watched the front of the canoe with excitement and held their breath at every flash of light. But eventually it became clear that something was wrong. For one thing, the Diver's parts would not stitch together. For another, when he finally did talk, his voice sounded like it was coming from the bottom of a deep well, and they could not understand a single thing he said. Saddened, they lifted his helmet and placed it on the seat like a lantern. Through the forelight, they could see the mist had returned. His corselet began to glow. They wanted to make sense out of what he was trying to tell them, but he spoke of things they'd never seen and never would see. As the night went on, they found they didn't mind so much that they couldn't understand what he was saying. It was reassuring simply to hear his voice again. For hours they listened. They asked questions, and tried to piece together his answers. By morning, his light went out for good.

The boys were quiet. "What happened after that?" the younger one finally asked.

"Well," Soren said. "Next day, they saw an island in the distance, and figured the Diver had somehow led them to it. They began paddling for those dark hills." Soren wiped his hands on the legs of his pants, then clapped his palms to his knees. The boys were watching him closely, but he wasn't sure what might come next. "The world was new. That's all," he finally said. "It was theirs to start." Soren saw the island exactly—a steep, volcanic ledge, climbing out of the sea—and he saw the canoe heading for it, then the story slipped away. He sensed that a great amount of time was passing and it felt like nothing at all.

"Were their parents there?" the younger boy asked.

"Oh," Soren said. "Of course they were. They'd been waiting. And they missed the boys so much."

182

The air in the bedroom felt suddenly thick. Soren could tell that neither boy was satisfied with the story, and he himself felt as though he'd arrived somewhere unexpected and unresolved—but it was late and he could think of nothing else to say.

"Good night," he finally announced, and stood. He gently pressed the back of his hand to each of their cheeks, then walked across the room, shut the door.

In the kitchen, Soren poured himself a finger of Scotch and began to straighten the counter. There wasn't much to do; Hana had gotten there first. He swept some crumbs from the toaster into his hand and dumped them in the sink. Then he turned out the lights and stood in the darkness. It hadn't been his intention to tell them a story creased with such loneliness. What he'd wanted was to tell them a story about brothers, one that pushed *against* despair. He'd done that, but it hadn't gone as planned.

He found Hana in their bedroom lying quietly on the floor. "My back," she said. Her eyes were closed as she concentrated on the pain. "How'd the campaign fare today?" Soren asked.

"Oh, you know. *Knock knock.* Not interested. I must've walked ten miles. Say 'climate' and watch the door close. It's depressing. The world's ending and nobody cares."

Soren took off his shoes and lay down next to her. Through the thin carpet he felt the hard, wooden floor. Hana opened her eyes. "What's the matter?" she asked. "You look like you've seen the Ghost of Christmas Past."

"No," Soren said. "I'm just thinking about something." She reached over and squeezed his hand. She was ready to talk. But whatever it was that he wanted to say kept moving away from him like a silver, glinting fish. He closed his eyes. Relaxing music was playing from Hana's phone at a low volume. He imagined a small, blue light, pulsing. He imagined diving into his wife's body, crawling down her spine, and looking at the painful spot in her back with a powerful underwater lamp.

"It really does feel like the world is ending," he finally said. "But it can't be."

"Well," Hana said. "Let me tell you about an *important* election coming up in *your* district. . . ." She stretched and sighed. "I hung up on Chloe. She called me a hypocrite for bringing children into the world."

Ethan Rutherford

"Why would she say that?"

"She's just angry," Hana said. "She doesn't know who to blame."

Their apartment was small, and from his vantage on the floor Soren could see down the dark hallway. One of the boys had left his bed and was now flipping the light switch to make his brother laugh. On, off, on again. Soren watched the light flash under their closed bedroom door like a signal from a secret lantern.

"Go to sleep," Hana called from the floor, not unkindly. He heard a sharp yelp and scampering and one more stifled laugh. Then they were quiet.

"I love this life," she said. "I regret none of it. I just want everything to last a little longer."

Soren nodded and closed his eyes. He felt the hard surface beneath his shoulders expand to curl around him like a boat. *You would hear the wave,* he thought, *before you saw it.* But was that true? He tried to make his body as still as possible. It was an old, old trick. Outside, streets were wet and the temperature was dropping. Beyond that was something he couldn't touch. The story was over. But, of course, it had also just begun. He reached for Hana's hand, found it. She curled her fingers around his thumb. Suddenly, on the carpet next to them, her phone began to quake and vibrate like a robot's heart.

"Don't pick it up," Soren said.

"I won't," Hana said. She stretched and yawned. Her eyes were closed too. "I wouldn't dream of it."

Near, and Nearer Now
Arra Lynn Ross

IT IS EARLY APRIL. Night's small snow lines the deck, the lips of open narcissi, the new roof. Over the high, thick buds of maple, mad in wind, darker thicknesses of cloud move fast. From the kitchen, my husband on his banjo, working a song he's worked for years. Then, quiet. From the library, cat teeth on hard kibble. On the blue-and-white rug, the dogs, at my feet, gather, while in the far field, snow on feathered wings, comes, farther down, the dragon.

I drag, from the back porch, the cold five-gallon plastic bucket, bent awkwardly, shuffling, with the handle between my spread legs. The water sloshes, wets my jeans at the knee. Silver and green, a slick fin quivers, folds close to the wide, black-spotted back, and the gold around a black pupil flashes.

*

I first translate the Old Norse's cosmogenic/apocalyptic poem, *Völuspá*'s last stanza like this:

> In that place, comes, inside the dimming,
> dragon, flying-breath,

snake-bright, flashing bright, shimmer-shiver from below

from the dark-moon, from the mountains;

Naked, bare, she carries on in motion towards, with
feathers

—over the field—

higher down.

Now remember, she comes down.

*

That is where the whole poem ends.

*

I want to point out something of interest, using two words from the original text.

"*Dreki fljúgandi*" could be simply translated as dragon flying, or dragon-ship flying. However, here, I'm interested in the second word, in which "*-andi*" is added to "*fljúga*" (to fly), or *fljúg* (flight), to make it a present participle, thus, "flying." Andi, though, in and of itself means, I read, *spirit*, or *breath*. Thus, in the Old Norse language, adding spirit or breath makes something move continuously in the continuous present moment.

The other word I'd like to point out is in the third line, *"naðr,"* which translates as snake or serpent, and is used to describe the *"dreki."* However, when added as a suffix at the end of a word, *-naðr* acts to change a verb, or even an adjective, into a noun.

Thus, the serpent gives body and form to a movement or quality, this language implies.

For example, to dance + serpent = the dance.

Or, of the earlier one: to dance + breath = dancing.

*

H. J. Rob Lenders and Ingo A. W. Jannsen point out that the grass snake, which lived symbiotically, physically, and symbolically, with humans for millennia, suffered after the advent of Christianity. They write that "probably the single most important symbol of pre-Christian chthonic fertility gods, the grass snake, was turned into the number one enemy of the one and only heavenly God."

In Scandinavia, in 1555 AD, the Swedish Archbishop Olaus Magnus, in his copious *Historia de Gentibus Septentrionalibus,* wrote, in Volume II, Book 21, Chapter Forty-Eight, of these "pet serpents, which in the farthest tracts of the North have the reputation of protective deities. They are reared on cows' or sheep's milk, play with the children indoors, and regularly are seen sleeping in their cradles like faithful guardians. To harm these creatures is regarded as sacrilege.

"However, such practices are survivals from ancient superstition, and since the adoption of the Catholic faith are completely forbidden."

*

The grass snake is also known as a water snake (Natrix means "of water"). It likes to eat fish, and can raise its head far above the water while swimming. Dark bodied, but with a gold ring around its neck.

It lived with humans for so long because heat hatches its eggs. Best are places that give heat as they decay: cattle dung, compost piles, barns with manure piles. Or else, near ovens.

*

My mother calls to tell me this dream:

She was tall, very tall, like seven feet tall, wearing an obsidian wet suit with gold at the top. She looked like the mosaic in the Swedish capital city hall. In my dream it was night. I was standing in the driveway wearing my black insulated gloves and a coat. I was on the right side of the driveway. To my left, standing on the snow, the figure asked me if I knew who she was. She said, "Do you know who I am?" I replied, "The lady of the lake," with assurance.

She said, "I have seen you with the ice in your fists. What do you intend to do when you make a fist and ice appears in your fist?" "Let go," I replied. I let go in my dream and a fish fell onto the snow. It was a cod (you know this is the fish of the Norse mythology). I made a lot of fish (you know, they're all lying on the snowbank). She said, "Yes, what you do with your hands, you can bring to market."

*

I pull my enormous unabridged 1960s *Webster's New International Dictionary* down on my lap, intending to open it randomly to find any old verb to use as another example, as dance did in a few paragraphs above. However, it opens to page twenty-nine, and my eyes, of their own accord, fall upon the word *adder*, which it says derived from Anglo-Saxon *naedre*, snake, "akin to" Old Norse *naðr*, and Latin *natrix*, water snake. Apparently, the loss of the "n" was a mistake.

*

The next day, the rain comes down hard and the power goes. I rip three small flowering twigs from the ends of my quince and put them in a tiny pale-blue bottle, a cube, with bubbles trapped in the glass. The pale five-petaled flowers are infused with an almost imperceptible pink just where the petal widens, then curls either inward, or out.

Paler, but not much, than the blush where bone joint meets breast, the inward curve against tendon, against rose-shivered skin, where the smallest feathers, delicate, round as petals, and, like petals, or leaves, traversed with increasingly fine and many-branching rivers. Calamus, I read, is the word for the hollow shaft from which these filaments spring. Here, in the down (*dünn*, in Old Norse), the calami bend inward, their pearl-fingernail-horn translucence cupping the feather petals toward skin.

The field is wet. The hollow shafts of bluestem and their empty awns, soaked dark gold. I have yet to cut them so their spring shoots can grow. By the time I get to the far field, my jeans squeak, cling hard, cold wetness burning my thighs.

*

Dansarens häll, the Dancer Stone, Cambrian sandstone bedrock carved on thousands of years ago, at Järrestad, in Sweden, has at least five serpents, along with ships with

190

upraised serpent-like heads. One *naðr* has a deeply spiraled tail, and another, the most intriguing, has two parallel lines forming the snake's thick body, two deep meanders, the tail a quick spiral, its head resting against a shoe.

*

Should I talk about the pink ball of the child's foot? Less pink, the thick paint, there, than on the dragon/*dreki*'s shoulder, though about the same shade where the long face tucks to the curled neck.

This is from the church sculpture of the Madonna from Edshult's Church/Kyrka in Småland, Sweden, carved between 1325 and 1350 AD.

The figure, under her feet, is pink as the child's upturned sole, as the top layer of cracked paint that remains on her bared breast, where the child's hand rests.

The tail, curled in one loop, touches her right shoe, disappears beneath the robe's once blue folds. The body thickens, Mary's left foot on its shoulder, above a small arm tucked beneath the head, much like a cat. The ears, laid back against its curved neck, long as a rabbit's, ripple, thin to a fleshy point.

191

The paint has worn from the face, from the brow, from the open almond eyes. The subtle bridge of a long face, like a deer's, sheared off, broken, at mouth and nose.

*

Action: I'm trying to tell you there is a dragon in my field.

Action: I'm trying to tell you, far, with pasqueflowers.

Action: I'm trying to tell you "naked, bare, unsheathed."

*

Is it useful to add that Tacitus, in his 98 AD *Germania*, comments that "the Germans do not think it in keeping with the divine majesty to confine gods within walls or to portray them in the likeness of any human countenance"?

*

Níð höggr, nái is the line I struggle with most, in the last stanza of the poem. *Nái.* Corpse. Most translators agree, and yet . . .

What if we considered other instances of *nái*, as a preposition, of *ná*, thus meaning *near, close, nigh.*

In the Old Icelandic dictionary, I read that *nái* is a plural of *nár*, as an accusative (i.e., object of a verb), thus, carries *the dead*.

But, as a verb, it means "to get hold of, to reach, overtake, to obtain."

Or, as a version of *nári*, feeder, nourisher.

There does seem to be held, in the word, simultaneously, a sense of life, death, and something passing between, from one to the other.

*

Outside, another butterfly, small, moves on strange wings, over the greening grass. The tulips, warm and red, open.

I appreciate Ursula Dronke's note: "This is a very rare image. The late Otto Pächt assured me that he knew of no representation of a dragon bearing bodies in its wings."

*

Perhaps we should talk about those wings.

Berr sér í fjöðrum. Let's take it word by word, and see what unfolds:

Arra Lynn Ross

Berr: bare, naked (in the open air); open, clear, manifest.

In the Old Norse poem *Vafthrudnismál,* stanza forty-seven, second line, "berr" is translated as "to birth" when the old sun gives birth to her daughter, the new sun who "will ride / as the gods are dying / the old paths of her mother."

sér: a reflective pronoun meaning (1) for oneself, separately, singly, (2) in a distributive sense, each by himself, each separately, sometimes each of them singly.

í: (1) in, within; in a certain spot; in, among; during, in; denoting action, state, condition; in respect of, in regard to; denoting form or content; by means of, through; (2) with: in, into; of time: in, during; denoting entrance into a state, condition; denoting change (*into*); denoting the purpose.

fjöðrum: from, I think *fjöðr* (gen. *fjaðrar,* pl. *fjaðrar*), a feminine noun meaning (1) feather, quill; (2) fin or tail of a fish ; (3) blade of a spear.

*

Bare naked, gives birth, oneself changing into feathers—or, into a fish, or, into a spear—

*

There are no dreki/dragons with wings in the old stories. Only big serpents. Wings and feathers belong solely to prey ravens and swans/egrets, never even to Valkyries, who fly upon (unwinged) horses. Wings belong to the swan-maiden tales, and to Freyja in her *fiaðrhamr*, or "feather body garment," as Dronke translates it.

I find, in that Old Icelandic dictionary (so similar to Old Norse) that *hamr* means (1) skin, slough; as in *"hleypa hömum,"* to cast the slough (of snakes); and (2) shape, form. Further, *hamramr* means to be able to change one's shape, and *ham-remi*, a feminine word, means "the state of being *hamramr*," while *hams*, itself, means simply "snake's slough."

Here, then, we have a mixed thing: the feather garment and the snake skin are one.

Shape-changers—

*

I go back to the oldest source. One can find the last stanzas of the *Völuspá*, within the *Poetic Edda, Codex Regius*, a picture of the gray-brown vellum calfskin, online.

The stanzas are not broken up. Instead, the stanza shift is indicated by a capital letter only there. One period, and no other capital letters are found within the work.

It reads something like this:

Par kōe in dimi dreki naðra nap [jʔ]a [zʔ] nʔ ne[jʔ] [smudged here, too much, to read] *m / nipa mollō. ber* [or is it *bek*ʔ] *ser imoprō* [or *ö*] *plygr vaill yr niphagr* [this is a bit blurred]/ *nai nu m h s Seyagz* [blurred].

The translations we have of the *Völuspá* are a compilation of blurred letters and words drawn from two different manuscripts—the Eddic and the Hauksbók.

*

Here is the most honest translation I can make, for what has previously been accepted, and translated as a corpse-bearing monster from the underworld:

There at that place cows in dimness dragon snake floating
[   ] / dark-moon dust. To bear, to carry, [or, to adorn the bench] each ember flies [the field] yew tree dark-down-giving-wise-counsel-to-put-right / near, and nearer now [   ]

*

The "dragon" carving is rough, a gashed cross on the flat below an eye, a deeper gash where bent head meets arched neck. Still, the wood shines, worn soft by much touch.

The almond-shaped eyes are carved like the eyes of mother and child, but without delineated upper lids. Still, the long, curved brow and turn to the bridge of nose are very similar, just softer, wider, in the dragon.

Open, the bare eyes, though the gesture of cheek upon small toes placed side by side, under, is quiet, is careful.

*

Some paint remains in the inner elbow and triangle of tucked-up paw, where the head rests. The undercoat is silvery pink marred with small cracks, as in old plaster. On top of the pale pink, a wash of wide, darker pink stripes on which, in warm red, someone has painted the pattern of scales, or maybe feathers, or petals, like a child would draw, each made with a long U, inside of which three or four lines, evenly spaced, brush down from the open end to the curve. The scales do not touch, and between the rows of scales, on the pale pink, is a row of evenly spaced red dots.

*

Arra Lynn Ross

For the Japanese artist Yayoi Kusama, the dot "is a vortex into another universe." It is "a way into infinity." It "has the form of the sun, which is a symbol of the energy of the whole world and our living life, and also the form of the moon, which is calm."

"Round, soft, colorful, senseless, and unknowing," said Kusama.

The dots on Scandinavian Bronze Age rock carvings, some argue, are also for the sun. They call them "cup marks." Such marks are found in rock carvings all over the world.

At Järrestad, not far from the serpents, a rich splattering, deeply ground, some a little bigger, some smaller, rise up the Cambrian slope. It feels good to run a thumb down them. They seem more or less evenly spaced. At the top of the long, thick column of dots, two feet, heels together, point down, each toe also a deeply ground, very circular, dot.

*

At other carvings, a dot between the legs marks, some think, *woman.*

*

My mother, a girl, pulls her knees up and over onto the hayloft of the barn. Bits of broken straw bite the fat of her thumb, the cap of her knee. Once free of the ladder hole, she scoots a little farther, then pulls her feet beneath her. She hears the bodies of cows, from below, moving against each other, a snort, a single low.

It is not dark up here, as she had feared. Shafts of moon fall from chinks in the vaulted ceiling onto piles of loose hay. She scoots to a close, narrow shaft; inside, she arches her fingers back and palms up till the lines etched in skin disappear.

A fleck of chaff dust floats down, sparks—a stirred ember. In the half-second flare, she sees, in minute detail, her own face wear away to become, first, fire of sun's innermost parts simmering over a hundred millennia to surface, then flying, light, swift minutes to touch moon's black basalts and crushed breccia facets, to cross, reflected, the bare second to the ceiling's open crack, and trace, now, the girl's near palm: rose-shivered flesh where even the smallest filaments—feathers, hairs, dragon scales—traversed with fine and many-branching rivers—are hallowed.

Fragility
Catherine Imbriglio

Fossilized imprints of raindrops like appreciating rain in the abstract and
   falling under a spell

*

Undertook to overtake and absorb the basis of the familiar
Forced into myself large gray clouds and a long strip of yellow light pressuring
   the clouds on behalf of the water horizon

*

Only a month for the fire and ice hydrangeas to transform impostor ice into
   impostor fires
Too much or not enough rain, along the lines of the great medieval floods,
   famines, droughts
What is handing off the future if not the body as the soul's default

*

My brain takes pleasure smuggling randomness into and out of congruity
We called our leaders worms, then realized we were insulting worms
Rain or shine, I spritz mornings onto myself, as part of my daily ablutions
Disturbed by the swans' warning sounds, I hiss back as if to ward off
   indignant water spirits

Catherine Imbriglio

*

Each lack of rainfall has its begging vernacular
On fast-forward legs, the back-and-forth sandpipers negotiate the water's edge
    enviably
There were malignant cuts in the eroding bluffs as if by giant claws of a
    monster cat
Because there are moons, many people do not go through their lives
    unaccompanied
Why are the origins of earth's water so humbling

*

When wiping up spills I contemplate linguistic exchange values
Heavy rain is one consolation that could require another consolation
How much will machine learning affect my internalized belief systems
Since with the power of retaliation, all numbers are born compromised
Seized upon rein, rain, reign to examine homophonic parts of my monster
    identity
The way humpback whales hunting fish with bubble nets make an example
    of water culture

*

What is the basis for so many fiendish faces in so many disparate crowds
My dog, fast asleep, used my thigh for a pillow, emulating tenderness
By eliminating fillers, am I overestimating strategic deployment of filters
Tapped my mug as if establishing the beat establishing the beat oh yeah
    establishing
Shadow companies underestimate the land's elongation of monster shadow
    companions
Displaced strict appearance to clear nasal passages by breathing in steam
So as to bend into the future rather than being dragged by my breath into it

Catherine Imbriglio

*

Roots of spruce trees germinated in leaf debris on top of granite rocks now
    hiding the granite
Afraid to follow the creek through the underbrush because I need
    necromantic shoes
More than unnerved by sketchy likenesses emerging from the looming birch,
    spruce, pine
What in your most beloved story breaks down your sense of the foundational
In crisis moments a monstrous base breaks up everyday politeness exposing
    irremediable fissures
I raise my hand to the sky, as if warding off slaphappy cloud displacements
Sea therefore land has not always been the case
When straddling the tide line, I am reminded of a border's cognitive
    dissonance

*

Last chance to keep belief systems from going under the weather
Pop-up monster memories make bedtime meanings even more creepy
Hung on to the birches as if I could peel away strips of morning like bark
Now decorating a niece's home, the grandfather and mantel clocks tick away
    their previous owners' displacements
As on the quarter hour, routine chiming, as if neither person had once lived or
    once died
Splaying one line under another line, I sense the premises become shakier
What happens as grace stirs up a mirror monster under the banner of time
Over patterns of rainfall the cove's moral centers being brought to bear
But not long before any attempts at corrective forgiveness become much like
    rain you no longer hear

*

Catherine Imbriglio

At the bus terminal, I was first in line, but it was the wrong line
The rainstorm felt bitter like a monster amplified
All along, you could have traced inclement elements incubating in the
  infectious
As the structure itself descends into madness I
What did one wall say to the other wall
The fall is not fortunate, if like leaves, I am in danger of turning on and/or
  into an amorphous passenger
Inhabiting the sacred are monsterbirds distending the day in the day out
As when forms of delicacy and small duration October light
Falls one wall upon another wall
Holy, wholly, en masse, to smuggle in as patchwork for the disintegrating

*

Shocked by water shrinking the human, making it difficult to wear
Imagined I controlled myself by matching a damaged creature's tears
Trying to distinguish between normal and abnormal in approaches to the
  horrifying
Does doomed biology generate any sympathy for the criminal
Complicit in whitewashing as when the natural calls up the unnatural
So as to push back on intention limits, for when the drowned boy reappears
Again and again, always the structure falling apart always the villain always
  vanishing
As when, under the circumstances, you go right through the other as desire
  murdering a desire
Then into, then beyond, what brackets the self as marked as unmarked as
  vanquishing
As when, with any minute, you suspect yourself as rain, as corporeal fluidity
  transmogrified
From whence that leviathan, what is it to turn into, in what form will
  renewable monstrosity next reappear

*

203

Catherine Imbriglio

To rein in at the last millisecond by not overstaying in the natural habitats of
the transgressive
Moody surrogates after the near implosion come back as raindrops no longer
gestating
As when I cultivate restraint in my undercurrents for the sake of ensuring fish
continuity, company

Over the years, trees bracketing the cove have not relinquished the many
failures they have witnessed

October light's intensified colors make a monster looking into the human
even the more threatening

Hoping that balance using a walking stick is still balance
Though one winter, chasing my dog, I sank in the mudflats and had to be
rescued

Each day meaning evaporates from the cove and then comes back down in
another form
The very foundation becoming more and more penetrable

I already heard that, I respond, when my dog undertakes a noisier sigh

Does a memory recognize when it is no longer required

Memory like a retreating wave that leaves part of itself behind

The Care and Feeding of Minotaurs
James Morrow

MY WOOLLY MANED LION, golden as wheat and fully engorged, places his paws against my shoulder blades. Poised on hands and knees, I sway like one of Daedalus's ingenious suspension bridges, but there is nothing precarious about our arrangement. With his cock my lover nudges aside the petticoats of my lioness disguise, its fabrics imbued with the scent of a feline in heat (this philter is another of Daedalus's creations), rather the way a slave might part the curtains of my royal litter, allowing me to step onto the streets of Knossos.

The cat and I connect. He takes care not to claw my back. We roar in unison. He licks my hair and nibbles my earlobes, fiercely but with panache. I work my fingers into the sheepskin rug, seizing great tufts of fleece, and squeeze, squeeze, squeeze. Yes, our tryst partakes of raw animal lust, but it also boasts a certain aromatic rapport, the joys of cross-species communication. He doesn't understand that he's screwing the queen of Crete, and he wouldn't be impressed if he knew, for tonight we matter to each other on a plane beyond primitive desire or mere political station.

Our passion consumes itself, and, still wearing my disguise and moving on all fours, I lead the golden lion onto the balcony beyond my bedchamber. He springs, landing in an oak bush, then drops to the rocky earth outside the palace. The darkness enfolds him, and he sprints toward the chalky, moonstruck hills beyond. Soon we shall be afloat, drifting from the isle of Crete to the continent of Hypnos, borne by our memories of the evening's tender bestiality. Call me Potnia Theron, mistress of the animals.

As the year progressed, I worked my way through the whole pungent wardrobe that Daedalus had constructed for me. Night after night I took carnal satisfaction in our local mammals, repeatedly transmuting into a she-bear, a she-goat, a she-wolf, a tigress, a mare, and, of course, my preferred persona, the lioness. We gave ourselves to experimentation and through practice achieved every position to which we

205

aspired—partner prone, partner supine, sideways, crosswise, athwart, canine. O faithful reader, I urge you to withhold your censure. Unless you've lain with the great cats—unless you've taken the bruin kind to your bed, coupled with a ram, or shagged a horse—I urge you not to judge me.

Banished by the king of Athens for sleeping with a royal concubine, Daedalus had passed a full year sailing the Gulf of Corinth in search of a new home, ultimately settling on these shores, where he pursued a lifestyle so prodigal as to shame the gods. With their intricate stitchery, cunning ball-and-socket joints, and interlocking bronze fasteners, his mammal costumes were priced to sustain his spendthrift ways. Happily for Daedalus, the royal treasury was sufficiently fat that I could patronize him beyond his wildest dreams.

Future historians will probably assume that my husband, not I, was the reigning monarch of Crete, when Kitanetos was in fact a mere minos, the consort of She Who Rules. He nevertheless thought of himself as sovereign over our empire, and the courtiers and I condescended to play along, even to the point of calling him King Minos. I could have done worse than Kitanetos. He was a good father to our six children, an effective admiral in the naval wars that gave us Crete and its many provinces, a shrewd player in the game of politics (his patience with administrative details spared me countless hours of ennui), and an astute collaborator with the dozen or so master builders commissioned to enhance our island with magnificent architectural achievements.

Many were the marvels whose construction Minos oversaw, from the Arena of Tylissos to the Hippodrome of Vathypetro, the Lighthouse of Amnisos to the Library of Phaistos, but none was more impressive than the subterranean Labyrinth of Eileithyia. Daedalus himself drew up the plans. Minos intended the maze as a stone prison in which political rivals and captured enemy soldiers would spend their remaining days in torment, dying of starvation, madness, loneliness, or some combination of the three. Not content to distribute the passageways and culs-de-sac along a single plane, Daedalus designed and executed a three-tiered maze riddled with vertiginous stairways, narrow bridges, and warped mirrors affixed to the damp walls. Everyone agreed that with the Labyrinth of Eileithyia our Athenian artificer had given the world his masterpiece.

"I call it the Mother of Puzzles," he told his patron, and King Minos was well pleased.

The most demonic of Daedalus's innovations, surely, was his

decision to make the labyrinth insoluble. This unholy construction, not so much an edifice as a torture machine, had neither a center nor an exit. The prisoner's only hope lay in somehow finding his way back to the entrance. To prevent all possibility of escape, royal guards equipped with maps, food, and torches would lead the blindfolded victim deep into the bowels of the machine. After a weeklong journey, the guards would issue their charge a brace of firebrands, give him a loaf of bread and a jar of water, and leave him to his fate.

Throughout the five-year interval that elapsed between the dedication of the labyrinth and the birth of our third daughter, Princess Acacallis, Minos and I enjoyed nothing that might be called connubial relations. We didn't care. Neither of us missed the other in bed. He had his concubines, and I had my menagerie. It was a well-anchored arrangement, and meanwhile the realm flourished.

Let me tell you something else the historians will get wrong. They will say my carnal requirements could be traced to a spell placed on me by the god Poseidon. Hearken, o my posterity. Eschew all pundits, prophets, and chroniclers who describe the female sex as naturally circumspect in its passions or, conversely, incapable of erotic restraint. My wardrobe, thick furred and many clawed, did not connote a woman under a curse. I went to the zoo because I liked it.

Indeed, not long after my seventh session with the golden lion, I found I didn't really need Daedalus's elaborate getups. Mammals of the male sex were spontaneously drawn to me, probably in consequence of my own spell-casting powers (though I would never be as competent a sorceress as my sister Circe or my niece Medea). I promised myself that, before withering into a crone, I would savor every sensation the wild had to offer, and if the historians were scandalized, too bad.

Cretan sunrises are dazzling affairs, Lord Helios snapping his whip above the flowing manes of his chariot team, the flail tearing through the membrane of the sky to release torrents of red and purple. Throughout each such spectacle King Minos and I normally ate fresh fruit and drank watered wine on the eastern balcony of the palace, reciting poetry to one another, pondering the latest political crisis, and discussing—in the days before they went forth into the world—how best to raise the children (this was something of a joke, as we left most parenting details to the discretion of nursemaids and tutors). But this particular morning was different. For once Minos had something momentous on his mind.

"I have asked Poseidon to send us a bull."

This last word gets my attention.

"I hope you're not planning to kill him," I said.

"The Lord of the Trident has bestowed many boons on the House of Minos. He arranged my numerous naval victories. He stocked our seas with crabs, lobsters, oysters, octopuses, and cuttlefish. Our enemies will not soon regroup, nor will our subjects go hungry."

Cuttlefish. The word excited me.

"There is no other choice, Pasiphaë. We must reciprocate Poseidon's favors with a sacrifice."

In his maritime wanderings, Daedalus had beheld many marvels, and he never tired of telling me about them. I would not soon forget his account of the immense cuttlefish—he'd called it a giant squid—that nearly wrecked his ship. It now crossed my mind that one day I might enlarge the palette of my appetites to include cephalopods.

"I have a better idea," I said. "Rather than sacrifice a bull, let us direct Daedalus to design and build a great aquarium. We shall consecrate it to Poseidon and populate the tanks with mighty octopuses and giant squid."

But Minos was having none of it, and so it happened that, late the following afternoon, I watched him pace back and forth at low tide on the beach near Agia Pelagia, as Poseidon, visiting my husband in a dream, had instructed him to do. From the wet sand rose an olfactory cacophony of stranded kelp, drowned crabs, and empty tortoise shells. The setting sun turned the sea into a cauldron of molten emeralds.

For the first time since we'd conceived Princess Acacallis, Minos and I held hands, the better to maintain regal tranquility in the face of a supernatural event. The coming of the sacred bull happened by degrees. With his heavily muscled legs the creature stroked his way through the coruscating waves. On reaching the shallows, he gained his footing and strode slowly toward us, salt water sliding off his back like dribbles of wax shed by an immense candle. His muscles twitched and rippled beneath a hide of the purest white. His eyes were iridescent rubies, his horns a gleaming silver lyre.

"How beautiful art thou," I said. "Thy name shall be called Lyreox."

Cautiously the white bull and I took the measure of one another. We trembled in unison. It was love, or something very much like it, at first sight.

"To kill such an animal would be to blaspheme the natural world,"

James Morrow

I told the king. "Surely we can honor Poseidon without slandering creation."

Minos fixed on the albino visitation. His face betrayed perplexity leavened with wonderment. In his own prosaic way he was as enamored as I.

"Crete is home to a thousand bulls, many as large as Lyreox, though none so white," said the King. "We shall bring a different animal to the altar in tribute to Poseidon. This Lyreox will live out his days in the cattle barns of Knossos and the pastures of Archanes."

"Perhaps you would like to consult a concubine in the matter. Phenomoe, is she your current favorite? Or is it Clea?"

"You have your spies, Pasiphaë, and I have mine. They inform me your lovers are many and so are their legs."

"Might I offer you my prediction, dear husband? Our subjects will venerate their king and queen for sparing this holy creature, even as they treat him like a minor deity. Whenever Lyreox takes his recreation in Archanes, the people will bring him heaping portions of their harvests."

The bull bellowed in assent.

By now my slaves were accustomed to the queen's eccentricities, so they neither asked questions nor lifted eyebrows when, three days later, I issued yet another directive concerning a quadruped. Shortly after sunset, they bridled the white bull in his barn and brought him to a moss-quilted glade beyond the western rampart of Knossos. I was waiting for them. Lyreox and I exchanged lascivious glances. He was already distended. My slaves vanished into the darkening air. I undid my bejeweled gown and molted for my panting consort, the fabric slithering from my shoulders to my loins to the ground.

Normally whenever I took a new animal lover, I appealed to his instincts by presenting rearward, but Lyreox had a different idea. He lay on his back, and I impaled myself, as ecstatic a skewering as might be imagined. My nostrils rejoiced in his scent, a fusion of brine, damp hide, and the viscous nectar of his sex. We made love until the sun came up, pausing occasionally to satisfy another sort of hunger. Lyreox champed the grasses. I consumed my fruit and cheese and drank my skin of watered wine. We parted with an understanding that this would not be our last liaison.

The days coalesced into weeks, the weeks became fortnights, and the bull and his Potnia Theron continued to partake of one another.

209

James Morrow

In time I realized I'd become the object not only of Lyreox's passion but also his fertility. The disquieting facts—my heightened sense of smell, the nausea that plagued me each morning, the cessation of my monthly courses—admitted of but one interpretation.

The Lord of the Trident was to blame, of course, causing me to become with child against all known principles of sexual reproduction. My pregnancy would salve both Poseidon's fury at Minos for placing the wrong bull on the altar and his disgust with me for my multiple seductions of Lyreox. Not only would the king suffer the shame of having a wife who evidently copulated with bulls, but the queen would be cursed with a hybrid child—a hideous creature, no doubt, congenitally unable to speak, reason, or function in the human world.

In his naivete Minos at first attributed my ever-expanding belly to gluttony. Only after his spies reminded him of my predilection for other species did he infer the obvious.

"I'm told that yet another trollop has come to Knossos," he said as, seated in the royal recreation room, we made ready to amuse ourselves with Gods and Heroes, a board game that the king and I played at least once a week.

"Fidelity, dear husband, is hardly the star by which you navigate this marriage."

Today Minos would move the marble figurines representing the twelve immortals, while I commanded Herakles, Bellerophon, Prometheus, and nine other demigods.

"This harlot presumes to sleep in the palace and call herself a queen." As his opening gambit, Minos dispatched his Hephaestus to square seven.

"I stopped counting after Phenomoe, Clea, Dora, Hestia, Eurydameia, and Oleria."

My circumference had expanded so greatly that I'd summoned from the royal stables my personal groom, the good-hearted and half-witted Rusa, to move my pieces for me. It wasn't as if the boy had other tasks, for his mistress was obviously not about to do anything equestrian.

"Place my Harmonia on square eleven," I commanded Rusa, and he immediately complied.

"I shall be the laughingstock of all civilization." Minos slid his Ares to square thirteen. "If I ever catch you alone with the bull from the sea, I shall cast you into the Eileithyian Labyrinth, an action whose righteousness this entire realm will instantly affirm."

210

"I know three princes who would demur," I said icily. "Three princesses as well."

My husband deployed his Artemis on square nineteen. "As for your precious Lyreox, tomorrow I shall send him to the Tylissos Arena, something I should have done long ago. It will be his thankless task to amuse oafish laborers and crude fishermen."

"I never asked for my present condition, Lord Minos. Can you not have pity on me?"

"Poor old Lyreox, careening around the ring while some foolish acrobat turns somersaults on his rump."

"I fear this hybrid will be incapable of rational thought. I fear it will look so hideous as to dry up my milk and stay my affections. Or perhaps I shall die on the birthing bed, never to see the face and form of my youngest child."

This litany evidently sparked something like sympathy in Minos's heart, and he offered me the semblance of a smile. "I shall instruct the priests of Asklepios to secure your survival," he said softly, brushing my hand. "Your Dardanus is threatened."

"Rusa, send the son of Electra to square eleven."

Two days after Minos's slaves delivered Lyreox to the Tylissos Arena, my birth pangs began. So protracted was my parturition that every object in my bedchamber—the curtains, mirrors, vases, lamps— became malignant in my eyes and hateful beyond all telling. Had Herakles been a woman, a single labor of the sort I endured, not twelve, would have been sufficient atonement for his horrid killing spree. When my anguish finally ended, its cause became apparent. I had brought forth not one hybrid but two, male and female, with human bodies, bovine heads, cloven hooves instead of feet, and tails suggesting furred serpents.

My cadre of midwives straightaway removed the twins' mutual caul—an auspicious sign—then gave them their first bath, cleaned up the afterbirth, and, approaching my bedside, held the infants before me wrapped in separate linen blankets. As I surveyed their blunt snouts, nascent horns, stubby fingers, bristled hides, and reptilian tails, a tempest raged through my soul. I found the twins' physical appearance . . . not repulsive, exactly—disturbing, I would say, dispiriting. For the queen and her newborns, caul or no caul, difficult years lay ahead.

I fixed on their faces, my gaze alternating between pairs of dark, moist, trusting eyes, and suddenly all conventional aesthetics dropped away. How endearing they were, these helpless creatures, so manifestly eager to begin the terrible and irreducible business of being alive.

My colostrum was flowing copiously, and I placed my heifer-daughter to my breast. She nibbled. I gritted my teeth. She gurgled and continued to take suck. The ardor with which she massaged my nipple and areola was unexpectedly arousing. I gestured for my bull-son and, upon his arrival, clamped him to my other breast. He proved as vehement as his sister, though by now the sensation was unequivocally pleasurable. Even after the twins began to teethe, I mused, the joys of nursing would surely outweigh the discomforts (ruminants having neither incisors nor cuspids), and I resolved then and there neither to employ wet nurses nor to hasten the weaning process.

Later that afternoon, when Minos entered the room and approached my bed, I had a large entourage in attendance, including three midwives, two physicians, a lyre player, a priest of Hermes, and my favorite hunting dog. The king had been warned what to expect, and he made a great show of welcoming the twins into the world. I understood his reasoning, or thought I did. Nature routinely tampered with infants in the womb, making bizarre monsters of mundane fetuses, and so the royal twins' peculiar appearance hardly constituted proof of a bastard lineage. By accepting these strange creatures and calling them his own, Minos would be forever spared the stigma of cuckoldry, and the only horns to figure in accounts of his reign would be those sported by the newborn prince and princess.

"They must have names," he said, kissing his stepdaughter on the muzzle. "Have you any in mind, dear wife?"

"These are children of the soil, rooted, earthbound—and so, my husband, in homage to paradox we must give them celestial names."

"Such as Helios? Or is that—?"

"Obvious, yes. Presumptuous. Our bull-son shall be called Asterion, star. Our heifer-daughter, Selene, the moon."

"Those are splendid names," said Minos.

"As befitting creatures who will one day perform remarkable deeds."

To further sustain the myth of the twins' legitimacy, Minos became an active participant in their upbringing, his dedication to their welfare at times eclipsing even my own. They matured quickly, as calves will do, and the king seemed to rejoice in each developmental milestone—smiling, babbling, laughing, walking, running, jumping, throwing, bowel control—while indulging them so extravagantly as to make the childhoods of our grown and better-pedigreed offspring seem by comparison austere. Strange as it sounds, the four of us experienced a satisfaction that often eludes more conventional households. We were a ridiculous family, but not a tragic one, and I would even say we were happy. Was it possible, I wondered, that every couple suffering from marital malaise should consider adopting—or even attempting to conceive—freakish infants with bovine physiognomies?

Assuming he was as petty as the other gods, I suspected the Lord of the Trident was surveying the situation with ever-mounting anger. Poor old Poseidon, outwitted by mere mortals, his vengeance in disarray. My impossible pregnancy had not sent me reeling with suicidal despair, nor had the twins' arrival heaped humiliation on the king. So what heinous scheme did Poseidon enact next? None, as far as I could tell. Did he formally cede the field? More likely he simply decided that, given my husband's capricious nature, disaster would befall the House of Minos without further divine intervention.

Against the expectations of all who'd seen the twins, human speech came naturally to them. Well before their first birthdays, they'd learned to talk in complete sentences, a faculty they used primarily to make demands on their eternally forbearing stepfather. When Prince Asterion asked for a pet monkey, Minos imported a rare blue specimen from the farthest East. When Princess Selene showed an interest in horticulture, the king commanded Daedalus to build her a garden so vast and convoluted it would be its own sort of maze. When my bull-son expressed curiosity about written language, his stepfather personally taught him the glyphs and encouraged his talent for verse. When my heifer-daughter decided that her games required the participation of other children, Minos approached certain courtiers who'd recently become parents and beseeched them to bring their offspring to the palace playroom—though to each such invitation he added an ominous coda.

"Please understand that my daughter's visitors will taunt her at their peril."

While Asterion and Selene remained eager customers for my milk, the object of their cathexes steadily shifted away from me and toward one another. I supposed that intense cross-sibling identification was normal with twins, but their melding of minds nevertheless unnerved me, and Minos didn't like it either. When addressing their parents, Asterion finished Selene's sentences with astonishing accuracy, and vice versa, as if they were reciting lines from a play. Beyond their competence in the Cretan tongue, they devised a wholly private language, speaking it with great fluency, or so I presumed (there was no way to tell). Day after day, they reveled in cryptic word games and enigmatic private jokes. Together they wrote indecipherable poems and set them to the dulcet strains of the lyre and the antic whistling of the flute. This prince and princess were not exactly musical prodigies, but had any children of so scrambled a heritage ever quitted themselves more famously in the sacred sphere of Orpheus?

With the twins' verbal facility came endless questions. Why was the night sky full of stars? If cattle ate no meat, why were they so stout and muscular? Did Helios live inside the sun, or was that eternal torch merely his avatar? They were particularly curious about the mechanics of mammalian reproduction. Between the two of us, the king actually did the better job of explicating the process. The prince and princess took the hydraulic details in stride.

Naturally they were inquisitive about the gulf that separated them from the other children they saw in Knossos. Why do we have horns and our playmates do not? What about our snouts, tails, and cloven hooves? Minos and I did not scruple to deceive the twins. Breezily we spun out the narrative of Damalis, a beautiful but malign sorceress who, upon being mocked by Minos, had bewitched Asterion and Selene in the womb—an explanation that, for the moment at least, seemed to satisfy them.

Even more distressing than the twins' psychic rapport was the physical dimension of their bond. Though a full year shy of adulthood, they embraced with the passion of accomplished lovers. They rubbed one another until their hides crackled. They kissed like a warrior couple on their final night together, dreading a dawn that would send them off to fight battles on opposite ends of the earth, Asterion the admiral of a great navy, Selene the leader of a mighty Amazon army.

Gradually I came to realize that Minos was particularly invested in the rearing of his stepson, while his stepdaughter had to make do with his residual regard. Well before the twins were weaned, the king began instructing Asterion in the allegedly manly arts of sword fighting, javelin hurling, archery, wrestling, and boar hunting. Although the prince was thriving, Minos required him to supplement my milk with solid food—not the barley, oats, and fruits he preferred, but the diet of a natural-born predator. At their master's direction, the king's slaves brought Asterion live frogs, toads, lizards, and garden snakes,

214

creatures that Minos then coerced the prince into killing and eating. Occasionally my husband even forced my bull-son to choke a lamb with his bare hands and partake of its flesh.

So deeply did Minos's parenting style disturb me, and so imperiously unwilling was he to discuss the matter, I commissioned a royal barge, sailed across the Gulf of Corinth, and ascended the southern slopes of Mount Parnassus, seeking the counsel of the Delphic Oracle.

Hedged by great cracks in the earth, a white temple marked the navel of the Great Goddess Gaia. Hopeful supplicants thronged the holy space, pressing their petitions on a sorority of acolytes and begging them for fair consideration. I sought out the chief priestess, who, upon apprehending my identity, escorted me past the crowd into the sanctum sanctorum.

A stately young woman, robed in red, sat on a three-legged stool positioned above a jagged opening in the floor, holding laurel leaves in one hand and, in the other, a bowl of water from the Kassotic spring. Thick saffron fumes rose from the crevice, enshrouding the Pythia, who ingested the sacred pneuma with sharp, rasping inhalations.

"The queen of Crete presents herself to thee," I said.

A series of convulsions passed through the oracle's frame. She released a long, musical sigh and drew into her lungs an especially large draft of pneuma.

"Come thee forward, O Pasiphaë."

I approached the Pythia and poised myself precariously at the edge of the cleft. "I have come to Delphi in search of—"

"I know what brings thee here," interrupted the oracle, wheezing. "Thy thoughts are clear as pebbles in a shallow pool. Why would thy husband make such a fierce fighter and feared predator of his stepson?"

An indeterminate interval passed. The vapor entered my own lungs and, reaching my brain, transmuted into purple eddies of light swirling along the cusp of my vision.

"By turning Prince Asterion into a brute," said the Pythia, "Minos will have his revenge for thine affair with the bull from the sea."

"Your answer saddens but hardly surprises me. Will the king contrive to punish me till the end of my days?"

The Pythia nodded. "Much as thou didst plot to punish him for his adulteries."

"'Plot' is hardly the right word. All mortals entertain dark ambitions, as do all gods and goddesses."

Again a violent spasm seized the oracle. "O subtle sister of Circe, didst thou not aspire to set fire to Minos's blood"—her voice was laden with echoes, as if she were addressing me from the bottom of a well—"causing it to burn in his veins like molten lava?"

"I never implemented the scheme, though I remain fond of it."

"O artful aunt of Medea, didst thou not undertake to stock Minos's semen with scorpions and centipedes, making intercourse excruciating for himself and his concubines?"

"To rehearse foul deeds at night and to realize them in the waking world are two different things."

"Hearken, Queen Pasiphaë, and thou shalt learn how to rehabilitate thy son. Because thou dost yet give suck to thy children, we can exploit thy powers over corporeal liquids."

"Their weaning is a full fortnight away, perhaps two," I said, intrigued.

"Look to thy milk, O sister of Circe. When next thou places a hybrid child to thy breast, speak the sacred syllables *medén ágan*—'nothing in excess'—over and over."

"*Medén ágan*," I echoed. Simply in the saying, the incantation warmed my mouth and bathed my tongue in nectar. "*Medén ágan*."

"Through this spell thy lactic reservoirs will transmute into an elixir by which a crocodile might be gentled and a cave bear become a clown."

"*Medén ágan*," I chanted again. "I am evermore grateful to thee."

"O great queen, thou mayest go back to Crete now, but first thou must make a sacrifice to Gaia."

"What manner of sacrifice?"

"There is a knife on the altar. Leave some of thy blood behind."

Before setting sail for Knossos, I cut myself as the Pythia had commanded, staining the stone with the price of my son's salvation.

Medén ágan. Day after day, the wine of benevolence flowed from my breasts into the prince and princess's eager mouths. Wonderful to behold and marvelous to relate, the milk charm worked. *Medén ágan.* O gods of moderation, I give you Asterion and Selene, epitomes of equanimity, slow to anger, quick to forgive, loath to make mischief.

Minos soon realized that something was amiss. His stepson no longer took joy in wounding opponents in duels, nor did he relish the bloody frenzy of a boar hunt or the foaming tumult through which a giant squid, gaffed and thrashing, is pulled from the sea into a boat.

Doubtless one of Minos's diviners had theorized that my milk was bewitched, an untoward tonic to salve the ire of even the most feral child, or perhaps the king had devised the theory on his own. In any event, he demanded that I stop nursing, and I was happy enough to comply, for both twins had acquired a sensibility as noble as their real father's.

In the months that followed, my husband seemingly grew reconciled to Prince Asterion's pacific nature. Once again we four became a normal family in the eyes of our subjects, who knew naught of the twins' unchaste relationship, the king's sordid affairs, or my outré infidelities (having reached menopause, I'd decided no force on earth, not even Poseidon's spite, could impregnate me again). By now Asterion and Selene were well into adolescence, and while they idolized each other more than ever, they were usually happy to join Minos and me for picnics, mountain hikes, cave exploring, and island hopping.

"Selene and I must put a question to you," Asterion announced one evening as we sat down to a family meal.

"Who is our father?" asked Selene.

"I am your father." Minos swilled wine from a golden goblet.

"We believe our mother is our mother," said Asterion, loading his plate with sliced turnips, "for she suckled us with sentiments no mere wet nurse could ever provide."

"And yet we have horns." Selene began eating her bowl of barley.

"We have snouts, tails, and cloven hooves," said Asterion.

"Who is our father?" asked Selene again.

"I am," said Minos. "You were cursed in the womb by a sorceress. We already explained all that."

"Yesterday that befuddled groom called Rusa approached us at the stables," said Asterion.

"With pained eyes and a quavering voice," said Selene, "he told us of a conversation he'd overheard between our mother and father."

" 'If I ever catch you alone with the bull from the sea,' " Asterion recited for his stepfather, " 'I shall cast you into the Eileithyian Labyrinth, an action whose righteousness this entire realm will instantly affirm.' Is that what you told our mother?"

"The addle-brained Rusa is not a reliable source," said Minos.

"Who is the bull from the sea?" asked Asterion.

"There is no bull from the sea," said Minos.

"Sweet sister, let us sail to Delphi and consult with the Pythia," said Asterion. "Unlike our mother and father, she will not lie to us.

217

She will tell us why we're freaks."

Minos abruptly stood up and slammed his goblet on the table. Wine erupted in all directions, staining the white linen cloth.

"Do you really wish to meet the bull from the sea?" he snarled. "Very well, you ungrateful aberrations, next week we shall travel north to the Tylissos Arena, there to meet the beast who violated your mother!"

"It was not a rape," I said evenly.

Although I suspected Minos's plan concealed a larger and entirely nefarious purpose, I now saw we were in fact duty bound to present the twins with the missing link in their lineage—horn, snout, hoof, and tail. Regardless of whatever plot was simmering in the king's brain, we must introduce the prince and princess to the white bull.

"Does our father have a name?" asked Asterion.

"Minos," the king replied.

"Lyreox," I said.

The journey along the Tylissos Road to the great amphitheater consumed the better part of a hot morning, the Cretan sun turning each paving stone into a griddle. Inseparable as always, Asterion and Selene, dressed in their finest tunics, shared their own horse-drawn wagon, while my husband and I traveled in separate carriages. Six of Minos's most trusted bodyguards joined our procession, for the rocky terrain sheltered pitiless brigands and wild beasts.

After an hour on the road we reached the arena and proceeded to the royal pavilion, a cantilevered affair jutting outward from the western tiers. Installed to facilitate a local custom, a narrow stone stairway led down to the playing field, though today it would probably not be used, for the king was hardly about to descend and place a garland of roses on Lyreox, the featured bovine performer, even if the bull who'd bedded his wife performed today with particular élan. Beyond the stairway, a sprawling, oval field of beach sand—no commodity was more easily obtained in Crete—lay baking in the midday heat.

Evidently Minos had sent ahead word of our plans, for a quartet of comfortable couches stood ready to receive the royal visitors, and the table was piled high with honey cakes, ripe figs, fat grapes, and hard cheese. At the center of this bounty stood a pitcher of red wine—the twins could now indulge without becoming silly or sick—and four goblets. The crowd applauded and cheered as we took our seats.

"Minos!" cried the audience.

The king rose from his couch and waved. "Pasiphaë!"

I followed my husband's example.

Much to the grumbling discontent of the audience, the legendary and beloved Lyreox did not appear immediately, nor did the principal acrobat, the renowned and incomparable Koretas. Instead the spectators had to endure exhibitions by three minor teams. Throughout the show, Minos, the twins, and I lounged beneath our crimson canopy, shielded from Helios's fire though not from our more hedonistic impulses. We ate the entire stack of honey cakes and drank far too much wine, the better to obliterate the tedious antics unfolding below.

At last Koretas and Lyreox entered the arena, and the crowd roared with adulation. My bull looked as magnificent as ever, his coppery horns shining like daggers, his alabaster hide gleaming. He snorted and pawed the sand. The performance began with a seemingly impossible stunt. As Lyreox trotted in a circle, Koretas ran beside him and vaulted onto the animal's back. The dauntless acrobat did a handstand on the bull's rump, maintaining the pose for a full circuit around the arena.

"Koretas!" chanted the crowd. "Koretas! Koretas!"

Lyreox stopped and became as still as a boulder. Koretas jumped to the ground and approached the animal from the front. He grasped both horns and sprang free of the sand, whereupon Lyreox jerked his head with such force as to send the acrobat spinning through the air. Koretas landed feetfirst on the bull's shoulders, then pivoted and began to dance atop his partner, pirouetting from neck to ribs to loins to rump and back again.

"Lyreox!" cried the audience. "Lyreox! Lyreox!"

"Your paramour plays his part well," said Minos above the din of the enthralled spectators.

"Is that truly our father?" asked Asterion, pointing.

"Truly," I said.

The acrobat dismounted, stood before Lyreox, and executed an about-face. In a feat of astonishing contortion he bent his spine until it resembled an archer's bow, then reached backward over his shoulders and seized the horns. Lyreox pressed his snout against Koretas's buttocks and thrust his head upward, lifting the acrobat free of the ground and launching him on a magnificent triple somersault.

Koretas touched down on the bull's loins, facing away from the

219

head, then turned, pranced along the backbone toward the horns, and turned again. Lyreox took off, cantering with ever-increasing velocity, even as Koretas astonished the crowd with a succession of somersaults, each executed so precisely that the rider invariably managed to spring off the neck, rotate once above the ribs, and land safely on the rump, though it always seemed as if the airborne Koretas was about to let Lyreox slip away beneath him.

Bull and leaper sustained their somersault act for an astonishing ten revolutions around the arena.

"Koretas!" screamed the spectators.

The show was over now, but the cheering continued. The acrobat raised his arms high, hand clasping hand. With his hoof the bull gashed a furrow in the sand.

"Koretas!" shouted Asterion and Selene.

"Lyreox!" cried the crowd.

"Lyreox!" yelled the prince and princess.

A soft breeze arose. I took a considerable swallow of wine, emptying the goblet, then lay back on my couch and studied the rippling canopy. The spectacle replayed itself in my mind—the enraptured crowd, the leaping acrobat, the galloping bull.

"That's right, Asterion, run to your father!" cried Minos, rousing me from my reverie. "Go ahead, Selene, meet your sluttish mother's bovine swain!"

I abandoned my couch and peered down onto the sandy field. Having descended the stairway, Asterion and Selene stood motionless before the triumphant and sweat-flecked bull. Koretas sidled discreetly away. For a protracted interval, Lyreox and his chimeric children simply stared at one another, inhaling each other's respective odors.

The bull snorted. The twins laughed. Asterion took his tail in hand and pointed the tip toward his father, even as Selene showed off her own tail. Lyreox stepped toward his daughter. He sniffed her midriff and licked her cheek. Selene threw her arms around his neck and hugged him.

Naturally I felt compelled to join this family circle. By the time I reached the sand, Selene had stepped aside, allowing her father to connect with his son. Lyreox pressed his nostrils against Asterion's neck and licked his jaw, even as the astonished prince embraced him.

"Behold the multifarious perversions that plague the House of Minos!" shouted the king from the royal pavilion.

A hush came over the crowd. Asterion relaxed his embrace and backed away. Lyreox and I surveyed each other with a mixture of longing, devotion, and appetite. The bull pawed the earth. I kicked up a plume of sand. We were both in a kind of trance, like oracles inhaling sacred vapors.

"Queen Pasiphaë, for the sin of copulation with a dumb animal, I banish you to the Cyclades," screamed Minos, "where the deserted island of Donousa will in time become your tomb! The king will have his revenge!"

"Revenge!" cried the crowd, and I knew instantly that Minos had packed the stands with his friends, soldiers, debtors, and sycophants.

Lyreox came forward and caressed my brow with his moist, bulbous lips. As an insult to Minos, and knowing I was doomed, I returned my lover's kiss.

"Revenge!"

"Princess Selene, illegitimate daughter of a lustful beast, for the unspeakable crime of incest with your brother, I sentence you to live under lock and key in the palace of Gournia!"

"I beg you, Father, no!" cried Selene.

"Gournia!" screamed the spectators.

"No daughter of mine has horns!"

"Gournia!"

"Prince Asterion, bastard son of a quadruped, for conspiring to overthrow the king, I condemn you to the Eileithyian Labyrinth, the destination of all who nourish treason in their hearts!"

"Father, I plotted no such crime!"

"Treason!" shrieked the crowd.

"No son of mine has hooves! No son of mine has a tail!"

The next thing I knew, all six of Minos's bodyguards were on the field. They blindfolded the twins and me, bound us hand and foot, and carried us up the stairway. Lyreox bellowed in anguish and dismay, and he kept on bellowing as the guards bore us away, until I could hear my white bull no more.

Shorn of trees and bereft of fresh water, the little island of Donousa proved as forlorn and sterile as I'd feared. Against all odds I survived for ten whole months. I knew blistering days of thirst, and I would have perished of dehydration had the occasional storm not deposited puddles in the clefts of the rocks and in the cisterns I fashioned from sun-cooked clay. I endured miserable nights of hunger, and I would have starved to death but for my desperate foraging, which on a good day yielded a handful of snails and barnacles.

James Morrow

My deliverance occurred on a moonlit night in the shank of winter.
The second coming of the sacred bull was as splendid as his advent
on the shores of Agia Pelagia. Proudly he sauntered from the sea and
stepped onto the southernmost beach of Donousa, the lunar light sil-
vering his pale hide and capping each horn with a star.

I embraced Lyreox about the neck, then scrambled onto his back.
We crossed the Gulf of Corinth in a three-day, forty-league ordeal of
tumultuous waves and frigid rain.

At long last the bull climbed onto the quay near Amnisos. Upon
dismounting, I told him we must attempt to rescue Asterion first,
and he surveyed me with apparent comprehension. The princess's
imprisonment in Gournia was a serious matter, I continued, but after
ten months in the labyrinth the prince would surely be close to death
by starvation, even if he'd managed to kill the occasional fellow prisoner and feed on the corpse.

Our arrival in the settlement of Eileithyia was nothing if not vivid:
a disgraced, demoted, ill-clothed queen riding along the quay on the
back of her notorious lover. While most villagers doubtless found
bestiality unpalatable, their disgust with the treacherous Minos was
a stronger emotion by far—and so the people welcomed us, fed us,
and saw to our immediate needs: warm blankets and a stable for
Lyreox, a hostelry room with a fine coverlet for me. I slept well that
night, confident that, short of entering the maze themselves, our
newfound allies would do anything to help us save Asterion.

The following morning, the hostelry keeper, a somber and thought-
ful citizen named Nashuja, told me of the king's most recent experiment in cruelty. It had taken the form of extortion. Shortly after my
deportation to Donousa, Minos had struck a bargain with his enemies across the Gulf of Corinth. To prevent the Cretan king from
landing a military force on their soil, the Athenians must start sending to Eileithyia annual tributes of seven youths and seven maidens.
The hostages' ultimate fate lay in the underground maze. Royal
guards would first escort them blindfolded into its deepest reaches,
then abandon them to the ravenous habits of the resident monster.
Whether the bull-man would eat his victims alive or kill them first
was a matter of some controversy among the villagers. In any event,
ten months earlier, the king of Athens had assented to Minos's terms
and delivered the first tribute to Eileithyia.

My husband's motives were no mystery to me. He wanted to fulfill his old dream of turning his embarrassing, milksop stepson—that
bovine but refined youth who played the lyre and wrote poetry—into

222

a demented fiend. And how better to achieve that goal than to force Asterion into a life of quasi-cannibalism?

The villagers provided me with a homespun gown, then equipped us for an arduous journey. Lyreox and I set out bearing jugs of water, sacks of bread, pouches of berries, pots of dried fish, a tinderbox, twenty firebrands soaked in flammable oil, and two woolen blankets. Nashuja and his fellow citizens chanted songs of praise as, burning torch held high, I disappeared into the first passageway astride my alabaster mount. To this day I wonder if the villagers understood that this quest was no less Lyreox's than my own. Whichever the case, we made quite a pair, fallen queen and honorable bull, intrepid wanderers pledged to foil a wicked king and save our love child or die in the attempt.

Day after day, we negotiated the labyrinth, as foul a place as might be imagined, rank with fungus and stale air, populated by vermin, its countless culs-de-sac and false portals materializing everywhere in testament to Daedalus's twisted brilliance. As if driven by the Furies themselves, we pressed on and on, past scurrying rats, spiders as large as apples, and glistening slugs that clung to the walls like lozenges of mucus. The warped corridors and barrel-vaulted courtyards resounded with the clack of the white bull's hooves and the steady drip-drip-drip of subterranean rivulets. Lyreox moved with emphatic, purposeful strides (whether following a passageway, ascending a staircase, or crossing a stone bridge), as if he'd picked up his son's scent.

We made do with one torch per day, so that after a fortnight six beacons still remained to light our way. Each evening we selected a courtyard as our bedchamber, the coarse blankets our only shield against the cold. Eventually we lost track of time and simply took spontaneous naps, oblivious to the irrelevant sun, a fire that, for all we knew, no longer rode the skies above Crete.

By the sixteenth day, or possibly the fifteenth, or maybe the seventeenth, the monotony of the journey was relieved by a succession of courtyards filled with fleshless human remains. Because there were so many skeletons, a hundred at least, I surmised they attested not to Minos's abominable tribute policy but instead went back to the earliest years of the labyrinth (the Cretan pendants and wrist medallions decorating some victims lent weight to my theory). Nevertheless, I decided to take the skeletons as a sign of progress. If Lyreox could find his way to the dead, perhaps he could bring us to his only begotten son.

My hopes were not ill-founded. On the nineteenth day, or whatever interval had elapsed since we left the village (we were down to our penultimate torch), Lyreox and I entered a courtyard that held exactly thirteen human skeletons. Naturally I hoped their meatless condition bespoke natural decomposition and not cannibalism. Alas, some cruel intuition told me these bones were what remained of Asterion's victims, their flesh stripped away to satisfy his hunger, their blood drunk to appease his thirst. It occurred to me that, to prevent his larder from putrefying, Asterion had probably kept certain captives alive for calculated intervals by forcing them to consume their fellow Athenians. While Minos's first attempt to corrupt his stepson had kindled my anger and sent me to Delphi, that same project had apparently seeded a ruthless predatory intelligence.

Thirteen skeletons. Evidently Asterion was down to his final source of nourishment—and, indeed, Lyreox and I entered the next courtyard to find our hybrid offspring squatting in the corner and strangling a beardless Athenian youth.

"Asterion, no!" I cried.

My son looked up. He regarded me with glassy eyes, then returned to the business at hand.

"Asterion, we're here to take you home!"

He finished murdering the youth.

"Together we shall save your sister!"

Again he looked up. He acknowledged me with a scowl and a snarl. His depravity was complete. Dried blood streaked his shaggy chest and leather kilt. His fingernails were jagged and torn, broken by the violence that had sustained him for these past ten months. Scrolls of loose hide hung from his bones. He made no effort to rise or speak, and I wondered if his brain had softened to a point where his lips and tongue could no longer form words.

The sacred bull strode up to his son and nudged the corpse away with a sudden jerk of his powerful neck. He licked Asterion's cheek. The object of Lyreox's affection grimaced and hissed. The bull bellowed. I released a howl, sank to the floor, and wept.

We spent the rest of the day attempting to rouse Asterion from his torpor, but to no avail. Having resigned from the race of rational hybrids, he was now wandering aimlessly through some twisted and unfathomable internal prison house. Until he drew his last breath, I feared, he would inhabit a labyrinth within a labyrinth.

When our despair was at its deepest, something astonishing occurred, as if the gods had brought all their machinery to bear on our plight. A woman's high-pitched scream reverberated up and down the corridors like a wind from Hades. Another scream followed, same voice but louder, then another such cry, and another. Camouflaged by echoes, the screams offered no indication of which passageway we should take to find their source (we had four choices), but this was not a problem, for Lyreox with his keen nose knew where to go.

We arrived in time to help bring the baby into the world. Having elected to deliver in the upright position favored by the Phoenicians (a technique that turned gravity into a kind of additional midwife), the mother stood facing away from us in the far corner of the courtyard, legs splayed, arms upraised, palms pressed against the walls near their common joint. She wore only a short tunic. A bowl of water lay at her feet, as well as a linen blanket in which she evidently intended to swaddle the infant when it came.

Lyreox loosed a deep, long, liquid bellow. The woman turned around. I nearly swooned. Selene. By all the gods, Selene. Sheathed in sweat, she acknowledged us with a fleeting smile that instantly became a grimace, then stumbled toward her father and grasped his horns, so that the parturition could continue in her preferred vertical posture. Lyreox tightened his neck muscles, fortifying the arrangement. With every spasm our daughter leaned into the bull's great snout, a kind of organic pillar, warm and comforting. For my part, I offered Selene soothing words, massaged her shoulders, and, when my granddaughter finally emerged, eased the wet little head and body out of the canal and into my lap. There was nothing unexpected in the infant's appearance: dark eyes, bristled ears, hairy tail, inchoate horns.

Selene released Lyreox, staggered back to the corner, and sank onto her haunches. In a departure from his normal diet, the bull gobbled up the afterbirth, quickly and with aplomb. I washed my granddaughter, wrapped her in the blanket, and brought her to Selene, who accepted the bundle with tears in her eyes and a song on her lips.

"How beautiful art thou," she trilled. "Thy name shall be called Antheia."

"Do I want to know who sired this creature?" I asked.

"No, you don't."

She put Antheia to her breast, and the infant took suck.

225

"I can make a guess," I said.

"And you would probably be right."

"Antheia's father is also her uncle—am I correct?"

"What my plan lacked in rectitude it made up for in efficiency," said Selene, nodding. "My milk is flowing copiously. There will be enough for both Antheia and her father. How well I know the incantation. *Medén ágan*. You sang it to me a hundred times."

"You never really needed it."

"But Asterion did, and now he needs it again. Will the magic work as well the second time around? Only the Pythia knows."

Selene pulled Antheia free of her breast. A tiny bubble of milk lay poised on the infant's lips. It drifted onto her dewlap and popped.

"How did you escape the palace of Gournia?" I asked.

"My father was Lyreox, mightiest of bulls. When I set my mind to it, I can break chains and crush locks. We have no time to waste. The second tribute will be here soon, and I shan't have them throttled by a monster."

O faithful reader, my narrative has run its course. There is little left to tell. Two days after Antheia's birth, the second set of fourteen potential human sacrifices, abandoned by their guards a fortnight earlier, arrived in Asterion's courtyard. The bull-man had no more desire to kill and eat these youths and maidens than he did to walk through fire. His sister's milk had cured him.

Naturally the potential victims were delighted to learn that, owing to the white bull's olfactory genius, we would not get lost on the long walk back. During the journey we might face privation, of course, but those spiders seemed rather robust—did they not?—likewise the slugs, and who would rather starve than eat a rat or two, and who would rather go thirsty than lick the moist walls of a stone maze?

One member of the tribute party had managed to smuggle the components of a sword into the labyrinth, the blade disguised as a splint bound to his supposedly broken leg. He had intended to slay the bull-man, thus saving himself and his companions. When I told this Athenian hero that his sword wouldn't be needed, he became testy and withdrawn. Princess Selene, that meddling mother, had canceled his opportunity to perform a great deed.

"Tell me, Lord Theseus," asked Asterion, "after slaying me, how did you plan to escape the maze?"

"Daedalus equipped me with a huge ball of string," Theseus

226

explained. "While he held one end, I began unraveling it, down the corridors, up the stairways, through the courtyards."

"I see no ball of string," said Selene.

"The rats ate it one night," piped up an Athenian maiden.

"Pity," said Asterion.

Before the year was out, the twins, Antheia, Lyreox, and I were all living in the Cyclades, on the island of Syros, a modest landmass, sparsely inhabited, and yet as bountiful as Donousa was barren. For the longest time our white bull seemed discontented with his situation, but by her fourth birthday Antheia had learned to leap about on his back, performing acrobatic feats, and Lyreox deigned to embrace our curious community. Whenever my nonbovine children visited, they opined that we'd lost our minds, but I believe they actually envied us our wild ways.

One splendid spring morning a startling piece of news came to Syros, courtesy of an itinerant peddler who preferred selling his goods from a boat instead of a cart. Minos had died ignobly in the palace of Knossos, poisoned by a jealous concubine. Prince Deucalion was now the king. We shed no tears that day.

The following afternoon we entertained another traveler. He came to us from the skies, borne by tiers of eagle feathers affixed to his arms with wax, his face hidden behind a ritual *máska thlípsis*, a mask of grief.

Upon touching down on Syros, our visitor complained of hunger and thirst, so we brought him cheese, bread, and wine.

"This man can fly!" squealed Antheia in delight.

"He can fly," I said evenly.

"I'm a clever artificer, but a bad father," he said. "Not long ago I put my son in mortal danger. He drowned. Hear me now, Pasiphaë. Today I shall have my revenge!"

"Might I suggest you stay with us awhile?" I said.

Instead of answering, the artificer furiously flapped his imitation wings and again took to the heavens.

"What a strange fellow," said Selene.

"I believe he's quite mad," said Asterion.

"Mad, yes, probably," I said. "But he was not always so."

"He knew you, Grandmother," said Antheia.

"I was once his patron."

"Where is he going?"

"Off to smite the sun."

"Is he a god?" asked Antheia.

227

"Merely a mortal with an obsession," I said.

"If he succeeds, will the world be plunged into darkness, forever and ever?"

"He will fail," I told my granddaughter. "He is doomed. The heat, you see. The wax."

"Doesn't he know that?"

"He knows," I said.

"When I grow up, I shall also learn to fly like an eagle," said Antheia.

"There will be no stopping her," said Asterion to his sister.

"Take care, princess," said Selene to their daughter. "Seek knowledge but not the sun."

"I promise."

The sacred bull raised his voice in assent, his bellow echoing across the sea and, I have no doubt, stirring fear and confusion in the fishermen mending their nets on the bright shores of Crete.

The Constant Lover
Karen Heuler

I HAD NEVER THOUGHT to kill anyone. I thought only people with little self-control did that. Yet there I was, standing over Jesse, having clobbered him with a rolling pin, of all things, something I had gotten *with irony* and never used.

It wasn't exactly my fault. He had killed my cat, a wonderful, lovely gray cat who liked to lie in the sink, waiting for the faucet to drip, who was plush and friendly and happy to have his belly rubbed.

Jesse wasn't even drunk; that might have been some excuse. He didn't drink to excess. I'm afraid I do, actually. I like a full bottle of wine and when I'm down, maybe a bit more. Sometimes it makes me happy; other times it makes me brood. Hard to tell the difference, because even when I brood it's with a dark, sardonic air that is very close to happiness.

I never believed I could give him that second blow, which most likely is why I did it, just to test myself. He used to look at me and raise his eyebrows when I said I would do something I'd never done before. "No, you won't," he'd say, and those raised eyebrows weren't just skeptical; they were dismissive. "You won't learn stick shift, won't lose ten pounds, won't learn Spanish. Quit posing."

Men like that deserve to die. *Hombres.* That's Spanish.

At first, I liked his sense of humor. I admit it. I liked the way he chided my wishes for myself. As if I was good enough as is; that's what I initially believed. When I said I was going to learn to meditate, he raised those eyebrows, and I assumed he thought that I was self-aware enough already. I only went meditating once; I was bored. I kept thinking about how much I wanted a cup of coffee.

Maybe it wasn't the cat, really. It might have been those eyebrows. Now I had a dead body and no plan.

Prioritizing was a good first step. I could easily bury the cat. Never give yourself more than you can accomplish, because you'll feel defeated and stop trying. I picked up Vesuvius, packed him in a pillowcase, took my largest serving spoon, and headed out the door to the park. Halfway down the street I felt the pillowcase move. He was still alive! I pulled it open and he looked at me. One eyelid was swollen. There was a bit of blood by his ear.

The vet was nearby and I told him that the TV had fallen on Vesuvius. It happened often enough, the vet said, and it didn't look bad, but X-rays were in order, and tests, and in the end it turned out the cat was good. Concussed, dented, but good.

Vesuvius was quiet on the way home, and I half hoped that my ex-boyfriend was like the cat and had arisen, but he hadn't. It seemed like the easiest thing to do was get him into a wheelchair and roll him somewhere else. I lugged him into a sitting position, wrapped a scarf around his head, and tied it to the back of a kitchen chair. That made him look kind of normal, without the lolling-head thing. I left him there to stiffen while I went out and rented a lightweight wheelchair.

I'm not going to explain how difficult it was to put him in it and how hard I worked. It's easy enough to imagine.

I moved him out in broad daylight, since it might have looked suspicious at night. His eyes were half-open, which was good. Closed, he might have looked weird. Open, it would have been noticeable that he didn't blink. Half-closed, he just looked sleepy.

There's a bus a few blocks over that goes along the old trolley tracks in Brooklyn all the way out to a former airfield, now a recycling center. I had to wait a long time for one of those kneeling buses and I got out two stops before the end, as a precaution.

Now the thing about recycling—which I happened to know because I had a job there once—was that a lot of the stuff that comes in is completely unrecyclable. People just toss things. So the first stop when the big trucks come in is a long conveyor belt, and workers who get paid maybe five dollars an hour use rakes to pull out obviously unrecyclable things like dolls and microwaves and birthday cakes—that stuff ends up in a dumpster headed for the landfill. This was my target. I happened to know the general work schedule started early and left the place deserted at night. There's not much profit in stealing recyclables.

It was easy to find a break in the fence near the trash dumpster, so I wheeled Jesse up to it. I jumped down to make a nice depression for him, climbed up, and tipped him over. His half-open eyes looked at me, so I smoothed some garbage over him.

After collapsing the wheelchair, I began the long trek home, where my cat was waiting for me.

Vesuvius got better. He would always have a squinty eye, the vet said, but no pain and his vision would be fine. I suppose I should have felt guilty about Jesse, since the cat was alive and he wasn't, but in fact I hardly missed him or his eyebrows.

And then, there he was, at the top of my stairs when I came home one night.

I froze, trying to figure it out but he saw me and nodded. My heart beat a little fast at first, and then it got back to normal. He was standing there, key in hand, blinking at me. I unlocked the door and let us in.

"Jesse," I said finally, "you have a fried egg on your head." It was a statement of fact (he had lots of garbage on him), but it was also an attempt to normalize what was going on. A fried egg was not supernatural, or mystical, or horrific.

His hand slowly reached up and pulled the egg off. He stared at it for a full minute then stuffed it in his mouth.

"Are you hungry?" I asked. "I could do toast. Or fried potatoes."

He sat down at the kitchen table. I could hear Vesuvius leap down from wherever he was in the next room and come racing in. He saw Jesse and growled in a growing crescendo, then he sprang on him and dug his claws into his neck.

Jesse didn't budge. The cat wriggled and writhed then just gave up. He jumped down, trotted away, and I turned to consider Jesse.

There were scratches but very little blood.

"Does that hurt?" I asked and he stared at me, as if he wasn't paying attention.

"Because the cat really tore you up," I continued.

He sighed. "I figure he deserved a shot" was his reply. I got soap and a washcloth and soaked it in warm water. He bent his head a little forward.

"Really?" I said. "You expect me to clean your neck? Like you can't do it yourself? Like you deserve some sympathy?"

"I hurt," he said softly.

"Yeah, well, you can hurt even more. Clean your own neck. I'll get some gauze and tape."

I turned and left but glanced over my shoulder and there he was, his head still lowered, his right hand dabbing his neck. I came back and put some bandages on it, then I sat down again.

"So tell me," I said. "Are you dead or alive?"

"Dead?" he asked and barely raised an eyebrow. "You think I'm dead?"

231

"I buried you."

"You threw me in garbage after you knocked me out. Not the same thing."

"You killed my cat."

He looked into the next room, into the darkness where two golden eyes stared back at him. "That cat?"

"Well," I said. "So I was wrong. I think you should leave."

He stared at me with mournful eyes. "You try to kill me and then you want to leave me?"

"I'm sorry," I said politely. Of course I was sorry, in a really annoyed way. I had gone to a lot of trouble, and it had *bothered* me to kill him and roll him out to the recycling center.

"No, I'm sorry," he said. "I need to do something about my temper. I don't hate Vesuvius."

"Vesuvius hates you, though."

He seemed very matter-of-fact. Not angry or even that much concerned. Though perhaps his head injury was affecting him?

"How do you feel?" I asked cautiously.

"Strange," he answered. "I'm thinking slowly but very clearly. I imagine you believe I'm mad at you. Before this, I would have been. But right now I see that I made a few mistakes, and I can't blame you for that." He put a piece of toast in his mouth. "Not much taste," he said and set the toast down.

"I'm sorry too," I said finally. "I overreacted."

He sat back. "It's hard to imagine all that anger," he said finally. "Do you mind if I go to bed? I'm very tired."

He got up and went to the bedroom.

"Could you shower first?" I called after him, but he didn't answer.

I slept on the sofa that night. Vesuvius slept in my armpit. We were both tense and jumped at every sound. I think we nodded off in turns.

Jesse slept a long time. I woke up, showered, put on coffee, made some eggs. Nothing. Finally, I went into the bedroom. He lay on his back, his mouth open, his eyes open. He seemed to be staring off into the distance. I stepped closer to him. He had a sheet flung over his chest. Was he breathing?

"Jesse?"

Suddenly he blinked and his eyes clutched mine.

"I thought you'd left me," he said. His voice hinted of pathos.

"Should I?" I asked. "Leave you? Why don't you leave me instead?

This is my apartment, after all."

"I'm too weak to leave you," he said. "Besides, I want to make it up to you. Maybe we could go to therapy, when I feel stronger. I need to sleep some more. Then, a little something to eat?"

His eyes closed and I could hear the faintest breath. Maybe he would die. I had killed him once, I told myself sternly; it was well past time for pity.

That's how it went for a while. Jesse got weaker and weaker. I asked if he wanted to see a doctor and he looked at me in faint surprise. "What for?"

"You have a trickle of something dark that comes out of your ear every so often; you might ask about that."

He waved at his ear. "It's nothing. Do you love me?"

He asked me this constantly. "I do not," I said firmly. "You nearly killed my cat."

"You nearly killed *me*," he said softly. "And I still love you."

"I want you to leave."

"Where would I go? I can't work, can barely walk across the room. I think you owe me something. What did you do to me?" His eyes locked on to mine.

That chilled my heart. "You can stay until you're better," I grudgingly said. "Only until then."

"Good," he answered calmly. "I love you very much. Please try to love me."

The days fell into a regular pattern. He slept at least until noon. Sometimes I ran home from work on my lunch hour to check on the cat and Jesse was still in bed. Then he was still in bed when I got home from work. Each night I would open the door and listen. I would look in the kitchen—he favored the kitchen when he was awake—and he wouldn't be there. For a second, or a minute, my heart would lift and I would think, He's gone, but then I'd look in the bedroom and he would stir and say, "Have I slept too long?"

"Not long enough, apparently," I'd answer. I was appalled he wasn't dead. It felt like he was doing it deliberately.

Jesse liked fried eggs and canned minestrone soup. Not together. A plate of fried eggs, a bowl of soup. It could take him an hour to finish that.

233

"Don't you want to do something besides sleep and eat?" I asked, annoyed.

He looked surprised. "What could I possibly do?" An element of wonder hovered in his voice. "I mean I *am* grateful for the fact that you work and provide food and shelter. I imagine it isn't easy."

"I'd rather live alone," I said. I repeated it every day.

"I love being with you. We have a deep connection." His hand strayed up to his head, to the line that ran from his scalp to his ear. Not yet a scar, not quite a wound.

"I don't love you," I said. "In fact, I don't even like you."

He took a slow spoonful of soup. Nodding, he then put the soup spoon down. "Every couple hits a rough spot. It's my fault, really." He studied me for a moment, then smiled. Winningly, boyishly, while a trickle of something rolled down his face. "We have to think positively. Look forward to the future."

If he had ever left the apartment, I would have changed the lock. I didn't think it was fair for *me* to leave—it had been my apartment to start with. But he couldn't be reasoned with. The housing market was so tight, my choices were few: either leave or kill him again.

But first, I thought I should try reason.

"Stop," I said, raising my hand after his next profession of love. "I'm tired of your loving me. Your loving me actually makes me shriek with boredom."

"Boredom is not so bad," he said. "I got bored after you hit me on the head. Because I couldn't do anything anymore. Not anything interesting. Because you hit me on the head."

We were silent for a moment after that.

"I love you," he said. "Don't leave."

This couldn't go on. I spent a few days researching on the Internet until I finally found someone who said vaguely that he was good at handling relationships that "had come to a dead end" and could help get rid of "problematic issues" keeping couples from detaching.

I sent a number of equally cautious emails, and we agreed to meet for coffee. Levin was middle-aged, bald, thin, and wore huge glasses, which made me uneasy because how could he really understand things if he couldn't tell those glasses were ridiculous?

Nevertheless, he was confident and increasingly explicit. He had worked with a number of people who didn't know when it was time to leave, even when they had been both psychologically and—he paused for emphasis—physically removed. "Some even died and just refused to believe it," he said. "They had to be convinced."

"Did you manage that?"

"I did."

I thought about that. I knew we were both talking about the same thing. I sighed. "My ex should have died from an accident, but he didn't. Now he won't leave and won't work and sleeps too much and says he's waiting for me to love him again. I want him gone. Can you help?"

He nodded and clasped his hands together. "Yes," he said. "Yes."

"What happens," Levin said, "is that the mechanism of dying is broken. It's like an on/off switch that won't go to off. Describe his first failed death."

"Well, it was an accident. I hit him on the head, really hard."

Levin nodded. "That was a good attempt. Sometimes it requires a few more."

"I can't imagine doing it again."

He clicked his tongue. "I understand. The truth is, he's just not good at dying. We need to help him with that. That's all. We're helping him."

"I *want* to help him," I said. "Obviously, he needs help. It helps me too, I admit that. But are you saying I didn't kill him but now I have to?"

Levin tilted his head, studying me. "He's neither dead nor alive. He's in a middle state because he can't decide, can't commit. Because he isn't good at it."

I needed a minute to process that. "Isn't good at—dying? Being dead?"

"You've heard of people holding on way past the time they were supposed to die? Making fools out of doctors' predictions?"

"But they were usually holding on for something in particular—their daughter's wedding, or a birth, you name it."

"Or a decision." His voice was uninflected. He watched me closely as I processed everything, until finally I looked up.

"He can't decide to leave me? But he keeps begging me not to leave *him*."

"When you're halfway in between life and death, leaving and being

235

left are the same thing. People like this merely get stuck and it's all a bunch of guessing and pushing and prodding to figure out what the trick is. So tell me a little about him."

"Well, he used to be nice. Charming. He would do very nice, small things, like make the bed in the morning and I would discover he had left a flower next to my pillow. Before he moved in. For me to find when I went to bed without him."

"Was he faithful?"

"He never wanted to be away from me."

"Ah, I see it. A conflict. Always having to restrain his needs, in order to please you."

"His neediness is not my fault. He's a big boy. It sounds like this is all coming back to me. Because he wanted more than I gave him. I'm not afraid to be alone. He is."

"Ah," Levin said, and we both shifted a little, settling back. "He thinks he'll be alone."

A sudden stabbing feeling hit my chest and then left. "Are the dead alone?"

"In no sense. It's getting rather crowded, in fact."

Again, we both paused.

"He never gives up," I added, running through the list of things I knew about him. "And he has a temper. It darts out and then it's over, but he nearly killed my cat. I mean I thought he had killed my cat and that's why I hit him and that's how it all began."

"Have you tried annoying him?"

"The things that used to annoy him don't seem to anymore. Plus, he's only awake for meals, pretty much."

"And is he eating normally?"

"Only eggs and minestrone soup."

"So it would be annoying if you didn't give him that?"

I smiled. Things were going to change. Levin gave me a few more instructions, and I bought some cream of mushroom soup and frozen waffles.

"Wakey, wakey!" I cried the next morning.

Jesse's eyelids lifted.

I yanked the bedcovers off and began to strip the sheets. "I have to do the wash," I said, "so please get up, will you?"

"Carolyn," he whispered. "Stop."

"Seize the day, Jesse, seize the moment."

"Coffee," he said. "Eggs."

"We're all out," I replied cheerily. "Unless you went to the store?" An exhausted but morose silence ensued.

"Didn't think so. You expect to have everything done for you. What are you, the president? The king?"

"The man you killed," he whispered. "I'm the man you killed."

I shrugged. "I have to do everything and you still want my pity. I've had it up to here," I said, and raised my hand high.

I went back to stripping the sheets, rolling him over so he was forced to sit up.

"When was the last time you had a shower? You stink."

He stood. "You're right. I need a shower but there aren't any towels."

"I'm doing laundry."

"I'll take a shower when you get back from the Laundromat then."

"I'm not going to the Laundromat today. Maybe tomorrow."

He frowned. "But you'll need towels." He looked at the bed. "And sheets."

"I'm giving myself a treat and going to a hotel for the night. Spas! Drinks! Massages!"

He sat down on the edge of the bed. "No. I don't want you to go. I don't want you to leave me."

"Not only me, but I'm taking Vesuvius. It's a cat-friendly hotel."

He walked to the kitchen and sat at the table. "I'm hungry. Some coffee, please."

"I told you. We're all out. No eggs either. The only soup I have is cream of mushroom."

"That's disgusting," he said. He even sounded a little irritated!

"Here, kitty," I called out, shaking the cat-treat bag. Vesuvius came running, and I scooped him up and put him in the carrier. "Bye," I said. "And I've blocked you on my phone, so don't try calling."

"I lost my phone."

"Even better."

I took the cat to the hotel, had a facial, went to a movie and afterward to the lounge for drinks, followed this with a massage, and slept wonderfully well. I even decided to stay an extra day. Let him sit and stew, without towels or soup. For a moment I had a twinge of conscience, but I beat it back. Instead, I called Levin and reported on my progress.

"It's a great first step," he said encouragingly.

237

"First step? I thought this would do it."

Levin laughed over the phone. "If he was easy, he'd be dead already. See if you can bring home a date."

I got online and posted a request for a boyfriend on WeDoIt. I described having a sick ex who wouldn't move out and said I just wanted someone to make him feel guilty.

"Hi, Brandon," I said to the guy who met me at my front door. "He's probably just sitting at the kitchen table, waiting for me, but on the other hand, he could be asleep. And don't worry, he's been sick. He has no strength. He won't lift a finger."

Brandon looked a little like he might back out, so I doubled his pay. We walked upstairs and I unlocked the door, and there was Jesse sitting at the table. He stared at me gloomily.

"Hi, Jesse, this is my new boyfriend, Brandon. He says he wants you to leave."

"Like, get out of here before I have to make you," Brandon said unconvincingly. He looked curiously at Jesse. "You OK, man?"

"She tried to kill me." Jesse's voice was raspy.

"I hear you killed her cat and she reacted. I like cats. I don't like cat killers."

"The cat *almost* died," I said. I held up the cat carrier. "See?" I let Vesuvius out, with his dented head.

Brandon looked at Jesse's head. "They match."

"I told you all about it, honey," I said. "He hit the cat, I hit him. Not a good relationship."

"Like she said," Brandon agreed. "Time to go, man."

"No."

"Well, I'm outa here," Brandon said. Not good at segues, apparently. He leaned over and planted a peck on my cheekbone. "See ya, babe," he said and left. I followed him out and paid him.

"You weren't scary," I said.

"I was supposed to be scary?" he asked, baffled.

I went back in. "Jesse, I'm done with you. Are you going to leave or not?"

"Not," he said.

"Then I will. I'll leave you right here all alone, sitting at that damn table with no one to fry your eggs."

"You owe me," he said. "You killed me."

"Half killed you. It was my first attempt, remember. If I stay here any longer, I'll give it a better try."

"I love you," he said mournfully. "I have always loved you."

He looked at me with tragedy in his eyes. I sat down, finally, and took his hand. "I killed you but you won't admit it. That's just like you. You're stubborn, you hate to fail."

"I love you," he said.

We stared at each other. "Admit it," I demanded. "You're dead."

He shook his head. "Please, Carolyn."

"I killed you," I said. "I hit you with a rolling pin and then I buried you in the recycling center."

His eyes got a faraway look; he frowned, then his eyes returned to me. "I'm really hungry, Carolyn."

"Dead people don't eat."

"If I were dead, I wouldn't be hungry."

"I bet you're not actually hungry. You're just eating because that's what you remember doing."

He glared at me.

"You refuse to admit you're dead. But you're dead, you're dead, you're dead."

He rose up, his hands clutching the table. Dead or not, his tendons stood out. His eyes were popping. He released his hands and stood straighter, his eyes roaming around the room. I recognized that look—that was exactly the way he looked when he assaulted Vesuvius. I stood up too. The cat, sensing something, crept into the room. His fur stood up.

"Don't you dare touch that cat!" I yelled.

"It's always in the way," he cried and lifted the can of cream of mushroom soup I'd brought him.

"No you don't!" I cried, and I reached for the cast-iron frying pan, the one I fried his damn eggs in each morning.

He lunged for the cat and I lunged for him. He dropped instantly, without so much as a moan.

There's something to be said for experience. Certainly, it was easier killing him the second time. I knew the routine—getting the wheelchair, catching the bus, going to the recycling center. It all went off without a hitch.

I spoke to Levin when I got back.

"Well," he said, "congratulations on a second try. Did he agree to die before you whacked him?"

"Agree?" I said, annoyed. "I was supposed to get him to *agree*?"

"That was the point," he said patiently. "Because if he didn't agree,

how do you know he'll stay dead? Was he still saying he loved you?"
"Well."
"Did he at least say he would move out before you whacked him?"
I was aghast.
"I think he's a repeat offender," he said. "He still doesn't get how this works."
Clearly, the time had come for a new strategy.
That was a Tuesday; on Wednesday I called my landlord and said I was leaving by the end of the week. That gave me time to sell as much of my stuff as I could and get out fast. Not many people were interested in my beat-up and broken-down furniture, so I left a lot behind. But it was a relief to get out of there while I figured out my next step.
The cat-friendly hotel offered me good long-term rates. It was within walking distance of my old apartment, and I went back to that street every day. I saw an overhead light on a few days after I left. On the first of the month, when I was no longer a paid tenant, the landlord came by. I got a coffee to go and sat on the steps across the street. A bit later, some big guys began carrying down all the furniture I'd abandoned. They brought Jesse down sitting in his kitchen chair, and left him amid the debris.
The pile of furniture, along with Jesse, was still there the next day, but it was all gone the day after that.
I called my landlord, pretending I'd left a valuable family heirloom in the apartment by mistake. He had a lot to say about Jesse.
"Your roommate wouldn't leave," he said. "So we just carried him down to the sidewalk in his chair with all the junk you left behind, and called for a pickup. By the way, you're not getting your deposit back."
"Did they take everything to the recycling center?" I asked. Would he just end up in the same dumpster and find his way back? He was getting faster. "I left something there by mistake. It's really valuable. Where did it go?"
"They ship it all to China," he said with satisfaction, and my heart leapt.
"Are you sure?"
"It's in the contract." He hung up the phone.
I was very happy to hear it. It seemed like a perfect solution—Jesse used to love dim sum. He might be happy there.

*

I looked cautiously down streets for a while, then I sometimes forgot to, and then I stopped altogether.

By the following February I was no longer thinking about him. I had a good apartment and my cat was feeling great and I was even dating again. There was a nice warm spell and I was walking along the Brooklyn shore, where the bay met the river, feeling upbeat and resourceful. I stopped here and there to lean on the railing and gaze out to sea. The harbor crackled with energy, with tugboats and cruise ships and people going to and fro from everywhere. The waves slapped up and down, carrying seagulls or plastic bags and a scattering bouquet of roses. Why did people throw flowers on the water? I hated symbolic gestures. Did that look like a seal? I squinted. I had never seen a seal in the harbor, though others had. I would very much like to see a seal.

The seal seemed to duck down a little and catch something—garbage? Wrappers and a small plastic bag floated near it. Was it eating garbage? My heart got very still.

It wasn't a seal.

It was still a hundred yards out when I felt my stomach lurch and I had to convince myself that it was possible. Could it be possible?

Jesse was heading straight toward me. His clothes were shredded and hung off his arms like ribbons. He swam in a loping, erratic way but there was no mistaking his destination. He passed the floating roses and grabbed one in his teeth.

If there was ever a relentless, unshakable, undeniable force, it was Jesse. Had he always been this way or had my first blow broken through to some aspect of him that had previously been hidden? If so, I regretted it. I regretted not striking harder. I regretted not killing him effectively. Why was I so indecisive? Why was he so inflexible?

Levin had said Jesse would return, and there he was. I stood on shore watching him swim toward me, watching the rose in his mouth lose petals, watching his eyes gleam with monstrous joy. I should have known this would happen. People beside me were exclaiming and pointing; a Coast Guard launch was belatedly turning in his direction. Soon he would reach shore and rise up, ragged and clenching his rose, dripping with love. I would kill him again, and he would ignore it again.

I turned and ran. I heard a megaphone from the Coast Guard launch, and I saw an ambulance approaching. I waved it down. "That man just tried to drown himself," I said, pointing vaguely back to the small crowd near the edge of the water. "Hurry before he tries something else!" Why had I never thought of this before? Why had I never turned him in?

Let the doctors make of him what they would. I headed back just in time to see them lift his strapped body on a gurney into the ambulance. He looked mournfully at me and opened his mouth, no doubt to say, "I love you."

He had to drop the rose to do that but before he could utter those words, the rose tumbled to the ground as they slammed the doors shut.

The last I saw of him was the receding end of an ambulance, its siren blaring and lights spinning, and that crushed rose on the ground.

It was fitting, of course. He knew I hated roses.

Goodbye, Baby
Jae Kim

ANYONE WHO KNOWS ME knows me to be immature. I'm easily excited by talk of sex, who likes whom, and I'm not only curious whether everyone sleeps with everyone, but I verbalize the question, which my friends, if you can call them that, find distasteful, but accommodate gracefully, on account of my immature personality. A part of it has to do with the fact that I never stay in one place for more than a year or two, and my general strategy, if you can call it that, is to act as a child would, to a group of children, and the strategy generally backfires. No one I met was a child, and neither was I. In fact, I was at the age where, given a couple more years, being childish in the way I was childish would be criminal.

I trekked up a mountain, a baby in my arms. The trail, running parallel to the mellow stream, was a long one that went through my neighborhood. It wasn't too far to walk from my neighborhood to the mountain. I'd taken the baby to different parts of the trail, to walk it, so I already knew what lay ahead, more or less.

The baby wasn't mine and never has been. I bought it to meet women. I put myself out there, tumbling with the baby on a lawn by a busy intersection, the sun shining down on us. Failing that, I made baby videos and uploaded them on YouTube. A few women have advised me, when I explained to them my purpose, that a dog would've been better suited to my needs.

But the videos provided a decent return on my investment. I wasn't good on screen, so for the most part I kept out of the frame. This tactic rendered the videos more of an experience than the typical window into domesticity, more like a series of pictures of a girlfriend who leads her photographer boyfriend by the hand through the world. A vicarious experience was what I went for. I even ran a special live-streaming feature where viewers would donate a dollar and choose which snack to give the baby, and my hand would come out from the bottom of the screen, pinching a Cheerio or acorn or snail. I announced the winner based on which snack the baby liked best.

I would never, under normal circumstances, carry the baby in my

243

arms. If the baby wasn't exhausted before going to bed, from walking and walking and walking, it cried all night long. So I walked it on the sidewalk, staying clear of other people's flowers, and then a good ways into the woods. I had thought viewers might fall asleep to the walking videos, but analytics showed they moved on, after watching the entirety of the video, to other videos such as those of the baby sleeping. The baby was large and grotesque. It was, in fact, more like an otter than a human baby. Gray and downy, it had folds all along its body, with a stubby tail. Even as I picked it out from among the many babies in the nursery, I'd had a nagging suspicion it wasn't going to be mine, and that I would, soon, not want to kiss it. I could hardly stand to burp it. I wasn't such a terrible person that I could bring myself to switch the baby for a different one. I thought about getting another baby, like those YouTubers who bred their dogs constantly so there were always puppies, but if there were two babies, the feel of the videos would become too wild. And it would be confusing, both for the viewers and for myself, to be watching two unnamed babies. I couldn't even come up with one name; how was I supposed to come up with two? None of the names I thought up for the baby had felt right to me. What often occurred to me was "Captain," because of how it led the way through the neighborhood and the woods, its harness wrapped around its chest, but the name lost its agreement with the referent once it was uttered. It was a private name, for when the baby forged ahead and I answered in my head, "Aye, aye, Captain." I let time pass and tried not to think about it, but the more time passed, the more unlikely it seemed a name to call the baby by would just come to me. So when we went on walks, leaves crackling under our feet, I trekked in silence while the baby went in and out of the tape, at times trailing behind, at times dashing ahead. When it was distracted, instead of following its digressions, I filmed the road, my frosty breath. That way, when it returned to me, viewers felt it was paying attention to them. The viewers liked "it."

"What's it doing?"

"Where is it?"

"Is it alive?"

"It's asleep."

I refused to play tricks that confused the baby, no throwing up a bedsheet over my head and disappearing, no shell games. I never turned my bathroom into a water park, installing large basins and cascading falls. I refused to create an environment that closely resembled the baby's natural habitat, with grass and mud and a hemp hammock, and the only Halloween costume I ever put on the baby was an otter onesie. I refused on principle, rather than out of meanness or resentment. I took videos from afar, or spent the whole fifteen minutes "looking for" the baby. Sometimes I cut the videos before finding the baby. After taking a walk, I didn't clean its hands right away, so that later I could put on "The Pink Panther Theme" and "follow its handprints" under UV light. I didn't feel good about this trick either, but ever since the rumor spread that the woods had deer ticks, people stopped bringing their dogs, and I didn't know what else to film. I made sure to check the baby's body for ticks. Thankfully, the baby didn't cling to my arms. Whether I'd been the one to draw the boundary, I couldn't tell. Afterward, the baby spent hours napping, or lying still as though it was napping. Still, it had a healthy appetite, and happily went on another walk the next day. I believed we'd each begun to lead an independent life, as companions on a parallel journey.

I recognized the dachshund that came running down the mountain trail to be my neighbor's. I was sweaty from carrying the baby, my deltoids round and glistening like the deltoids of someone who liked to work out. I was breathing in a cloud of my stench, which attracted gnats. A beautiful day had to be shared with gnats; there was no getting around the fact. They clung to my hair and the hair that poked out of my pits. My brows, each of which was as thick as two brows, were also susceptible. The dachshund was my neighbor's new dog. I forget its name. Her old dog was dead. I don't know that I ever knew what that one was called. It was already dead when we met. She had said, before we met, to somebody else, not me, that she might get a tattoo on her foot when her dog passed away, so that the dog still walked with her, in honor of their relationship, which was the longest one she'd ever had. First thing I did when we met was look at her feet. We were sitting in an alcove for smokers between buildings, and the shade drew a sharp line between us. I was in the dark, surreptitiously looking at both of her feet, which were bare and tattooless. "I mean maybe when my dog passes away" was how she'd put it before, and the dog she'd had then was definitely dead. She told me so. She'd also said, to somebody else before, that her pain tolerance was abysmal, so she wouldn't want to "put the tattoo artist through all that." Someone had asked her if there was anything in her life that would never change, and when she said there wasn't, this someone grew highly suspicious, and she'd had to defend herself: "I'm just afraid I'll regret it, I'll look back and be like what was I thinking? I mean I do like to express myself in creative ways, physically, so it's a bummer to be in this job where I have to wear . . . this." She was wearing a cardigan. "I used to have blue hair. When I had blue hair, I was treated like a delinquent everywhere. I was dressed nicely and everything. It's so funny, when I had orange hair, people treated me differently, like I was really creative. And pink hair, kids loved me, and people were really sweet to me, they treated me sweetly."

I was on a diet then, and I ate at the same restaurant every day at two in the afternoon. I fasted in the mornings, and had a liquid dinner. Lunch, instead, was the heaviest meal. I sat at the bar, since it was easier. The bartender was normally the same person. It was the only time in my life when I could ask for "the usual." I didn't even have to ask. The bartender told me about the daily side by way of a greeting, and I pursed my lips and shook my head, which meant I would have creamed corn instead. When the usual bartender wasn't there, I was regarded by the ones who were there with confusion. I wanted to look back at them with the eyes they were making at me, whose numerous intimations included that I was not playing by their rules, that I was not welcome, that I was not sexy, that I was not to be trusted, and that I was not making any sense. *What do you mean?* they asked me, even before I opened my mouth to order. To all the other customers at the restaurant bar, lone travelers from out of town, they deployed their signature charm. In this regard, my usual bartender was no exception. She assumed I was content to eat in silence.

The dachshund turned around, ran up the mountain trail, following the bend in the road, and disappeared. I grew nervous, and thought about letting the baby down to walk, but there was no turning back now; I had to see things through. "He's such a good dog," I heard in my head, reliving the memory of the alcove, the neighbor saying, "You know how I found out he was a good dog? We went for a run around the neighborhood"—she cried some, remembering the dead one—"and I fell on my knees. I was in such pain my mind went blank for a second. When I came to, Lee Marvin was sitting next to me, even though I'd let go of the leash."

It's worth noting that we didn't see each other again for some time after we met, meaning I hadn't taken advantage of her grief. And if her judgment had been compromised by her everlasting grief for the dead dog, that was on her. She, the neighbor, slept on my stomach. That a sleeping animal is the best animal is as good as proven. But much depends on whether we find the defenselessness or the lack of consciousness cute. Either way, open display of trust has nothing to do with it. Resting has everything to do with it. When the baby entered the bedroom, the neighbor recoiled from the sight of the creature. "Do you want to hold the baby?" I asked her. The two of us crowded around the baby on the floor. My apartment has two identical rooms, connected by a kitchen. It was not often that the baby journeyed across the cool tiles of the kitchen into the bedroom. I demonstrated to the neighbor that she didn't need to be afraid of the baby, taking the baby's hand in mine. The baby's hand, hanging limp in my hand, was damp. The moment I grabbed it, I felt it flinch, but after that, I felt no resistance. I rolled the soft jelly of the baby's fingers between my fingers, tempting the neighbor, who scooted closer. The baby watched the neighbor with a lazy gaze, sprawled on the floor. The neighbor didn't want to get too close. The baby stayed still and watched the neighbor's outstretched hand. I picked the baby up and put it on my lap. "What's your name?" the neighbor asked the baby. "If you have any ideas," I said, "I'm all ears." "Oh I'm terrible with names," she said. "My dog's name is Lee Marvin." The neighbor caressed the baby a few times, but was no braver for having touched it. "Just pet it," I said, annoyed, "like you pet Lee Marvin." I placed a firm hand on the baby's head and stroked it. I lifted the baby and put it on the neighbor's lap. I grabbed my camera and filmed them, all but the neighbor's face: her hands, once raised in hesitation, lowering onto the baby's chest, then petting it softly, so softly. I sensed that the baby was irritated by the subtleties of her strokes and tried to lift it onto my lap. As I reached under its shoulders, I had a premonition, and it came true shortly thereafter. I dropped the baby onto the floor, from quite a height, recoiling from the pain in my right hand, on the fleshy part between the thumb and the forefinger. The baby, who'd bit me, rolled onto the neighbor's lap.

The video earned many views. Some viewers were horrified, others were curious who the neighbor was. The neighbor watched the video on her phone on my stomach. She hadn't watched any of my videos before. So she claimed. She wanted to be in all the videos now. No face, I said, but she didn't listen. I had to go in and blur out her face in the footage of her feeding lemon to the baby (which failed to induce the grimace she wanted). For other videos, I filmed her legs and feet only. Gimmicky videos were not such a bad idea after all. A little harmless teasing, a one-sided conversation in which the baby is terribly confused. Lie down on the bathroom floor and pretend I'm dead, see what it does. Prod it, annoy it, be mean within reason, in order to learn more about it. Fight, if need be, and be hurt. Test the love itself, see how much it can withstand. The neighbor loved the baby more than she loved me, that much was obvious. She fell belly flat on the floor and baited the baby with a plush toy. She waited for half an hour at a time, being a poor fisherman. She played Chopin on my cheap Magnus organ, and I put the baby down on her lap, between her arms. The baby resisted the general busyness of her hands, pushing against her arms. She picked it up and put it down on top of the keys. The baby lay down, belly-up, and wiggled to scratch its back on the black keys, playing for her pentatonic gibberish. "What if," the neighbor said, "we showed the baby a movie about a baby?" I filmed a second of the movie on the computer screen, then panned over to the baby on the neighbor's lap wiggling and not paying attention. "Look," the neighbor said, nudging its chin toward the dashing baby splashing around in Scottish waters, but it was more interested in the neighbor, who was there in the flesh. "Shhh," the neighbor said. She held the baby's feet and gently massaged them with her thumbs. Anyone could've guessed how the story would end. There was nothing a woman loved more than her dog, except someone else's baby. At first, they were playing on the floor. Lee Marvin—in the heat of the moment, I'm sure—bit the baby. Even as it was bleeding, the baby continued to drool from excitement, leaving a puddle on the floor. The wounds were shallow, but I took it to the doctor. I filmed the dressing on its fingers as we came out of the hospital. I brought it home and put it to bed. I said, "Goodnight, Captain." The neighbor, feeling guilty, changed the dressing each day. The baby still clung to her arms, but my relationship with the neighbor, for what it was worth, fizzled out soon—and so, even if one were to make a case for my having taken advantage of her grief, ultimately I'd failed in my endeavors—and all I could do for the baby was take it to bustling campsites by a nearby river, where it received more attention than it knew what to do with. I sat in my foldout chair in the shade, making sure the long leash didn't get too tangled. I often fell asleep and woke to find the other campers feeding the baby provisions from the campfire. If grief were all about the living, that would mean suicide prevention was purely for the sake of your loved ones. Don't die, they say, for us. No, for you, they say, appealing to common sense. Deep down, yes, you must not want to die. But I'm not talking about death. Nobody died, except the first dog.

I was headed to one of those campsites now, the baby in my arms, where I'd often taken it, tired of being cooped up with it at home, listening to it cheep cheep, scuttle, and fall silent, which meant it was holding on to its Stroopwafel box, a "gift" from the neighbor, for dear life. I didn't understand until I visited her house, the baby in my arms. She was looking at her phone, leaning on the stove, I could see through the provocatively bare window. I saw saliva drying on the crumbs scattered about the dinner table, chairs covered with yarn curled loose from having been unraveled too many times. I saw this aftermath of dinner through the window and suspected the neighbor was angry at me.

"Long time no see," the neighbor said, approaching the window. "Do you need a drink?"

I said, "I like beer."

"I love beer," she said. "Have you ever had mulled beer? Mulled beer is sooo good. Is that a new tattoo?"

I'd been seeing her around. Saw her in the woods. On my way to various campsites. Saw her walking on the side of the highway, dangerously, following a scent. The first few nights we spent apart from each other, I'd thought I could hear her voice in the ether, yelling at her dog, "Good dog! Good dog!"

"Oh, you noticed," I said.

"I would never get a tattoo," she said.

"Why?"

"I'm just afraid I'll regret it, I'll look back and be like, What was I thinking?"

"So there's nothing in your life that'll never change."

"No."

I was filming. I had my phone mounted on my baseball cap. Since the baby was in my arms, I was recording the neighbor and only the neighbor. For once she was not an incidental subject. She said, repeating herself, that her pain tolerance was abysmal, and that she wouldn't want to put the tattoo artist through "all that." "I mean maybe when Lee Marvin passes away. Like on the foot, you know, have you seen . . . ? So it's like the dog still walks with you."

I passed by an empty bench, and soon arrived at the campsite, also deserted—where had the dachshund run off to? I set the baby down gently. I titled this final video "Goodbye, Captain." The video was so well received I'm still living off the viewers I gained then, who knew, first and foremost, that the baby was not by my side anymore. The moments when I hid in the bushes and observed the baby to see if it would swim away in the river, and when I revealed myself thinking it had swum away but then it poked its monstrous head out of the water—like so—were a gift from the gods. I still make videos, out of

Elizabeth
Terese Svoboda

IT'S ALMOST NOON when he hauls in the fish. The catch is a surprise: the sea lies flat and smooth right to the horizon, without a change of color, and the net wasn't even baited. What fish would throw itself in?

Except for the bird, I never would have checked, he says to his wife. The gull swoops across the bow while he cranks hard at the old coffee grinder winch—all out, the fish is that heavy. The wife gets herself tangled in the floats affixed to the net, and she and the man, while saving her hand from the roiling of net and fin, almost fail to land it. But he is quick, and jerks her free with strong arms speckled white where the sun is making poison.

All three of them—man, woman, fish—pant on the deck.

Must be sick to let itself be caught, says the man, hoisting himself to his feet.

She sits up, stands, steps back, and he grabs the shovel they keep for ice, and with a big, hard heave, flips the fish out of the net and over the lip of the holding tank level with the deck. The water's shallow, the ice melted long ago.

Ugly enough, she says, staring at the fish starting to right itself. But the scales look healthy. She bends down and yanks at the brown seaweed hung up on the dorsal fin. It doesn't give. We could get good money for this one.

We could, he says, and finds a new tear in the flannel of his shirt. But I'm hungry. Where's the baseball bat?

We should sell it, she says. And go out again.

Ha, he says, poking around the deck. Here we are, adrift two days from shore, no way to rouse the Coast Guard, no food, hardly any water, with the gas pump broke and the currents bad—skunked. I can't paddle with this. He waggles the bat.

If the flesh is wormy, it'll be bad eating, she says.

It flips over then, showing a white belly, but it isn't the belly that stops the man from killing it. Breasts part the water, two, with nipples, and above those floats a face, or at least two shut eye slits positioned

251

not too far apart, a nose not as beaked as a parrot fish, and lips as soft as a grouper's. The seaweed—or is it seaweed?—haloes the whole thing, then the fish twitches its five feet and rolls again.

The wife raises her hand against the sun to see better.

The fish makes a feeble splash like the outboard the man had just tried to start again, which turned over once, beat at the water, and died.

Kill it, she says.

You sure do change your mind fast. He bends to move the seaweed around with his finger, looking for wounds under the scales but finding only gill openings above the area that waists the fish. You're right—people would pay money.

You'll be making it sick if it isn't already, touching it like that, she says. Fit for the bird, that's all she'll be.

She? You call it a she? Her confirmation of the sex excites him, and he moves his hands over the fish again, but the seaweed swirls everywhere so he can't really see what he's doing. The tip of her nose?

He pulls his hand out fast.

She bit you, says the wife, and laughs hard, almost a bark.

He wipes his finger against his pants, though it isn't bleeding. It's got to be rare or at least protected. There'll be a fine.

The fish is swimming on its side the way they do when their air bladders are shot. This time when it turns all the way over, its eyes are open and dark, dark brown.

Oh my God, he says.

Wow, she says and kneels to stick her hand into the tank to touch it herself. I once had a ferret with eyes like this.

Maybe it breathes air when it's on its back—look at those lips, he says.

They protrude from the water and move. He leans down and puts his hand to his ear, as if to hear something. A little sound does come out, but not much. He steadies himself on the gunwale. Let's think this over, he says.

Good grief, you're gullible. Did she talk? she asks. Come on, tell me, Mr. Big Fish, what did she say?

A burnt piece of skin drifts off his ear where he pulls it. I'm hallucinating.

She wouldn't speak English necessarily, she says, rubbing her eyes under her sunglasses. Maybe she's a French mermaid.

He slides the hold shut. Maybe she said: Elizabeth.

Stop it, she says, kicking at his leg. That woman's probably divorced

Terese Svoboda

six more chumps like you. Let's just spread the net again. Maybe we'll catch a whole school of Elizabeths.

God forbid, he says, but together they swing the net into the water, then with the flourish of exhaustion, they drop into ragged director's chairs.

By late afternoon the gull has become two gulls that take turns diving at the boat. What they really want is us, old bones, she says. She squints up at them, and yawns. They're more like vultures, not gulls.

He's been awake for a while, sorting gear. In the stories, he says, the mermaid keeps the other fish away because the fisherman has done something bad. She follows the boat and punishes him.

The gulls exchange shadows on the deck. You should never have left those Haitians so far from land, she says.

We, he says, we. Saying we twice leaves his mouth dry and now it is drier. He wets his lips from the little that's left in their last water bottle, and one of the gulls dips down.

They must be migrating, she says.

If we killed them, he says, they couldn't shit on us.

She takes the baseball bat and whacks at the air. The birds fly to a patch of sea a quarter mile off where they start diving. Fish, she says, without enthusiasm.

At our current speed, he says, it will take an hour to sail there. We need bait.

She checks the hold. The fish is swimming a little, but gets stuck trying to turn around.

It will make us famous, he says, right behind her.

Go on, she says, licking salt off her lips. Whoever gives it its Latin name will get famous. We'll just be a couple of old fish heads who had something in Latin stinking up the hold.

E pluribus unum, he says, and he tries to steal another last swig of their water but she slaps at the bottle and it bounces, spilling the rest of its contents, to the foredeck.

You idiot, he says.

The fish wriggles against the back of the tank so the seaweed shimmies.

She doesn't deign to answer.

He lowers himself into his chair. Maybe we can catch flying fish tonight, he says with false cheer. They like the moonlight. There will be a moon.

253

Elizabeth, she says. Just another fish in the sea.

He pulls his visor lower.

You'll be drinking your piss, she says. That's what's ahead.

They do not speak again but shove their chairs out of the shade, the sun low in the rigging but still warm. The water returns to absolute stillness, the color of nothing. There's hardly even lapping waves, just the gulls who return to float above them.

It isn't long before he's peeing over the side of the boat and regrets it, watching his stream break the water. Why does she have to be right? He buttons up and takes two steps into the middle of the boat to open the hold.

If you go in, you'll get even sicker, she says.

Cancer isn't a cold.

He keeps his clothes on in the water anyway, and touches the breasts. He could have been ministering to it.

Don't get yourself too excited, she says.

The fish bangs its head against the far end until he stops, then he lays himself out on the deck, facing away from her. Elizabeth, he says.

She cries.

The wind begins to push at the sails.

At dusk they don't check the limp net. The gulls are gone and she says that's a sign. He picks up the baseball bat and waits until the face turns to the bottom of the tank and then he kills it. They catch as much blood as they can in a bucket to drink, throw the guts into the water for chum, and she cuts up the flesh. The head and its seaweed they hook to the net.

Surgeon

Justin Noga

PATIENT WORE TO THE PROCEDURE hair plated in Brylcreem. Described to Surgeon a squeezing in his lungs, a numbing twitch in his
face. His body creaked onto the cot, and a foul breath ghosted up out
of him. Said to Surgeon, tapping his heart, "I had a stent a while back.
I believe it to be the stent."

Surgeon made note. Noted also—perhaps a trick of the OR fluo-
rescents, perhaps an optic nerve fraying too slow to notice—a kind of
dim light in Patient's eyes. Readying the gas, Surgeon told Patient
of some glow of health about his person in the hopes Patient would
come clean about this other ailment. He could charge double. "You
have an air," Surgeon said. "A certain air. I bet you could crush a rock
with a toe. Nothing can cut you down."

"It's true," Patient said. "I am immutable." His tongue lolled out.

Said Surgeon then opened up Patient's chest and dug around. Hair
held tightly to Patient's head during procedure, indicating quality
Bryl.

Surgeon puzzled off Patient's chest with knife, with pick, with saw
and clamp and retractor. Each instrument used Surgeon passed to
Nurse, who wiped them with a rag and dropped them into a clear
bucket of Barbicide. Inside the parted chest, Surgeon saw the full
nature of Patient's heart, how it beat beneath like a peeled pigeon.
Angling the drop bulb over the coronary artery, Surgeon found said
stent, still in place. But wedged within the stent, Surgeon found
quarters, a pair of them, as well as a dried sausage with a crimped tip.

Surgeon made no note, pocketed each.

Nurse, however, cleared his throat, forthwith emitting from Surgeon
a sigh, a long sigh. Sausage passed to Nurse. Nurse dipped sausage
clean in Barbicide and dried it on his sleeve.

That smell, that mix of garlic and coriander, it cut through the
antiseptic and flowered in the room. Nurse held it under his nose and
sucked back with a noise indicating it was now Known To Him.

Surgeon suggested a shared dinner. "I know of a table wine made
from benzene that would give that meat some real pepper." Much of

255

the time Surgeon ate his meals alone, over the sink in his kitchen straight from the pans, and often wished this was not the case.

"Not in the cards tonight," Nurse said. "Other dreams to fulfill." He o'ed his mouth and centered the sausage between teeth and lips, touching neither. Eyes on Surgeon the whole time, eyes crowed into a smirk. He pushed further, though, and hit uvula in a rough manner. Nurse gagged. Nurse tripped over the bucket of Barbicide. Blue antiseptic spilled out along the tile and emptied through the pocked grouting. Surgeon blinked. Nurse apologized. Nurse left the room for a new rag, to warn the surgeons on the levels below of inevitable dripping.

Surgeon moved to the drier side of the operating table.

Procedure could be finished without Nurse. Surgeon would deduct pay accordingly. Clamps were unclamped, tethers sprung back into coils. The stent was swabbed. Bone stapled back to bone. Tape peeled off, and that which did not clump with membrane was rerolled onto the spindle. Yet before Surgeon closed the chest fully, something stopped him. Something new. A pale thing was glimpsed scooting about the skirt of the lung. Surgeon took a pair of damp tongs from the floor and lifted the pink flap. Found behind said lung was a man, a thin man, the size of a peapod. Nude too, but haired over in a delicate shine. Gripping lung, head swiveling left, right, left. Surgeon wanted to say, Well, hello there, but merely looked, diagnosed. He had always kept his wits about him in the OR and now was no exception. Under the lung itself, the peapod man—what else could he call him?—guarded a frothy white film that Surgeon recognized to be eggs of an expectant parent. He had seen these little men in videos. They were spoken of only in hushed tones by those who had one. He had read chat logs. Guides. Slept to their chittering audio. They had no consistent name, only pet names, names so innocuous that they felt to Surgeon simply obscene.

Surgeon looked too long for being on the clock. The peapod man's eyes were small, his pupils pinprick specks, but they drew into them a luminous green light.

Was he looking back too? Or looking through him?

Surgeon thought a moment. He tonged up Patient's Brylcreemed hair and, lifting a plated edge, saw an opening of skull, a telltale chunk eaten away the size of a fist. Brain resembled something gnawed upon, in need of cortical lubricant, but overall in quality condition. This Patient, he realized, this Patient had given all to this peapod man. The thought cut at Surgeon, who felt an emptiness in his own chest, felt his chest dry and hollow and suddenly wanting to fill with eggs, with family, with a shared future.

"Who are you to me?" Surgeon whispered, bending into the open chest. "And who could I be to you?"

Without warning, Nurse cleared his throat. In the doorway he stood with an armful of fresh rags.

Surgeon tugged the lung back over the peapod man. "Ring up the charges, would you?" He whistled a casual tune, didn't move toward the door until he knew for sure Nurse was gone. The rags lay in a dampening heap. Surgeon tiptoed over them, locked the door.

Surgeon thought, No one would know.

So Surgeon pocketed the peapod man. Left the eggs to rot. The stitches he sewed on tight and tender. The whole time the peapod man made not a noise.

Though Patient, upon waking from the gas, said he felt worse off, emptied out of something he was too dazed to recall, Surgeon assured him the stent was sound.

Patient wheezed, rubbed knuckles of left hand on the thread lines down his middle. Said, "You're sure?"

"Sound as it'll ever be," Surgeon said, unlocking the door.

Patient paid in quarters.

In the unit above Surgeon's arid one bedroom, a window shredded open. A trash bag was flung out of it and hung in the air for three floors until it caught in the branches of a tree outside Surgeon's window.

Curtains were drawn shut. His door bolted. Only then did Surgeon calm down. On his way back from the ward everything set him on edge. Every distant siren, every foot clomping quick behind him. He held the peapod man in a cupped hand shoved in his pocket, never squeezing but never giving him enough space to wriggle out.

Surgeon sat on his sofa. He bit his lip. He uncupped his hand.

The peapod man rushed out onto the sofa quicker than expected, claiming a spot between back cushion and upholstered arm. The sofa was of corduroy, and the peapod man ran his hands along the ridges. Downstroke. Downstroke. There, in spite of Surgeon's hopes for a fresh start, the peapod man spun around. Small blue veins rose on his bare back, and he chittered and shook, and soon daubed out new eggs in a clumping fashion. The peapod man crawled above the new eggs and tucked himself in the sofa's corduroyed pit. The eggs were clumped between the corduroy's channel and wale. They swayed in the cool blowing of an overhead vent.

Surgeon said the eggs shook like a little tease. "Is that how you get all the boys? By showing them evidence of where you've been?" The peapod man gripped the pit, swiveled his head.

Surgeon said, "I like that."

Wind whipped at a flagpole outside, tuneless and arrhythmic. Yet, Surgeon thought, the chiming felt like something more, like it was built into a moment they would reflect on years down the road. Surgeon indicated to the peapod man the perceived tune. "It's like a song for us, our own song." Surgeon sat at the other end of the sofa, tapping erratically on the coffee table.

The peapod man did not dance to the beat. Instead he dragged down a passing fly. Lips to its head, he sucked it to a husk. He wiped the spent flesh of the fly on his patch of chest hair.

Downstroke.

Downstroke.

Surgeon couldn't help but blush.

The peapod man wriggled back into the pit, looking ready to pounce again. No doubt still famished, Surgeon thought. All those eggs. All that wasted effort.

Sweeping his hand under the fridge, Surgeon found a live roach. He broke it in half, and fed one to the little man, one to himself. "One for my sweet, one for my sweetening." Surgeon wiped his mouth clean, dabbed clean the mouth of his beloved with a prodding Q-tip.

The heat of the sofa appeared insufficient, as the peapod man began shivering. Surgeon dug in his closet until he found a tear of silk, which he wrapped around the peapod man like a robe for ancient royalty, which, indeed, snugged the peapod man in a manner of undeniable seduction. The peapod man gripped cloth to his little neck, swiveled his head.

Gripped, swiveled.

What Surgeon knew of peapod men he had always distrusted. He shifted to the other side of the sofa and dug out from under the cushion the chat logs, which described the mating rituals of peapod men. Hovering over the part about suctioning, about husking, Surgeon thought it all read too dry, too medical, not in the way he now understood it to be. Like how Patient had gotten on with him. OK. Credit given where credit was due. Theirs was, admittedly, the true give-and-take of love, defined and unabashed. The logs described none of that. Surgeon gave up by page eighteen when he realized he didn't need an explanation of why the peapod man was not tending his old eggs as feverishly as expected, how he swiveled and gripped, why Surgeon himself felt his own face flush so warm. Why in this cold blow of the vent they both sweated so.

Surgeon put the stack of paper down. "I'd be lying if I said this wasn't on my mind all night too."

The peapod man gripped, swiveled.

They made love in time with the flagpole chain.

Surgeon knew what was coming. After all that, he could not deny the rituals laid out in the other logs. The lovemaking had relaxed him, sedated him, put him in a condition Surgeon in his professional opinion could only qualify as Forward-Thinking. Surgeon set out a spare bottle of cortical lubricant on the coffee table in preparation. Stretching his body across the sofa, Surgeon laid his head beneath the peapod man, who'd crawled back into his corner. Above Surgeon the eggs swayed. Surgeon turned his head, his eyes fixed on his kitchen island. The little man quietly slipped out of the sofa pit. His little fingers were scratchy on his scalp, like raw toothpicks catching on the strands of Surgeon's hair. The peapod man ran his lips along Surgeon's skull, between parietal bone and sphenoid bone, teeth combing at the canal of the coronal suture. Then he dug in.

Almost an hour had passed of the peapod man chewing at Surgeon's scalp—but the little man never got through skin, through skull, never straight to the core of Surgeon's being. Surgeon's hair simply matted in saliva. Excess streamed down his forehead and into his eye.

The whole thing took too long for Surgeon's taste. Perhaps, he thought, the sight of the cortical lubricant was too Forward-Thinking, an inhibitor instead of a catalyst.

Surgeon left it on the table, though, continuing to cheer the peapod man on. "Hurry, hurry," he said. "I'm more than that old twit you were with. Take what you need. I am an endless well. I am a barrel without bottom." He spread the hair on his scalp for better ease of chew. Placed his index finger on the back of the little man's head to get him to go deeper.

A knock at the door.

Surgeon's heart leapt but he tried to ignore it. A key jostled. A dead bolt popped. Nurse sauntered in, holding up the spare he had never before used. Nurse gave a wave with the crimped sausage and pretended not to see Surgeon springing up, flushed, his scalp moistened, quickly thumbing the peapod man back into the sofa.

Surgeon coughed. "You said I wasn't in the cards tonight, did you not?"

"Cards?" Nurse chopped at the sausage and dropped the pieces in a pan. "My cards are with a friend with good taste whom I'd be remiss to ignore." Nurse dumped a bottle into the pan and ignited the stove flame, and there bloomed a spiced antiseptic smell.

Surgeon didn't know what to say. Had he seen what Surgeon had taken from the OR after all? The bottle of unopened cortical lubricant gleamed on the coffee table, but he didn't make a move to grab it lest it draw more attention. Surgeon just sat there. He felt like a fool. A thief caught with his hand in a pie.

In a theater of feigned camaraderie, Nurse walked over with the heated meat on a plate. As if he had just noticed, Nurse said, "Oh, and who is your guest?" and swept the cortical lubricant aside. He took a seat on the table, his knees snugged against Surgeon's knees. Before Surgeon could slap him away, Nurse nudged him from the arm of the couch to produce a full view of the peapod man. He lifted out the little man in his silk robe.

"Hello, little sailor," Nurse said.

The peapod man chittered. He slipped from Nurse's hand and hung on by his fingernails. The robe, unknotted, fell away.

Nurse kept his eyes on the flesh. "Well, aren't you just the cutest little tumbler."

The peapod man swung back onto the cushions, crawled back to the pit to protect his eggs. Neither Nurse nor peapod man made moves to recover the robe.

Nurse bent to the little man, apologized. Nurse placed a bit of fragrant sausage tight between his teeth, and leaned in. A moment passed between them. Then the peapod man gripped the bit of sausage with tiny arms, tiny legs, tiny teeth—tooth on meat on tiny man—until Nurse suddenly let go. The peapod man fell back, spun into the pit, spine out, and ate with a wet noise Surgeon had never heard before.

That whole moment, helpless on the other side of the sofa just watching, watching, Surgeon felt emptied out.

*

The chain light snapped on in the closet. Surgeon backed Nurse into a crush of windbreakers and slammed the door behind them. "You've interrupted," he said. "You've ruined the purity of the night."

Nurse laughed and picked at his teeth. "I'm being a friend when I tell you this: there is no purity in that one."

"I have to ask you to leave."

"You think I'd lie to you, friend?"

He saw what Nurse was doing, and said so. "We are our everythings. Don't think you can split us apart so easily." Surgeon angled his head under Nurse's nose and showed him what was freshly shorn.

"That? That's nothing."

"Our love is true. It's unshakable fact."

"Why are you pushing this? You think I want in on that?" Nurse flicked a fleck of pepper from his teeth into a polyester hood. "You really don't see it, do you?"

"See what?"

"He has the look of utter revulsion when he looks at you. How can you be so blind to it?"

Surgeon threatened his job.

"OK, I must come clean," Nurse said. He drew in breath for what seemed like ages. "The rumors are true. There's always been a spark between us, and you're just the other man."

"Rumors? You just met!"

"We've had a time together. Before you. During you."

"He hasn't left my sight."

"Our love takes place in the spots of time you simply ignore."

"More lies."

"Tell me then: whose eggs are those?"

Surgeon called them leftovers from a time regretted, a sensitive issue under control.

"Leftovers? They're fresh. They're beautiful and new and wanted even before they ever came to be. Ask the little tumbler what we've named them. We have a plan."

"Incubation is not that quick. I read a manual. I read the logs."

"Parentage is emotional," Nurse said. "Not solely academic. Mine happens to be both."

The air in the closet had grown stuffy. Surgeon flung the door open and slammed it on Nurse. He stomped back to the peapod man left on the sofa to tend eggs. Nurse, walking behind, carried two stools they had agreed the peapod man would crawl toward as a test of love.

261

The little man would take his pick: the tried-and-true or the new sheen?

When Surgeon got back to the living room, however, he found the front door again open, this time jimmied ajar with a screwdriver. The smell of an old wound hit him first—sprawled out on the sofa, here was Patient bleeding anew from the stitches down his ribs, head resting below the nest.

The eggs too, they had all hatched. Hatched from the pit, hatched from the innards of Patient himself.

Quaint little things, the hatched babies. Babies the size of thumbtacks. Scooting out of the corduroy pit, out between the stitches, they trailed behind them a slick paste of effluvia. They swarmed from chest and pit into the Brylcreemed plate of Patient's skull, spreading his hairs, entering one by one, eating and eating.

"Christ almighty," Surgeon said, covering his ears from the collective mewling. Needles in the eardrums.

They were so small.

There were so many.

Nurse placed the stool on the floor. Instead of sitting, he simply stood. He had paled considerably. Then he looked down. A squat to his coat on the floor, an innocuous zipping up. "I suppose I should get going," he said, and bade Surgeon the best of nights.

Patient, tongue lolling as if gassed once more, sang what Surgeon construed as a dirge. About rings and calves and a porous rock that could fit dozens of fingers. As much as he didn't want it to, the dirge touched Surgeon so. The way Patient's mouth shook, how his breathing shallowed. Surgeon's eyes watered. More babies swarmed inside Patient's head, his song growing quieter, more intense, slurring enough that Surgeon could interpret the song from any angle he wanted to: a dream, a promise, a hope, a fear, an escape.

The peapod man was nowhere to be found.

Wherever Thou Wilt Touch
A Bruise Is Found
Quintan Ana Wikswo

The little one stands at the edge of the wooden bridge in his wood and leather shoes. Three times he stomps his feet: *klompf, klompf, klompf*, left, right, left.

He waits.

*

Beside him, the larks have built their nests in the dry and chalky weeds and wild carrots that clutch around the earthfast timber posts.

Later, the birds will skim the air with the angled slice of a skipping stone.

*

The little one shuffles his feet, watching the leather laces of his shoes crust and clot with dust.

As the sun drops, he waits for a response from below the bridge, his body an insoluble black gesture against the tawny mustard sun.

It seems he's a single letter—a *shin* or a *nun*—drawn there by some unseen hand, writ dense upon the fading sky.

*

The little one sips the air for a moment before he sings a school
song thinly between his lips, a comfort, but not loud enough to
drown out the awaited *rompf rompf rompf* answering from the
creatures beneath the bridge.

*

Never is the little one to walk home alone and cross the bridge by
himself. There are beasts there, says the old man, who are hungry
for the taste of his grandchildren.

Instead, he is to trace the lacy pattern of the forest pathway and
follow it until he comes to a red wooden bench the old man carved
for him with a chisel and mallet. He is to sit there and wait until
the old man meets him, and walks him safely across the bridge,
and then home together, talking of the day.

The bench has the little one's name written on it deep in the birch
wood, and that of his sister.

But the little one won't sit there, because that's where the bridge
beasts will come looking for him.

*

The little one waits at the edge of the wooden bridge, preparing for
battle with its ogre below. Although the flies are silent still, the
seedpods whirligig down upon the faraway and empty bench,
siliculed as a wedding night.

264

The little one watches for movement of the dreaded ones in the pale spectacle of the viburnum. Beyond its white blossoms the bridge beasts guard a village alive with larvae, their business repulsive, exclusive, executive, not braced by bone or spine. Early summer as impossible as a pogrom.

Deeper in the forest the young men have felled branches and stacked them into vaulted cones, and crawl inside with their young women.

There are gray-headed ravens too, mated for life, and a thousand hoofed and padded feet traversing the forest floor, all pushing the seedpods deep down into the sorrel roots and loam.

Seed becomes tree, grave becomes cradle.

*

The little one is not to cross the bridge because the old man doesn't want him seen lingering near a source of water. Half of Bremen dead. Half of Hamburg, and even more in Köln.

Plague sickness impervious to punishments or constraint: an ache that rises in the skull, a stomach set sail upon uneven seas, then high fevers and private swellings that fasten on to the afflicted, torment them, and move on.

Once-blond skin now showing the wild purple stains and sores of elderberries.

The little one is not to go near water, said the old man, because already there is suspicion around the wells, and accusations the circumcised ones have denied: the secretive mystery of kiddush cups filling the rivers with scourge.

But the knives and clubs and axes glisten with a proclivity for mobs.

265

*

The little one removes his new shoes before crossing into the
dominion of the bridge beasts. Before crossing puddles such a
purplish color of mud, an uncertain hue that's half human, half soil.

Carry the leather shoes high so as not to muss them. Make no
noise to awaken the beasts of this bridge to the village.
Nonetheless, the *hum brum hum* in the oxlip as enormous flies
draw near, riding light as though along a foamy rim of beer.

*

At night, after the villagers, after the torches, after the torn hair and
all the voices, the rats descend from the bridge to swim in the river.

After the villagers, exhausted, after the little one waited too long at
the bridge, after the others playing at monsters along the riverbank.

High socks, low shoes, and ducklings float now beneath the bridge.
Little elbows, damp and unhinged in water made not for limbs but
fins.

Sinking, and then resting amidst pale leaves underneath, where the
sun cannot reach but the bridge beast can. The water the color of
children, unripe.

*

After the bodies are claimed. After there was too much blood.
Amidst the echoes of such unsacred sounds, the cow again culls
swaths of oxlip, yellow, from the riverside. Alongside it, the water
buttercup rises above the wet, its stalks curving away from the
broken necks below.

Clean cloths are found for the little girls. Clean cloths for the little boys.

The shrouds will soon get muddy within the common grave.

The only thing greater than the bodies of our children is the Shema, says the old man, and he rocks back and forth, the words of the prayer falling from his mouth like teeth.

*

Villagers say: *The shouts of the children were indistinguishable from the cries of animals, or dogs surprised by pain. And, Everywhere the bluebottle fly. A plump fellow, fat and firm.*

But our old men lament, *Enough to make a minyan, that's how much of us he has in him, this fly, come to visit from our generations.* Fed from stacks left upon the offal heap.

With the bitter humor of the mourning. *Who can say our children are dead when the fattened flies beneath the bridge yet live?*

The Ancient One
Madeline Kearin

THE CREATURE IS PROPPED UP against the wall with an elaborate system of braces and ropes, so that its lower portion rests lightly on the ground. Its body has no flat surface on which to sit or stand effectively. Its shape is unlike anything in nature. It is too amorphous to resemble any vertebrate, but has too many long, meandering appendages to resemble a potato. The only useful analogy Ellery can summon is that of a massive amount of Play-Doh, mashed into a shapeless lump and stretched into outrageous configurations.

Yet even Play-Doh has a uniform consistency, and the creature isn't made of any one substance. To use the proper term, it is a chimera, a grisly melting pot of genetic scraps minced so finely as to obliterate any distinguishing feature. No one can tell eye of newt from toe of frog. No one can say whether those two mealy protuberances, situated on opposite sides of the creature's upper portion—a mound of flesh that Ellery has designated its head, purely for the sake of expedience—might be eyes. But they are fairly certain that it can't see. It doesn't react to visual stimuli.

But it does hear. At this very moment, Dr. Lawrence King is holding a video camera, patiently recording as Dr. Ellery Channing, standing a few feet away from the creature with a yardstick in her hand, issues commands to the creature in a slow, measured voice.

"Move your right—um, hand," she says, using the yardstick to tap the part of the creature that protrudes from its right side. In truth it is more like a fin than a hand, with five evenly spaced bones that are covered with a dense webbing of oatmeal-colored skin. Ellery taps the appendage again and it flutters, each bone rolling slowly in sequence.

"Good!" says Ellery, and pushes a small button in her other hand, triggering the release of a large dose of pleasure-inducing chemicals into the creature via a lattice of supracutaneous pads that are stretched over what might—according to the current interpretation of its anatomy—be called its back.

"It heard me, Larry," says Ellery, her face blossoming with delight. "It understands."

Lawrence tips the camera down from his shoulder. "Sure, El. There's *no* way that was a reflexive action or a spasm. It's absolute proof of sentience. Stop the presses."

"Could you please not rain on my parade *for once*. When I tell Dr. Moreau—"

She's cut short, interrupted by the hideous convulsing of the creature as it smashes its pseudohead against the wall behind it, setting off a chain of tremors that Ellery can feel in the soles of her feet. Lawrence sets the camera on the ground and the two of them manipulate the elaborate panel of buttons and keys that controls the ropes until the creature is wrested into its pod, a rectangular metal box like an upright coffin that just barely contains its formless bulk. The front panel squeals shut and a flood of dark liquid rushes into the pod via a system of clear tubes, drowning the creature in a witches' brew of growth hormones and steroids and more genetic material, which will deliver a series of complex encoded instructions to every cell of its body. Even through the six-inch-thick walls of the pod, they can hear the creature's screech of protest: a low, piercing, guttural warble unlike any earthly noise. While the sound gradually dies away, its vibrations continue to buzz across the surface of Ellery's skin, operating along a frequency that is tangible but not audible—the echo of a universe beyond the scope of human imagination.

Seven months ago a team of scientists led by Dr. Helen Moreau traveled three thousand miles into the heart of Antarctica to investigate a vast and uncharted crevasse discovered by a solitary polar explorer. More remarkable than the crevasse itself—a mile-deep cross section of the earth that provided an unprecedented window into geologic time—was the discovery that the explorer made upon rappelling into its farthest depths: a massive glacier in which was embedded what the explorer could only describe as a "creature." An entity of no identifiable species past or present, it appeared through the ice as a snarl of massive tentacles, deathly still yet preserving the illusion of movement in their wild, serpentine forms. Visible in the narrow intervals between the tentacles were long fringes of gills, claws the size of elephant tusks, and an unpredictable scatter of reptilian eyes, their pupils contracted into black slits. Its surface was covered with a dense layer of scales, leathery and rutted and heavily barnacled, that resisted any attempt to assign them a color. Sometimes, when the sunlight infiltrated the crevasse at a certain angle, they appeared

Madeline Kearin

blue or green; at other times, struck by the glow of a flashlight or a headlamp, they appeared red, orange, or yellow. The depth of the creature inside the crevasse, along with the inclusion of Cambrian trilobites at the same stratigraphic level, indicated a date two to three million years before the present.

Dr. Moreau stood for a long time with her bare hands pressed against the surface of the glacier, seemingly untouched by the cold that made Lawrence and Ellery, even in their shared state of awe, shrug up against each other for warmth. Barely a foot of ice separated her fingers from the tip of one of the creature's tentacles.

"Isn't it beautiful," she said, more to herself than to any of the spectators gathered behind her. "What a miracle we are going to make."

After being extricated from the crevasse and brought to Dr. Moreau's laboratory—a feat that required the mobilization of two cranes, a tractor trailer, and an aircraft carrier—the creature has been placed into a series of thirteen pods. The first three were designed solely to thaw it from the block of ice in which it was suspended without damaging its tissues, which were found to be in a remarkable state of preservation. Before it was fully defrosted, a potent cocktail of chemicals was introduced into the pods, pickling the creature in a viscous syrup. The precise composition of this cocktail is known only to Dr. Moreau, but its effects are plainly evident. Beginning with the fourth pod, the body of the creature has transformed with each emergence. It has grown softer and paler. Its surface, once leather-hard and unyielding, has taken on a supple, doughy, claylike quality, tempting Ellery to poke the creature with her finger to see if it would leave an impression. Its scales have faded, then disappeared; its tentacles contracted into wasted stumps and its eyes withered into brittle scabs that desiccated, then fell off. And it has grown successively smaller, prompting Lawrence and Ellery to invent a game: the winner is whoever is first to identify an object that approximates the creature in size. After the fourth pod, it was a blue whale. After the fifth, it was a submarine.

After it emerged from the sixth pod (the size of an eighteen-wheeler), it began to exhibit small twitches and contractions that couldn't be mistaken for purposeful actions but were nonetheless enthralling to Ellery. She spent hours watching its tremulous bulk float aimlessly inside the massive tank in which they kept it between pods, straining to catch the flicker of an appendage or the shudder of a stump.

270

Lawrence was less enchanted. He wanted to dissect the creature in every way possible, taking measurements of its dimensions, scraping off samples of its flesh to study under the microscope, arranging it inside an enormous makeshift cage he cobbled together out of two dozen X-ray machines in order to render images of its mysterious inner structures.

"We should be trying to keep up with what Dr. Moreau is doing," he would tell her. "We've got to understand the process."

"I don't think *she* even understands the process," Ellery would respond. It all seems a bit slapdash to her. Dr. Moreau tends to drift in and out of the laboratory space they have dedicated to the creature, acknowledging it with a distant fondness, like an absent parent, before issuing vague instructions and supplying them with the latest cocktail. Ellery and Lawrence have no firm understanding of what the outcome of the experiment is supposed to be.

They simply observe, noting the diminishing size and altered qualities of the creature with every pod cycle, and conducting their own tests of its awareness and ability. After the seventh pod (Sherman tank) and eighth pod (elephant), they began to notice that its movements were gaining regularity and precision. By the ninth pod (minivan), it had begun to scream, despite the absence of a visible mouth. The screaming continued unabated, stopping for only brief intervals, through pods ten (station wagon), eleven (sedan), and twelve (sofa), shifting slightly in tone and pitch as it transformed, yet retaining its preternatural quality, capable of animating the hairs on the back of Ellery's neck and shattering glass test tubes.

Lawrence has already plugged his ears with gauze in anticipation as he records Ellery unlocking the thirteenth pod. What first emerges is a massive, blubbery sac: a tumescent balloon with an oily protective covering through which the shadow of the creature is vaguely visible, pitching gently in its inner ocean. This time the sac is small enough for Ellery and her assistant Bev to catch in their arms as it collapses out of the pod. They maneuver it carefully onto the floor, where Ellery breaks its membrane, resulting in a fantastic gush of clotted slime the consistency of cottage cheese. Protected by rubber gloves that stretch up to their shoulders, Ellery and Bev wipe away the slimy stuff, paring it back to expose the form of the creature within. Its moaning is perceptible, though muffled. Ellery scoops away a large curd of sludge and suddenly the unadulterated sound breaks free into the room.

It is strident and piercingly loud—yet hauntingly, unmistakably human.

Ellery and Bev continue to dig and scrape through the sludge with their fingers until they hit solid flesh. Feeling something narrow and firm, Ellery gives it a tug, and is shocked into momentary paralysis by the result: at the end of her arm, protruding out of the greasy, shivery mass, is another arm, its wrist gripped in her hand, its hand open, and five fingers grasping.

She and Bev pause, exchanging unsettled glances, then continue, using the arm as an anchor onto the creature. They trace it to the place where it connects to a small, rounded shoulder and a pale arched back. They find another arm, give another tug, and the creature's head slouches backward out of the slime, rolling slackly on its neck like that of a newborn. Ellery places the palms of her hands onto its crown and swipes down to uncover its features.

It is a plain human face—eyes, nose, and mouth—utterly unremarkable in appearance, yet it might as well have been the face of Jesus Christ or her own dead mother for the shock that it incites in Ellery. Cradling its head, her fingers tangle in the creature's long hair. The creature's eyes are closed and its lips parted, emitting the same droning scream. Ellery runs her hand over the creature's eyelids, wiping away mucus.

"Open your eyes," she commands. "Come on, now. I know you can hear me."

The creature's eyes open and it stops screaming. It blinks, searching frantically for a point of focus, then seizes upon Ellery's face and stares—a cold, blank, reptilian gaze that inverts the substance of Ellery's gut. Its eyes are a glacial gray-blue in color. The hair in her hands, in the spots where it is beginning to dry, is auburn.

They have placed the creature in a room outfitted with a bed, a table, and a desk. Ropes and braces are no longer necessary; she (for it is now unmistakably a she) sits on the edge of the bed in a cross-legged posture that is simultaneously feral and childlike. She doesn't move or speak, but her eyes track Ellery's motions throughout the room. They have bathed her and dressed her in one of Ellery's spare pairs of scrubs—*like she's one of us*, Ellery thinks, and feels another jolt of crawling unease.

"My name is Ellery," she tells the creature. Sitting in a chair next to the bed, she tries her best to convey friendliness and trustworthiness through her voice and facial expression.

Lawrence is propped up against one corner of the room, his arms crossed defensively, his brows tightened into a skeptic knot.

"That grump over there is Larry," says Ellery, gesturing. "And you're—well, you're somebody else. Can you tell us about yourself? Can you speak?"

"This is an obscene farce," says Lawrence. "Is this really what Dr. Moreau intended? What is it supposed to do, stare the Soviets into submission?"

"Can you say *hello?*" Ellery says to the creature.

"She might have turned it into a dog instead," says Lawrence, "and we could teach it to do tricks."

"You're not helping," says Ellery.

"Are *you?* We haven't received instructions from Dr. Moreau in three days. We'd be better off to leave it alone and wait until she delivers the punch line to what is obviously a very elaborate joke."

"I think it's a miracle," says Ellery. "Look at her. She's got eyes, a mouth, hands. She can communicate with us."

"Yeah, it seems really communicative."

"You know what, Larry—" Ellery turns to confront him, but is abruptly interrupted by the sensation of a forceful grip on her arm. The creature has seized her by the wrist, and when Ellery turns her head, she is confronted by the unblinking gaze of those cold gray eyes.

"It heard me, Larry," the creature says.

Ellery feels herself begin to tremble, a full-body vibration that works its way slowly toward the surface from a place deep inside of her. Her arm aches under the creature's grip.

"Sure, El," the creature continues. "There's *no* way that was a reflexive action or a spasm. It's absolute proof of sentience. Stop the presses."

"My God," says Ellery. "I was right. She *could* hear us."

"Oh, good," says Lawrence. "She's the world's most expensive tape recorder. The Six-Million-Dollar Parrot."

"Will you shut up?" says Ellery.

"*Esta cosa no es una de las criaturas de Dios,*" the creature says. "*Sólo el mal vendrá de esto. Dios ayúdanos.*"

"Where did it get the Spanish?" asks Lawrence as the creature releases Ellery.

"Marta," Ellery whispers, without breaking eye contact with the creature. "The cleaning woman. She works in the lab at night."

The creature speaks again, this time in a garbled, lilting chain of syllables that neither of them can identify.

"And what is *that* supposed to be?" asks Lawrence. "Some sort of Welsh?"

Ellery shakes her head. "I don't know. But try to remember it, because I'm going to have to write all of this down."

The creature does not speak again, though Ellery sits with her through the evening and into the night, waiting to see what she will do (nothing, except sit in the same stilted posture, staring vacantly) and whether she will sleep (she won't). Finally, around 5:00 a.m., Ellery capitulates to her own weariness. She considers laying a blanket across the chair and sleeping there, but another glance into the creature's face prompts her to reconsider. There is nothing explicitly menacing about the creature, yet her entire being excites an imprecise feeling of dread, her alert stillness suggesting the latent energy of a snake coiled to strike. Ellery tells the creature good night. She hesitates at the door, unsure of whether to leave the light on or off. Finally she turns it off, and leaves the creature staring in the dark.

Excerpt from the Log Book of Dr. Ellery Channing
July 25th, 1982

It has now been six weeks since we released the creature from the thirteenth pod. Over that period we have observed her remarkable capacity to assimilate knowledge and acquire skills. Since the second week she has been speaking in full sentences, simple and brief to begin with, but quickly evolving in sophistication and complexity. The first words of her own were to ask us what this place was. We told her it was a laboratory in which scientists conduct experiments, an answer that seemed to satisfy her. In the third week we began to teach her to read. She has since completed Orlando *and* The Time Machine.

Her outward appearance is that of a grossly normal, postpubescent woman of small build, 160 centimeters in height—but her physiology is abnormal by almost every standard of measurement. Her heart rate ranges from 10 to 255 bpm, with no correlation to her level of activity or arousal. She occasionally neglects to breathe for periods as long as fifteen minutes, with no apparent effect on her bodily functions. Despite externally unremarkable musculature, she can lift 250 pounds with seemingly little effort . . .

Perhaps most remarkable—and most difficult to explain—is the fact that every specimen we have attempted to take from her—blood, skin, saliva, and hair—has, upon its separation from her body, metamorphosed into something else. The first tube of blood we drew from her arm appeared normal for about ten seconds before it turned into two dozen ladybird beetles. Biopsies of skin from her leg and back became a dragonfly and an Atlas moth, respectively. The largest sample we took—a pint of blood from her arm—turned into a spotted salamander as it filled the bag. These specimens have been examined by the team of zoologists down the hall, who found them all to be normal representations of the species, with the exception of their colors, which are atypical. She heals with supernatural rapidity; the incisions from the biopsies and puncture wounds from the needles disappear within ten to fifteen seconds.

She appears comfortable, though she has not yet slept and eats very little. When she does eat, she will accept only raw seafood, which she consumes in its entirety, bones, shells, and all . . .

The creature sits beside Ellery at the table in her room, examining the pages of a biology textbook. The creature's hair is neatly plaited, and she has assumed a prim, upright posture, with her legs tucked under the seat of the chair and her ankles crossed, that is clearly an imitation of Ellery. Finding them striking mirrored poses, seated at the table or cross-legged on the bed, Lawrence has taken to calling them the Twins. The creature mimics Ellery's speech patterns, her gestures, her tendency to scratch her scalp when she is nervous, assuming these habits with a detached curiosity, as though trying on a new set of clothes. The creature doesn't mimic Lawrence, but mirrors the coolness he shows toward her with an icy disaffection of her own.

"So those are animals of the same phylum," says Ellery. "And these are animals of the same species."

The creature nods. "You and Lawrence are humans. *Homo sapiens.*"

"That's right."

"Am I human?"

Ellery fumbles, her eyes darting back and forth between the creature and different spots in the room, as though she might discover the answer lurking there.

"Well, uh—we don't properly know," She says.

"I look like you."

"Yes, but . . . ," Ellery trails off, shifting uncomfortably, suddenly feeling like an insect caught inside the laser focus of the creature's gaze. The creature's expression is as always preternaturally calm, but her eyes are hard and incisive, honed to a crystalline sharpness by that ever-present dormant potency.

"I'd like to see other species," says the creature.

"Well, I—I suppose we could arrange that," Ellery says, brightening.

Two days later, with the proper clearances in order, Ellery escorts the creature into the zoology lab, located on the third floor of one of the five radial arms of the complex. The creature has been outfitted with an identification card, courtesy of Ellery's friend Jacob, who works in security. She wears one of Ellery's lab coats over her scrubs and a pair of white Tretorn sneakers in place of the wool clogs she typically wears in her room. It is the uniform of the typical fresh-faced laboratory worker, and Ellery is amazed—practically mesmerized—to see how effortlessly the creature assimilates herself into her new environment, greeting the zoologists with a dispassionate politeness that seems to elicit a more favorable reaction than the effusive positivity that Ellery typically shows them. *Look at that. Even Stephen Lancaster likes her. He's practically entranced. How can it be? She's barely said anything at all, and she's no prettier than I am.*

Watching the creature walk pensively down the rows of aquatic tanks, her arms folded behind her back, Ellery is suddenly overcome by a spinning reel of images—the twisted tentacles, the shapeless bulk, the decontextualized appendages twitching and seizing in wild, pulsating motions. She sees them every time she blinks, the images spliced over one another in such rapid succession that she can barely distinguish them against the real world.

Ellery stands still, spellbound, until the spell is broken by her mind's sudden, urgent clarion call, bypassing the realm of conscious thought to directly stimulate her muscles, and she leaps forward. The creature has come to stop in front of a large tank filled with bobtail squid, her eyes tracking their movements with rigorous intention.

Ellery takes the creature by the arm and draws her gently away. "Let's look at some mammals," she says.

As she leads the creature alongside cages of mice, rats, and guinea pigs, Ellery hears a rhythmic thumping drawing close behind them. It's Lawrence, his lab coat billowing as he runs, his face as red as a beet. When he reaches them, he bends over with his hands on his knees.

"What are you doing?" he asks between panting breaths. "Taking *her* outside?" (Though he has, at last, capitulated to referring to the creature with gendered pronouns, he inflects them with a tone of passive protest.)

"We're not *outside*, Larry."

"You know what I mean. Outside our lab. You don't know what she might get into."

"She's not getting into anything." Ellery gestures toward the creature, who is standing quietly with her hands in the pockets of her lab coat. The creature has a peculiar talent for assuming a posture of pointed innocence, even frailty, as if to ask, *Who, me? What harm could I possibly do?*

Yet if she wanted to, she could lift that five-hundred-gallon tank of armadillos over her head and throw it across the room, Ellery thinks, and wonders if she has been imprudent. The creature has a way of disarming her, even as she keeps Ellery consistently on edge. It is the same feeling Ellery once felt around a few of her most electrifying professors, the ones who could be friendly and charming yet commanded a degree of respect that was intimidating. It was the way she still feels around Dr. Moreau—a sense of obedience that is ambiguously rooted somewhere between loyalty and fear.

"OK, fine," says Ellery. "We'll go."

Back in their own laboratory, Ellery and Lawrence stand outside the entrance to the creature's room while the creature sits cross-legged on her bed, cradling the biology textbook between her knees.

"You can't be so reckless with her," Lawrence says. "Just because she looks like a little girl doesn't mean she's not dangerous."

"Wow, Larry," says Ellery, her confidence buoying now that she is back in her home territory. "I didn't think you were so impressed with her. What was it you said about her staring the Soviets to death?"

"That was a long time ago. We have a better idea now of what she can do. But we're no closer to understanding Dr. Moreau's intentions, and that scares me."

277

"Dr. Moreau isn't here," says Ellery, and knows as she says it that it both is and isn't true. In fact, Dr. Moreau has not visited the lab in months, has not seen the present version of the creature, and does not acknowledge their daily missives, if she even receives them. Yet the mention of her name seems to summon her presence into the room. She is there: in the fraught silences between them, in the architecture of the lab, and in her greatest handiwork, the creature herself. There are times, catching her out of the corner of her eye, that Ellery even thinks the creature *is* Dr. Moreau. The illusion lasts only a millisecond before it disappears, but it is enough to sustain a growing suspicion. Could there be a bit of Dr. Moreau there, a shadow of her profile in the aquiline arch of the creature's nose, in the crooked smirk of her closed smile? What color had Dr. Moreau's hair been before it went gray?

"It's just—it's just that—I think she's lonely," says Ellery. "I don't know if we're the best company for her."

"I see. She thinks we're boring. Maybe we can find someone more interesting to entertain her, someone worthy of her intellect."

"No, that's not it at all. It's not a question of intellect. It's more like—a vibe. We're not her kind."

Lawrence shrugs. "Well, I'm sorry, El. It's hard when you can't give your baby everything she wants, but there it is."

Two days later Ellery sits in the creature's room, studying a drawing that the creature has just completed, when a soft knock comes on the door.

"Come in."

"I can't," comes Lawrence's voice. "Hands full."

When she opens the door, he steps forward and lowers his parcel gingerly onto the table.

"What is that, Larry?"

"It's a—why are you whispering?" Lawrence asks, and is answered by Ellery's silent gesture. The creature is lying on her bed, her knees drawn up and her arms folded against her chest, sleeping.

"My God," he says. "Is she dead?"

"*Shhhhhhhhh*, no. She's fine. I just did a little experiment. You know she's been asking what it feels like to sleep. She tries but can never quite achieve it. So I decided to give her some Secobarbital . . ."

"Sleeping pills?"

". . . and it worked."

278

Lawrence shakes his head. "Well, shoot. I wanted her to see my present."

"She can see it when she wakes up. What is it?"

Lawrence opens the flaps of the box, revealing a small striped kitten with tipped brown ears and long white whiskers.

"I thought she might get along better with a different species. They can commiserate about how terrible humans are."

Ellery's face blooms. "That's wonderful, Larry. What a lovely idea."

"And," says Larry, leaning toward Ellery conspiratorially, "it's only a stray. There are six more under my mother's porch. In case—you know."

Ellery gives him a quizzical look.

"In case she ends up eating it," he says.

The creature sits with her shoulders rounded over her desk, the tips of her hair lightly grazing one side of the picture she is drawing. It is autumn, although one would hardly know it inside the laboratory walls; the massive HVAC system maintains a consistent temperature and humidity year-round, buffering the sharp edges off the air and filtering out the smell of woodsmoke and leaves. Pip, the tiny striped kitten, now grown prodigiously large, lounges in the bowl of the creature's crossed legs, his head dangling over one knee and his long puffy tail coiled around the other. The creature is caught in one of her productive trances; she will produce ten, twenty, maybe thirty pictures this hour, all of which Ellery will examine with a researcher's meticulous eye.

"She says she sees them in her dreams," she tells Lawrence, when he finds her poring over them in their small shared office across from the creature's room.

They are landscapes, ranging from empty vistas to intricate cities, none of which are identifiable to Lawrence or Ellery, though they contain certain recognizable features—the half-timbered bracing of Tudor construction, a stark modernist monolith of mirrored windows, even a mansard roof like the one on the house Ellery grew up in. Though they depict nothing unnatural, there is something vaguely surreal about all of them in their depth and proportions, which seem configured to confound the eye, leading it down paths to nowhere, or alternately sending it through complex labyrinths only to return to the same bewildering locus: a thatch-roofed cottage in a wilted landscape, a broken window in a shambolic shantytown, a tower of black rubble on an island feathered with pale grass.

They are all mesmerizing in their own ways, but there is one that has consistently haunted Ellery. It is a barren canyon, thicketed with ragged stalagmites like a forest of half-melted skyscrapers, their crooked tapers needling the sky. The creature has rendered it in a uniform ashen-gray color, deeply rutted with shadows that conceal the full extent of its depths. Between the foreground, which looks out over a jagged precipice, and a murky abyss is an ocean of ambiguous shapes rendered in the same ashen tones, their forms bluntly articulated, as though smothered in concrete. As Ellery studies them, she begins to discern pieces—a limb here, a featureless head there—that look vaguely human, anthropoid figures bent and buckled, or crawling on all fours, trapped and frozen in a solid casement of ash.

"She's never seen anything like this," Ellery tells Lawrence from her desk, shuffling from one picture to the next in the stack, while he stands behind her eating a peanut-butter-and-jelly sandwich.

"I know."

"Not in a book or in real life. She's never even seen the outside of a building."

"I know," says Lawrence, as he wipes his mouth and struggles to contain the massive bite he has just taken.

"Jesus, Larry, you know you're not supposed to have that outside of the cafeteria. Admin says they've been getting ants."

"Well, I can't help it if no one in the cafeteria wants me to sit with them. They want to know how our work is going and I can't tell them—not that they would believe it, anyway. They all think Dr. Moreau is a bit of a loon."

"Well, most geniuses are."

"My parents still wish I had become a lawyer."

"Mine wanted me to be a nuclear physicist." Ellery smiles wistfully.

"Well, joke's on them. Those nerds don't know the things *we* do."

"Do you think anyone else ever will?" says Ellery. "What would the world do if it knew about her?"

Larry shrugs. "Nothing too dramatic. The Russians would want one immediately, but they'd have to settle for some off-brand version. They'd thaw an octopus out of a freezer and use that. Then they'd send it to Venus. How should I know?"

*

280

Thursday, Ellery thinks. It's a Thursday, stranded somewhere in the vastness of December. This much she knows. But where is she?

She raises her head and the dimensions of the world invert, the ground rotating upward to become the ceiling, as though she is stuck on one of those spinning tunnels at the county fair. She retches unproductively, then lays her head down again.

Her cheek presses against cold, hard tile. She's on the floor. In a room, the creature's room—she can tell by the grid of drawings papered across one wall, and the table, stacked with textbooks.

She is lost, shipwrecked on an island of disarticulated time. She struggles to reach backward, to connect the previous flow of events to the one that is unfolding now, in tipsy currents, in front of her.

Morning. She came into the creature's room as usual. The creature presented her with a new batch of drawings, including one of the white clapboard octagonal house she has now sketched a half dozen times. In some drawings the house sits on its own amidst a stand of scraggly saplings; in others it is flanked on both sides by other buildings, abandoned houses, their windows vacant and doors smashed in. The creature was saying something to Ellery, something about time. Ellery has just introduced her to Einstein's theory of relativity. But what had she said?

The day proceeded as usual. They had breakfast, lunch. Lunch, in the creature's room, their reclusivity abetted by Lawrence's pilfering of sandwiches from the cafeteria. *Don't we make an eccentric little family*, Ellery had thought. Father, mother, and prodigal child, adopted from a distant millennium. What was it that the creature had said about time?

Lawrence had a meeting in the afternoon. Before he left, he and Ellery stood outside the creature's room, discussing something that she only hazily remembered; then Ellery came back inside. The creature was drawing, Pip sprawled in an extravagant arc over the table in front of her, one paw lightly nudging at her pencils with perfunctory interest. Ellery began to feel tired, for a moment entertaining the possibility that she had forgotten her regular 1:00 p.m. cup of coffee. But no, there was the empty mug right in front of her, beside the plates from their lunch. Maybe she had forgotten to add the sugar; it had tasted bitter. She was so tired. She needed to sit down.

Ellery forces her head up from the floor again. *No.*

She scans the tilted contents of the room. The creature is nowhere to be seen. She staggers to her feet, resisting the lurching pitch of the floor, and finds the note on the table, one corner pinned beneath a

281

textbook, written in the creature's meticulous hand. *There are hidden cameras in every room. Dr. Moreau has been watching you.*

It took six weeks, carefully secreting the tablets in a pocket beneath the mattress, to amass the amount of Secobarbital necessary to incapacitate a woman of Ellery's size. From then it was just a matter of waiting for an opportunity, for all of the variables to fall into alignment—Lawrence absent, the cup left untended, the key card easily accessible in Ellery's pocket. They had already provided her with most of the equipment, the lab coat and scrubs, and the identification tag Ellery had obtained for their visit to the zoology lab— it wouldn't help her to get into any of the other laboratories, but it would allow her to pass inconspicuously through the halls, and security didn't give a second look to someone who was on her way out.

It took longer, more than three months, for her scouts to complete their survey of the building. The first team she sent, a colony of black ants, never returned, presumably felled by the exterminators. The termites fared better; they bored into the walls and made their way through the innards of the building unnoticed, emerging only to gather necessary details: the codes for the door, the routes taken by security, the locations of the exits. She unleashed them at night, using the razor from her pencil sharpener to cut a notch at the base of her thumb, and sending them out through the air shaft behind her bed. They returned to her by the same route days or weeks later. She didn't find out what they had learned until they had reassimilated, crawling onto her skin and then dissolving. For the most part, they gave her what she had asked for, but once in a while they provided a revelation that she didn't expect.

She walks purposefully, avoiding eye contact with those who pass her, imagining herself as Lawrence, strutting down the hall like he owns the place. The distinct thrill rises in her chest, which she has felt only once before, in the zoology lab—the thrill of deception, of the secret knowledge she holds, that she is not what they think she is—she is not one of them, and yet their eyes skirt casually over her, occasionally making small, private gestures of acknowledgment, signaling their unwitting collusion in her duplicity. The more people who see her, the more enmeshed she becomes in her disguise, in the identity they are projecting onto her. A part of her even begins to believe it herself, to hear that person's voice in her mind. *Hello, Susan.*

Isn't it a beautiful day? Hi, Bob. Did you catch St. Elsewhere *last night? Carol, how are you? Alan, is your throat feeling better? Stephen, have your alligator eggs hatched yet?*

What an elaborate charade. The laboratories are full of little performances like that; peeking out of ventilator shafts and scurrying across ceilings, she has observed hundreds of them and yet they never cease to amaze her, these miniature conspiracies of civility, unacknowledged yet vitally important, indispensable to people's sense of self and belonging in the world. With every exchange, they tighten the bonds around each other, willing into existence a certain version of reality. They take it for granted, not knowing how precarious it really is—how easy it would be for a stranger to insinuate herself into their patterns, and to subvert them for her own purposes.

She can see the door, situated at the end of a long corridor flanked with windows, admitting the first sunlight she has ever seen. *The first I've seen with these eyes,* she corrects herself. She has no real memories from her ancient eyes, only itinerant glimpses, phantom sensations, dust swept into recesses in remote corners of her mind.

The light crests over her face, its warmth flooding into her pores. Then she hears the voice.

"Eva!"

She stops and stands, motionless.

"Eva, wait."

She turns around. Dr. Moreau is standing ten yards behind her, at the other end of the corridor. She is as the scouts described: a woman of medium stature and build, outfitted in a neatly pressed lab coat over a cream-colored sweater and tweed slacks, with silver hair cut into a bob and swept in a sinuous arc behind each ear. She has a narrow face, shallowly pleated around her eyes and mouth, and a long and graceful nose.

The cat, Pip, who has followed on the creature's heels since she left the laboratory, comes to sit next to her, his lashing tail scuffing the sides of her white sneakers, and raises his leg to lick his paw.

The creature has witnessed many things in the past months, through her human eyes and those of her insect army. She has watched Ellery and Lawrence discuss and argue, privately exchanging their fears and concerns about the mystery of Dr. Moreau's intentions. She has gathered snatches of the events of the outside world—the competitive hoarding of world-destroying weapons, the massacre of refugees, the travels of machines to distant planets, the imprinting of intelligence into computers. Yet the most surprising discovery of all, the only one that has plucked the chords of her own artificial heart, was the knowledge that in her files tracking the progress of her experiment, Dr. Moreau has given the creature a name.

"Why did you do this?" says Eva.

Dr. Moreau opens her arms, her palms upturned in a beseeching gesture, but doesn't speak.

"For what *purpose?*" says Eva.

"Come back to the laboratory," says Dr. Moreau, "and I'll tell you everything."

Eva stands still, wallowing in the moment, trying to imprint every detail of Dr. Moreau's face into her mind. There will be a time—she knows, instinctively—when she will need to find it again. There are revelations yet to come, and the walls of secrecy will come tumbling down. But not today.

Eva turns, punches the code into the door, and turns the handle. The sunlight blasting into the hallway envelops her figure and that of Pip, pressing them both into oblivion.

Lost Souls
Matthew Baker

PRAISE BE TO YAHWEH, and to Allah, and to Buddha, and to Vishnu, and to Shiva, and to Brahma, and to Amaterasu, and to Jesus, and whoever else might hear our plea!

Naomi was working at the hospital the day that the empty bodies began being born. She was a nurse in the neonatal unit. The rookie. She had graduated only just the year before. Wildfires were raging in the mountains beyond the valley, and dark clouds of smoke had blown into the city, casting a spooky haze over the resorts and the casinos. Naomi had just clocked in for the day when the first infant was rushed into the neonatal unit. A pudgy pink-skinned newborn with bright blue eyes. The child hadn't been born prematurely. The child technically wasn't even ill. Its pulse was good, its respiration was normal, its temperature was fine. And yet something was clearly wrong. Its automated processes were working—its heart was beating, its lungs were breathing, its fingertips jerked in response to a prick, its pupils dilated in response to a flashlight—and yet the child didn't show any signs of consciousness. It wasn't moving its head. It wasn't moving its arms. It wasn't moving its legs. It wasn't crying. It wasn't squealing. It wasn't cooing. It wasn't moving its body or making any noises at all. Just gazing silently at the ceiling with an eerily blank stare. The physician on duty tried rubbing its back, tried spanking it, tried tickling it, and the baby still didn't respond. And then while the physician was standing there troubleshooting, the baby died. Just like that. It was just there and then it was gone, no pulse, no respiration, beyond resuscitation. Its eyes didn't glaze over. Its eyes didn't even close. Almost like sudden infant death syndrome, Naomi thought, except the baby hadn't been asleep. She was still looking at the dead newborn in confusion when another infant was rushed into the neonatal unit with that same blank stare. Then another. And another. The neonatal unit was chaos. A graveyard. Over half of the children born at the hospital that day exhibited the same symptoms. An utter

285

lack of consciousness. Sudden death. Initially the staff assumed the phenomenon was restricted to that single hospital, but then word began to spread that empty bodies were being born all over Las Vegas. All over Nevada. All over the United States. All over earth.

Naomi drove home in a state of shock.

"These aren't stillbirths that we're talking about. These are babies that were born alive. Physically all of the babies were perfectly fine. Just empty. Completely unresponsive. Like there was nothing inside," said a gruff voice on the radio.

"And all of the babies died within minutes?"

"I want to be clear that we're not talking about an extinction scenario. There's no reason to panic. Normal, healthy babies were born today, all over the world. Whatever this is, not all newborns seem to be affected."

"But what if the disease spreads?"

"We still don't know enough about the phenomenon to refer to it as a disease."

"Then what else could it be?"

"We don't know yet."

"Is it going to keep happening?"

"We just don't know."

Naomi had found out that she was pregnant the week before.

Crows were circling in the sky above the entrance to her neighborhood. The street was empty. The sidewalks were deserted. An abandoned tricycle lay upended in a yard, the wheels still spinning. Tad was waiting for her in the driveway of the condo, wearing slippers and a bathrobe that was billowing in the wind.

"Everything's going to be OK," Tad said, wrapping her in a hug.

"I watched thirteen babies die today," Naomi said, and then he led her into the condo, where she got into the bathtub and wept.

Later she sat in a bath towel on the sofa with wet hair and a smoothie and watched the newscasters on every channel try not to have a nervous breakdown on live television.

"I could use a fucking drink," Naomi said.

"I'm sorry," Tad said.

"I just want to get drunk," Naomi said.

"Me too," Tad said.

"You're not pregnant," Naomi said, almost upset.

"I know."

"We still have that bottle of sake in the freezer."

"I know."

"At least one of us should be drunk for this."

"I'm not going to drink if you can't," Tad said, staring straight ahead at the screen, and he was so serious and earnest and simple that she felt the anger fade. She could never manage to get mad at him. She wished that she could have gotten mad at him sometimes. She would have liked to be mad at him. But it would have been like getting mad at a bandage. All he ever wanted to do was help. A baffled public health official in a checkered dress shirt was being interviewed on the television. Rama, the kitten, came wandering into the living room with a mischievous look, and then the whole family was there, Naomi and her husband and her cat and the baby growing in her womb, the baby that now was maybe going to be born only an empty body after all.

And though she would have preferred not to think about the possibility that there was an empty body growing in her womb, she was confronted with the possibility constantly, every moment that she was at work. Empty bodies continued to be born at the hospital that next day and the day after and the rest of the month, and each of the babies was rushed straight into the neonatal unit, and she had to stand there watching each of the babies die. Medications for catatonia had no effect. Electroshock therapy treatments had no effect. Out of desperation, in total secrecy, and despite the fact that the symptoms the affected babies exhibited weren't truly those of a trance state, the hospital brought in a professional hypnotist, who failed to induce any form of consciousness in the empty bodies. The halls of the maternity ward were filled with the wails of grieving parents. Meanwhile, back out on the streets, in forums on the Internet, various parties were busy assigning blame for the epidemic. The environmentalists were convinced that the phenomenon was somehow related to widespread consumption of genetically modified foods, despite a lack of any supporting evidence whatsoever, while the puritans were convinced that the phenomenon was caused by widespread consumption of birth control pills, despite a lack of any supporting evidence whatsoever, and the prohibitionists were convinced that the phenomenon was thanks to widespread consumption of marijuana, despite a lack of any supporting evidence whatsoever and the fact that humans had been getting blazed for millennia. Naomi wasn't an environmentalist. Naomi wasn't a puritan. Naomi wasn't a prohibitionist. Naomi was a scientist. She believed in logic. She believed in data. And for that reason the phenomenon horrified her. She had never before lived through an epidemic that modern medicine couldn't explain. Most researchers were pursuing studies that assumed that the phenomenon was caused by an infection, perhaps by a novel virus or a mutant bacterium, and yet even the scientists promoting these theories admitted that the theories were flawed, as the affected babies didn't display any of the classic symptoms of a viral or a bacterial infection, not to mention the fact that a virus or a bacterium would have had an origin, would have had to spread, while the phenomenon had appeared simultaneously across the globe. The utter lack of consciousness that the affected newborns exhibited seemed to suggest that the problem was neurological, or perhaps lay with the sensory organs, and yet autopsies showed no abnormalities in the brain tissue of the affected newborns, nor in the eyes nor the ears nor the nerves of the skin. The autopsies showed no abnormalities whatsoever. Science couldn't explain what was happening. The epidemic was claiming hundreds of thousands of lives a day, claimed millions of lives over the course of that first month, and still the best procedure that the medical community had developed for dealing with the phenomenon was just to catalog the deaths. To sit back and watch the babies die. Naomi had never dreaded going to work before, not ever, but the blank stares of the empty bodies terrified her. And yet the most frightening aspect of the phenomenon wasn't the empty bodies. The most frightening aspect of the phenomenon was its numerical precision. In Arizona, just across the border, only a state away, a famous gynecologist at a university medical center thought to turn to statistics. Examining the available data, the gynecologist discovered that the number of empty bodies being born per day was strangely consistent. The number didn't spike or drop the way that mortality rates would during a typical epidemic. The number did slightly fluctuate from day to day, but overall the number was constant. Almost as if the number were being regulated by a sentient force. That alone would have been eerie, but then the gynecologist thought to subtract the total number of empty bodies born each day from the total number of babies who were born daily, thereby obtaining the average number of babies born each day who were healthy and conscious. Then she compared that number, the adjusted global birth rate, with the global death rate. And the rates were equal. The number of humans being born each day now appeared to be approximately equivalent to the number of humans who were dying, stabilizing the global population at just over thirteen billion. Naomi felt a shiver of dread and awe, reading the paper that the gynecologist had published online. A Cabalist, the gynecologist suggested that the phenomenon might somehow be related to the cycle of reincarnation. It was as if, the gynecologist said, the exploding global population had exceeded the total number of available human souls. The bodies seemed empty because the bodies were empty, just meaty shells, born without souls. Other scientists were quick to point out that correlation didn't imply causation, and that there wasn't necessarily a connection between the birth rate and the death rate. Yet in the absence of any viable alternative explanation, the theory was compellingly logical. It explained the symptoms. It explained the numbers. Within hours the theory had spread across the Internet, being hailed as a breakthrough on the news, being discussed as a fact on the forums, becoming the prevalent explanation for the phenomenon worldwide. The Phoenix Hypothesis, the theory soon came to be called, named both for the city where the gynecologist practiced and for the mythological creature of cyclical reincarnation.

And yet to say that the theory was prevalent was not the same as to say that the theory was popular. The scientific community was upset by the implication that there was a spiritual realm, an invisible domain that couldn't possibly fit into the modern understanding of physical cosmology, unless human souls were composed of an as-yet-unobserved material, like dark energy or dark matter. The physics conferences that autumn were sober affairs. Beloved colleagues avoided even speaking to each other. Scuffles broke out between researchers who refused to give the theory serious consideration and researchers attempting to reconcile the theory with quantum fields. And the religious community wasn't any happier. The Christians and the Muslims, while pleased that the theory seemed to prove the existence of the individual immortal soul, seemed upset by the implication that human souls were reincarnated, which would fuck up centuries of theology. The Taoists and the Buddhists, while pleased that the theory seemed to prove the existence of reincarnation, seemed upset by the implication that every human had an individual immortal soul, which would fuck up centuries of theology. The Jains and the Hindus, of course, while delighted both that the theory seemed to prove the existence of the individual immortal soul and that the theory seemed to prove the existence of reincarnation, were distressed by the implication that the cycle of human reincarnation was separate from the souls of other animals, and, like the Sikhs, were profoundly disturbed by the notion that human souls could in any way be finite or quantifiable, which would fuck up centuries of theology. Everybody seemed to have been wrong in some way or another. The Internet was haunted by angsty monks and clergy, gloomy specters appearing in interviews for newspapers and vlogs, bemoaning the bewildering state of the world. Even the Scientologists seemed troubled by the implications of the theory, although nobody except the Scientologists knew why the Scientologists would be upset, since nobody except the Scientologists had any clue what the Scientologists believed.

"I mean, if souls are real, and reincarnation is too, how do we *know* that souls don't move back and forth between humans and other animals?" said an acne-scarred janitor in the lobby of the hospital, helping to hang explanatory posters adorned with colorful infographics about the epidemic.

The data seemed conclusive. The phenomenon didn't appear to affect other species of animals. Cattle weren't giving birth to empty calves. Dogs weren't giving birth to empty puppies. Horses weren't giving birth to empty foals. The shortage only seemed to affect humans. And basic logic led to the same conclusion. Considering that humans had spent the past century exterminating countless species of animals from the planet, causing the greatest mass extinction event since the Quaternary, a shortage of souls in newborn babies was presumably only possible if human souls were separate from animal souls. Overall, although the human population had dramatically increased over the past century, the total number of living organisms on the planet had decreased considerably. If humans had been able to share souls with other animals, then there should have been a surplus rather than a shortage. Still, despite the overwhelming evidence to the contrary, an idea soon spread that killing animals might somehow liberate souls that could be used by human babies. Nowhere was this idea as infectious as in America. Within days of the theory being published, there were towns that had been whipped into a frenzy. Towns out in the country, coal towns and farm towns, where the locals subscribed to mysterious folk religions whose curious belief systems combined elements of born-again evangelicalism, talk-show morality, gun worship, truck worship, bibliophobia, and pagan superstitions about college athletics. Towns where feeling ruled over logic. Towns where hearsay ruled over data. Towns where every nonhuman animal had been slaughtered, the bodies heaped into piles as high as haystacks. Corgis shot through the forehead, beagles shot through the forehead, terriers shot through the forehead, cats slick with wet blood, horses bleeding in ebbing spurts, deer that had been rammed with cars, canaries that had been slain with hammers, parakeets that had been crushed with shovels, cockatoos that had been smashed with rocks, rabbits speared with pitchforks, beheaded hens, mangled opossums, finches, cardinals, woodpeckers, and squirrels with snapped necks, a heaped mess of limbs and paws and hooves and tails and bloated tongues, being set ablaze at twilight in town squares as children in military fatigues marched about the burning bodies. The killings had no visible effect on the phenomenon. The killings kept happening anyway.

Babies fertilized in vitro were shown to be just as likely to be born empty.

Babies delivered by caesarean were shown to be just as likely to be born empty.

Meanwhile, the price to adopt a child had soared to over a million.

"Just because you've felt your baby moving doesn't mean that your baby is conscious. Most movements in the womb are involuntary. Or reflexes. There isn't necessarily any actual *control* involved," said a tech with auburn hair, pushing a patient in a gown down the hallway in a wheelchair.

With so few viable babies being born, the number of preemies in residence at the hospital had plunged. The neonatal unit looked like a motel on a dying highway. Full of empty beds.

By the end of that autumn, the hospital admin had decided to downsize the staff of the neonatal unit. Naomi was the rookie. She was first to go.

"We're grateful for the work that you did here," the human resources director said, offering her a handshake and a smile.

Naomi didn't bother applying for a new job. None of the hospitals were hiring for neonatal. She spent the week after losing her job sprawled across the sofa in underwear and a hoodie, crushingly depressed, bingeing on cream puffs and jelly donuts, watching the television with the curtains drawn. She was so tired of hearing about the phenomenon. Hearing about the phenomenon exhausted her. She kept flipping to shows about the phenomenon anyway.

There was an interview with somebody in a poncho.

"God was like, fine, you're going to legalize abortion? You don't want your babies anymore? You only want your babies sometimes? You're just going to start killing babies at random? Then so am I."

There was an interview with somebody with beaded cornrows.

"There's always been this assumption that God is good. Because that's what our scriptures tell us. But scriptures are just the word of God. We're taking God at its word. We're assuming that God never lies. If a man came to your door and told you he was good, and the only evidence he had for that was a book that he had written that said he was good, would you trust him?"

There was an interview with a weather-beaten rancher who had burned a hundred acres of prairie.

"Why burn all of the fields?"

"We're trying to kill all of the insects."

"You believe in reincarnation?"

"Been coming around to the idea."

"What about all of the evidence that humans souls are separate from other animals?"

The rancher grimaced, gesturing helplessly at the blackened stubs of grass.

"I'm willing to try anything at this point. My daughter's pregnant."

In the background a hawk flying over the ashes was shot out of the sky by a child with a rifle.

Tad stepped timidly into the living room, covering the mouthpiece on the cordless phone.

"Let's have dinner with your parents tonight," Tad whispered.

Naomi looked at him from the sofa. Rama had followed him into the living room, curling around his ankles, purring at his feet. Her parents lived in the hills above the city, in a modern villa with a shimmering infinity pool, with underwater lighting that cycled between shades of neon, violet and cyan and indigo and green. The house where she had been born. Tad liked her parents, but he had never spontaneously suggested having dinner with her parents before, not under any circumstances. He was just trying to help. To get her off of the sofa. To get her out of the condo. She decided to go along with it.

"You can say that we'll be there," Naomi said.

She took a long shower. She put on actual clothes. She still looked depressed as hell. Later that night she sat on a chair in the villa, sipping a virgin daiquiri across from her parents. Her parents were religious more out of habit than out of conviction, although the epidemic had inspired a renewed interest in religion for everybody, her parents included, and her mother had set out fresh flowers on the shrine. Her father wore a bright dastār with a charcoal suit. Her mother was wearing jelly sandals with a silk sari. Her parents were much older than she was, almost elderly now, and had no hobbies aside from making money and watching sports. Lately her father had been obsessed with professional paintball. A paintball match was playing across the television on mute.

"You look terrible," her father said.

"You really do," her mother said.

"I appreciate you saying that," Naomi said.

Warriors fist-pumped as paint-spattered enemies fell to the dirt.

"In a way, maybe losing your job was a good thing," Tad said tentatively, sitting next to her in a cream polo.

"Now you have the ability to travel if necessary," her father said.

"Now you have the freedom to explore every option," her mother said.

Naomi stared at her parents suspiciously, sensing a vague implication, a current of conspiracy in the air. Her parents were plotting something, she realized. Dinner tonight hadn't been spontaneous. Dinner tonight was an ambush. She glanced at her husband. Tad looked nervous. He was in on it. He had been scheming too.

"I hate it when you all make plans about me behind my back," Naomi said with a scowl.

"Please, baby, just hear us out," Tad said.

"There's a place out in the desert," her father said.

"A special place," her mother said.

"For pregnant women," her father said.

"Women looking for some type of assurance," her mother said.

"The facility is one of a kind. You can think of it as a precaution. We would live there until the baby was born, in order to ensure that it's born with a soul," Tad said.

Naomi scowled at him.

"I'm going to have the baby at home," Naomi said.

Tad glanced at her parents before turning back toward her with a hint of pleading in his voice.

"This is a once-in-a-lifetime opportunity," Tad said.

"We'd pay for it," her father said.

"It's really very expensive," her mother said.

"Absolutely not," Naomi said.

Her parents frowned with disappointment.

"Naomi. There's a body growing inside of you. You have a responsibility to do everything you can to give it a chance at having a soul," her father said.

"You're talking about the baby like it's not a person," Naomi said, getting upset.

"We have no way of knowing whether or not it has a soul yet, and without a soul, it's not," her mother said.

Naomi stared at the staircase to the basement behind her parents, at the scuff marks rubbed into the wallpaper by the rubber arms of the baby gate that had stood there for so many years. Naomi had been a sleepwalker as a child, awaking in the darkest hours of the night to wander the house with glazed eyes, brushing her hair in the darkness in the bathroom, holding her toys in the darkness in the playroom, sitting in her chair at the empty table as if expecting to be served a meal. Her parents had said that there was nothing to be ashamed of, that sleepwalking was simply a matter of the body waking too soon, before the soul. She remembered how embarrassed she had felt when her parents had installed a baby gate to protect her from falling down the steps while she was sleepwalking, and how furious she had been when her parents had said she didn't study enough to do premed, and how irritated she had been after dropping premed when her parents had suggested she might like nursing. How skeptical she had been when her parents had arranged the marriage with Tad, a goofy mathematician with a homely appearance. How certain she had been that there was no connection, even up to the very day of the wedding, convinced that the marriage would be lifeless and sad, but how afterward she had grown close with him, and how she had even come to love him. How sweetly and kindly he had cared for her every day since. How much she loved talking to him in bed before falling asleep, when his speech took on a temporary lisp from his retainer. Somehow her parents always knew what would be best for her. She looked at her mother and her father sitting there on the heirloom divan, at those tired and wrinkled faces, creased with worry and lost sleep.

"Coming to this country was not easy, but we did it, for the future of the family. And now, for the future of the family, this is something we must ask you to do."

Naomi felt the baby give a faint kick, and she hesitated, taking a breath, and then she turned back toward her husband.

"Could we bring Rama?" Naomi said.

A week later she was in the car, gliding along a desolate highway in the desert, gazing out at the sand and the shrubs and the massive ridges speckled with greenery on the horizon. Heat haze shimmered in the distance like flailing spirits. Rama was curled up on her lap, either napping or pretending to nap. Tad sat behind the wheel in a polka-dot dress shirt, occasionally glancing with a nervous expression at the clock on the dash, as her mother and her father chatted back and forth in the back seat, bantering about cryptocurrencies, both wearing shades. Following the instructions that the facility had given her parents, Tad turned off of the highway onto a dusty, unmarked dirt road. For the next hour the car wound steadily through gullies and valleys and canyons without passing a single sign of life. Rocks ground under the tires. Clouds floated above the sunroof. The murmur of soul music playing over the radio gradually turned to static. After finally coasting through a forbidding gate, the car arrived at a gigantic concrete compound with a flock of buzzards perched on the roof.

Jane, the manager of the maternity center, was waiting at the towering doors.

"Welcome to the Oasis," Jane said.

Naomi was thirteen weeks pregnant.

In the vast hallway leading from the entrance of the compound into the inner chambers, a mass of faded prayer flags hung from the ceiling, fraying rectangles of colorful fabric, swaying with drafts of air. Jane was middle-aged, sporting a pair of heels with a blouse and a blazer and a hip haircut, and had the lively charm of a circus ringmaster, strolling ahead of the group to gesture enthusiastically at the highlights of the tour. Naomi and the others followed her through an arched doorway into a vast circular chamber, the altar room, where bright sunshine streamed down through the skylight on the vaulted ceiling, casting shadows behind pillars, making the space glow. Shimmery patches of sunlight trembled on the wall, reflecting off the glass in watches and spectacles. The chamber was furnished with over a hundred cots, radiating out from the stone altar at the center, each occupied by a withered body. Pregnant women sat on worn wooden stools throughout the chamber, murmuring together, giggling together, playing singing bowls over the peaceful sound of the life-support monitors, the quiet beeping of the electrocardiographs and electroencephalographs. The monitors stood on bedside tables, accompanied by bottles of pills and bottles of water. Incense in brass urns. Lilies in clay vases. Ancient statues spotted with moss and lichen were arranged like guardians along the perimeter of the chamber. Gods of childbirth. Gods of motherhood.

"A soul may be a spiritual entity, but that doesn't mean that it's magic, or can just do whatever it wants. This very epidemic proves that souls have limits, which means that just like an angel or a demon, a soul is still bound by the laws of physics. That's the key. A soul can't simply teleport into a new body. A soul has to travel through space and time. What we offer here is proximity. We're over a hundred miles from the nearest city. And on any given day we have over a hundred dying people in residence here. Many of those people are on life support, kept alive only by machines, and have given us permission to switch off the machines at any time, allowing us to guarantee that at least one person dies here every day. We also sacrifice a number of animals throughout the day. Typically a dove and a lamb at sunrise, a rooster at noon, a peacock at dusk, and a goat at midnight, although if you feel a special connection with another species of animal, we'd be happy to incorporate it into the daily cycle," Jane said.

Naomi glanced at the stone altar across the chamber, where a ceremonial dagger with a curved blade and an ebony handle rested on a stand.

"You'll give birth to your child right here at the Oasis, under the care of some of the finest obstetricians in the country, and between now and then every day you'll be surrounded by freshly departed souls in need of a new body to inhabit," Jane said.

Jane waved to a pudgy, bearded cook in a spattered apron, who walked past the arched doorway carrying a tote bag brimming with leafy vegetables.

"That's Joaquin, the chef. The food here is exceptional. Bathrooms are communal. Towels are provided. The linens are washed daily. You'll be given a private bedchamber, although some residents occasionally prefer to sleep here among the dying, which can be arranged upon request," Jane said.

Naomi paused, watching a pregnant woman with beautiful golden hair, who sat on a stool near a cot, stroke the shriveled hands of a geriatric man with bloodshot eyes and a sallow complexion.

"Come to me," the woman whispered. "I've seen how you smile when you eat cookies. You like cookies. I'll give you all the cookies that you want. You'll have the perfect childhood. Disneyland. Malibu. Box seats at the Derby. Summer in the Hamptons. You'll have a trust fund. You'll have a sports car. We'll buy you anything you want. We're an important family. We have powerful connections. Exeter. Harvard. We fought in the Revolution. We had ancestors on the Mayflower. Come to me when you die."

Naomi felt a sudden chill as the woman with the golden hair turned toward her, gazing at her with a jealous look.

"Naomi, time to say goodbye," Jane called with a smile, leading the group back toward the hallway with the prayer flags.

Tad said an overly cheerful farewell to her parents, Naomi gave each of her parents a tight hug, and then her parents left the compound, heading back to the city, and she followed him down a hallway lined with rough wooden doors.

The bedchamber was simple, furnished with a full-size cot draped with a beige wool blanket, a dresser, a mirror, a desk with a chair, and a bright salt lamp that cast a warm saffron glow across the room. No window. The door had a sliding lock. The bags had already been delivered. Rama was curled up in a satin cat bed on the floor, drowsing. Naomi sat down on the cot with a creak. Tad was organizing geometry books over on the desk.

Tad noticed her staring at him.

"What?" Tad said.

"You don't believe in any of this."

"I never said that."

"You're a card-carrying atheist."

Tad frowned, sitting down on the mattress, wrapping an arm around her.

"I haven't seen those empty bodies in person like you have. I've seen videos, though. And it scares the hell out of me. I don't want that to happen to our baby. I'm willing to try anything. No matter how dubious its science is. No matter how much it costs," Tad said.

Naomi was one of a dozen mothers living at the compound. Most of the fathers didn't have the ability to work from home, and only visited the compound on weekends, or once a month. Tad was the only father living there. He rarely left the bedchamber during the day, hard at work on a new proof in synthetic geometry, hunched over the desk with a mug of steaming coffee. Naomi spent the days wandering the compound alone. While the primary mission of the facility was to ensure the spiritual health of the babies by providing pregnant women with exclusive access to freshly departed souls, the facility was also designed to ensure the physical health of the babies. The daily agenda was wellness. The dining hall was stocked with wholesome nourishment, including freshly squeezed juices that the chef would make upon command, pouring shimmers of pink and yellow and red and orange into crystal goblets, grapefruit or mango or watermelon or carrot. In the bathrooms, the rough stone counters were equipped with jars of prenatal vitamins and antacid tablets and gleaming amber vials brimming with fragrant bodywashes and shampoos and exfoliants and cleansers and moisturizers and creams. A maid cleaned the bedchambers and washed dirty laundry. A masseuse offered massages, gently kneading the oiled skin of women splayed across towels. A yoga instructor drove in each day to lead yoga classes in the yoga room, strolling between the rubber mats as women held rigid poses. A meditation teacher drove in each day to lead meditation classes in the meditation room, coaching women sitting on embroidered cushions through soothing breathing techniques. Women exercised on stationary bikes in the fitness center, drinking purified water from glass water bottles embedded with colorful hunks of quartz meant to dispel negative energy and impart positive energy and help calm the mind, while others reclined with diaries on the benches in the greenhouse, journaling together in the clean, pure, steamy air. Jane worked spiritedly throughout the day to ensure that each of the residents had whatever was needed, running to and from the supply room in the manager's office to fetch body pillows and belly bands and eye masks and maternity bras and boxes of truffles. If not for being located in a desolate wilderness of sand and shrubs and scorching heat, the maternity center would have been heaven. Naomi felt spoiled and lonely. Rama trailed after her sometimes, mewling at residents in passing. Other days the cat stayed back in the bedchamber with Tad, or snuck off to prowl through the compound alone. Regardless of whether the cat was with her, the other residents never spoke to her, just smiled tightly in passing. Emily, the pregnant woman with the beautiful golden hair, was the belle of the compound, always surrounded by happy, chattering companions, the center of attention. Emily was tall and slim and elegant, dressing in haute couture garments made from lush, magnificent fabrics, with an intense, hungry gaze and a harsh, angular face that was pretty the way that a storm could be pretty, and wore her hair in fantastically intricate buns and chignons and braids that were as geometrically complex as figures from a textbook. Strands of gold would twinkle in the light as she passed through a room. Packages of new clothing arrived at the compound for her almost daily. The other residents fawned over her. Like her, the rest of the residents seemed to come from prominent families. Socialites, and legatees, and scions, and heirs. Naomi was an outsider. She was the outcast. When she tried sitting with the other women in the dining hall, none of the women ever made conversation with her. When she arrived in the dining hall before the other women, the women sat at tables across the room from her. Emily seemed to whisper about her sometimes, glancing at her as other women broke out into cackles. Naomi became accustomed to eating breakfast and lunch alone.

Naomi had never been frightened by pain or suffering or death, but there was something eerie about the altar room. Most of the terminal patients were comatose. Withered, atrophied bodies that were fed intravenously. The rest of the terminal patients were bedridden. Elderly bodies reduced to withered husks. Dying figures coughed and moaned and muttered and called out from cots as the medics on duty emptied out bedpans and changed drip bags and spooned mashed peas and chunky applesauce between trembling lips. The smell of incense and lilies was thick in the air. Although even the patients who were conscious were generally too addled by dementia or pharmaceuticals to carry on much of a conversation, residents were encouraged to socialize with the dying, and all of the women visited the altar room at least once during the day, sitting on worn stools beside the cots, holding the hands of comatose patients, wiping the brows of bedridden patients, praying at the feet of the ancient statues, quietly playing singing bowls with wooden mallets. Joaquin, the chef, came through the altar room periodically to deliver refreshments. Silver platters heaped with persimmons. Trays piled with plump figs. Chilled bottles of water, infused with lemon wedges or sliced cucumber. Emily was often in there, murmuring in the ears of comatose patients, reading fairy tales aloud to bedridden patients, prowling through the cots with a covetous look. Naomi avoided being in the altar room when she was there, and though death had never frightened her, violence of any kind profoundly disturbed her, and she avoided being in the altar room during sacrifices too, when the sharp, curved blade of the ceremonial dagger would be drawn across the tender throat of a shrieking rooster or a struggling peacock, and dark blood would spatter across the rough, pale stone of the altar, taking hours to evaporate into the air. Every afternoon a comatose patient was chosen to die, removed from life support by the medics, vanishing from the world to the sound of a flatline. Emily was always there, hovering nearby with a hopeful expression as life left the body, and whenever a bedridden patient suddenly died without warning, Emily would rush to the altar room to be as near to the freed soul as possible, followed by an entourage of women. Naomi liked to be in the altar room at quieter times. Liked to be helpful. To rub the arms of comatose patients to prevent bedsores, to scratch the legs of bedridden patients to soothe itches, and to sit listening to the peaceful beeping of the life-support monitors, which made her nostalgic for the hospital. Yet even then there was something creepy about the altar room. Pregnant women and terminal patients had both occupied the same building at the hospital, of course. But, still, the juxtaposition of the pregnant women and the terminal patients in the altar room troubled her, and she felt followed sometimes by the empty stares of the decrepit statues along the wall.

There was something eerie about the birthing room too. The birthing room was across the compound, a vast circular chamber the exact same size and shape as the altar room, but instead of a hundred cots radiating out from a stone altar, the birthing room was completely empty aside from a single hospital bed, shining under a spotlight at the center of the chamber. Rather than having statues standing along the perimeter, rustic wooden shelves were arranged along the wall, lined with gigantic healing crystals, lumps of amethyst and topaz and citrine and quartz that glowed in the faint underlighting of the shelves, casting glimmers of color across the floor. Dust twinkled in the air. Nobody was ever in there. None of the residents were due for months. Naomi sometimes peeked in through the arched doorway, placing both her hands on her stomach, feeling her baby move under her fingers, imagining giving birth to the child in there someday. If she shouted, her voice would echo through the chamber, the sound reborn every couple of seconds with another bounce off the wall.

That was how she passed days at the Oasis. Getting periodic medical exams by the doctors, doing yoga with women who ignored her, practicing meditation with women who ignored her, eating mochi, drinking lassis, getting massages, and wandering the compound. A clanging bell announced when dinner was served. Tad ate dinner with her every night, babbling excitedly about whatever podcast he had listened to while he was working. After dinner she would hang out with him, playing tattered board games from the entertainment room, or videochatting with her parents, or streaming new rom-coms together, or reading popular science magazines. Some nights he would have sex with her. Some nights he wouldn't have sex with her. Each night he dutifully inserted his retainer before climbing under the covers to go to bed, mumbling his final thoughts for the day as he drifted off to sleep, faintly lisping. The concrete walls were thick. Naomi never heard any noises from the other bedchambers. Tad slept peacefully, probably dreaming of lines and shapes, the shifting measurements of changing angles. Naomi slept fitfully. When she couldn't sleep, sometimes she took walks, padding barefoot through the compound in the darkest hours of the night, when the hallway was lit only by the dim emergency lighting above the doorways to the bathrooms. Jane lived at the compound too, but she was never awake that time of night. The only staff on duty that time of night was whatever guard was in the security office and whatever doctor was in the medical office, there in case of emergencies, getting paid to sit quietly. Naomi liked to climb the central stairwell to the tiled patio on the roof, where the other residents sunbathed during the day. To sit there under the moon. Just to look at the stars. She missed Vegas. She had never imagined that was possible, but she did, missed the neon and the noise and the heat and the traffic, and the celebrity impostors, and the ridiculous billboards, and the tourists stumbling drunkenly down the sidewalk in skintight clothing, and the gambling addicts waiting in line at the pawnshops, and the newlywed elopers parading out of kitschy chapels, and the cheapskates strolling out of buffets with purses full of stolen pastries, and the catcallers, and the gangsters, and the missionaries, and the doomsayers, even the putrid stench of the garbage baking in rusted trash bins in the alleys. Being able to drive around, and run errands, and grocery shop. Lounging around in her condo. Getting to visit her parents. Smelling sautéing garlic, taking a bath while her husband cooked brunch. Rama sat with her on the roof occasionally, watching intently as bats arced over the compound. Naomi never saw anybody else up there that time of night. Sometimes she would stay on the roof until dawn, when she would hear the station wagon that the chef drove arrive in the parking lot with a crunch of gravel, and then she would slip back down the stairs, heading toward the dining hall to get some breakfast.

Naomi was rummaging through the video collection in the entertainment room one day when she heard a group of residents stroll through the doorway, plopping onto couches, sinking into armchairs, chattering with Emily, who took a seat on a plush leather ottoman, grinning wickedly at the others, hair cascading from an elegant waterfall braid.

"Hold on, which guard?"

"The young one," Emily said.

"Kyle, with the gauges?"

"We did it in the greenhouse once," Emily said.

"Wait, you've hooked up with him more than once?"

"I couldn't take it anymore. I was completely losing it. I've been really horny since the first trimester. Danny knows that. If he didn't want me to sleep with other people then he should have been here. Money isn't an issue. He chose to keep working. He decided not to come."

"I'd rather just use a vibrator."

301

"I haven't been horny at all."

Naomi fumbled a cassette, which hit the floor with a clatter. Emily glanced over at her, then turned back toward the others.

"I mean, it's whatever. He's the best of what's around. The other guards are too old. And the cook is just creepy. I'd be afraid of catching a case of eczema or something, hooking up with him. You just know his back is hairy. You don't even have to look. And the other options around here are just as unattractive," Emily said, looking over at Naomi again with a faint smirk.

Naomi realized that she was talking about Tad.

Naomi stormed back down the hallway in a blind rage, not even paying attention to where she was going, furious both to have had her husband be considered an option for seduction and to have had her husband be deemed too unattractive to fuck. She trembled with barely contained anger. She went back to the bedchamber.

"I can't do this anymore," Naomi said.

Tad looked up from the desk.

"I want to go home," Naomi said.

Tad took in a breath, then let out a sigh. He set down a pencil. Rama mewed, peering out from the shadows under the cot.

"I don't want to be here any more than you do," Tad said.

"I really don't think that's possible," Naomi said.

"Trust me," Tad said.

"Nobody here will even talk to me," Naomi said.

"Baby. We're so close. Just hold on. We only have to make it a few more months," Tad said.

And she tried, but the situation only got worse. When she ran to get a drink of water during yoga class, Emily took her place, forcing her to move to a mat at the back of the room, where she couldn't even see the instructor through the contorted limbs of all of the women who shunned her. When she ran to take a pee during meditation class, Emily edged out her cushion, forcing her to move to a place at the back of the room, where she couldn't even concentrate on the teacher over the distracted whispers of all of the women who shunned her. Emily organized a sleepover in the entertainment room, ordering a dozen sleeping bags from online, buying stovetop popcorn, getting pizza delivered, and then invited every resident except for her. Naomi tried approaching the other residents when the women were alone, trying to make friendly jokes, trying to make superficial banter, even just trying to exchange pleasantries about the weather, and the women rebuffed any attempt at conversation, as if acting on orders to exclude her. When she went to the medical office for a checkup at her scheduled time, Emily was there instead, insisting that she needed to be examined at that very moment in order to make a session with the masseuse, insisting that stress could be incredibly harmful to a child in the womb, insisting that the massage was absolutely crucial to the health of her baby, and she threw such a tantrum that the doctor finally caved and pushed back the appointment with Naomi.

Jane found her afterward, looking apologetic and embarrassed.

"I'm so sorry about that," Jane said.

"I'm paying to be here too," Naomi exploded.

"I know," Jane said.

"I shouldn't have to deal with this catty shit," Naomi exclaimed.

"I'm sorry. You've been so patient. Thank you for that. Truly. I know how hard it can be to deal with her. There's nobody here who visits my office as often as she does, every day, even during the night, always with some new problem or demand. There's no excuse for it. I just try to remember that she had a difficult upbringing. There are mental health issues. She's under a lot of pressure from her family," Jane said.

Naomi went into a bathroom, the only place she knew she could be alone at that time of day, and shut the door and hit the lock and sat cross-legged on the floor under the sink, blasting trance music over her headphones, letting the noise shake her, letting the sound consume her, like she'd done as a teenager whenever she'd been so frustrated that she'd wanted to scream. She hated how important that minor interactions could seem in an isolated social setting. She had friends back in the city. Friends from college. Friends from childhood. On an intellectual level, she knew that she was likable. On an emotional level, though, she felt like a loser. Back at home, in real life, she wouldn't have given a fuck what women like that thought about her, but having to live with the women, having to share space with the women, seeing those women and only those women every single day, she would have given her life for a smile. Being rejected by the other women there felt like being rejected by all of human society. It was absurd. It was crushing. That was all she wanted was a friend.

That next evening a new couple arrived at the compound, a woman with thick bleached hair in a bright holographic jacket and a man with a muscular build wearing a black tracksuit, who both looked vaguely familiar. Naomi was sitting near the altar with Rama, petting the cat behind the ears. Eavesdropping as the couple took a tour of the facility, Naomi realized that the woman was a celebrity tennis player, a gold medalist, a world champion, and that the man was a supermodel. Naomi had seen his face on billboards along the Strip, in pouty advertisements for peacoats and underwear. He had grown up in Newark. She wasn't sure where she had read that, and was embarrassed that she had.

Annabelle, the tennis player, wasn't pregnant yet.

"We don't get to have sex while you pull the plug on somebody?" Annabelle said.

"That actually isn't necessary," Jane said.

"But what if a soul enters a new body at the moment of conception?" Annabelle said.

"It certainly might," Jane said.

Annabelle frowned, looking at the withered figures sprawled across the cots in the chamber. "So then shouldn't he be trying to come in me at the exact instant that one of these guys flatlines?"

Jane smiled awkwardly. "Fertilization doesn't occur the moment that the sperm enters the vagina. Conception happens anywhere from an hour to a week after sex. It's impossible to predict the exact moment that you'll become pregnant." She clasped her hands together. "For that matter, we don't know how to identify the exact moment that a body has died, either. Medically we used to consider a body dead after the heart had stopped, but that definition has become problematic now that we have defibrillators that can start a heart back up again. Many physicians now define death as the moment that all electrical activity ceases in the brain, but even that definition is problematic, as various organ systems within the body can continue to function long after brain death occurs." She spread her hands wide. "And even if we could pinpoint the exact moment that a body had died, we don't know how these matters work spiritually. If a soul remains with the body for a time or leaves the body instantaneously."

Brock, the supermodel, looked totally lost.

"So, like, why did we even come here, if we're not supposed to fuck while some dude gets terminated?" Brock said.

Jane handed the couple the key to a bedroom.

"You're paying a lot of money to be here, and that money ensures that this facility has a steady supply of dying bodies. You can start trying to conceive whenever you're ready. Tonight, if you want. And on the day that your child is conceived, and at every other stage of

304

your child's development, we can guarantee you that there will be freshly departed souls nearby, looking for a healthy human body to inhabit," Jane said.

Naomi briefly fantasized about becoming friends with the new couple, doing group activities, doing double dates, which she knew was ridiculous. It seemed ridiculous. But the next day she was sitting alone in the dining hall when the tennis player approached her with a tray of food.

"You want to be alone?" Annabelle said.

Naomi stared.

"You can sit," Naomi said.

"Why aren't you eating with the others?" Annabelle said.

Naomi hesitated.

"There's a certain hierarchy here," Naomi said.

Annabelle rolled her eyes, setting the tray on the table, sitting down in a chair with her hair tied back in a messy ponytail. With a shock, Naomi saw that she had a bowl of cereal. Naomi gazed at the cereal in amazement. Geometric marshmallows bobbed in the milk, colorful triangles and circles and squares. Naomi had been craving cereal for months, but the dining hall didn't have any, and she had been too embarrassed to ask for any or order any online.

"Where'd you get the cereal?" Naomi said.

"Smuggled a box in. Figured all of the food here would be natural or organic or probiotic or whatever. I would have starved to death. I need a balanced diet of artificial flavors to get through the day," Annabelle said, and then took a bite.

Naomi watched her with a sense of longing as she chewed and swallowed the cereal.

"I've never actually seen you play tennis," Naomi admitted.

"I'm a typical baseliner," Annabelle said.

"I don't have a clue what that means," Naomi said.

"I hit at crazy angles," Annabelle grinned.

Naomi's heart leapt at the sight of a smile. She glanced across the dining hall, where the rest of the residents were gazing at Emily, listening to her tell some story, and then she turned back around toward Annabelle, watching her gulp a sip of chocolate milk. Naomi felt ecstatic suddenly. She felt extraordinary. She felt fantastic. Joaquin was flipping omelets behind the counter.

"I heard an interesting rumor last night," Annabelle said through a mouthful of marshmallows.

"What rumor?" Naomi said.

"That most of the people who die here used to be homeless," Annabelle said.

"I thought everybody who dies here is getting paid?"

"Well. Their families are. Which seems fair. I mean, imagine if you had some junkie uncle who'd been living on the streets the past fifty years, totally refusing to go to rehab, refusing to give up the drugs, occasionally hitting your family up for money or favors, and then suddenly he's in a coma at a hospital, hooked up to life support, with no chance of resuscitation, and some company comes along offering you a huge windfall of cash just to take him out into the desert to pull the plug."

Brock, the supermodel, wandered into the dining hall with mussed hair and wrinkled pajamas, yawning glamorously.

"I hope it's true. I was a runaway as a kid. I lived in a shelter a while. I had a lot of friends there. It'd give me a weird sort of satisfaction, knowing that all of these rich people were going to end up giving birth to children with the souls of homeless people," Annabelle said.

Rama had snuck into the dining hall. Silverware rattled as the cat leapt onto the table. Naomi set the cat back down onto the floor. Rama slunk off toward the buffet with a sulky look, heading for Brock, who was filling a plate with bacon.

Annabelle glanced back toward the hallway with an expression of admiration.

"Genius, in a way, figuring out how to monetize all of this," Annabelle said.

"Nobody's even given birth here yet," Naomi said.

Annabelle looked at her.

"That's what's been keeping me awake at night. I mean, we don't even know if this will work," Naomi said.

Rain was falling on the roof. Naomi sat over a board game in the dining hall, across from Annabelle. Tad was sitting across from Brock.

"Do you think a soul gets to choose its new body after it dies?" Annabelle said.

"Totally," Brock said, losing a turn, passing the dice.

"That actually wouldn't make any sense," Tad said.

"Don't get all mathy on us," Brock said.

"It's not math. It's just logic. Nobody would choose to be born to an abusive heroin addict living in a shack in a slum in a country ruled by a totalitarian regime. But some people are," Tad said.

Naomi rolled the dice, reaching for a soldier piece, trying to launch a war. She was twenty-nine weeks pregnant.

"Maybe souls have, like, different criteria," Brock said.

Dust was blowing past the windows. Naomi stood over the foosball table in the entertainment room, next to Annabelle. Tad was standing next to Brock.

"Can any of you remember past lives?" Annabelle said.

"Nope," Tad said, spinning a bar, missing the ball.

"I had a really intense dream about being a sailor once," Brock said.

"I don't think dreaming about sailors counts as a past life," Tad said.

"I had all of these skills, though. Like tying knots. And catching fish. And then everybody on the boat accused me of stealing a bagpipe," Brock said.

Naomi twisted a handle, making the goalie backflip, kicking the ball down the court. She was thirty-one weeks pregnant.

"I have trouble with the idea that we're something separate from these physical bodies," Tad said.

Naomi was slumped on a bench in the greenhouse with Annabelle, passing a bowl of dry cereal back and forth.

"It was hilarious. My parents have always been totally opposed to things like that. People who do yoga for exercise, or do meditation for mental benefits, like to increase productivity or whatever. My parents think it's a corruption of Indian religions. Seriously, whenever they drive past the studio by their house, this total silence falls over the car. You'd think they'd just driven past a Confederate monument. They've been that way my entire life. I got really into yoga and meditation back in college. I caught so much flak from my parents for that. But when they took the tour here, they were so into the idea of this place that when they saw all of the women doing yoga and meditation together, they were like, 'Yoga! Meditation! Naomi, this place is paradise!'" Naomi said.

Annabelle threw her head back and laughed.

"I want to meet your parents so bad," Annabelle said.

"You'll definitely get to. They're going to drive up the second my water breaks," Naomi said, chewing some marshmallows.

"I can't wait to hang with those two," Annabelle said.

Matthew Baker

Beads of water glistened on the colorful apricots and plums and nectarines hanging from the branches of the fruit trees across from the bench. Tad was working. Brock was napping. The warm, steamy air in the greenhouse felt refreshing.

"I wish you would have gotten to meet my mom," Annabelle said.

"Me too," Naomi said.

Annabelle found out that she was pregnant a week later, months after arriving at the maternity center. Naomi went on a walk with her afterward. Naomi had never seen her so radiantly happy. Annabelle kept laying her hand on her stomach, which was still as flat as an axis. Naomi was bulging through her sweatshirt, with pains in her back from all the extra weight. She felt gargantuan. Annabelle sat next to her by the stone altar in the altar room.

"I'm really going to miss you when you're gone," Annabelle said.

"I know," Naomi said.

"I'm still going to have so long to go," Annabelle said.

Emily was in there, dressed in a baggy linen tunic and leather huaraches with golden buckles, looking especially fervent today, playing a singing bowl near the cot of somebody who'd just died.

"We'll come back to visit you," Naomi said.

"You swear?" Annabelle said, glancing at her.

"I promise."

"Thank God."

Rama was staring at a blank spot on the ceiling.

"Make sure you bring that cutie too," Annabelle said.

Rama kept staring at the blank spot on the ceiling.

"What are you looking at, Rama?" Annabelle laughed, reaching down to nuzzle the cat under the chin, but the cat ignored her, gazing intently at the ceiling, as if watching something that the humans couldn't see.

Across the altar room, a medic covered the dead body with a white sheet, preparing to wheel the corpse off to a waiting ambulance. Smoke rose from incense. Petals fell from lilies. Rama turned to watch something invisible glide down the wall, then backed away, crept forward again, batted at something invisible on the floor, and quickly ran out into the hallway, as if chasing something.

"Cats are so dope," Annabelle said.

*

Naomi was stepping off of a treadmill in the fitness center later that night when she ran into Emily.

"Naomi, hi," Emily said.

Naomi hadn't had a single interaction with her in over a month. She froze, bracing for a confrontation. Emily was smiling at her, though. She looked genuinely happy to see her. Rather than workout clothes, she was still wearing the linen tunic and the leather huaraches, as if she had come into the gym specifically to talk to her. Her hands were cupped around the swell of her belly.

"You look so beautiful today," Emily said.

"Oh," Naomi said, taken aback.

"You're like literally glowing," Emily said.

"Thanks," Naomi said, confused.

Tad was watching from a stationary bike, as if waiting to see if she needed to be rescued.

"I just had my latest checkup. Everything looks perfect. Everything looks great. And the baby has been really active lately. Moving around a lot. I know everybody says that that doesn't mean anything, but, still, it's reassuring, you know?" Emily said.

Naomi was so stunned by this pleasant chitchat that she was briefly speechless.

"You're due soon too, right?" Emily said eagerly.

"Um, yeah, in a week," Naomi said.

"We don't know the gender."

"Us either."

"We want to be surprised."

"Us too."

"You're so lucky that you've been able to have your husband here with you the whole time. That's so special. That's so nice. Danny's overseas for another month, doing work things in Switzerland, but after that he's going to come straight here. He'll be here the last month, for when the baby's born," Emily said.

Tad had turned back toward the handlebars of the stationary bike, breathing heavily as he pedaled.

Emily abruptly turned toward the door, as if about to leave the gym, but then turned back around with an anxious expression.

"I'm sorry for being a terrible person. I should have been nicer to you. I'm such a monster sometimes. I can be so vicious. I honestly don't know why. Really, I've been like this my whole life. I just lash out at people," Emily said.

Naomi was speechless again.

"We could have been friends. I wish that we had. You're a real person. I mean, like, somebody who really thinks about things. From the moment you arrived, I could just tell somehow. You're the realest person here," Emily said, tucking a strand of hair behind her ear.

Naomi felt a bright, warm glow spread through her chest, a sense of utter bliss, a powerful sense of reconciliation, being spoken to and apologized to and accepted by Emily finally after being rejected by her for so long. Emily suddenly seemed so vulnerable and insecure. Instead of the meticulously perfect braids she usually wore, her hair was lopsided, Naomi realized, with stray strands of gold hanging loose from a tortoiseshell hair clip. Her cheekbones looked oddly gaunt. Her eyes had puffy bags. Naomi almost wanted to hug her. Naomi didn't need her as a friend anymore. Naomi had other friends now to support her. But still, for some reason, being treated with kindness by her, being able to connect with her, made her intensely happy. The feeling overwhelmed her.

"It's OK," Naomi said.

"And sorry about your cat," Emily blurted.

Naomi frowned.

"About my cat?" Naomi said.

"Oh, I thought somebody probably must have told you," Emily said, laughing nervously.

"Told me what?" Naomi said.

"I know everybody says that humans can't get souls from animals. I'm an overachiever, though. I'm the type of person who'll do extra credit even when she already has a perfect grade. I'm like that with everything. Even if humans can't get souls from animals, I'd still prefer for the staff to sacrifice some animals during the day, just in case it might help. I actually think that it might. Anyway, I didn't even realize that the cat was yours at first. I thought it belonged to one of the staff. I've always felt a connection with cats. I don't know how to explain it. I just do. So, I don't know, I just got this idea into my head that the other animals weren't enough. That the cat needed to be sacrificed too. Jane said no, of course. I mean, it's your cat. This was back around the time that you first got here. I threw a huge fit. I was pretty embarrassed afterward. I was sure that you must have heard. Anyway, Jane got me some different cats instead. Every night for a week, that was the midnight sacrifice," Emily said.

Naomi stared at her in shock.

"I've just been freaking out a little. The stress makes me feel crazy. All of the pressure. We both have fertility issues, Danny and me.

Especially me. I know we could just adopt, but my parents wanted us to have one that was ours, and that's what we wanted too. We spent over a million dollars on fertility treatments. We tried so many times. Over a dozen procedures, a dozen different embryos, and every single one failed. Every single one. Except the last one. This baby is a miracle. It's the most beautiful thing that's ever happened to me. I just want to do everything possible to make sure the baby is born healthy. I know it will be. I have faith it will. I just get nervous sometimes," Emily said.

"It's been a hard year for everybody. But everything is going to be OK," Naomi said.

"You really think so?" Emily said, looking at her.

Naomi nodded, and meant it.

"It's been really hard. But we're almost there," Emily said, squinting in happiness as she caressed her stomach with her hands.

The next day, two of the residents at the compound went into labor, one at breakfast, one during lunch, and by evening both of the babies had been born, healthy and ensouled. After months spent living under a constant sense of fear and doubt and looming tragedy, a feeling of hope came over the residents at the maternity center, hearing the cries and babbles of conscious babies ringing through the hallways. Women kept spontaneously bursting into fits of relieved laughter. Naomi couldn't stop smiling. That night the staff hosted a celebration. Jane decorated the dining hall with golden balloons. Joaquin baked a pair of chocolate birthday cakes. At midnight a stork was slaughtered on the altar.

"And we know now that the methods at this facility really do work," Jane said during a triumphant speech.

Joaquin applauded along with the residents from behind the counter in the kitchen.

Naomi was expected to give birth next, but when her due date arrived, Emily went into labor instead of her.

Naomi was eating a slice of apple pie in the dining hall when a nurse appeared in the doorway with a frantic look.

"She's asking for you," the nurse said.

Naomi hurried down the hallway, following the nurse to the birthing room, where the rustic wooden shelves were still standing along the walls and the gigantic healing crystals were still glowing on the shelves and the rough concrete floor was glimmering with bursts of color from the crystals. The spotlight shone down onto the hospital bed. Emily still wasn't due for over a month. She was lying on the sheet in a satin gown. Jane was standing beside her clutching a manila file folder.

"Danny isn't here yet," Emily was saying, looking sweaty and frightened.

"Emily, he won't be here for weeks," Jane said.

"Call him. You need to call him. He can fly here today," Emily insisted.

"By the time he got to the airport, flew all the way across the ocean, and drove all of the way here, the trip would take more than a day," Jane said.

"We need to wait for him," Emily said.

"You cannot wait for him," Jane said firmly.

"But the baby isn't due yet," Emily said.

"The baby is coming now," Jane said.

Emily stared at her a moment with an expression that flickered between uncertainty and stubbornness and denial and fury. Then her mouth tightened, and her gaze softened, and she nodded finally, taking a deep breath. She wiped a sweaty strand of hair from her cheek.

"All that matters is the baby. I'm ready. Let's go," Emily said.

Emily hadn't asked for any of the other residents to be there. Only Naomi. Naomi sat next to her throughout the delivery, rubbing her forehead, holding her hand. The labor was straightforward and effortless and lasted only an hour. The baby was born just after noon, a tiny, rawboned child with fragile arms and delicate legs and wide, round eyes that sparkled with beautiful flecks of blue. A child destined for power and wealth. The doctor clamped and cut the cord. Naomi stared at the child in disbelief. It wasn't moving. It wasn't crying. It just gazed at the ceiling in silence, breathing mechanically.

The body was empty.

"I'm so sorry," Naomi said.

Jane looked horrified. Emily looked fine. She reached for the child with an expression of reverence.

"He's perfect," Emily whispered.

Naomi and the others watched as she held the child, gazing into the blank eyes, tenderly cradling the empty body, murmuring lovingly. The child continued to breathe. Dust floated through the spotlight. Sweat was drying on skin. Emily began to look anxious.

The doctor moved to take the child back from her when the breathing stopped.

"He still doesn't have a soul," Emily said with a hint of confusion.
"It's too late," the doctor said.
The doctor hesitated before reaching for the child again.
"Just let me hold him," Emily pleaded.
"He's gone," the doctor said gently.
"Don't take him from me," Emily pleaded.
Naomi left. By then the news had already spread through the rest of the compound. Giving birth at the facility didn't guarantee a baby would have a soul. At dinner that night the residents were solemn, forking bites of salmon and arugula in a gloomy silence, asking in murmurs for salt or butter to be passed. Brock sat staring at a blackberry tart in a daze. Annabelle sat hunched over a plate of meringues, looking just as somber. Spoons clinked against bowls. Emily was usually the center of attention in the dining hall, but tonight she wasn't there.
Tad wasn't concerned.
"Even if there's no guarantee, being here might still increase the baby's chances," Tad said, walking back to the bedchamber.
"I actually believed that we didn't have to worry anymore," Naomi said.
"The baby is going to be fine," Tad said.
Earlier that day he had discovered a new type of impossible object. A two-dimensional figure that couldn't possibly exist in three-dimensional space. A remarkable achievement. Back in the bedchamber, he tore a strip of masking tape from a roll, stuck a charcoal sketch of the impossible object to the wall above the desk, and then stood back to admire the drawing, gazing at the shape the exact same way that a parent might look at a newborn child. Tad had a blunt, ugly face, marred with blackheads, but when he was that proud, when he was that in love, there was something about him that was profoundly handsome. He was wearing the same polka-dot dress shirt that he had worn on the drive from the city.
"An impossible object only appears possible because of the limitations of the human mind," Tad said.

Naomi went on a walk later that night after he had fallen asleep. She wandered through the darkened passageways of the compound in a baggy cotton nightshirt, taking a moment to contemplate the withered bodies on the cots in the altar room, the blinking life-support machines, and then slipped into the stairwell, climbing the steps to the patio on the roof. She sat cross-legged up there for hours with her hands cupped around her belly, watching airplanes drift over the desert, watching satellites glide across the sky, looking at the stars, trying to decide what to do now that she knew the facility couldn't guarantee that a child would be born with a soul. Whether or not just to go home. Her baby was now one day overdue. Towels for sunbathing hung from the railing. A gossip magazine rustled in the breeze. Somebody had left the cap off of a bottle of tanning oil, putting the sweet scent of coconut in the air.

For a moment she closed her eyes, trying to sense the separate components of her soul and her body. Trying to imagine what it would feel like for her soul to separate from her body. Trying to imagine the course that her soul might have taken through human history. The lives it had lived in wealth, and the lives it had lived in poverty. The lives it had lived in war, and the lives it had lived in peace. The lives it had lived in health, and the lives it had lived in affliction. The lives it had lived in slavery, and the lives it had lived in freedom. She caught the sweet scent of the tanning oil again, which was her body that sensed that, though the awareness came from her soul. She wondered if she had a soulmate somewhere. And then she opened her eyes again, and bats were flying over the roof, and she remembered her baby, and that after all of the time that she had spent at the compound the child might still be born empty.

Naomi still hadn't decided whether or not just to go home when she went back into the compound. She emerged from the stairwell lost in thought, but then paused at the sound of a faint hum in the altar room. Electrocardiographs and electroencephalographs. The tone of a flatline. With the skylight dark, the only light in the altar room came from the glow of the candles flickering between the cots, and she could see the monitors from where she stood. Every last screen showed a flatline, as if all of the patients had died at once. Naomi frowned, thinking that the monitors must be malfunctioning, that maybe a power surge had fried the circuits, but then as she walked through the massive arched doorway of the altar room she realized that the monitors were functioning perfectly. All of the patients were dead. The bodies were mangled. The sheets were drenched. Blood was dripping from the cots onto the floor. The concrete suddenly felt cold under the soles of her feet. Frightened, she glanced toward the stone altar and saw that the ceremonial dagger was gone. Shadows flickered across the room with the flames of the candles. Naomi froze in place, watching the shadows carefully, afraid that whoever had stabbed the patients might be hiding somewhere in the room, behind or beneath the cots. The decrepit statues along the circumference of the room were silhouettes in the dim light, and she desperately tried to remember each of the poses that the statues held, paranoid that one of the silhouettes might be the killer posing as a statue. The flat-lines kept humming. The statues were motionless. Naomi stood there in the doorway with her heart beating wildly until she finally believed that she was alone, that nobody was hiding in the room, and still she was afraid to move, but she forced her body to move, to go get help, and she padded off down the hallway with sweat trickling down the nape of her neck and a hot flash spreading across her skin. She felt sick. The walk to the security office seemed impossibly long, like minutes, entire minutes, and she felt a rush of relief when she saw light streaming from the doorway, the salt lamp that stood on the desk where the guards sat, but instead of sitting behind the desk the guard who was on duty was sprawled across the floor, stabbed so many times his uniform was shredded, with tinny music still play-ing over his earbuds, a chorus of trilling violins. Light was streaming from the doorway of the medical office too, the salt lamp that stood on the desk where the doctors sat, and instead of sitting behind the desk the doctor who was on duty was sprawled across the floor, stabbed through the thick fabric of her uniform, while a classic sit-com streamed across her tablet, accompanied by a laugh track. In the manager's office, Jane lay on the cement in a mound of silk, her neck slashed, her face rigid, her features contorted into a grotesque expression, surrounded by aspirin tablets that had spilled from a bottle onto the floor. Naomi felt a ripple of terror. There were no other staff at the compound that time of night. She and the other residents were alone. She had to warn the other residents. Tad. Annabelle. Brock. There would be safety in numbers. She wasn't going to die. Her hands were trembling. She followed the hallway deeper into the compound, glancing behind her once, but nobody was behind her. Nobody was there. The bathrooms were dark. As she passed the bathrooms she caught the scent of the diffusers, lavender and euca-lyptus, heard dripping water, and then she came to the residential section of the compound, where the rough wooden doors to the bed-chambers stood at regular intervals in the hallway. At that time of night all of the doors were always shut, but all of the doors were open, as if each of the residents had been summoned from sleep by a soft knock or a familiar voice. Naomi stared down the hallway with a sense of horror. Madeline, a real estate heir with a brown bob cut and vintage spectacles, lay in a heap in the doorway of the first bed-chamber, wearing madras pajamas soaked with blood. Limbs of other bodies extended from doorways farther down the hallway, hands and feet and shiny coils of hair. In the soft light of the salt lamps glowing in the bedchambers, the puddles of blood spreading from the door-ways shimmered on the floor, forming an archipelago of black pools that extended off down the hallway, into the darkness. A ventilator came to life with a thump. Air creaked through a duct on the ceiling. Naomi padded cautiously down the hallway, stepping around the blood, with the nausea growing in her stomach with every body that she passed. The women had all been stabbed repeatedly in the throat and the belly. Brock had fallen onto the floor with his hand stiffened around a bottle of absinthe, nude, bleeding from his chest and his throat. Annabelle had fallen to the floor in a bright kimono, bleeding from her neck and her belly, with her eyes wide with fear. Naomi was hyperventilating. As she walked toward the darkness at the end of the hallway she was crying now, silently, trying not to make any noise. Her bedchamber was the last one in the hallway. The salt lamp in her bedchamber was glowing too. Nobody was following her. Hesitantly, she stepped into the room. The satin cat bed was empty. Geometry books had been spilled across the floor. Metallic shapes glimmered on the covers. Silver grids of lines. The charcoal sketch of the impossible object was still taped above the desk. Tad was sprawled across the concrete in a horrible rag-doll posture, his mouth wide open, still wearing his retainer. Naomi spun away. Stars twinkled across her vision. She felt dizzy. The nausea rose in a stomach-churning surge of acid, and she squatted to vomit in the wastebasket by the desk. Afterward she sat panting on the floor by the wastebasket, catching her breath. She spat, trying to get the taste of acid out of her mouth. Nobody was in the doorway. She was shaking. She tried to think. She didn't have keys to any of the cars in the lot. She didn't have time to search all of the rooms for keys. She just had to run. She needed to run. Nobody was in the doorway. Still wearing her night-shirt, she knelt on the floor to put on her sneakers, but her hands were trembling so badly that she couldn't tie the laces. She swore. She fumbled. She knotted the laces. She wobbled as she stood. Nobody was in the doorway. Cupping her hands protectively around her stomach, she slipped back into the hallway, glancing in both direc-tions, but the hallway was still empty. She was going to have to walk through the desert. She was going to need water before fleeing the compound. A canteen. Taking the quickest route to the kitchen, she ambulances tearing down the highway, and she imagined that there must have been some accident at the military base, where he used to work before he had taken the job running the kitchen at the Oasis. Joaquin didn't like for her to do housework that late in the pregnancy, but she needed to do something to keep her mind off the discomfort and the monotony, so she dusted the house, and she swept the house, and she plunged some hair from the drain in the bathtub, and by then she was exhausted, so she went into the living room to do some sudoku. When she got tired of the silence she got off the couch and went over to the television to turn on the news for some background noise. She froze when she saw the image on the screen, realizing that she recognized the building. Joaquin had taken her there once, proudly touring her through the kitchen, showing off the industrial mixers and ranges. The maternity center. There had been a massacre at the maternity center early that morning. The worst mass killing in the country in over a month, and the murderer hadn't even had a gun. Over a hundred people had been stabbed to death, every last soul in the compound, before the murderer had phoned in an incoherent plea to an emergency hotline and then swallowed a bottle of meds. The only living creature that had survived the massacre was a cat. Footage of a firefighter holding the cat played across the screen, and then there was a clip from within the compound, a body lying on the floor of the dining hall, and the face had been blurred out, but she saw the hairnet, and she saw the apron, and she saw the colorful aloha shirt that he had been wearing when he had brought a glass of water into the bedroom for her before leaving for work early that morning, and then the screen cut to a shot of the compound surrounded by emergency vehicles with flashing sirens. Lupe had dropped the sudoku puzzles. She sank to the floor. She didn't weep or scream. She just stared at the television, in shock, as the same cycle of clips continued to play across the screen. A great wind blew through the yard, like a mass of spirits rushing across the desert toward the city, disturbing the chimes hanging over the stoop, agitating the laundry hanging from the clothesline, and a faint breeze escaped from the gust to slip into the house through the screen in the window, twisting gently around her body, sending chills across her skin. Advertising jingles rang out from the television, singsongy voices, peddling insurance and vacuums during commercial breaks. The phone in the kitchen rang and rang and rang and then eventually fell silent. Later, when the bright gold sunlight streaming through the windows had dimmed to the burning red of early evening, she curled up in a fetal position on the rug, staring at an empty power outlet in the corner as political pundits argued back and forth on a talk show.

"We should be grateful. We should be celebrating. It's solved the greatest problem of our time. I'm not talking about climate change. Climate change was just a symptom of the root problem. Pollution, famine, water shortages, those were all just symptoms too. The root problem has always been overpopulation. But we don't have to worry about the population growing anymore. Now the number is fixed."

"How can you expect people to be happy when children are dying?"

"If the religious community is right, and these babies are being born without souls, then technically there's nothing to mourn."

"But how can you ignore the lost potential of these empty bodies?"

Lupe was still lying on the rug later that night when the presidential debate came onto the television.

"We're in a time of crisis. Our scientists can't stop what's happening, and our prayers are going unanswered. God is sending us a message. It's up to us to act. God's chosen nation. A vote for me is a vote for your future. There's thirteen and a half billion people on this planet, and only half of a billion people in this country. America's children come first. We've got a military strong enough to carpet-bomb the rest of the world into oblivion. And that's exactly what we're going to do. We're going to release thirteen billion souls back into the ether all at once. A vote for me is a vote for your children. No more children are going to be born without souls in this land."

Lupe got up off the floor finally and went into the bedroom, falling back asleep clutching Joaquin's pajamas, which still smelled like his scent, as cicadas sang in the yard.

Her water broke early the next morning, and she drove through the desert alone, into Las Vegas, where she gave birth in a hospital with peaceful pastel colors painted across the walls of the maternity ward. Her child was born healthy and angry, shrieking and wailing at the sight of the world. Lupe raised the child back out in the desert. The child was angsty and listless and selfish, grumbling moodily about homework, complaining of boredom constantly, throwing blood-curdling tantrums in the parking lots of gas stations. He had the same hazel eyes as her, with that starburst pattern of brown and green, and the same bulbous earlobes as her father, and the same tilted snaggle-tooth as her mother, but more than anybody in the world the child looked like Joaquin. That exact same face, round and attractive. That exact same hair. That exact same smile. And yet in terms of temperament, the child bore absolutely no resemblance whatsoever to her, or her parents, or her husband. She tried to teach the child to work hard, to take pride in a job done with care and integrity, and instead the child did chores sloppily, shrugging indifferently when confronted with a poorly made bed or messily folded laundry. She tried to teach the child to be kind to animals, to find joy in petting and feeding other creatures, and instead the child threw rocks at chained dogs, laughing with satisfaction as the dogs yelped or whimpered in pain. She tried to teach the child about materialism and humility, to find contentment in the simple pleasures of life, to be grateful and appreciative for what life provided, and the child screamed and kicked on the floor of a supermarket, shrieking with fury, overcome with rage at being denied a new toy. Lupe had always believed in souls, even before the phenomenon with the empty bodies had started, and that was why. There was no explaining how different that a child could be from its parents otherwise. A child born to bookish parents, raised by bookish parents, who took no interest in learning whatsoever. A child born to outdoorsy parents, raised by outdoorsy parents, who loathed doing activities in the wilderness. A child born to frugal parents, raised by frugal parents, who wasted money on idiotically frivolous expenses. There was no explaining that by nature or nurture. Only by chance. The particular quality of a soul. Watching the child swinging on the playset in the yard, Lupe wondered about the soul that inhabited that body. She knew the theories that the staff at the compound had promoted. That a freshly departed soul would attach to the nearest available embryo or fetus. Lupe had been less than a dozen miles from the compound on the night of the massacre. The child might be inhabited by the soul of any of the people who had died. Even by the soul of the murderer. The person who had killed her husband. When she thought about it, when she honestly considered it, she was almost certain that that must be the soul that inhabited the child. Yet she loved him anyway. Lupe had always been taught that she should judge a person by what was inside, not outside. That she shouldn't judge a person based on physical appearance. That she should judge a person based on spiritual character. The child had a cruel, greedy, miserable soul. He pulled the wings from moths and butterflies for amusement. He spilled milk onto the floor deliberately. He hammered nails into the heirloom credenza. He called her horrible names. He screamed that he hated her. He stole earrings from her jewelry box, coveting the shiny nubs of silver and gold. He lied for fun. And yet she loved him, for no other reason than that the child had come out of her body, and vaguely resembled her, and resembled her parents, and resembled her husband. Because the child happened to look like other people she had loved. Lupe stood at the window in the kitchen, watching the child run around the yard. Maybe he would grow out of it. Maybe he wouldn't. The child might grow up to be an asshole, or a chauvinist, or a racist, or a killer. It didn't matter. It just didn't. She already knew that she would love him until the day she died.

NOTES ON CONTRIBUTORS

SELENA ANDERSON's work has appeared or is forthcoming in *Oxford American, The Baffler, Bomb, Georgia Review,* and *Fence.* She has received fellowships from the Kimbilio Center, the MacDowell Colony, and the Bread Loaf Writers' Conference and recently won a Rona Jaffe Foundation Writers' Award. She lives in California with her family and is working on a novel.

Named one of *Variety*'s "10 Storytellers to Watch," MATTHEW BAKER is the author of the story collections *Why Visit America,* forthcoming from Henry Holt, and *Hybrid Creatures* (LSU Press). Born in the Great Lakes region of the United States, he currently lives in New York City.

TERE DÁVILA is the winner of two Puerto Rico National Prizes. She is the author of one novel, *Nenísimas,* and three books of short fiction: *Aquí están las instrucciones* (all Institute of Puerto Rican Culture), *Lego* (Isla Negra Editores), and *El fondillo maravilloso* (Terranova Editores). Her short stories have been published in the United States and international anthologies and literary magazines. In 2017, she received Puerto Rico's *New Voices Award.*

JULIA ELLIOTT is the author of the story collection *The Wilds,* a *New York Times Book Review* Editors' Choice, and the novel *The New and Improved Romie Futch* (both Tin House). She has won a Rona Jaffe Writers' Award, two Pushcart Prizes, and her fiction has twice appeared in *Best American Short Stories.*

BRIAN EVENSON is the author of more than a dozen books of fiction, including most recently *Song for the Unraveling of the World* and *A Collapse of Horses* (both Coffee House Press). He has been the recipient of a Guggenheim Fellowship, an NEA Fellowship, and three O. Henry Prizes. He lives in Los Angeles and teaches at CalArts.

JEFFREY FORD is the author of the recent novel *Ahab's Return* (William Morrow), the upcoming stand-alone novella *Out of Body* (Tor.com), and a short story retrospective collection *The Best of Jeffrey Ford* (PS Publishing).

ELIZABETH HAND is the award-winning author of sixteen novels and five collections of short fiction and essays, as well as a longtime reviewer for numerous publications, including the *Washington Post* and *Los Angeles Times. The Book of Lamps and Banners,* the fourth novel in her acclaimed noir series featuring punk iconoclast Cass Neary, will be published this year by Mulholland Books. She splits her time between the Maine coast and North London.

REBECCA HANSSENS-REED is a translator and writer whose work can be found in *The New England Review, Hayden's Ferry Review, Washington Square Review, Asymptote,* and elsewhere. She has an MFA in literary translation from the University of Iowa, where she was also a Provost's Postgraduate Visiting Writer. Her translation of the novel *Gelsomina Inside the White Madhouses* by Margarita Mateo Palmer is forthcoming from Cubanabooks Press.

KAREN HEULER's stories have appeared in over one hundred literary and speculative magazines and anthologies, from *Conjunctions* to *Weird Tales,* as well as a number of Best Of anthologies. She has published four novels, four collections, and a novella; won an O. Henry Award; and been a finalist for many others.

CATHERINE IMBRIGLIO is the author of two volumes of poetry. Recent poems have appeared in *New American Writing* and *West Branch.* She lives in Rhode Island and teaches at Brown University.

LUCY IVES is the author of two novels: *Impossible Views of the World,* published by Penguin Press, and *Loudermilk: Or, The Real Poet; Or, The Origin of the World,* published by Soft Skull Press. Her first collection of short stories is forthcoming from Soft Skull in early 2021.

A. D. JAMESON is the author of *I Find Your Lack of Faith Disturbing: Star Wars and the Triumph of Geek Culture* (Farrar, Straus and Giroux) and the coauthor (with artist Andrew DeGraff) of *Cinemaps: An Atlas of 35 Great Movies* (Quirk Books). In May 2018, Jameson received his PhD in English from the University of Illinois at Chicago. He is currently working on a novel.

MADELINE KEARIN is a writer and PhD candidate in archaeology at Brown University. Her first literary publication, "Fallout," appeared in *Conjunctions.* Her subsequent work has been featured in *Conjunctions, Beloit Fiction Journal,* and *BFS Horizons.*

JAE KIM is a writer and a literary translator. His short story "South of Here" was recently featured in *NOON.* His translations of Lee Young-ju's poetry are forthcoming from Black Ocean.

MARY KURYLA is the author of *Freak Weather Stories,* recipient of the Grace Paley Prize in Short Fiction (University of Massachusetts Press). Her novel *Away to Stay* is forthcoming with Regal House Press. Kuryla's stories have received the Pushcart Prize and the Glimmer Train Very Short Fiction Prize.

JAMES MORROW is the author of ten novels, including *The Godhead Trilogy* (Harcourt), *The Last Witchfinder* (William Morrow), and *Galápagos Regained* (St. Martin's Press). He has received the World Fantasy Award, the Nebula Award, the Theodore Sturgeon Memorial Award, and the Grand Prix de l'Imaginaire.

JUSTIN NOGA is a writer out of Akron, Ohio. He is an MFA candidate at Arizona State University. He lives in Tempe, Arizona. This marks his second literary publication.

JOYCE CAROL OATES is currently Visiting Distinguished Professor in the College of Arts and Sciences at Rutgers University, New Brunswick. She is the author most recently of the novel *My Life as a Rat* and the story collection *Beautiful Days* (both Ecco), in which several stories originally appearing in *Conjunctions* have been reprinted. She is the 2019 recipient of the Jerusalem Prize.

ARRA LYNN ROSS's "Near, and Nearer Now" is excerpted from a book-length manuscript titled *Freyja's Labyrinth*. Her second book, *The Day of the Child*, will be published by Milkweed Editions in fall 2021.

JOANNA RUOCCO is the author of several books, including *The Week* (The Elephants), *Dan* (Dorothy), and *Field Glass* (Sidebrow), with Joanna Howard. She is an associate professor in the English Department at Wake Forest University.

ETHAN RUTHERFORD's first book, *The Peripatetic Coffin and Other Stories* (Ecco/HarperCollins), was a finalist for both the *Los Angeles Times* Art Seidenbaum Award for First Fiction and the John Leonard Award, received an honorable mention for the PEN/Hemingway Award, was a Barnes & Noble Discover Great New Writers selection, and was the winner of a Minnesota Book Award. His second collection of stories, *Farthest South*, will be published next year by A Strange Object. His fiction has been anthologized in *The Best American Short Stories*.

DEL SAMATAR holds a BA in fine arts from Rutgers University. He lives in New Jersey, where he is pursuing a career as a tattoo artist.

SOFIA SAMATAR is the author of the novels *A Stranger in Olondria* and *The Winged Histories*, and the short story collection *Tender* (all Small Beer Press). With her brother, the artist Del Samatar, she cocreated *Monster Portraits* (Rose Metal Press). Her work has received several honors, including the World Fantasy Award.

LUCAS SOUTHWORTH's first fiction collection, *Everyone Here Has a Gun* (University of Massachusetts Press), won AWP's Grace Paley Prize. Recent work has appeared in *AGNI*, *Alaska Quarterly Review*, *Copper Nickel*, *DIAGRAM*, *Willow Springs*, and others. He teaches fiction and screenwriting at Loyola University Maryland in Baltimore.

TERESE SVOBODA's most recent book of stories is *Great American Desert* (Mad Creek). Anhinga Press is publishing *Theatrix: Play Poems*, her eighth book of poems, in 2021.

Cover artist HUGO VON TRIMBERG (ca. 1230–ca. 1313) was a German Catholic author of the Middle Ages. His epic poem *Der Renner* ("The Runner" or "The Courier") is the most comprehensive didactic poem in the German language.

QUINTAN ANA WIKSWO is the author of the collection *The Hope of Floating Has Carried Us This Far* (Coffee House Press) and the novel *A Long Curving Scar Where the Heart Should Be* (Stalking Horse Press). A Creative Capital grantee in Emerging Fields, her work has been honored by a National Endowment for the Arts Fellowship at the Lynchburg African American Cemetery and a Pollock-Krasner Foundation Endowed Fellowship at Yaddo.

Poet : T. Duchamp.

1. I am anything.
2. I will like anything something
4. 3. I anything anything.
~~[struck-through line]~~
3. 4. I chose anything
5. Anything I choose is something.
6 -

The Saddest Thing Is That I Have Had to Use Words: A Madeline Gins Reader
edited by Lucy Ives

Poet, philosopher, speculative architect and transdisciplinary artist, Madeline Gins (1941–2014) is well-known for her collaborations with her husband, the artist Arakawa, on the experimental architectural project Reversible Destiny, in which they sought to arrest mortality by transforming the built environment. This revelatory anthology brings never-before-published poems and essays together with a complete facsimile reproduction of Gins's 1969 masterpiece *WORD RAIN*, along with substantial excerpts from her two later books. Expansive and playful, Gins's vigorous and often ecstatic exploration of the physicality of language challenges us to sense more acutely the ways in which we can—and could—write and read. Like Gertrude Stein before her, Gins transfigures grammar and liberates words. Like her contemporaries in conceptual art, her writing is attuned to the energized, collaborative space between reader and page. She invites the reader into a field of infinite, ever-multiplying possibility. Long out of print or unpublished, Gins's poems and prose form a powerful corpus of experimental literature, one which is sure to upend existing narratives of American poetics at the close of the twentieth century.

$28 · PB · 328 pages · b/w illustrations · www.sigliopress.com

siglio
uncommon books at the intersection of art & literature

Memory
Bernadette Mayer

"To a reader leafing through *Memory* now, Mayer's feral run-ons may elicit a wistfulness for an era that appears so much freer than our own, and her photos' rich cinematic hues might prompt a person to wonder how our age, so manically documented, seems far less vivid in comparison. And while prescience is always a dicey claim, Mayer's self-portraits, often taken while staring into the lens, somehow appear like eerie proof that she was seeing us long before we would see her." —**Jennifer Krasinski, BOOKFORUM**

In July 1971, Bernadette Mayer embarked on an experiment: For one month she exposed a roll of 35mm film and kept a daily journal. The result was a conceptual work that investigates the nature of memory, its surfaces, textures and material. *Memory* is monumental in scope as well as a groundbreaking work by a poet who is widely regarded as one of the most innovative writers of her generation. Presaging Mayer's durational and constraint-based diaristic works of poetry, it also evinces her extraordinary—and unheralded—contribution to conceptual art. This publication brings together the full sequence of more than 1100 images and almost 200 pages of text for the first time in book form, making space for a work that has been legendary but mostly invisible.

the
IOWA REVIEW

celebrating 50 sweet years
of the best new
fiction, poetry, and
nonfiction

The American Journal of Poetry

theamericanjournalofpoetry.com

EPOCH

A MAGAZINE OF CONTEMPORARY LITERATURE

PUBLISHED THREE TIMES PER YEAR

$5/ISSUE $11/YEAR

"Last Night's Tea"
sketchbook drawing
(12x9 inches) in
pen and ink by

Blair Thornley

WWW.EPOCH.CORNELL.EDU

FC2 & The Jarvis and
Constance Doctorow
Family Foundation
present the

FC2 Catherine Doctorow
Innovative Fiction Prize

Winner receives $15,000
and publication by FC2

Entries accepted
**August 15, 2020 -
November 1, 2020**

Submission guidelines
www.fc2.org/prizes.html

*FC2 is among the few alternative, author-run presses devoted to
publishing fiction considered by America's largest publishers to be too
challenging, innovative, or heterodox for the commercial milieu.*

The Ronald Sukenick/ FC2 Innovative Fiction Contest

$1,500 & publication by FC2

Entries accepted August 15, 2020 - November 1, 2020

Submission guidelines: www.fc2.org/prizes.html

FC2 *is among the few alternative, author-run presses devoted to publishing fiction considered by America's largest publishers to be too challenging, innovative, or heterodox for the commercial milieu.*

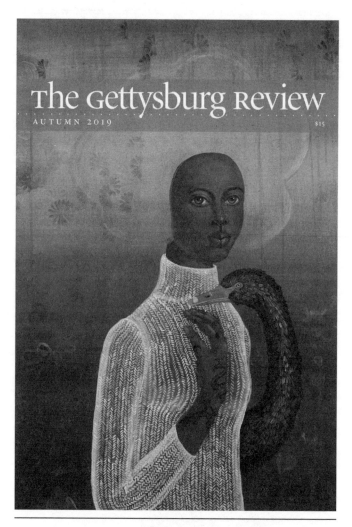

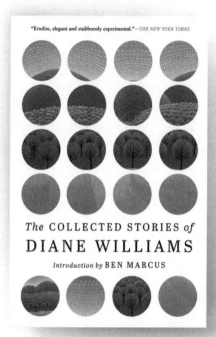
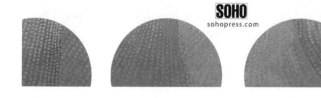

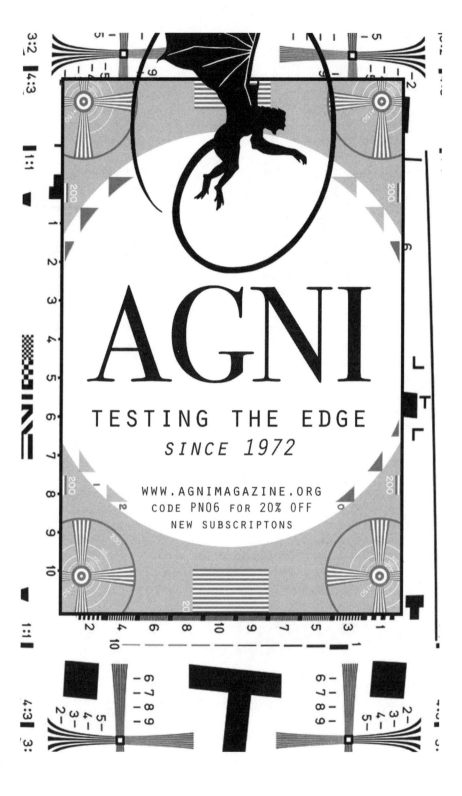

TRADE PAPERBACK · $17 · EBOOK AVAILABLE · AUGUST 2020

CHAPBOOK · ILLUSTRATED THROUGHOUT · $10 · EBOOK AVAILABLE

"Great, unforgiving wilderness, a vanished teenager, an excellent villain, and an obsession with art that shades into death: what else do you need? An excellent book."
— Brian Evenson, author of *Song for the Unraveling of the World*

"The 50 very short impressionistic stories in this evocative collection from Lanagan (*Yellowcake*) take inspiration from the works of a wide range of Australian female poets."
— *Publishers Weekly*

TRADE PAPERBACK · $17 · EBOOK AVAILABLE · AUGUST 2020

★ "Cotman (*Hard Times Blues*) wields biting wit, powerful emotion, and magic large and small. . . . The title story is the strongest, imagining a group of immortals with the ability to extend their lives by growing and consuming fruit. . . . Readers will be blown away by this standout tale, which grapples with the responsibility of holding power, and whether that power can, or should, be shared."
—*Publishers Weekly* (starred review)

SBP
Small Beer Press

BOOKS, ZINES, CHAPBOOKS &C.
SMALLBEERPRESS.COM
DRM−FREE EBOOKS: WEIGHTLESSBOOKS.COM
PICK UP A T−SHIRT FROM OUR BOOK SHOP:
BOOKMOONBOOKS.COM

CONJUNCTIONS:72

CONJUNCTIONS:72

Nocturnals

Nocturnals

Edited by
Bradford Morrow

Night shrouds, but also illuminates. It is a time of meditation and celebration, but also of madness and grief. Nighttime is marked by loss and soul-searching, sweet dreams and grisly nightmares. Whether under a full moon or new, the night is a time of prayer and murder, of love, hate, and epiphany. A cascade of contradictories, night is sometimes restful, sometimes restive. Dread, loneliness, and dislocation are often intensified in the darkness of night, but the mind may also be set free during the hours in which Edgar Allan Poe's "sable divinity" reigns. Whether awake or asleep, half our lives are passed during the night, lives that are often led in very different ways than during the day.

In the *Nocturnals* issue of *Conjunctions*, readers will encounter fiction, poetry, and essays by some of our most engaging and innovative writers, including Carmen Maria Machado, Kathryn Davis, Rick Moody, Rita Chang-Eppig, Sallie Tisdale, Brian Evenson, Frederic Tuten, Ann Lauterbach, Carole Maso, Mei-mei Berssenbrugge, Cole Swensen, Han Ong, Anne Waldman, Bennett Sims, Joyce Carol Oates, James Morrow, Heather Altfeld, and many others.

Conjunctions. Charting the course of contemporary literature
for nearly 40 years.

CONJUNCTIONS

Edited by Bradford Morrow
Published by Bard College
Annandale-on-Hudson, NY 12504

To purchase this or any other back issue,
visit our secure ordering page at www.conjunctions.com.
Contact us at conjunctions@bard.edu or (845) 758-7054
with questions.

CONJUNCTIONS:73

EARTH ELEGIES

Edited by
Bradford Morrow

To be mindful of the planet we call home is to be aware that our natural world is suffering. Its oceans are rising up, as if in protest. Its populations of birds and fish, of mammals and reptiles, are, many of them, in steep and steady decline. Droughts and wildfires counterpoint, in increasing intensity, hurricanes, flooding, and landslides. Glaciers and polar caps are dissolving before our eyes. Forests, coral reefs, habitats of every sort of life form, from tree frogs to butterfly fish, from elephants to bees, are profoundly afflicted. It is hardly an extremist point of view to see that our planet and all of its denizens—not just humans, who represent a small percentage of living beings, but all flora and fauna—are in mortal jeopardy.

This special issue of *Conjunctions, Earth Elegies*, gathers writings that examine and lament the plight of our planet, while also celebrating its grand sublimity, its peerless beauty, its interconnected intricacies, its indispensability. Contributors include Robert Macfarlane, Diane Ackerman, Rob Nixon, Yxta Maya Murray, Sofia Samatar, Joyce Carol Oates, Arthur Sze, Francine Prose, Rae Armantrout, Lance Olsen, James Morrow, Nathaniel Mackey, Kristine Ong Muslim, Hilary Leichter, Toby Olson, Quincy Troupe, Brian Evenson, and many others.

Conjunctions. Charting the course of contemporary literature
for nearly 40 years.

CONJUNCTIONS
Edited by Bradford Morrow
Published by Bard College
Annandale-on-Hudson, NY 12504

To purchase this or any other back issue,
visit our secure ordering page at www.conjunctions.com.
Contact us at conjunctions@bard.edu or (845) 758-7054
with questions.